6/06

BLACK MARKETS

In direct response to indefinite delays on the national transplantation wait-lists and an inadequate supply of organs, a growing number of terminally ill Americans are turning to international underground markets and coordinators or brokers for organs. Chinese inmates on death row and the economically disadvantaged in India and Brazil are the often compromised co-participants in the private negotiation process, which occurs outside of the legal process or in the shadows of the law. These individuals supply kidneys and other organs for Americans and other Westerners willing to shop and pay in the private process. This book contends that exclusive reliance on the present altruistic tissue and organ procurement processes in the United States is not only rife with problems, but also improvident. The author explores how the altruistic approach leads to a "black market" of organs being harvested from Third World individuals as well as compelled donations from children and incompetent persons.

Michele Goodwin, B.A., J.D., LL.M., is an Associate Professor of Law and Wicklander Fellow at DePaul University College of Law. She is the Director of the Health Law Institute and the Center for the Study of Race and Bioethics. In 2002 she was a visiting scholar at Berkeley School of Law in the Center for the Study of Law and Society. Her primary research interests are tort theory, property relationships in the body, bioethics, and biotechnology. Prior to joining DePaul, she was a postdoctoral fellow at Yale University, conducting research on the antebellum politics of sex and law. Her op-ed commentaries have appeared in the *Los Angeles Times, Houston Chronicle*, and *Chicago Sun Times*.

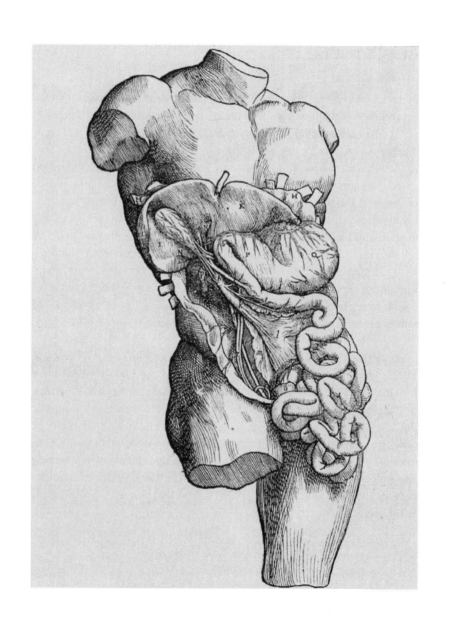

Black Markets

THE SUPPLY AND DEMAND OF BODY PARTS

MICHELE GOODWIN
Depaul University College of Law

CAMBRIDGE
UNIVERSITY PRESS

CAMBRIDGE UNIVERSITY PRESS
Cambridge, New York, Melbourne, Madrid, Cape Town, Singapore, São Paulo

Cambridge University Press
40 West 20th Street, New York, NY 10011-4211, USA

www.cambridge.org
Information on this title: www.cambridge.org/9780521852807

First published 2006

Printed in the United States of America

A catalog record for this publication is available from the British Library.

Library of Congress Cataloging in Publication Data

Goodwin, Michele.
Black markets : the supply and demand of body parts / Michele Goodwin.
    p. ; cm.
Includes bibliographical references and index.
ISBN-13: 978-0-521-85280-7 (hardback)
ISBN-10: 0-521-85280-3 (hardback)
1. Transplantation of organs, tissues, etc. – Corrupt practices.   2. Body, Human.
3. Homografts – Moral and ethical aspects.   4. Medical ethics.
[DNLM: 1. Tissue and Organ Procurement – methods.   2. Altruism.   3. Coercion.
4. Ethics.   5. Fraud.   6. Informed Consent.   7. Tissue Donors – supply & distribution.
8. Tissue and Organ Procurement – legislation & jurisprudence. WO 690 G657b 2006]
I. Title.
RD120.7.G66   2006
362.19′79500688 – dc22   2005037985

ISBN-13   978-0-521-85280-7 hardback
ISBN-10   0-521-85280-3 hardback

For Louise, Nina, Selena, and Theresa

"Organ transactions today are a blend of altruism and commerce; of science, magic, and sorcery; of voluntarism and coercion; of gift, barter, and theft."[1]

Nancy Scheper-Hughes

Contents

Chinese woman advertising her organs for sale. Chinese woman Liao Xiuyan begs with a sign reading "Sell my organs to save daughter" in Guangdong Province, China. Liao, 42, said that her 17-year-old daughter is suffering from leukemia and waits for marrow transplantation. The surgery, which costs almost RMB 500,000 (USD 61,652), is far beyond what Liao and her husband can afford. (Photo by China Photos/Getty Images)

Preface

Organ poachers and distributors have developed international networks and some are more sophisticated than others. In October of 2005, police in Pakistan arrested a group of organ robbers from Afghanistan shortly after the devastating earthquake that killed more than 57,000 people and left more than half a million people homeless in that region.[1] The four men were caught carrying a cooler that contained 15 organs from victims who did not survive the devastation.[2] The victims' corpses were left in the rubble, emptied of the precious kidneys.

Americans live with the understanding that thousands will die each year because too few organs are donated in our present procurement system. Our demand for organs is soaring and the supply is very low. How we resolve this conundrum will reflect our values for autonomy, human dignity, and life-saving efforts.

The interrupted journeys of a few individuals who bravely fought (and later lost) their battles against treatable diseases helped to inform this book. Quite a few had been dropped from transplant waitlists or were misinformed about the benefits of transplantation versus dialysis. In particular, the willingness of some of these individuals to pay for organs to save their lives was a profound statement, particularly because they were African American.[3] They presented an interesting juxtaposition to the race-based rationale for a ban on organ selling. For years, commentators based their opposition to markets in organs on the theory that organ selling resembled slavery. They predict that organ markets would hurt African Americans. Some scholars suggest that an open market in organs could result in familial homicides. They also argue that financial incentives could lead to economic irresponsibility (for the sellers). Some argue against financial incentives in organ procurement, opining that all financial transactions with the human body are coercive and could destroy the integrity of African American communities. Such fears have, in my opinion, limited the discourse and inquiry about how to increase organ supply. We may not know the impact on African Americans as participants in a market system, but statistics reveal how they have been disproportionately "hurt" by the current "altruistic" transplantation model.

In writing this book, I carried a number of stories with me. Some of these stories were more than mere interviews with patients about their experiences on dialysis; they were an oral history of people who influenced the lives of others and whose absences now reveal voids in their communities. Other stories were gleaned from legal cases, briefs filed by attorneys, and investigative reports. The personal experiences of dialysis patients interviewed as part of this project – Jerry, Tim, D. J., Emogene, and others – shed light on the racial dynamics of dialysis treatment, as well as organ transplantation and rationing. Their personal accounts helped to humanize an otherwise scholarly pursuit.

I found other stories equally interesting. These were the "after death" stories. Dead bodies do not speak; but their relatives can be quite expressive. Cadaver stories gripped my imagination, and led me on an interesting journey that included the review of hundreds of cases involving the mishandling, misappropriation, and unlawful burial of cadavers. In particular, the claims made by individuals who took legal action against companies for mishandling, moving, and otherwise disturbing their dead relatives presented unsettled nuances in the law as to property ownership in human bodies. The early legal history and analysis of body part appropriation and misappropriation seemed a logical extension of study and research on questions of institutional change in organ transplantation. Addressing system tolerance and institutional choice in procurement systems inevitably turns us toward the limits of our past engagement with body parts, how we value the deceased, and the level of our tolerance for institutional change.

Two civil cases intrigued me. The first case, *Moore v. Regents*,[4] dealt with the question of conversion and more specifically whether Mr. Moore could sue his doctors for what amounted to his doctors misappropriating his cell line. Moore's doctors made millions of dollars based on patents they developed from the nonconsensual use of Moore's genetic material. The California Supreme Court answered in the negative; they argued that an individual has no ownership or property interest in his or her body! The second case, *Carney v. Knollwood Cemetery*,[5] was more obscure. This was a Cleveland, Ohio, case that involved the mishandling of a deceased person. In this case, the Knollwood Cemetery instructed its employees to destroy a buried vault, including the casket within it, and to toss the remains in a trash heap behind the cemetery office to make room for a grave. Later, visitors reported seeing bones, a skull, and other body parts in the trash pile. News cameras captured footage of the macabre scene. In *Carney*, the court held that the plaintiffs (the sister and grandchildren of the late Mrs. Carney) had a viable cause of action against the cemetery for causing them emotional distress.

Yet another story intrigued me. This was slightly more personal, as it took me back to my childhood days visiting relatives in the South. My great-grandfather, a farmer wedded to southern soil, was nearly 100 years old at death. He was committed to the South and never left it except to bury his children in the North. As a little girl, I listened attentively to his fantastic stories, which as it turns out, often involved two subjects, the land and the dead. Within those two domains my cousins and I learned about harvests, moons, and tides. We also learned about "the value" of things buried: people and money. However, one story came back to me while I was in law school. It was a story he shared often about how Black graves were pillaged for body parts that were used for research and medical school anatomy classes. During summers in Mississippi, those stories seemed like interesting folklore. Only later, I researched his claims, and as shared in Chapter 8, you will see that his tales were true. The supply and demand challenge for body parts is not a new question.

It became clear to me that the law was not settled on body ownership questions. From state to state (and internationally), questions about property ownership in bodies and body parts were answered differently by courts. In some states, relatives were recognized to have "quasi-property right interests" in their deceased relatives' bodies. Therefore, relatives could determine organ donation, burial location, disposition of the body (cremation, burial, whole body donation), and even instigate litigation for violation of their quasi-property rights. On the other hand, in even the most egregious cases of body parts misappropriation, including a hospital's failure to return a prematurely born baby for burial,[6] a two-headed fetus kept in a bottle on display at a circus,[7] or nonconsensual removal of corneas for transplantation,[8] the notion of property interests in human bodies was flat out rejected by some courts.

For me, the question of body ownership was relevant to the issue of organ transplantation. Body ownership was one way of looking at rights connected with the power to donate. Who has the power to donate? An individual may choose to donate her organs, but the state cannot force her to do so. The next of kin also possess a recognized legal interest in their deceased relatives' bodies. They too can decide whether to donate a dead relative's organs. But from where do their rights spring? The recognition of "quasi-property" right interests in bodies, specifically for purposes of body disposal dates back centuries in English common law. English courts initially applied this legal theory as an affirmative duty on relatives to properly bury and dispose of their kin. Early U.S. cases involved nuisance actions against relatives who improperly interred their relatives in stoves, fireplaces, and furnaces.[9] However, "quasi-property rights" theory is inconsistently recognized and applied by courts. Some U.S. courts refer to it as a "legal fiction." Indeed, as with all rights, there are also limits. In this book, I parse out these questions of ownership and how we might address an overburdened, underserving, organ procurement system.

Acknowledgments

My journey was aided by many. For more than a decade, John Paris has been a great mentor. He and Dean Hashimoto provided guidance and encouragement during the conceptual periods of this project, long before it was ever imagined as a book. John is an outstanding bioethicist and his willingness to respectfully challenge, inquire, and probe complex, nuanced medico-legal problems is inspiring. His spirited yet thoughtful engagement with sensitive issues taught me early on to courageously engage on bioethical terrain.

I am also most deeply indebted to Dorothy Roberts and Dorothy Brown, both of whom have been incredibly generous with their time and guidance. I am fortunate to have both as mentors. Marc Galanter's contributions to this project are also appreciated, particularly his critiques in its early stages when he encouraged me to follow through with my then-developing theory on market systems and how they could relate to organ procurement. Research assistants are invaluable to all academic endeavors. This book is no exception. For this project, Tamara Hobbs provided outstanding research assistance and I am most grateful. She along with Rakeena Payne, Cora Smith, and Michael Bankhead helped me to reach the Black community of and throughout Chicago for comment on dialysis, organ transplants, and community health in general. Pamela Koszut provided invaluable research support for this project. Erin Crow, thank you for being an extra set of eyes and performing cite checking. Glen Weissenberger provided the research funding to help bring the project to its next step. Special thanks to John Berger, my editor at Cambridge University Press and his great team. Any and all flaws in this text are my own.

Andreas Philippopoulos-Mihalopoulos, thank you for allowing me to present a chapter of this book as a keynote lecture at Westminster College of Law. I am also very grateful to Patricia Werhane and the Institute for Business Ethics. Receiving the Wicklander Fellowship was a great honor and I am most indebted. I owe a debt of gratitude to the Institute for Law and Society at the University of California at Berkeley. The faculty and staff helped my research stay to be a rich experience. Blake Morant is ever a great supporter. I thank him, the Frances Lewis Law Center, and his colleagues at Washington and Lee Law School, for inviting me to present a chapter of this book as part of their 2004–2005 lecture series. Versions of various chapters were presented at MAPOCC meetings; thank you all in the Mid-Atlantic for comments and criticisms. I would also like to thank Dr. Sandra Jackson and Dr. Fassil Demissie for inviting me to share a chapter of this book at the Center for Black Diaspora at DePaul University. I would like to thank Guido Calabresi for his encouragement during my drafting process.

Finally, there are the family members who make our journeys through life meaningful. I must express my deepest appreciation to Nancy for providing an underground railroad of sorts. Memories of those years will always bring gratitude and warmth to my heart. In the end, this was not possible without you. Ann, Vata, Julie, and Todd, thank you for being there. I owe much to Ingrid Hillinger and Margit Livingston. To my godfather, Daniel Kunene, thank you for inspiring such beautiful poetry and for supporting my endeavors. Lastly, my daughter and son, Sage and Brook, and husband, Greg, provide year-round inspiration and help to place life in perspective. Journeys are only as valuable as the homes to which we return.

– Michele Goodwin

BLACK MARKETS

SUNDAY
PERSPECTIVES
A daughter waits

My daughter was placed on the list for a heart and double-lung transplant when she was 20 years old. She was born with a badly deformed heart, which ruined her lungs. It took one week after the evaluation for the transplant team to decide she was a candidate. We were told that it might take up to four years to have the surgery because she needed multiple organs and that she needed to "put in time on the list."

That was two years ago. Did Gov. Casey get preferential treatment? You bet he did!

Saying that his sudden death could occur was a copout. People are not placed on that list unless their condition is incompatible with life and nothing else can be done. My daughter has been in a dangerous cardiac arrhythmia for a year and her oxygen blood level is nearly incompatible with life. Still, she waits on the list, non-priority.

I'm not begrudging Gov. Casey a transplant, but I certainly think that he should have waited his turn. Yes, he's an important man, but there are thousands of people on that list who are under 30.

We've heard that people, angry over this incident, are tearing up their organ-donor cards. This will not punish the powers that be; it will only punish people like my daughter who desperately need transplants.

LINDA BURNS
Harmony, Pa.

A family snubbed

I can't stand the umbrage I felt when I discovered that the members of William Michael Lucas' family, who so nobly donated their son's organs for transplantation into Gov. Casey, were denied forgiveness of their son's hospital and burial expenses.

Of the hundreds of thousands of dollars expended in this endeavor, I feel the Lucas family did not receive the consideration it deserved.

Gov. Casey
Did he jump line?

Gov. Casey and Mayor Masloff were elected to oversee the community welfare. When public servants become recipients of the organs of violent-crime victims, one is left wondering, "To whom is protection being rendered?" Perhaps, murder in the streets has found its ultimate good. What a sad commentary!

ROLAND C. BARKSDALE-HALL
Lincoln-Lemington

Let us sell before dying

Gov. Casey's recent heart and liver transplant, and the inordinately short waiting period he experienced, serves by contrast to emphasize the long waiting period ordinary folk endure.

Did Casey skip the line?

1 Introduction

A. A Tale of Two Cities

The politicians can have our organs, but they can't give us jobs.

(Mr. Giles)[1]

All week long, we've been trying to get someone to pay attention to this (beating), and nobody wanted to hear it ... The police have not been cooperating with us. They haven't been investigating. All of a sudden, they want to speak.

(Yvonne Lucas)[2]

There is a book of rules that controls the placement of organs and the rules under which they're transferred from donors to recipients, and I said I want to be sure, and you've gotta assure me now, each one of you that those rules are gonna be followed to the letter, – and they were.

(Robert Casey, former governor of Pennsylvania)[3]

It was a Sunday night, June 6, 1993, when Mrs. Frances Lucas discovered her semiconscious son. William Michael Lucas, 34, had sustained an unmerciful beating.[4] Covered in a pool of blood, Michael had somehow managed to struggle from the front door to his mother's kitchen floor. Despite his urgent medical condition, police and ambulance were slow to respond.[5] One lone officer finally arrived, but would not call for an ambulance to the home.[6] So Mrs. Lucas dragged her son into her car, placing him as gently as she could in the backseat and drove off to the hospital.[7] One week later, two very different men would be fighting for their lives. Michael would lose, but the Governor, Robert Casey (Pennsylvania), would survive with a pair of new organs.[8]

Days after his brutal beating and shortly after being declared brain-dead, Michael's heart and liver were delicately inserted into the waiting caverns of Governor Casey who was dying from amyloidosis.[9] Michael was the "wrong guy" caught in a vicious cycle. Michael Lucas was a victim of mistaken identity, bludgeoned by a drug gang that "beat up the wrong man."[10] Local police described the attackers as a fleet of gang members from Pittsburgh who swarmed into this small Monessen town looking for trouble.[11] Beaten by life, unemployed, but searching for work, Michael was the second of two sons to die violently.[12] Most of his attackers were never found. Michael's forgotten contribution to the state of Pennsylvania was saving the life of Governor Casey. The story made headlines in part because of Michael's brutal death, poverty, and the toll of racism on a small town and local Black communities. The story also became newsworthy because transplant patients and their families were outraged that the governor skipped over hundreds of patients on liver and heart waitlists. A reporter from the *Washington Post* described Michael as a product from a dying steel town, "a man who had vowed to escape but never could."[13] The fated timing of Michael's death and the governor's dual organ placement on the waitlist illuminated uncomfortable realities about organ procurement and transplantation. The political, economic, and social ironies read like *A Tale of Two Cities*.[14]

Michael Lucas was yet another Black male statistic among many, demonstrating how he was not able to pull himself from the mire, but also how a state could not or did not resuscitate his dying community, ravaged by poverty, unemployment, drugs, and lacking healthcare to offer him an opportunity for success. Casey, on the other hand, a 61-year-old White male, would have another opportunity to live, contemplate running for president of the United States, and complete his term as governor. A social commentator characterized the irony of Michael's fall and the governor's rise: "so it was that a man marked by every scourge of his times – violence, drugs, joblessness, racism – saved the life of the governor of Pennsylvania."[15] The "tragic irony," he notes, "was that it was supposed to be the other way around."[16]

Keeping vigil over her son, even passing a birthday, turning 64 during her watch, Mrs. Lucas prayed as her son's condition worsened. The following Sunday, June 13, 1993, as soon as Michael was declared brain-dead, an organ procurement specialist approached his mother. Thinking that perhaps another life could be saved, she consented to his organ removal. Yet the contrasts between how Michael Lucas and Robert Casey were treated when both needed medical attention is instructive, reminding us that "[Michael Lucas] waged [a fight] against [the] odds"[17] and the quiet role his race and circumstance played outside of the Black community. Indeed, those outraged by the governor's immediate transplant were more concerned that he had not spent fair time on the waitlists, really ignoring the more subtle and complex issues of urban violence, racism, and disillusionment.

Michael Lucas, however, had a story like so many young Black boys whose visions for the future shattered. His story is full of false starts and tragedies piling and collapsing on each other. Michael's athletic prowess and hopes for college play were dashed by a hip and leg injury that left him in a body cast for over six months when he was 12. The next year, Michael's idol, an older brother, was shot in cold blood by a White tavern owner. His half brother described the options left to young people trying to live in Monessen: "there were three choices for anyone young who stayed, death, drugs, or jail."[18] Through a series of ups and downs, including unmarried fatherhood and dropping out of college training programs, in 1987 it appeared that he had landed on his feet. It was also the year Casey took office. That year, however, would end like many others, with compounding social hardships, compiling debt, and his introduction to drugs while living in the only neighborhood his sister said he could afford. Drugs devastated the small mill communities just as it did in the larger urban areas.[19]

Casey's first stop on the postcampaign trail was Monessen to make promises he surely hoped could be achieved, and to some degree progress was made.[20] Yet despite his laudable gubernatorial efforts, Casey's progress was overshadowed by double-digit unemployment, even then twice the national average. As Yvonne Lucas lamented, her brother was just as devastated and vulnerable when Casey visited in 1987 as he was six years later, writhing in pain on his mother's floor.[21] According to his job counselor at the job services center, "a Casey-Wofford initiative," Lucas applied for "easily 100 jobs" the year before his death, but came close to getting only one.[22]

The events immediately following Michael's beating illustrate the complex labyrinth of race, class, and medicine. Mrs. Lucas called the police twice before an officer appeared.[23] Mrs. Lucas, a medical receptionist, drove her son to Allegheny General Hospital "in her own car."[24] She donated his organs that Sunday after being informed that he would not come out of his coma and that he was officially brain-dead.

Governor Casey, on the other hand, son of an attorney, and well educated himself, was called on Sunday and told that "he would need a new heart as well as liver transplant to try to beat amyloidosis," an organ-destroying disease, and that both were waiting for him.[25] That day, he "was flown to Pittsburgh in a state plane and driven by state police car to the University of Pittsburgh Medical Center, where reporters waited to record every step in his treatment."[26]

Casey's doctors claimed that he did not receive special treatment because he was the governor, but because he "needed" two organs. However, tragedies mark many parts of the joined stories of Michael Lucas and Robert Casey; although Casey waited only one day for Lucas' organs, others continued to wait over 200 days for a heart and 67 days for a liver. Indeed, if the story were turned around, would Michael have received aggressive treatment? Because of procurement and allocation policies at the time, hundreds were passed over for the governor to obtain Michael's organs.[27] For the Lucas family, their tragedy played on as only two of the fifteen involved in his murder were convicted, and police called an end to the investigation, claiming that it was "stalled." Reverend Giles, a minister and cousin of Michael who performed the eulogy at Lucas' funeral, summed up the consternation of local Blacks: "They can come to our community and say how great things are, but they can't lift us up."[28]

And then there was J. D. . . . .

J. D. was the first African American to chair the Fayette County School Board in Lexington, Kentucky. He took this role quite seriously, bringing about investigations into the proper treatment of children with disabilities, shutting down a school that had been a dumping ground for boys with behavior problems and replacing it with a model alternative school, and supporting what were considered "radical" efforts to eliminate sexual harassment at the professional and student levels in the district's schools. His exceptional accomplishments as the leader of the school board were considered milestones in a community where implementation of the mandates from *Brown v. Board of Education* was under federal watch as late as 1999, the year of his death.

J. D., like thousands of other African Americans who preceded him, and many more since, died from complications arising from end-stage renal disease. Although placed on dialysis by his physicians, when I interviewed J. D. in 1998 and 1999, and asked whether he qualified for a kidney transplant, he thoughtfully expressed, "they never told me about transplantation."[29] J. D. was referring to his doctors. By the time of our conversations on organ transplantation, it was too late; his death was not an if only a when. J. D.'s death had a profound impact on his community; without him there were no other persons of color on the school board (the second largest district in the state). The African American community no longer had a voice on the school board. Another important community role model had died.

Although separated by miles, culture, education, and economic status, J. D. and Michael were Black men connected by end-of-life transplant stories. Neither story is unique. Ashwini Sehgal's illuminating study on organ transplantation in the United States revealed that Blacks were more likely to be organ donors whereas Whites were more likely to be recipients.[30] In the investigation, Sehgal, a nephrologist and director of the Center for Reducing Health Disparities at Case Western Reserve University, examined data from over 100,000 transplants performed in the United States during the period of 1996 to 2001.[31] The results confirmed long-suspected disparities. Blacks were more likely to be donors and Whites recipients for six of eight types of deceased donor transplants (kidney-pancreas, liver, lung, pancreas, intestine, and heart-lung).[32]

Commentators have long alleged inequitable treatment in the allocation and distribution of organs. Annual reports from the United Network for Organ Sharing (UNOS)[33] repeat the tale that has become all too predictable: *Blacks wait longer than all other ethnic groups for organs such as kidneys, and have the highest death rate (while on the list) of all populations in the United States.* The list does not share anything about those like J. D. who are not given information or presented options about transplantation. Those Blacks never make it onto the list, but spend their last months and years hooked to dialysis machines several days per week. They are the forgotten ones.

Some commentators allege that inequitable distribution of organs is caused by racial profiling and "cultural incompetence" that impedes the fair distribution of organs.[34] African Americans have a greater need for kidneys, where the acute shortage is felt most. As of July 12, 2005, the Organ Procurement Transplantation Network (OPTN), which gathers data on transplantation, reported that there were over 66,000 Americans waiting for kidneys and African Americans comprised over one-third of that list.[35] Currently, there are 23,042 African Americans waiting for kidneys, making them the largest per-capita ethnic group on this list.[36] Yet how many of these waitlist candidates will ever receive an organ? How many more will be passed over because the matching criteria is too restrictive? What is the solution? I have come to the conclusion that the altruistic procurement process is inadequate, creating problems for all those who seek organs because it simply does not generate an adequate supply. The current altruistic procurement system that supplies organs is problematic for Whites too. Even if organs were equitably distributed, there is still a dramatic shortage in the number of organs available for transplantation.

The stories of Michael and J. D. speak to the significance of status and the troubling nuances of contemporary organ procurement and allocation. From whom will we capture organs and to whom will they go? Biotechnology provides methods to increase life span. However, biotechnology cannot (at least at this time) address the supply and demand of human resources. We are at a crossroad where institutional sufficiency must be measured and tough choices are to be made. If we continue with the present altruism-based procurement strategy, one thing can be predicted with certainty; thousands will die annually.[37] Disproportionately, morbidity will be greatest among people of color.[38] In particular, African Americans will wait longer than other ethnic groups and suffer the highest rates of death.[39] Such predictions are alarming, but not surprising; they are based on current practices and trends.[40] Each death will have an impact on a family and local community.[41] Those who can avoid America's transplantation system will do so. They will bypass the American waitlist process for greater access abroad, even if that choice involves paying a destitute living donor and violating the law.

B. Black Markets: Altruism's Limits

In this book, I contend that exclusive reliance on the present altruistic tissue and organ procurement processes in the United States is not only rife with problems, but also improvident. The death toll resulting from organ failure is high – it is not declining – yet more people are added to the organ waitlists each day. Let us examine what this means in real terms. Each day, 18 persons on the UNOS waitlists die before ever receiving the anticipated organ.[42] They are replaced by another 110 persons who will enter that list by the end of the day.[43] This number rises each year.[44] The dramatics of who enters and exits would be far less onerous if there were equilibrium between who enters and exits. If we consider the demand only for kidneys, notice the number of candidates added to waitlists each year between 2001 and 2003, respectively: 64,280 (2001); 68,333 (2002); 72,132 (2003).[45] One person becomes a waitlist candidate every 13 minutes. These figures help to place in context the gravity of our organ demand.

The crisis in U.S. organ transplantation is only partially addressed by the actual organ shortage. The balance of the equation requires us to honestly consider the limitations of our procurement system and strategy. Rationales once used to justify the prohibitions on incentives in organ donation may be less persuasive in an era where demand for transplantable organs is exponentially higher than nearly 40 years ago when the Uniform Anatomical Gift Act (UAGA)[46] was originally drafted and in 1984 when the National Organ Transplantation Act (NOTA)[47] was enacted. At the time of the U.S. ban on organ sales, transplantation was slightly better than an implausible reality. Transplants were episodic as relatively few transplantations occurred in the 1970s and 1980s. In 1984, a transplantation system based purely on altruism was compatible with our medical capacity and social trust of biotechnology. Moreover, the medical technology to sustain transplants, cyclosporine, and other drugs were yet to be developed. Thus, the collective concerns of urgency, biotechnology, and social confidence in transplantation are far different today than 20 years ago.

In addition, we have learned in considerable measure that the market pitfalls predicted by Richard Titmuss in his seminal study, *The Gift Relationship*,[48] were overstated and wrong. A generation ago, Titmuss suggested that market systems in human blood would attract "skid row" participants who would infect the blood supplies of Europe and the United States. In particular, Titmuss noted that many of these skid row types were "negro" because the commercial banks "are better placed" in "Negro and Ghetto areas."[49] His concern about the disproportionality of "Negro" involvement in the blood supply reverberates in contemporary debates about financial incentives in organ supply. *The Gift Relationship* is concomitantly laudable and troubling; it develops a thesis praising the value of human relationships developed through altruistic gestures. On the other hand, Titmuss equates racial and economic status with diseases that would infect a blood supply pool from which Whites would draw. Titmuss forewarned the Western world that blood commodification would lead to insalubrious plasma entering the supply and incapacitating the blood procurement system. He pointed out, for example, how one commercial blood bank in Newark, New Jersey, collected 12,680 donations in 1968, but that "85 percent of its donors were male, Negro . . . part-time workers."[50] The significance of this fact was not lost on legislators and readers of the early 1970s. The United States was highly segregated at the time and the reality of integating blood supplies in a nation resistant to school and housing integration must surely have caused concern. Titmuss highlighted such donation scenarios as dangerous for the blood supply and an incongruent redistribution of blood (i.e., from poor to rich supply).[51] And what was the solution? Should Blacks have stopped donating? One way to read Titmuss' warning about "bad" donors is that Black males are less ideal donors only when compensated. It is difficult to know whether Titmuss was leery of poor donors or poor "Negro" donors. In other words, Titmuss might have believed that all poor donors potentially placed blood supplies at risk. If so, his solution to forbid payments to poor donors addressed only one aspect of the tragedy he predicted, because poor donors were not excluded from altruistic blood donations. What Titmuss does make clear in his writings is that Negroes were potential polluters of the American blood supply. Ironically, Titmuss assumed that blood would flow *only* from Blacks to Whites. Did Titmuss forget that Blacks needed blood too?

The Gift Relationship garnered significant praise and recognition, but its racial undertones have largely been ignored. Titmuss described the worst aspects of a market – and in that he was not incorrect. There are harmful downsides to unregulated market – based approaches, including coercion of unwitting participants, the incapacity of markets to respond adequately to certain social dynamics, and the potential for disparate class relationships to emerge.[52] What Titmuss did not predict nor account for was acquired immunodeficiency syndrome (AIDS) and the very generous donation patterns of gay men unaware of their human immunodeficiency virus (HIV) status, which threatened the American and Western blood supplies in the 1980s.[53] A crippled blood supply had nothing to do with the wealth of those who donated, but rather their health. The correlation between wealth and health in that context is far too narrow. Moreover, Titmuss erroneously assumed that altruistic behavior positively corresponds to physical and psychological health. In this, only unhealthy people engage with markets; healthy people avoid markets and are more altruistic. Altruism does not respond to status in the manner in which Titmuss predicted. The health emphasis in any procurement system is better placed on screening, testing, and documenting social histories. Reliance on the gift relationship model ignores biological shortages and unhealthy gifts from very generous people.

Recent health crises involving organ donation further demonstrate the unreliable correlation between altruism and health. On October 6, 2005, the Centers for Disease Control (CDC) in the United States announced that three individuals who received organ transplants from a single donor were infected with West Nile virus. Two of the patients were comatose at the time of the CDC announcement. The New York City donor was declared brain dead on August 26, 2005, after suffering a traumatic head injury, and within two days, his liver, kidneys, and one lung were harvested for transplantation. However, this was not the first incident in which West Nile, a flu-like virus, was transmitted through transplantation. The first instance involved a donor contracting the virus through a blood transfusion, and later after his donation, four recipients of his organs contracted the disease. The infected donors in these instances were not "skid row" menaces to society, focused only on financial reward. Rather these altruists were among the very classes Titmuss suggested would be infection free and safe. Ultimately, it is not a matter of class that determines whether the donor's organs or blood are safe, but rather effective tests.

Altruism may be the noblest form of giving, especially in the context of organ donation, but how many people need die before we rethink our procurement strategy? A Gallup poll indicates that whereas 85% of Americans support organ donations, only 20% carry donor cards. Americans are very generous people, but they refuse to volunteer their organs at a rate that accommodates national demand. Their generosity must be placed in context with what they are willing to "give" and to whom they are willing to provide it. Despite aggressive public service campaigns and more than a billion dollars spent over the past decade to promote organ donation, Americans are unmoved. As the death toll mounts, demand for organs continually outpaces the supply, resulting in rationing that at times could be considered arbitrary and capricious.

The most noticeable flaw in the altruistic procurement process is system incompetence. By this, I am suggesting that if altruistic procurement is designed to meet the overwhelming need for organs, it is a numerical failure. In this way it closely resembles a sophisticated lottery system rather than a reliable supply system. I am not suggesting that altruism should be abandoned. That would be foolish; we don't wish for the supply pool to drop. Nor am I suggesting that the dedicated procurement specialists at organ procurement organizations (OPOs) or the regulatory staff at the United Network for Organ Sharing (UNOS) are failing in their responsibilities. To the contrary, they have been very innovative in their efforts to increase supply within a limited framework.[54] What I suggest, however, is that exclusive reliance on altruistic procurement will perpetuate organ shortages and an avoidably high death rate for patients.

The altruistic procurement system veils other pitfalls and problems. Biotechnological developments, such as organ transplants, fetal transplants, cloning, and tissue transplants, outpace legislative regulation and judicial inquiry, and thereby create gaps in the rule and role of the law. Where such gaps exist, secondary and alternative systems can develop, undermining public awareness and affecting health, safety, and public trust. The law has yet to catch up with subsystems that exact a harmful toll on vulnerable populations. Often, subsystems develop in response to incompetent primary systems.[55] Let's consider some of the system by-products of our current organ procurement model.

1. The Black Market

Consider first that altruism veils the existence of thriving black markets. In direct response to indefinite delays on the national transplantation waitlists, unease about pressuring relatives, and an inadequate supply of organs, a growing number of terminally ill Americans are turning their backs on the U.S. waitlist process. Instead, a growing number are turning to international underground markets and brokers for organs.[56] Americans receive hearts, lungs, kidneys, and other body parts through the underground or *black market* process. Chinese inmates on death row[57] and the economically disadvantaged in India[58] and Brazil[59] are often compromised co-participants in the private negotiation process, which occurs outside of the legal process – or in the shadows of law.[60] Many countries prohibit organ selling, but enforcement is often weak, difficult, or subject to corruption. Increasingly, it is reported that even Iraqis are selling organs, not to Americans, but to other desperate patients.[61] The black market is an open secret. Once perhaps considered an isolated occurrence unworthy of public note, black market organ transactions are part of a robust international industry with brokers traceable on the Internet. Third world or developing country participants supply kidneys and other organs for Americans and other Westerners willing to shop on the black market.[62] In the new lexicon of organ transplantation, black market shopping is known as "transplant tourism" or "organ tourism." The Third World transplantations cost less abroad and patients wait a fraction of the time anticipated on U.S. waitlists.

For years, commentators and some bioethicists have been in denial about the underground markets in human body parts. They dismissed the personal narratives of people of color in third world countries who have sold organs. However, congressional reports reveal that the federal government has long been aware of black markets in organs, including the abuse of prisoners for organs.[63] On June 27, 2001, the Congressional Subcommittee on International Operations and Human Rights, chaired by Henry Hyde, reported that "the evidence gathered throughout the last two decades clearly shows that China . . . has found a lucrative industry in the field of organ transplantation."[64] The Congressional report notes that harvesting from Chinese prisoners "began in 1979 with the issuance of a document from China's Public Health Ministry entitled Rules Concerning the Dissection of Corpses."[65] Several years later, in 1984, the Chinese government issued new regulations entitled Provisions for Regulations on the Use of Dead Bodies or Organs from

Condemned Criminals.[66] According to the Subcommittee, the 1984 report "detailed instruction on the conditions and the procedures for harvesting organs from executed prisoners, including the coordination between health personnel and prison and public security officials."[67]

2. Exploitation of Living Donors

Both domestically and abroad, living donors are pressured for their organs. As described earlier, the black market process involves compensation to organ donors and thus may be rationalized as less nefarious and invasive than if individuals were forced by the state to supply body parts for organ tourists. However, living-compensated donations are not uncomplicated nor free from coercion. These transactions are complicated by the coexisting vulnerable statuses of both the donors and the donees. For sure, there is a double bind for transplant patients. If they adhere to the U.S. waitlist process, their waits could be interminable. Yet, if patients engage in what appears to be a voluntary paid transaction between individuals, they are circumventing U.S. laws and encouraging poverty-stricken individuals to undergo nontherapeutic operations. Patients are caught in their own death traps; death may be imminent when they decide to circumvent the U.S. transplantation process. Their choices are terribly circumscribed.

Both black market living-donations and those within the U.S. altruistic system exact pressure on donors. In the case of third world donors, their vulnerable status is revealed by relatively how little they are paid for organs and the lack of postoperative medical care provided to them. These Brown and Black donors are preyed upon by Americans too frustrated with our domestic transplantation policy. Sadly, these black market exchanges can be easily perceived as a modern form of colonization. However, let us consider our domestic system.

Altruism is defined as "the belief in or practice of disinterested and selfless concern for the well-being of others."[68] As the cadaveric supply pool stagnates, Americans increasingly seek altruistic responses from relatives, children, friends, and coworkers to supply organs and bone marrow. That living donation outpaces cadaveric donation in the United States is instructive. It could indicate that Americans embrace altruism as a necessary part of transplantation, but why doesn't that level of altruism carry over at death? Some commentators suggest that guilt and pressure exacted on family members is the cause for rise in living donations in the United States.[69] Moreover, in some U.S. cases and abroad, families are "building babies" to create "perfect matches" for transplantation.[70] Such actions may fit outside of the ethical and moral expressions of altruism, which I analyze later in Chapter 3. Recent studies support donation, but conclude that not all organ donations were made out of love, but rather self-interest, guilt, or coercion.[71] These studies indicate that years after the transplantations, donors experience anxiety, frustration, and even regret.[72] Children donors report nightmares, fear of hospitals, and even guilt if they are found to be incompatible for donation.[73]

3. Compelled Organ and Tissue Donation from Children

Federally mandated altruistic procurement severely constrains parental ability to seek alternative, viable sources for children needing organ or bone marrow transplants. The weaker, less desirable options become the exclusive options, quite unnecessarily. In Chapter 3, I argue that children and the mentally ill are not viable replacements for an incompetent, struggling organ procurement system. Their involvement is symptomatic of the deeply embedded procurement strains on altruism. Their participation should be limited to the narrowest possibilities.

Currently, siblings account for more contributions to the living donor pool than all other groups.[74] Adults are the primary organ donors in this category. However, legally incompetent minors figure prominently in this practice as they continue to be represented among living donors. Sibling organ and tissue donations outpace all other donor groups. Living donation cases, particularly those involving children, are deeply nuanced and may be influenced by a host of factors difficult to monitor and predict. Unfortunately, with limited judicial intervention, children are harvestable entities as demonstrated by the *Hart*[75] and *Ayala*[76] cases. Courts presume children are psychologically benefited by the organ harvesting that saves a sibling's life.[77] My research suggests that federal guidelines and the jurisprudence in this area must become more nuanced in light of the potential for coercion, confusion, manipulation, and conflicts of interest not only among physicians, but also parents.

How should courts respond to compelled living donation? Biotechnological advancements create further complicated nuances, including opportunities to create children for harvesting. A Colorado couple recently disclosed that they took advantage of such an opportunity to save the life of an existing child.[78] Through in vitro fertilization and genetic screening, parents can design babies to fit specific genetic profiles.[79] How do we balance the desire to preserve life versus the desire to protect life from unnecessary harm and interference or intrusion, particularly for children? Chapter 3 investigates these questions and makes policy recommendations regarding compelled donation from children and reproductive altruism, or the practice of reproducing children to harvest their biological resources to improve the health or save the life of another child. This chapter draws on cases involving competing interests among parents, physicians, courts, and children.

4. Bias and Fraud: Who Gets Priority Status?

Two major problems exist with organ allocation in the United States: shortage and bias. Even if bias were not a factor, the organ shortage would still exist. J. D.'s case is informative on this point. Even if he had been placed on a waitlist, J. D. might not have received an organ. Blacks wait longer than any other group for kidneys and experience the highest death rate while on the lists.[80] Commentators and scholars are sometimes defensive on this point, choosing to believe that race disparities in transplantation are functions of science and not discrimination (i.e., if more African Americans were perfect "matches" they would receive kidney priority). Blood matching is important; however, so are individual patient narratives. For some commentators, if there is no smoking gun, such as racist remarks from physicians (presumably overheard by patients or epithets in bold on treatment charts discovered by a nurse) then claims of bias are unfounded. However, accusations of bias in the transplantation system deserve serious consideration. Bias undermines confidence in the transplantation system. Bias and fraud may also motivate individuals to operate outside of the U.S. transplantation system or avoid transplantation, which is a death sentence.

Consider the case of several Chicago-area transplantation centers. In 2003, the University of Illinois paid the United States and the State of Illinois $2 million to settle a lawsuit that alleged the "University's Medical Center at Chicago improperly diagnosed and hospitalized certain patients...to allow them to become eligible sooner for liver transplants."[81] The lawsuit resulted from a "whistle-blower" lawsuit brought by a liver transplant surgeon and professor at the University of Illinois College of Medicine (UIC), alleging fraudulent practices at the University of Illinois Hospital.[82] The lawsuit alleged that the University of Illinois Hospital falsely diagnosed patients and placed them in intensive care to make them appear more sick than they were. Those patients placed in intensive care were positioned ahead of others who were waiting for organs in the transplant region. The lawsuit further alleged that "two of the patients received liver transplants despite failing to meet the criteria established by a national organ sharing network for priority among eligible patients."[83] Another patient who received a transplant had been ineligible because she had liver cancer.[84] According to the settlement agreement, UIC denies and claims valid defenses to all the allegations of the lawsuit.[85] However, the suit was settled for twice the amount of actual damages.[86] Similar lawsuits filed and settled against other Chicago-area hospitals, including the University of Chicago and Northwestern Memorial Hospital, indicate that fraud and bias are not isolated occurrences in the U.S. transplantation system.

There is no science to organ allocation in the United States, at least not at the initial stages.[87] Indeed, it is the lack of uniformity and clear standards in the early stages of coordinating waitlist efforts that permits bias to enter and influence decision making. The federal government steps in only when federal dollars are misappropriated, as in the UIC case. In the UIC case, the Attorney General alleged that from 1996 to 1998 "at least three federally insured patients were admitted...to intensive care, which was not medically necessary at the time."[88] Their stays were lengthy and taxpayers footed the bills. For patients who are not federally insured through Medicaid or Medicare, but who are willing to pay out of pocket for intensive care services, their priority status and arrangements would fly under the federal radar. St. Vincent Medical Center, one of the largest organ transplant centers in California, suspended its liver program in September 2005 after discovering that its doctors arranged for a Saudi Arabian candidate to jump ahead of others on the waitlist. The Saudi government paid $339,000 for the transplant. Though we may abhor the very thought of bias and fraud in our transplantation system, it exists. How we address it is another matter. Chapters 2 and 4 further scrutinize our allocation system.

5. Presumed Consent: An Underground Process

Presumed consent laws are another by-product of our strained procurement system. Over the years, legislators have proposed a "compelled altruism" model otherwise known as "presumed consent" and "legislative consent" to increase organ and tissue supply. Presumed consent laws were passed in 28 states and most were promulgated during the mid-1980s. Corneas[89] were needed for transplantation and relatively few Americans were taking advantage of the opportunity to donate. Presumed consent statutes are compulsory measures that obligate individuals to donate certain tissues. States presume that individuals would have wanted to donate and ostensibly substitute judgment (and give consent) for the deceased donors. Presently in use to procure corneas, eye tissues, and heart valves, presumed consent is an open secret.[90] Legislatures are not shielding state regulations that authorize presumed consent from the public. On the other hand, public service announcements never indicate that some states have imposed laws that provide for nonconsensual tissue harvesting.

The statutes authorizing presumed or legislative consent for use of select tissues permit a medical examiner or justice of the peace (or their agents) to extract the corneas and sometimes other tissue (including the entire eye) from cadavers if a mandatory autopsy was scheduled to be performed and no objection to the removal is known.[91] Autopsies are mandatory in homicide and catastrophic death cases.[92] The medical examiner may delegate this right to a physician or eye bank.[93] Its proponents suggest that presumed consent increases tissue supply while respecting "donor" autonomy and individual choice by virtue of an "opt out" provision for prior refusal.[94] However, the "opt out" provisions are more illusory than real. How can a dead person opt out? How can the uninformed relatives opt out? There is no "opt out" card for unsuspecting potential donors to carry. Without a real opportunity to refuse donation, presumed consent looks more like a compulsory form of donation or forced acquisition of human tissue. Compulsory donation makes transplantation problematic. Forced use of others' tissues is justifiable only if donation is viewed as a civic responsibility or if our bodies are property of the state. Donation as a civic duty is an interesting concept, but is not supported by social custom or an American legal tradition.

Presumed consent legislation is also burdened by existing legal and ethical pitfalls and problems.[95] Courts struggle with how exactly to treat the growing litigation resulting from nonconsensual body part appropriation.[96] Lawsuits alleging due process violations, negligence, and interference with corpses result in different verdicts depending on jurisdiction and whether the case was heard in state versus federal court.[97] Some eye bank officials, including those from California and Alabama, credited presumed consent laws with increasing corneal tissues available for transplantation in their states.[98] Indeed, data from these states indicate that corneas available for transplantation increased, particularly as more tissues were available from victims of trauma and homicides.[99] Disproportionately, the homicide victims were Black and Latino and, in California, they comprised the primary pool of unwitting donors. Over 80% of nonconsensual cornea harvests in Los Angeles were from Black and Latino cadavers.[100] In some instances surpluses were created that allowed for tissue banks to sell "leftover" tissues to medical research laboratories sometimes at tremendous markups.[101] Doheny Eye and Tissue Bank and the L. A. Coroner's Office developed an arrangement whereby the Coroner's Office was paid "an average of about $250 for a set of corneas, which [were] then sold to transplant institutions for a 'processing fee' of $3,400."[102]

Thus, whether presumed consent has always worked effectively is debatable.[103] Problems regarding tissue extractions without consent and the possibility of transmitting communicable diseases where health or social histories have not been obtained, transplanting low-quality biological materials, and failure to obtain consent highlight some concerns of presumed consent opponents. Presumed consent opponents also argue that any policy that limits donor autonomy and ignores family consent is fundamentally flawed. Chapter 6 further scrutinizes presumed consent legislation and articulates reasons to avoid such a system for organ procurement.

6. Tissue Sales and Donor Betrayal

Other by-products of the current procurement system also transpire in the shadows of the law, including a robust commercial market in which human skin, tissue, valves, brains, bones, and other body parts are traded commercially between university hospitals, brokers, and biotech firms. Here too there is a supply versus demand disparity, but donation requests are not made by the Fortune 500 companies that financially benefit from these transplantations. Greater communication and transparency in this industry might illuminate that donors have been misled. For example, what happens to the nonviable organ donated to organ procurement organizations (OPO)?[104] Is it buried? Returned to relatives? Most policies allow hospitals and OPOs to dispose of the body part. Most altruistic donors presume that the cadavers they donate for medical or scientific purposes will never enter the stream of commerce nor move from the institution to which they donated the body or body part. Perhaps in this biotech age such assumptions are not wise. As noted earlier, federal law prohibits the sale of human body parts, yet, from California to Maine human donations enter altruistically and exit commercially. Altruistic human donations are part of a nearly *billion dollar* per year industry whose rapid expansion can be traced on the New York Stock Exchange.[105] Altruistic procurement is not to be blamed for a renegade marketplace. Rather, a business industry has developed that capitalizes on free body parts and donor ignorance. Ironically, in the case of private, commercial transactions in body parts, only the donors are expected to act altruistically.

Concerns involving the private commercial transplantation industry briefly came to light in 2004 when a body parts broker and an official at the University of California at Los Angeles' (UCLA) Willed Body Program were arrested for selling frozen body parts to medical research laboratories.[106] For over six years, twice per week, a body parts broker, Ernest Nelson, had an arrangement with the chief of procurement for the UCLA School of Medicine, Henry Reid, whereby Nelson dissected body parts from cadavers and sold them to his corporate sources.[107]

According to reports, Nelson collected "knees, hands, torsos, and other body parts needed by his corporate clients involved in private medical research."[108] Among Nelson's clients was the Fortune 500 pharmaceutical giant, Johnson & Johnson.[109] Johnson & Johnson's subsidiary, Mitek, obtained tissue from Nelson in the 1990s.[110] UCLA's program was scandalized; apologies were issued by university officials, donors filed a class action lawsuit, and reporters from across the globe investigated the allegations. However, UCLA is simply the canary in the coalmine. Other medical schools, university hospitals, and organ procurement organizations are known to engage in such clandestine transactions.[111] In fact, not-for-profit donation centers, including hospitals, are sometimes linked to for-profit, commercial tissue banks. Transactions in the tissue-processing industry are problematic, but seemingly protected by a loophole in the National Organ Transplantation Act, which provides for reasonable fees to be used in the transporting and processing of human body parts. Tissue procurement and organ procurement are more closely linked than either the organ procurement organizations or tissue banks disclose.

The Food and Drug Administration reports that over 200 private companies that treat and reprocess human body parts operate in the United States.[112] What the federal government has not asked is from where the body parts are coming. Failure to aggressively regulate in this area will be problematic. When defective body parts enter the stream of commerce, as discussed in Chapter 8, courts will have limited guidance on how to proceed and who should prevail – the unsuspecting donee or the manufacturer that created the new part? Does a family have standing to sue for misappropriation of a body it has donated? Are the purchasers of products derived from diseased human body parts such as knees out of luck against manufacturers for negligence when the parts are defective? Tissue purchasing is hardly isolated. Bodies have been purchased by the U.S. military from Tulane University to test ammunitions.[113] Bodies have also been used for product-safety research, including for crash-test dummies.[114] Most replacement knees today are a product of reprocessed donated human tissues subsequently sold to hospitals.[115] To be sure, the services provided by the commercial industry are very important: Reprocessing human bones to create knees, heart valves, and replace bones destroyed by cancer enhance the quality of life for thousands each year. Yet what information, consideration, and mutual bargaining power are owed donors?

C. Reform: An Alternative Vision

Exclusive reliance on altruism in organ procurement is a losing battle. Waitlist delays and the rising death tolls of those waiting for organs indicate that the current transplantation system has stretched far beyond its capacity.[116] This system failure has real, painful meanings for the critically ill, their families, and society. The problem is not a shortage of human tissues, bone marrow, or organs. Rather, legal options for obtaining human tissues, organs, and bone marrow are limited, thereby reducing medical consumers' real options to only one possibility: altruistic procurement.

How many people need die or experience exploitation domestically or abroad before we are willing to consider alternative transplantation approaches? This book offers an opportunity for dialogue and transparent communication about organ and tissue procurement in the United States. It encourages alternative visions for the U.S. transplantation system. It challenges legislators, scholars, and bioethicists to think beyond present procurement strategies and recognize the limits of altruism. This book describes the current altruistic procurement process and its companion, the allocation regime. It analyzes the pitfalls and problems in the current approach but acknowledges specific benefits derived from altruistic procurement. The book scrutinizes the legislative and judicial history of organ transactions, providing the reader with a view of the inconsistent case law developed in recent decades. The cases presented herein bring us closer to understanding the personal challenges and journeys of families attempting to reconcile duties to the living and responsibilities to the sick. I offer a different vision for organ and tissue procurement that involves a hybrid model. Along those lines, I scrutinize the presumption that markets are necessarily and always detrimental to people of color, particularly African Americans. The book argues that a limited market in body parts would not resemble slavery and that such antimarket rhetoric obscures the real challenges in procurement, including overcoming racial and socioeconomic bias.

Alternatives

There are three alternatives more immediately available to enhance organ procurement: presumed consent, directed donations, and commodification. Each could potentially increase organ donations. A fourth, cloning, is a biotechnological possibility, but it is far less certain how individuals' bodies would respond to cloned organs. Other technologies seem promising in helping to address America's organ shortage, particularly stem cell therapy[117] and even xenotransplantation.[118] However, the technology for both therapies is too premature to guarantee success, and thus cannot resolve the present shortage of transplantable organs.

Each model – presumed consent, directed donations, and commodification – might be described as a more competent organ procurement model than our present system. Yet, these regimes are not without controversy. Prior scholarship scrutinizes presumed consent.[119] Some of that scholarship squarely addresses race.[120] The second alternative, directed donations, which would allow African Americans to donate to other African Americans to increase both their confidence and participation in the transplantation system, will nevertheless pose due process and equal protection problems. These problems, as well as benefits, are worth investigating. The third alternative, commodification, is outlawed in the United States. Few scholars have seriously debated its merits or drawbacks.[121] Guido Calabresi, Margaret Radin, Gloria Banks, Michael Gill, Bill Sade, and more recently Rhadiko Rao have written in this area. Reproductive technology provides one persuasive example of Americans' willingness to utilize markets to both procure and allocate human resources.

Hybrid System

I recommend a transparent, hybrid system that supports altruistic procurement. The book argues for reform in the form of a hybrid commoditization system that would allow for altruism and commoditization to mutually thrive. The proposed system embraces a transparent but limited market approach. It is clear, however, that the introduction of alternatives requires making tough choices and considering unattractive possibilities. By acknowledging past criticism of commoditization, I address both the moral and instrumentalist arguments put forth by market opponents. Commoditization alternatives are more familiar to us, yet currently transpire in nonideal ways outside of the law. Private organ negotiations occur in the shadows of law as organ sales to individuals are prohibited by federal statute, but occur anyway in and outside of the legal gaze.[122] These black market institutions are not the types of systems worthy of replication, but they indicate that a failed altruistic system will drive individuals to market-based approaches.[123]

This proposed market model would be restricted to posthumous harvesting (after death), avoiding the murkier and problematic issues involved in living donations. The coexistence of the two approaches would be a narrow but inventive first step toward resolving our organ crisis. Under the proposed model, individuals would not be compensated for providing a live donation. Rather, this proposal would allow for individuals to negotiate for organ transfer upon death. Family members or a decedent's estate could be compensated for organ donations, as well as charitable organizations.

Slavery Debate

Lastly, and most importantly, this book squarely challenges the liberal notion that a market model in organ transplantation is "just like slavery." This book debunks the notion that a posthumous market in cadaveric organs will necessarily harm African Americans and their domestic interests. Commentators who offer such practiced refrains have not studied the question of supply and demand among African Americans deeply enough. This book argues that a hybrid system, which transparently engages the public and private aspects of organ procurement, will likely help African Americans whose needs for organs, particularly kidneys, exceed all other ethnic populations.[124] The slave/organ comparison is provocative, but not constructive.

American slavery was a gross form of involuntary servitude targeted almost exclusively at Blacks from Africa.[125] The injustice of American slavery has much to do with the nature and construction of the horrible practice. Slave policies were sanctioned and legitimized by legislatures and courts unwilling to recognize the humanity, citizenship, and human status of Blacks (as distinguishable from Blacks' legal status as chattel).[126] Thus, there was no system within our tripartite government from which equitable relief could be sought and rights asserted; there were no enforceable "slave rights." Thus, if a slave were harmed, her "master" could bring suit, but not the slave because she had no legal standing in American courts.[127] However, these particular legal conditions are not part of contemporary Black life.

To be clear, American slavery was a barbaric system of engagement, in which religious thinkers,[128] politicians,[129] judges,[130] and even presidents[131] were complicit in its perpetuation and the denigration of Blacks. That slavery was a system designed to harvest Blacks from Africa and forcibly transplant them to the United States gives only one point for comparison to our contemporary debate about organ transplantation. It is a historic fact of great significance. This point, however, is not persuasive enough to foreclose a legitimate study of market options in transplantations.[132]

D. Research Framework: Law and Status

In the larger picture I explore how the introduction of market systems will affect marginalized or vulnerable groups; in this instance organ candidates. In a corresponding and equally important frame, I explore the same questions, but study them from the perspective of racial minorities. In doing so, I adopt a law-and-status approach to critique how current and past rules governing ownership of body parts affect organ waitlist candidates, particularly African Americans. African Americans are a central research focus of this project as they demonstrate a disproportionately high rate of organ failure (and thus demand) that exceeds all American ethnic populations. They are the ideal population on which to base research and policy recommendations regarding organ transplantation and systems for procurement. The supply and demand questions, therefore resonate penetratingly clear for that group as they are the canaries in the coalmines. By bringing to light the injustices and disparities that are more evident when studying African Americans in the altruistic system, the entire system is better exposed and appropriate, functional alternatives can be sought.

Law and status is not a unique or new method to explore legal questions.[133] In recent decades scholarly examination of law and organized labor,[134] law and race,[135] feminist jurisprudence (exploring the law and status of women),[136] elder law,[137] and more recently law and sexual orientation scholarship[138] demonstrated the value of making legal inquiry relevant to social problems and institutions. Law and status is perhaps a more comprehensive model than simply utilizing a normative or positivist framework to discuss whether altruism is a functional organ procurement system or has reached its limits. Rather, using a law-and-status approach provides an opportunity to employ different legal schools of thought, including doctrinalism (or formalism), legal process, and law and economics to scrutinize how altruism as an organ procurement procedure (or methodology) affects those who are shut out, but on the other hand could potentially be exploited, coerced, or defrauded in a commoditized organ procurement regime. Law and status focuses on how all law and social rules combine to create particular outcomes for particular groups. As part of that type of inquiry, this book examines prior case law, social movements or trends, legislative efforts, and incorporates interviews with organ procurement specialists (both within and outside of traditional legal frameworks), and surveys of hundreds of African Americans who were asked to respond to questions regarding organ donation, body ownership, and states rights versus individual autonomy.

The data in the following chapters are based on the most recently available information from the Organ Procurement and Transplantation Network (OPTN) and the United Network for Organ Sharing (UNOS). At times the data between the two organizations is not consistent, although OPTN operates under the guidance of UNOS. Every effort has been made to ensure that the data is up-to-date and accurate.

Understanding the Strain on Altruism

> Since there are too few organs to go around, how we distribute the organs that are available decides who will live and who will die.
>
> Senator Bill Frist (2000) (R-Tenn.)[1]

Part I of this book studies the strains on the altruistic organ and tissue donation model in the United States. This section examines organ supply and demand by critiquing what "altruistic" organ donation has come to mean in terms of social perception. Part I scrutinizes the use of "The Gift of Life" marketing concept, arguing that it is far too attenuated to promote broad-scale participant confidence. Highlighted in this portion of the book are two separate studies involving African Americans. The first of the two studies examined African Americans' perceptions about organ transplantation more generally, including incentives versus compulsory and voluntary procurement strategies. The second study asked a diverse cross-section of African Americans about their willingness to participate in different transplant regimes. Part I highlights perceptions from study participants who shared deep-rooted concerns and fears about organ donation as we currently know it.

Emptied corpse: organ trafficking at Lefortovo, Russia. The lonely, naked, cadaver lies on the basement floor of crowded Morgue No. 2. The Lefortorvo Morgue was the sight of scandal and corruption. Whistle blowers exposed its black market sales of eyes, kidneys, and other cadaveric body parts. Russia's presumed consent laws make bodies available for harvesting, but are also linked to the black market. Body parts from Lefortovo have been linked to American companies. (Corbis Images)

2 Institutional Supply, Demand, and Legitimacy

INTRODUCTION

In Chapter 2, I analyze the limits of altruism and the "gift" model concept. It argues that we should rethink our exclusive relationship with altruism. Chapter 2 uses empirical data to explore institutional choice and why it seems we are wedded to particular institutional models at certain times. The "ethic" of volunteerism is what drives our altruistic procurement system.[1] Indeed, the strategic information campaigns, promoting donation as a courageous act that is so valuable that it is priceless, transformed the language of organ donation, but has not reached its mark to increase participation from potential donors. In doing so, marketing experts created a metaphor trapped in its own cloak or rhetoric. The "gift of life" is a fallacy according to Siminoff and Chillag.[2] Organ donation, according to the authors, is more like creating a fettered "creditor-debtor" relationship with the inability of donors or recipients to ever fully come to closure with the transaction.[3] The issues examined in Chapter 2 extend beyond donors and recipients, and thereby involve questions of equitable redistribution and sharing, faith, and confidence. Fully comprehending the strains on altruism requires situating the model within this broader social context and exploring its physical capacity to accommodate medical needs.

This chapter begins by examining institutional efficiency and legitimacy. What are the goals of our procurement process and who will evaluate whether those goals are met? What are the pitfalls or promises of having only one institution weigh in on that type of decision making? In particular, this section begins with the question of medical trust in government-sponsored relationships. It argues that a legacy of pernicious medicine in the United States must come to light and perhaps in the process of acknowledgment, trust might be restored. The next section provides an empirical overview of organ demand in the United States over a 15-year period, from 1990 to 2005, utilizing data collected from the UNOS (however, the data for 2005 reflects available information as of July 2005). This chapter concludes by examining faith and confidence in the altruistic system, particularly from the focus of African Americans. Data collected from a qualitative study involving African Americans in Chicago help to illume their hesitation, fears, reluctance, and lack of confidence in the current procurement model. Their concerns are complex, residing not exclusively in the procurement process. They also expressed deep misgivings about how organs are distributed and government involvement.

A. Medical Trust and Government-Sponsored Medicine

Black bodies often found their way to dissecting tables, operating amphitheaters, classroom or bedside demonstrations, and experimental facilities.[4]

Most Americans support organ donation in theory, but in practice individuals are reluctant to participate in the altruistic process.[5] For African Americans, the notorious syphilis study sponsored by the U.S. Public Health Service (PHS) and carried out by government doctors speaks to a legacy of medical abuse and betrayal[6] that must be acknowledged if modern medicine, including organ transplantation,[7] clinical trials,[8] and other therapies,[9] are to gain legitimacy within Black communities.[10] The syphilis study is but one stop on a long journey of pernicious medicine involving Black Americans that reaches back to experimentation on slaves[11] to eugenics (sterilization) practices in the second half of the last century,[12] which lasted beyond the syphilis study, and recent cornea transplant scandals.[13] Some commentators might dismiss the relevance of past breaches of medical ethics against African Americans, but doing so is a grave mistake.

The infamous syphilis study, commonly known as the Tuskegee Study, was conducted on 399 Black men in the late stages of syphilis from 1932 until 1972.[14] Researchers purposefully targeted these men. They were uneducated, mostly illiterate men, the majority of whom were sharecroppers in one of the poorest rural counties in Alabama. Participants in the study were never informed about the disease, how it destroys the body, or its cure. In fact, most were told they simply had "bad blood." Study participants suffered from tertiary syphilis, which can result in blindness, tumors, heart disease, insanity, paralysis, and ultimately death. The purpose of the study was to collect data on the corpses of men ravaged by syphilis. Thus, the men were meant to die during the period of observation because research was intended to truly begin postmortem at the autopsies.

The Tuskegee experiment is thought to be the longest nontherapeutic medical study on human beings in the world. By the time President Clinton apologized for the government's complicity in conducting this study in 1997, only eight survivors remained. Others died directly from syphilis or syphilis-related diseases. Twenty-eight men died from syphilis and 100 died from related complications. This toll was excised on their families too; 40 of their wives became infected and 19 of their children were born with congenital birth defects resulting from syphilis.

Coercion, fear, and social manipulation were the modus operandi for collecting and retaining the men in the Tuskegee research study. In fact, the men were promised free medical care, and were often sent communications reading, "last chance" for free medical care. The medical care provided were painful spinal taps and special pink pills, which were only aspirin.[15] Among the information withheld were the critical after-death studies on their corpses and the dissecting of the syphilis-ravaged bodies. On the other hand, the study participants were commended for good behavior and checking in with their physicians. The U.S. Surgeon General sent certificates of appreciation to the men who lasted in the study for 25 years.

The Tuskegee Study lives in the memories of African Americans, not only because the victims were coerced by doctors in their unfettered pursuit of syphilis-ridden corpses, but also because the experiment continued in the wake of international criticism of Nazi experimentation. Indeed, government doctors and lawyers criticized Nazi doctors for engaging in notorious human studies. The PHS attempted to justify the study and their conduct, explaining the great need to confirm that White bodies and Black bodies respond differently to diseases and even medical treatments. The study continued despite which political party occupied the White House or led Congress, through liberal and conservative administrations, the establishment of the Nuremberg Code, and other national and international medical ethics protocols. The study continued even beyond the discovery of penicillin, which cures syphilis.

According to former president William Clinton, "The United States government did something that was wrong – deeply, profoundly, morally wrong. It was an outrage to our commitment to integrity and equality for all our citizens... clearly racist."[16] Thus, it should not be a curiosity that African Americans are leery of government-sponsored or related programs involving the body. Clearly, there are two different prisms through which Blacks and some researchers and those in medical communities have come to value Black bodies. For example, Dr. James Marion Sims, considered the founder of modern gynecological medicine, wrote that Blacks endured pain far better than Whites. Sims based his respected assertion on numerous medical experiments and gynecological surgeries he personally carried out on his women slaves, Lucy and Anarcha, without any anesthesia.[17]

In testifying before a congressional subcommittee, Dr. Benjamin Payton, president of Tuskegee University, urged lawmakers to understand why "African Americans exhibit a disproportionately large amount of cynicism and lack of confidence in the U.S. health and research establishment.[18] Some studies link that mistrust to a long history of medical abuse extending back as far as slavery. Others assert a more recent and direct relationship to what has come to be called 'The Tuskegee Experiment' that was conducted by the Public Health Service... on poor Black males in Alabama."[19]

Thus, African Americans are justifiably cautious about the type and quality of relationships they seek to develop with the medical community and government-supported medical programs. Racial discrimination in medicine is not easily forgotten for them, particularly as patterns of disparities in access and treatment continually emerge.[20] The Institute of Medicine Study in 2002 and the subsequent book, *Unequal Treatment*, provide compelling evidence of contemporary discrimination in medicine. For this reason, the past lives on, including the medical experimentation on slaves. Slaves were involuntary subjects of early American experimentation.[21] Goodson writes that the Medical College of the state of South Carolina "like other Southern medical schools, used live Africans extensively in medical demonstrations, and dead ones for dissection."[22] Francois Marie Prevost "introduced the cesarean section operation to doctors in Louisiana" and for five years, between 1820 and 1825, "he operated exclusively on enslaved women."[23] Other medical accomplishments born on the bodies of enslaved Blacks were the removal of ovaries by Ephraim McDowell and James Marion Sims' notorious but largely uncontested experiments on enslaved women, which resulted in the creation of the speculum and earned him the distinction, "Father of Gynecology."[24] Sims became famous for mastering the repair of vesico vaginal fistula. However, his "ideas about the Black woman's ability to withstand pain and about her coarser constitution converged with ideas about the need for the development of gynecological surgery."[25]

In his autobiography, *The Story of My Life*, Sims speaks passionately about regularly experimenting on his female slaves year-round.[26] In one passage he describes taking a "three week break" from his experiments on enslaved Black women and the clamorous anxiety in the house because of the break.[27] Sims preferred to perform surgeries without anesthesia or at least he refused to use it on the enslaved women, although postoperatively, he provided opium. One slave, Anarcha, suffered through 13 operations to correct her vesico vaginal fistula, which resulted from deprivation of a healthy diet.

I was always anxious to see the result of all experiments; but this was attended with such marked symptoms of improvement, in every way, that I was more anxious now than ever. When the week rolled around – it seemed to me that the time would never come for the removal of the sutures – Anarcha was removed from the bed and carried to the operation table. With a palpitating heart and an anxious mind, I turned her on her side, introduced the speculum, and there lay the suture apparatus just exactly as I had placed it . . . I had made . . . one of the most important discoveries of the age . . . [28]

The past continues to inform the present for African Americans.[29] Ironically, in Sims' home state, South Carolina, tensions continue to exist among Black women, the medical community, and the state. Nowhere is that more crystallized than in the case of Regina McKnight and dozens of other Black women whose doctors selectively turned over laboratory test results of their urine to prosecutors. The women sought and were encouraged to receive prenatal services through a public service announcement campaign. The program, however, was in actuality focused on prosecuting women who used drugs during pregnancy. It would appear that it was racially motivated as well, as only Black women and two White women with Black boyfriends were prosecuted. Nurses and doctors at the hospitals sponsoring the program created an agreement with prosecutors that they would provide evidence of their patient's drug use by taking urine samples and releasing the results to prosecutors. Regina McKnight continues to serve a 20-year sentence reduced to 12 years for birthing a stillborn child.

Overcoming the dynamics and perceptions of discrimination in medicine and medical research will prove essential for the promotion of African American participation in organ procurement regimes. If African Americans are to be taken seriously in the organ procurement process, medical conflicts must not be treated as simply a part of the past. For some, this concept might be difficult to grasp, particularly because it involves race, class, and memory. For example, a researcher at an annual meeting of the Law and Society Association asked me, "what have eugenics, slave experimentations, sterilizations, and non-consensual cornea removals to do with organ transplantation?" The relationship between organ transplantation and some of these medical inquiries is more obvious than with others. There are many answers to his question, including the fact that all medical instances mentioned involved mining Black bodies for a "social" good, whether to rid society of potentially degenerate offspring or to give sight to others. The violations of trust and episodic instances involving abuse of power create a pattern that stretches across generations, which for Blacks becomes systemic. One of the fundamental tensions underlying these issues is the desire for some to move on and others to protect themselves by remembering.

African American participation in organ procurement may not be served by the present organization of the altruistic model, which relies on governmental actors convincing families at their most sensitive moment before a relative has passed, to donate an organ.[30] African Americans, as you will observe later in this chapter, are highly suspicious of that process. Secondly, the altruistic model undervalues the importance of information; generally, donors do not know to whom their organs will go. And although protecting recipient identity is laudable, it fails to address this particular concern for African Americans. African Americans assume that doctors will not attempt to save their lives (if they pre-consent to organ donation), that Whites will be the beneficiaries of their organs, and Blacks will be passed over. Interestingly, the desire to know more about the recipients is shared not only by African Americans, but also other groups. African Americans desire greater transparency in medicine, particularly in nontherapeutic procedures. Effective procurement regimes must be information focused, and promote greater individual autonomy and control in order to secure African American trust and participation.

Ultimately, for the transplantation system to work competently, individuals who can supply must match effectively with those individuals in demand. Although the proposition may seem obvious, recognizing matching as fundamental to the process helps us to better grasp how best to link the parties for effective outcomes. Currently, we attempt to push triangles, circles, and trapezoids into square holes. What this means is that we have not tested African Americans' (or for that matter any other group's) style for donating outside of our rigid rubric of altruism. We cannot assume that African Americans wouldn't be more viable participants under a different organ procurement model. A focus on matching experience with institutions also helps us to recognize which institutions or systems are best suited to address these demands. Those with demands or needs have vested interests in participating with institutions that will meet their needs. Participation in systems that are perceived as biased, perpetuate delays, and involve high risks is less attractive. Potential organ suppliers are likely to have limited interest in participating in systems wherein they anticipate limited or no reward. Thus, joining the disinterested or reluctant potential supplier with the needy will result in poor outcomes. Such outcomes characterize the present altruistic system.

B. Institutional Competency

Neil Komesar's philosophical examination of the rule of law in *Law's Limits* is informative for the purpose of studying transplantation regimes, particularly supply, demand, and institutional capacity.[31] Komesar's approach to comparative institutional analysis and its applicability to other forms of institutional dynamics, particularly private versus public institutions, seem clear. In *Law's Limits*, he argues that alternatives must be sought when institutions reach their capacity and can no longer operate effectively. The difficulty is often deciding what institution should make the decision to move on to another system.

Komesar uses property disputes to demonstrate the difficulty of a single institution approach. Specifically, he recommends that alternatives to the judicial process must be sought for addressing harms arising from property disputes when institutional capacity becomes overtaxed, resulting in judicial inefficiency, delay, and impairment of its substantive abilities.[32] In his opinion, the considerable demands for adjudicative lawmaking in property disputes strain the ability of courts – on the simplest level with financial costs.[33] The costs, however, are more than financial. These processes are highly political, and the judicial (or court) alternative, like altruism, is a "known," less controversial – "accepted" model. Such models, like courts in property disputes or altruism for the procurement of organs rock the boat far less, but increasingly pose greater risks for participants. In the case of altruism the risks are high, including death. Inevitably, courts cannot competently address the growing public and individual demands to create new law through the adjudicative process. Likewise, altruistic procurement cannot efficiently meet the current nor it appears future demands for human organ and tissue supply.

Choices are to be made, and all choices are not equal, nor do the best choices come without controversy and tension. According to Komesar, "[a]ll institutions are imperfect and choice between alternatives can be sensibly made only by considering their relative merits."[34] Although Komesar analyzes what the law is and can be for addressing property disputes, his comparative institutional approach is refreshing. The model he lays out is useful for exploring and analyzing supply and demand in an organ transplantation system. The growing demands on altruism to answer the call for organs has overtaxed a system that is now incapable of fully or competently responding to a fraction of patients' needs. As we discuss later, altruism is burdened by a number of uncontrollable variables, including volunteerism and mixed perceptions about government-sponsored programs that involve harvesting body parts.

Institutional Goals

The primary goals of any institution controlling the supply of precious goods should be efficiency, fairness, and legitimacy. These goals are not complicated. By efficiency, we need to generate an adequate supply of organs to generally meet demand. Let us not forget – this means generating organ supply. Efficiency does not portend that all demands should be met, but rather based on equitable criteria we will attempt to reduce the social costs of people living with terminal illnesses by providing a life-saving alternative. Efficiency in this case (i.e., supplying organs) cannot be measured by good intentions, but rather by the number of organs brought into the supply pool. Drawbacks of low performance and efficiency in altruism are the rationing models that naturally develop from them. When the supply of anything is low, rationing occurs and the methods by which this is done are not always fair.

By fairness, we should desire to adopt policies that reduce the likelihood for racial, gender, and other forms of discrimination based on immutable characteristics and other social biases. Nor are the first two simple goals difficult to identify. Yet the body (or "oversight arm") that determines the operative goals of such institutions (in this case UNOS) influences how those institutional models like altruism are evaluated and how their successes are measured. Unfortunately, oversight arms are at times too wedded to their institutions and therefore unable to effectively evaluate when their institutional models strain beyond capacity. In other words, recognizing the need for institutional change varies according to the prisms through which different groups and organizations study institutional efficiency. Here is a tension. Specifically, wedding to one model becomes a political choice and the very goals of the supply model can be neglected. For this reason, institutional legitimacy cannot be disregarded as it tracks the long-term relationship an institution will enjoy with its public. If institutions are perceived as untrustworthy, inefficient, and biased, they will lose participant trust and confidence.

The black market in organs and the grey market in tissues, along with other problems highlighted in Chapter 1, give evidence of altruism's unconquerable strains. Not all strains in any given institution indicate system failure. However, in this case, the by-products of our limited approach influence the creation of nefarious secondary procurement systems and result in thousands of deaths each year. Altruism is no longer an efficient model for organ supply. When systems fail, alternatives must be sought. Strains on the altruistic model have produced tough individual and institutional choices. Allocating resources properly means considering demand as well as supply and assessing institutional value based on a broad set of factors including the ability to meet social demand. This, in the context of legal demands, means looking at more than courts.[35] By comparison, in the transplantation context, it means looking beyond altruistic regimes. Meeting organ demand necessitates studying other procurement models and their attendant health, social, moral, and economic considerations. The coexisting factors necessarily include distribution, autonomy, safety, efficiency, and ethics. Such a dialogue must also scrutinize the roles of racial and ethnic status and the political process.

Institutional Supply and Demand

My purpose here is not to suggest the elimination or the scaling down of altruism in human organ and tissue supply. Its institutional strengths are well established despite very acute drawbacks. Altruistic procurement may be the least morally offensive of all possible procurement strategies. Altruism serves a fundamental purpose in the procurement of valuable human biological supplies by permitting individuals to consensually share their physical resources (or that of their relatives) with individuals in need.

Rather, the effort in this chapter is to critique altruism's viability, efficiency, and competence in light of demand and public perception. Altruism cannot resolve the American organ demand problem. The reality of an alternative procurement system will only come about if commentators critically examine the deficits in our present model and the costs associated with exclusively engaging in a procurement paradigm plagued by incertitude, lack of participation, mistrust, perceptions (grounded or not) of patient abuse, and impaired confidence. Law-making in this regard will be slow until legislators unblind themselves to the risks of altruism. Altruism's weaknesses compromise the legitimacy and, ultimately, the competency of the procurement system, not simply because of their existence, but by a failure to respond in light of thousands of preventable deaths each year.

Since 1988, organ donations have plateaued, becoming a reliable pool of a certain dimension, but overall relatively stagnant in light of demand.[36] The pool is continually reconstituted to a certain sustained but insufficient supply, which inevitably holds promise for only some waitlist patients, but not all. The altruistic pool is divided between living and deceased donors and within each of these frameworks different dynamics exist as discussed more extensively in Chapters 3, 4, and 5.

Within the deceased pool, organ providers tend to be anonymous donors and their motivations may be very different from living donors whose actions may be motivated by familial affiliations as well as a range of emotions from love to guilt. Nearly half of all deceased donors are the arbitrary victims of motor vehicle accidents, homicide, child abuse, and other causes not defined by the Organ Procurement and Transplantation Network.[37] The other half represents deaths by diseases and natural causes.[38] Figure 2.1 illustrates the compositional characteristics of the deceased donor pool.[39]

UNOS and OPTN data reveal minimal annual gains nationwide, but also from state to state in deceased or cadaveric organ donation. Indeed, the numbers are shockingly low.[40] By examining state data from particular regions of the country, we might be able to determine whether the organ shortage is confined to one area of the country or more pervasive. For example, in New York in 1988, 224 organs of deceased persons were

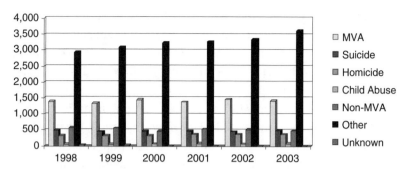

Figure 2.1. Deceased donor pool graph.

donated to the organ procurement organization.[41] That figure increased only slightly by 2003; only 353 deceased donations were recovered in that year.[42] Thus, the increase was only 129 organs in the course of 15 years. How do we evaluate the significance of that data? On one hand, these figures demonstrate an almost 50% increase in the volume of organs donated, which in the abstract could be celebrated as a remarkable gain. However, the reality of this slight improvement leaves much to ponder.

If we are to consider context, and measure altruism's value in light of demand, we might reconsider the meaning of incremental increases in organ donation even at local levels. Assessing procurement needs at the local level might assist individual regions, states, and cities in determining the efficiency of altruism and its dynamics. It might also point us in other directions for particular cities and states based on particular needs. For example, although 353 deceased donors provided organs in New York in 2003, there were over 7,000 candidates awaiting organ transplants.[43]

In Virginia, 67 organs from deceased persons were recovered in 1988. According to the 2004 OPTN Annual Report, 77 organs were recovered from deceased Virginians in 2002.[44] In California, 648 organs were recovered from deceased donors in 2002.[45] Fourteen years earlier, in 1988, the state organ procurement organization recovered 496.[46] Despite efforts from members of Congress, an aggressive campaign by the former Secretary of Health Donna Shalala, public service announcements, media campaigns, and significant state involvement, donations in the altruistic system remain relatively low. UNOS statistics demonstrate that altruism lacks the supply capacity to meet the demand for organs.

Physical Capacity

The inefficiency of the altruistic system could loosely be illustrated by a bowl, filled with goldfish, but with only a few ounces of water at the bottom. Those at the bottom, in this case, may survive, although the obvious pressure and strain to reach the bottom where there is a limited supply of water surely takes its toll, and whether the water will be of significant benefit once there is questionable. Along the way others strain to reach the life source; it is clear that few will survive and most others will not. Many will die. Those who are in the bowl at least have the hope that perhaps more water will be added, but this possibility is more idealistic than real. If the fish must rely exclusively on the kindness of weary, reluctant volunteers to transport water and all other avenues are closed off, it is terribly unlikely that the bowl will ever sustain an adequate water supply. Moreover, the bowl itself, even if filled with water, still would not adequately meet demand as others wait outside for inclusion. Relative to demand, the capacity of altruistic systems or institutions is constrained.

Nevertheless, participants might hope that other alternatives become available, perhaps other bowls will be supplied or tanks with fewer fish and more direct water resources added. The tragedy in this scenario, as in real life, is that many will die although other alternatives are readily available. Such risks are inherent when relying exclusively on altruism or blind goodwill in organ donation.[47] When competent institutions are overstrained, they naturally fail to meet their ultimate goals in efficient and equitable ways. There are institutional as well as collateral risks, which become readily apparent. The institutional risks include added costs, delays, and a larger but ineffective bureaucracy. Patients who cannot receive kidney transplants are placed on dialysis, which costs more than $65,000 per patient per year, which does not include pharmaceutical drug costs.[48] In addition, there is the potential for these matters to be settled in the least appropriate venues, including courts.[49]

The personal or collateral costs include deaths of individuals who give meaning to their communities.

One need not promote the eradication of altruistic donations as a resource, as those most in need of organ transplantation with very limited resources should have primary access to that system.[50] Other alternatives should be available for those with greater resources who can gain access to supply through other institutions, thereby freeing altruism to work for those who are truly the most vulnerable, particularly economically disenfranchised patients. Altruism's competence will be restored only through balanced collaboration and support with other institutions with better supply. Altruism alone has not met the demand for organs and likely will not in the future. Its incompetence has meant service for some and death for many others. The altruistic system cannot competently meet the incredible demands for organs by terminally ill patients as demonstrated by thousands of waitlist deaths occurring each year. Nor, it seems, are we prepared to turn our backs on those suffering from illnesses for which medical cures are available.

C. Competency and Altruism: A Statistical Overview

Organ donation and procurement are at the highest levels ever recorded.[51] These increases must be placed in context, however, as demand dramatically overshadows supply. With aggressive efforts at state and federal levels, organ donations have only incrementally increased.[52] The statistics are daunting. Consider kidney donations. In 1988, a total of 5,688 kidneys were donated and that number more than doubled to 12,221 by 2003.[53] Although that increase in kidney donation is impressive, it must be understood that over 50,000 Americans were waiting for roughly 12,000 kidneys in 2003. Table 2.1 illustrates kidney, liver, and heart donations from 1988 to 2003.[54] Not all donations will be viable; thus an organ donation does not always translate to an organ transplant. Nonetheless, dramatic increases can be traced between the periods recorded. Notice the increase in living donations, as discussed earlier; special dynamics attend those figures.

TABLE 2.1. Table of kidney, liver, and heart donations, 1988–2003

YEAR	Kidney Cadaveric	Kidney Living	Kidney Total	Liver Cadaveric	Liver Living	Liver Total	Heart Cadaveric	Heart Living	Heart Total
1988	3,876	1,812	5,688	1,833	0	1,833	1,784	7	1,791
1989	3,810	1,903	5,713	2,372	2	2,374	1,781	9	1,790
1990	4,306	2,094	6,400	2,868	14	2,882	2,167	12	2,179
1991	4,268	2,394	6,662	3,165	22	3,187	2,198	4	2,202
1992	4,276	2,535	6,811	3,334	33	3,367	2,246	1	2,247
1993	4,609	2,851	7,460	3,764	36	3,800	2,442	2	2,444
1994	4,797	3,009	7,806	4,093	60	4,153	2,525	3	2,528
1995	5,002	3,387	8,395	4,334	54	4,388	2,491	0	2,491
1996	5,036	3,670	8,706	4,460	62	4,522	2,461	1	2,462
1997	5,082	3,929	9,011	4,599	85	4,684	2,426	0	2,426
1998	5,338	4,410	9,748	4,844	92	4,936	2,449	0	2,449
1999	5,386	4,692	10,078	4,974	251	5,198	2,316	0	2,316
2000	5,489	5,447	10,936	4,997	385	5,382	2,283	0	2,283
2001	5,528	6,012	11,540	5,106	506	5,612	2,276	0	2,276
2002	5,636	6,236	11,872	5,293	355	5,648	2,222	0	2,222
2003	5,754	6,461	12,215	5,679	314	5,993	2,122	0	2,122
2004	6,326	6,648	12,974	6,321	323	6,644	2,096	0	2,096

The American shortage in organs available for transplantation could perhaps be more appropriately described as a newer phenomenon with a significant impact from the skyrocketing demand generated by patient-consumers and their doctors. This is well illustrated by the total number of organ transplants (liver,[55] kidney,[56] lung,[57] heart, pancreas, kidney-pancreas, and heart-lung[58]) performed from 1988 to 2003. Data from OPTN's 2004 Annual Report reveals that over a 15-year period, 1988 to 2003, organ transplantation increased by 103% from 12,618 to 25,076.[59] The data inform us that patients utilized available technology to secure life-saving treatments. Both deceased and living transplants increased, however, the significant gains experienced in living procurement enhanced growth in living transplants.[60] Transplants from cadavers increased by 69%, from 10,794 to 18,270, whereas living donor transplants nearly tripled, from 1,824 to 6,806 during that 15-year period.[61] Accompanying this growth was an increase in level of involvement among people of color in donor pools; from 1994 to 2003, organ procurement from Blacks, Asians, and Latinos increased.[62]

TABLE 2.2. Donors and candidates by organ[67]

Year	Heart Donors	Heart Candidates	Kidney Donors	Kidney Candidates	Liver Donors	Liver Candidates
1994	2,528	2,891	7,806	25,852	4,153	3,996
1996	2,462	3,640	8,706	32,310	4,522	7,351
1998	2,449	4,079	9,748	38,772	4,936	11,764
2000	2,283	3,978	10,936	44,719	5,382	16,505
2002	2,222	3,803	11,872	50,855	5,648	17,306
2003	2,121	3,529	12,221	57,211	6,000	17,515
2004	2,096	DNA	12,973	60,369	6,643	DNA

With such encouraging data, proponents of altruistic procurement may be slow to recognize its limitations, risks, and inefficiencies. The data obscures the system's failures. Despite the gains in recovered organs and increased transplantation, the number of available organs continues to fall short of the great demand.[63] Each year, the gap between the number of donors and candidates grows considerably (Table 2.2).

Thus, deciding who will be first in line once on the waitlist is part of an intense national debate as discussed later. Whereas the waitlist process provides less opportunity for subjective decision making, troubling racial disparities in distribution are nonetheless apparent.[64] These disparities relate to waiting time for organs and high death rates for non-Whites, particularly Blacks.[65] The disparities are commonly attributed to two main factors: biological differences between races and low donation rates among Blacks.[66]

Racial Disparities, Distributive Justice, and Waitlists

In 2004 OPTN released its annual report that chronicled the previous 14 years of organ transplantation waitlist data. The OPTN report is an informative guide, detailing donor and recipient data by race, gender, state, organ donated, and whether the donor was living or deceased. Those statistics, along with information gathered from interviews with Joel Newman, Jack Lynch, Scott Helm, and Dr. Mary D. Ellison, enhance the discussion that follows.[68] Between 1993 and 2000 the OPTN waitlist more than doubled, from 33,014 registered candidates to receive organ transplantation to 69,057.[69] By the end of

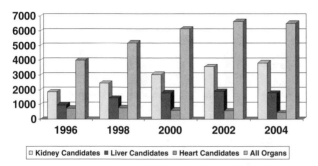

Figure 2.2. Death removals by year.

2003, 86,355 Americans were registered on organ transplant waitlists.[70] Other striking statistics also characterize contemporary challenges in organ transplantation. For example, waiting times consistently increased for all organ transplants, exacerbated by an influx of potential recipients on waitlists. This trend includes the increasing morbidity rate among patients dying before ever receiving the needed transplant.[71]

The alarming number of Americans waiting for organs steadily grows[72] while lawmakers, ethicists, and physicians grapple with best practice proposals[73] Unfortunately, state and federal proposals and media campaigns have yet to yield meaningful national (or even significant state) results.[74]

Of the patients registered in 2004, over 6,529 died while on the waitlist,[75] others died but were not included in Figure 2.2, because they were never provided the option of being on a waitlist due to severity of illness, age, or social screening. Of those most likely to die while awaiting a transplant were kidney patients, followed by liver, heart, and lung patients respectively.[76] Scott Helm agrees that these figures are troubling, particularly because "a lot of these people [on waitlists] won't ever see a transplant," referring to the growing number of African Americans waiting for kidneys, livers, hearts, and other organs.[77] African Americans have the highest death rate among all Americans on the waitlists. In comparison to other ethnic minorities, to date African American death removals are almost twice that of Hispanics and nearly seven times that of Asians.[78] To date, there have been 12,747 African Americans removed by death from waitlists; 6,492 Hispanics and 1,802 Asians.[79] Of

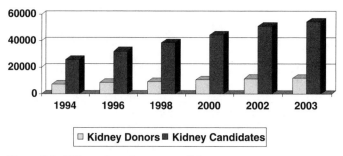

Figure 2.3. Kidney donations v. candidates.

the reported deaths in 2003, 59% were kidney patients, 27% were liver patients, 7% were heart patients, and 7% were lung patients.[80]

a. Kidney Waitlists

The gravity of the organ procurement process may be better understood as we examine the actual waiting lists. The problem, according to Coleman, is put into perspective when observing the potential kidney patients' death rates. For example, every four hours a patient awaiting a kidney will die.[81] At the turn of the last century, 44,719 people were waiting for kidneys.[82] As of July 17, 2005, 62,550 Americans waited for kidneys.[83] For kidney patients, the waiting lists more than doubled over the past 10 years.[84] In 1994, 25,827 persons were waiting for kidneys; by the close of 2003, that number had doubled to 54,231 as shown in Figure 2.3.[85] The median waiting days also increased substantially.[86] In 1994 the waiting time for a kidney was 836 days; by 2000 (the most recent year available) it had substantially increased to 1,199.[87] Nearing the end of the 1990s, so few kidney transplantations had occurred compared to need that OPTN found it "impossible... to calculate an overall median waiting time for 1996 and 1997 registrants" for its report in 1998.[88]

As for African Americans, although the number of Black patients receiving organs has increased, so has the alarming death rate of those on waitlists.[89] Registrants of color constituted 46% of those waiting for kidneys in 2003.[90] The overwhelming majority of those patients were Black.[91] Their high number reflects the fact that the number of Blacks registered for kidney transplants had increased, which indicates a growing health concern for African Americans.[92] This increase was twofold however, because Black patients' wait time also increased.[93] Blacks waited on average twice as long as Whites for kidneys; over 1,891 days for Blacks as compared to 840 for their White counterparts.[94] For Asian and Latino Americans the figures are equally troubling. Asians waited for 1,550 days and Latinos for 1,357 days for organ transplantation.[95] Perhaps most troubling about these figures is that unidentified people of color never make the waitlist and die without being counted.[96] Data collected by OPTN 2000 to 2001 shows that fewer than half of all African American kidney candidates received an organ that year. In the 1999 calendar year, Whites who received kidney transplants had waited 840 days compared to 1,891 days African Americans waited.[97] Over 3,266 African Americans have waited over five years for a kidney.[98]

The gains experienced by people of color in organ transplantation must be viewed in context with their wait times and frequency of death while on the waitlists. Commentators concerned about equity in health-care delivery should be skeptical about what the future holds since the number of kidney recipients of color peaked in the mid-1990s, only to drop toward the end of the decade.[99]

b. Liver Waitlists

The liver waitlist is the second largest patient pool for organ transplan-tation. According to the most recent UNOS data, over 17,424 Americans are registered on the liver waitlist.[100] The median waitlist for liver trans-plants for Whites increased dramatically from 656 days in 1997 to over 801 days in 2002.[101] For Blacks, the waitlist increased from 492 days in 1997 to a total well over 600 days in 2002.[102] Moreover, the number of individuals waiting for liver transplants has increased dramatically over time as shown in Figure 2.4, from 616 registrants in 1988 to 17,515 in 2003.[103] Of the total number of patients on waitlists, who represent only a fraction of those in need, over 32,902 died while waiting for liver transplants during that period.[104] Much of the increased demand can be attributed to improvements in technology, specifically with regard to immune suppressant drug therapy that has allowed for improved organ retention and lessened rejection rates.

Racial disparities extend beyond liver transplantation and affect both waitlist times and death rate statistics for persons of color. For example,

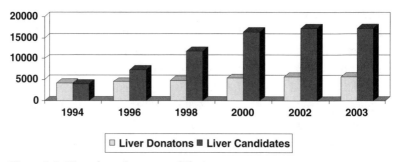

Figure 2.4. Liver donations v. candidates.

people of color, on average, have longer wait times on liver transplant lists.[105] Racial implications also extend to the death rates on the liver waiting list. Consider, for example, that over the past few years, Blacks experienced the highest mortality rate of all groups waiting for organs followed by Latinos.[106] On average, Latinos can expect to wait more than 1,263 days on a liver transplant waitlist.[107] Although Blacks and Whites waited nearly the same length of time for liver transplants, the death rate for Blacks was significantly higher, pointing out once again the unresolved racial and perhaps economic implications in the healthcare experiences between Whites and Blacks. Blacks may experience a higher rate of death because their illnesses are diagnosed at more progressed stages.

c. Heart Waitlists

Those waiting for hearts accounted for the third largest patient group dying on the lists.[108] As with other organs, the demand for hearts dramatically increased over the past 10 years as shown in Figure 2.5. The waiting list for hearts more than tripled between 1988 and 2002.[109] Near the close of the 1980s, heart registrants accounted for just over 1,000 persons on waiting lists.[110] However, by 2003 the number of heart registrants grew to 3,519.[111] By the end of 2003, over 65% of registered potential heart recipients were waiting more than a year.[112] Moreover, whereas Asians and Latinos waited on average less than Whites, Blacks remained longest on the heart waitlists.[113]

Commentators claim that the prolonged waiting times and high death rates among people of color on the waitlists are evidence of

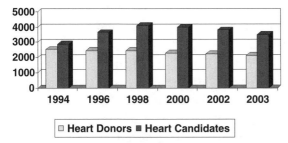

Figure 2.5. Heart donations v. candidates.

institutionalized racism in healthcare, and more specifically, in organ transplantation. The impact of racism in the American healthcare industry inevitably creates inequities that result in disparate treatment in organ transplantation.[114] Barbara Noah argues that strategic efforts to resolve the increasingly threatening prospects of more people dying while awaiting another's organ are undermined by another type of "pernicious" rationing that occurs.[115] Although such allegations might be dismissed as an oversimplification of a more complex issue, notions of justice and equity require compelling justification for these disparities. UNOS' statistics, highlighting many racial disparities, seem to demonstrate that persons of color are least likely to be informed about healthcare options and once they are notified, they may be too sick to qualify for high-tech treatments.[116]

D. Confidence and Donation

You know, like your mother or your father or your friend or somebody might pass away unexpectedly, and the first thing they do is they try to rush in and offer you like condolences for a brief moment. And then they'll say, did you think about organ donation? I mean, that's within the same breath. And it kind of makes you wonder, like, man, what's more important here, my grieving or the organ?[117]

Let us consider confidence as well. Systems that are competent but lack group confidence and buy-in are also doomed to fail and clearly those that lack participant confidence ultimately fail. Confidence in any system may be the most critical ingredient in system success; it is necessary for its sustainability and growth, and particularly for medical models, which invite invasive procedures and cross the boundaries of privacy and control. However, what is confidence comprised of and can it be located in the altruistic model?

The most recent Gallup Poll on organ donation explained that although over 85% of Americans approved of organ donation, only 20% were registered donors. Whereas this could possibly be explained 30 years ago by registration obstacles and other minor barriers impeding mass registration, such would not be true today. Organ procurement has been a federal priority with its importance trickling down at the state level in significant ways, including aggressive campaigns sponsored by organ procurement organizations (OPOs), public service announcements, and unusual efforts to pair donors with recipients in magazine and newspaper articles. Yet, statistics continue to demonstrate a marginal commitment among Americans to voluntarily, without compensation, contribute their organs.

The reluctance to donate organs could be attributed to the breach of confidence and lack of trust in the current transplantation and procurement systems. This is particularly true of African Americans who explained their distrust and lack of confidence in the altruistic model in two recent research studies conducted over a two-year period (2002–2004) in Chicago, Illinois.[118] African American Organ Transplant Study I (AAOTS I) involved 588 participants. This survey was facilitated with the assistance of local clergy in the greater Chicago area.[119] Surveys were disseminated at churches, community organizations, senior centers, and community development organizations. Chicago clergy were critical to the successful administration of the survey in African American communities because churches and religious communities have been central safe havens for Blacks in America. Clergy of African American churches assume a unique role in African American communities, particularly in Chicago where they represent religious as well as local political leadership. Rather than overcoming a trust deficit, this research benefited from the confidence parishioners invested in their clergy.

Churches in the African American communities serve a vital multipurpose role by providing spiritual guidance, political empowerment, and education. For example, until recently, some churches provided health and legal services for their congregants. Olivet Baptist Church, once one of the nation's largest churches, housed a legal service bureau and a medical clinic for its congregants. Catholic churches on the south side of Chicago were equally helpful. The churches I worked with collectively represent one of the few institutions where African Americans report having a trust relationship. Rather than target particular religious affiliations, I targeted churches in seven zip codes, which according to census data showed the greatest concentration of African Americans in the city of Chicago. Those zip codes included 60616, 60653, 60615, 60637, 60649, 60619, and 60617.

The first study (a 23-question survey), AAOTS I, involved 588 participants. The survey was designed to assess participant knowledge about kidney-related illness, treatments, including dialysis and organ transplantations, and perspectives on the law's role and function in organ transplantation. Specifically, they were asked whether the state should assume legislative authority over individuals' body parts, if commodification in organs should be legalized, and whether selling organs was like slavery. AAOTS II was a qualitative follow-up involving 40 African Americans who were interviewed during the winter and spring of 2003 to 2004. AAOTS II participants provided additional insight about African American perceptions, trust, confidence, and attitudes about organ transplantation in general and specifically the law's role and function in assessing various procurement approaches.

When asked about why fewer African Americans participate in organ donation, overwhelmingly those interviewed posited that distrust, fear, and being undervalued by physicians contributed to low donor registration. Participants perceived the altruistic process to be manipulative and a veiled effort to sacrifice African Americans to save White Americans. For example, a 27-year-old resident physician urged, "We first need to help African Americans feel more comfortable [and] trusting the healthcare system in the sense that when we say we are going to help them we are actually helping them and not manipulating them and misusing them."[120] The Director of Education at a local private college responded, "I think there's a...lack of trust of the medical community."[121] J. M., a state supreme court law clerk, opined, "There's not a lot of understanding in the Black community or Hispanic community as to what happens during organ donation. You know, there's a fear that they're going to be basically cutting you up or chopping you up, taking parts out. What are you going to look like when you get buried?"[122] J. M. added:

> You get people that say I want to get buried with all my stuff. You know, I don't want anything missing, a fear of where is this stuff going to go to. There's also some type of concern recently from shows – there's been a "Law and Order" show that comes to mind that if you're an organ donor, the doctors will sometimes take steps more so in an effort to save your organs than in an effort to save your life. I have a cousin that this happened to – that they believed it happened to – ... I think there's a big strong belief in the African American community... and maybe it's in the world at large that somehow the doctors are more concerned about harvesting the organs than what's best for the patient...

Another participant, a career coach, answered, "[African Americans] don't participate because they fear. They have myths about donating organs."[123] A local business manager confided, "I believe [they] fear because I, myself have a strong fear of donating. I still have that fear and I know people – several other people who also have that fear."[124] H. C., a day porter, remarked, "Fear, not caring. That's basically it, fear and not caring."[125]

   Others, including K., were quite direct about lack of confidence, indicating fear of a pernicious conspiracy against African Americans. She suggested that efforts to encourage African Americans to donate were part of a conspiracy "because they were going to use Black people as spare parts. You know, when White people are sick or whatever, they'll have a means to get their organs."[126] M.M., 33-year-old computer technician echoed a community-wide sentiment, "Well, the concern I've heard is that a lot of people feel that your organs will be harvested before you actually die. So if you're borderline, you could go either way, they won't do as much as they could to save your life in hopes of, you know, getting organs. So I think that's the biggest fear."[127] D.W., a 35-year-old electrician shed both humor and light on his skepticism of the transplantation system, "You went in there complaining about a little cold, a little back pain, your toe hurting. The next thing you know they're talking you died. He had gangrene. His toe fell off. He had diabetes. He didn't know..."[128] Ironically, D.W.'s cynicism is not entirely off the mark. In the 2003 Institute of Medicine Study on health-care disparities, the only category in which African Americans received more care than Whites was in amputation.[129] African Americans were six times more likely than their White counterparts to be the subjects of amputation.[130]

Although fear and mistrust were common themes, others raised the concern of community education and lack of knowledge, indicating that although African Americans are aware of the effects of high blood pressure and diabetes, and most participants knew individuals on dialysis, there were few African Americans whom they knew to have been transplant recipients. Thus the value of transplantation may be lost on communities that often find themselves symbolically if not actually shut out. U.J., a third-year law student, suggests:

You know, there's just different cultural experiences...Maybe because it was something that was probably never an option for Black people at some point in time. You know people were ill or sick, and if something failed, it just failed and they died. You know, it wasn't an option of, well, you have money to get a transplant for this...it never was an alternative..."[131]

D.J., a conductor for a major railroad, offered:

In order to get good information, you have to have good access to a doctor and the way to get good access in this country unfortunately is to either have the cash to pay for that or the insurance. So a lot of times African Americans may not have benefits at their jobs or they may have HMOs as opposed to a PPO and they may not have a doctor who is willing to give them that information for what they are getting in return. So, I don't think they have the opportunity to have knowledge passed on to them from a health provider.[132]

The feeling or experience of being shut out can have a double bind effect, the dilemma of excluding African Americans can also lead to self-exclusion and doubt about worthiness to participate. In fact, N. suggested that African Americans are "scared" about donating organs, but that she also was concerned about whether her organs were "good enough." "That was my personal feeling that my organs may not be good enough...And I really think that a lot of African Americans would say that, well, I've done this and I've done that throughout my life, and how could I possibly benefit someone else?"[133]

AAOTS II interview participants consistently raised concerns about mistrusting the organ donation process and the medical system. From a nurse sharing her personal observations on the mistreatment of African American patients in the hospital where she works to general speculation and conspiracy theories, Blacks have passed on an intergenerational fear of the altruistic procurement process. Such fear also indicates a perception that they lack control in the altruistic process and this is seemingly confirmed by the low number of registered donors.

Registering to become a donor demonstrates planning and preparation for death, much like buying a life insurance policy and cemetery plot. There appears little incentive to prepare for a process that is perceived to hasten one's life and siphon organs out of the "community." Moreover, participant comments also signify a lack of faith in the altruistic system to promote distributive justice. For example, in AAOTS I when survey participants were asked whether they are registered to donate, only 36% answered affirmatively. However, when asked whether they would be willing to donate if the recipients were Black, over 58% answered positively. Thus, the concept of organ sharing is not the problem; fewer than 10% of those surveyed opposed donation. Indeed, Blacks were more willing to donate when they believed African Americans would be treated equitably in both the procurement and allocation processes.

Several participants expressed that African Americans are not "selfish," rather their hesitation is a response to a profound mistrust of the medical system, and the procurement process in particular. One striking insight is that participants like J.F., a young banker, believed that organs were not something that African Americans would receive. He suggested that African Americans may be less concerned about organ donation because "they are not going to get them."[134] His concerns were echoed by Y.W. Y.W., a home health care nurse perceived low donation to be the result of inequities in the allocation process, noting, "usually if they would take their organs and give them to other nationalities and not African American people."[135] Her perception was shared by many others, including D.W. II, a 32-year-old assistant principal, who suggested that "the biggest concern [is] the fact that [organs] aren't being given to African Americans who need transplants. They go to the individuals who can afford and people who can afford it are usually Caucasian."[136]

Whether fear and lack of confidence would dissipate in a commoditization system and how that system would be tooled or designed differently to promote equitable outcomes are discussed in Chapter 7. Ultimately, fear and mistrust affects African American willingness to participate in the current altruistic organ procurement regime. Such fear does not seem resolved by greater information about how to engage in the process. African Americans interviewed seemed very well informed about where and how to register to become organ donors. One participant noted the Illinois Secretary of State Jesse White has been very proactive in this regard. Others referred to commercials, personal encounters at churches with donor solicitors, or advertisements in their communities. Moreover, they understand that lives are saved in the process. Nor could one suggest or affirm that their access to the altruist procurement system is blocked. Rather perceptions about injustice in the process and its companion regime, allocation, influence their opinions about its legitimacy, efficacy, and competence. Procurement and allocation are intimately interwoven in the United States. The system cannot give what it does not have, and how it presently gives (rations) has been characterized as pernicious, unfair, and inequitable. Confidence in a system indicates one's perception that the system is competent, effective, and trustworthy. Yet, if altruism is perceived as lacking in certain capacities (to the point of seriously discouraging participation), what are the alternatives?

CONCLUSION

Less frequently explored but absolutely central to the present debates about institutional choices involving altruism and organ sales are the issues involving status, race, and culture.[137] Most commentators are possibly unaware of the marked racial disparities in organ referral, transplantation, and "the waiting game." This perhaps contributes to the conspicuous absence of race in the discourse on organ commodification. This void may unfortunately imply that race is not a significant factor in the debate about the efficiency of altruism or the benefits of organ sales, consequently mistaking the issue as color neutral, which it clearly is not. Ironically, race, although ubiquitous in other discourses about health access, has been conspicuously absent from the dialogue on organ commodification, with the exception of observations comparing organ sales to African American enslavement in the United States.

Arguments that lifting the federal ban on organ sales is an act akin to endorsing a system of neomillennial slavery are political lightning rods. Potentially, such commentaries reduce intelligent debates on organ procurement to sensationalism and soft rhetoric while masking critical issues such as the high incidence of organ failure in African American communities. For example, could organ sales benefit African Americans? How would African Americans participate in a market regime? Would transfers be limited to postmortem harvests? How would such a system be regulated? Are all market schemes necessarily coercive to African Americans? Could equitable, noncoercive transfers result from informed decision making? What protocols might be necessary to ensure informed decision making?

Reports suggesting that organ alienation might entice America's poorest, ethnic minorities to subject themselves to market forces that ultimately benefit those more affluent are not entirely unpersuasive. Such apprehensions contribute to general misgivings about organ and other tissue commodification.[138] Fears pertaining to racial exploitation in a more transparent organ industry indicate the invariably troubling status of race relations in America and suggest that a commercial market in organs would further devalue people of color and the poor, thereby exacerbating preexistent patterns of social stratification.[139]

Anxieties about legal and economic exploitation of African Americans underscore problematic race relations in the United States and disparities that extend beyond the socioeconomic.[140] The question of organ sales has also shed attention on anxieties related to how the proceeds from market sales would be distributed, and to whom such funds will flow. Could a market in organs inspire illegal or immoral conduct, ranging from intrafamilial homicide to withholding lifesaving treatments? People of color, especially African Americans, figured prominently in the exploration of such questions. Undoubtedly, they would be targets of some compensation-based programs, in part because of a perceived broad socioeconomic need, but also due to historical involvement in human biological supply, consensual or not.[141] Lastly, how organ market contributors would spend the proceeds from organ sales dominates a considerable part of the larger debate, which unfortunately detracts from perhaps the more critical ethical, moral, and legal issues. These issues are explored in greater detail in subsequent chapters in Part II of the book.

Ernest Nelson (top) and Henry Reid (bottom). Both men were arrested for selling body parts donated to the University of California Los Angeles Medical School. (University of California Police Department)

3 Nuances, Judicial Authority, and The Legal Limits of Altruism

INTRODUCTION

This chapter analyzes the legal case history of organ and bone marrow transplantation. It asks how might judicial considerations be framed and what values are most essential to preserve in establishing a framework for compelled living donations? Currently, federally mandated altruism procurement constrains parents' ability to seek alternative, viable sources for children needing organ or bone marrow transplants. The weaker, less desirable options become the exclusive options quite unnecessarily. This chapter argues that children and the mentally ill are not viable replacements for an incompetent, ineffective, organ procurement system. Their involvement is symptomatic of the deeply embedded procurement strains on altruism. Their participation should be limited to the narrowest possibilities.

The chapter focuses primarily on living donations, which means the donor is alive when she donates. This chapter explores a series of questions. How should courts respond to compelled living donation and reproductive altruism? How do we balance the desire to preserve life versus the desire to protect life from unnecessary harm and interference or intrusion? John Rawls' analysis of a just society being bound in utilitarian ethics indicates morality and equity as being core principles of an optimally functioning legal and social system. How do such principles fit pragmatically in the context of organ and tissue donation, particularly with regard to children? This chapter scrutinizes these issues.

In keeping with the theme established in Chapter 1 and carried throughout, I argue that exclusive reliance on altruism to meet increasing demand for sophisticated, life-saving medical therapies forces strains on the altruistic organ and tissue transplantation system, and drives individuals to create unregulated, living-donor subsystems, some that are legal and others that are not. The altruism subsystems addressed in this chapter, *compelled living donations*, which demands organs from people either unwilling or incompetent to donate, and *reproductive altruism*, producing children specifically for organ and tissue harvesting, operate on principles inapposite to the legal values associated with altruism. These subsystems lack voluntary participation, informed consent, and mutual bargaining power, subverting the intention of altruism, with heightened possibilities for coercion, pressure, guilt, and unequal positioning. Thus, these systems are overshadowed by ethical, moral, and even legal doubts. The "gift of life" is a fallacy according to Siminoff and Chillag and perhaps they are right.[1] Organ donation, according to the authors, is more like creating a fettered "creditor-debtor" relationship with the inability of donors or recipients to ever fully come to closure with the transactions.[2] Recipients may later feel unworthy or guilty about receiving the organs, and the donors, according to a study conducted by Cheyette, may be regretful.

Section A briefly explores the language of altruism and its loaded connotations. Section B provides a brief empirical overview of living donations. It then examines the limited but often scandalous body of case law where courts struggle for guidance in an attempt to craft precedent or a reasonable test to guide compelled donation. Can we force cousins to donate bone marrow? What about half-siblings – can the courts force 3-year-olds to appear for bone marrow harvesting to save the 12-year-old brother they don't know? Section C focuses on a theory of reproductive altruism. It applies the term reproductive altruism to volitional procreation for purposes of harvesting. It cautions against such practices although it points out the lack of legal regulation to proscribe such activities. Section D concludes by suggesting that only an alternative vision for organ procurement will reduce parental demand to harvest from their children.

A. The Language of Altruism

Despite the degree to which this metaphor pervades transplantation practice, our studies have demonstrated that "gift-giving" or altruism is not necessarily the primary motivation when families decide to donate. Families often donate for nonaltruistic reasons, for example a desire to see their loved one live on in the recipient.[3]

There is the presumption, at least used by some courts, that explains living donations of children to siblings as providing a "psychological benefit" for the child donor. Such rationalizations and invoking the term "benefit" to a process that requires nontherapeutic medical intervention seems consistent with a preexisting, problematic paradigm. The presumption here is that all gift-giving is good, and that altruism as a concept in organ donation is pure and unspoiled by secondary or spurious motivations. This reasoning, as we will discuss, is seriously flawed. Far worse, however, is the problem of vernacular in organ transplantation that extends beyond terminology. Language is powerful and to the extent that children are involved in organ donation, the language of the "gift" may obscure manipulation, coercion, and downright abuse. Compelled organ donation from children is but one additional problematic by-product of the "gift" or "altruism" model. Section A addresses these concerns along with a look at individualism and its importance to a critique of altruism and status.

Individualism, according to Rawls' social contract model, should be supplanted for the betterment of the whole community.[4] Social Security is a model of altruism within a social contract framework as are the municipal benefits resulting from the taxes we pay.[5] Fletcher emphasizes a normative view of social solidarity, communal concern, and a sense of togetherness, all of which can be satisfied only in a moral community that is premised on the value of mutual responsibility. In this way, decision making for the benefit of society enures benefit to the individual.[6] Dorothy Brown, however, challenges the operation of this type of altruism, noting that it is not impervious to the social criteria otherwise used to exclude or punish those considered more marginalized, less desirable, trustworthy, or of value to society.[7]

The social contract assumes equal bargaining and acquisition power and in our present altruistic donation system we perhaps presume the same.[8] However, this view of altruism in the transplantation and broader body parts industry does not ask whether all individuals are situated similarly, even within families, particularly children and the mentally ill.[9] Theories of altruism, including Rawls' theory of social justice and fairness, are intended for democratic societies that adhere to nondiscriminatory principles. However, such altruistic theories, even if appealing, do not consider law and status as we know it in our society. So they tend to overlook preexisting imbalances in society and the compromised status of those traditionally marginalized or discriminated against.[10] Understanding the nuances of status and language are critical to the study of organ transplantation, particularly donation and why as Siminoff and Chillag assert, the "gift" concept does not work.[11] These nuances are indicated in the law's treatment of these issues as described and analyzed herein.[12]

The power of altruism resides in the performance of selfless, voluntary acts, which deprive us of some value or object that inevitably has some worth associated with it, in order to achieve a social good.[13] These deprivations are usually tangible and may be financial such as salary, labor, and stocks or those instruments that are more personal, such as a home, car, clothes, shoes, or time. At times these deprivations are temporary owing to the fact that we might inherit or be the eventual beneficiaries of our own "selfless" good deeds.[14] Perhaps the jewelry we buy our grandmothers will one day be worn by our daughters or the paintings we donate to a museum will be viewed and enjoyed by all in our community.[15] In some instances, perhaps we are motivated by other benefits such as tax credits.[16] Those motivations, however, indicate the nebulous nature of altruism; acts otherwise perceived as selfless may have underlying motivations. Through our taxes we support educating children, hoping they are better prepared to administer our government and cities when we become older and vulnerable, thereby investing in a future type of social safety.[17] In these instances, the gifting is not entirely altruistic.

At other times, our utilitarian acts are irreversible, philanthropy of a rare kind, which involve anonymity and limited if any direct benefit in our personal or professional lives.[18] These acts are perhaps the purest forms of altruism, inuring only self-satisfaction and pleasure found through others' transformations resulting from our deeds. In the realm of organ donation, such deeds are often referred to as "gifts" and "miracles."[19] Indeed, therein exists the power to love and the will to be generous absent our own desires. The enormity of such emotions can never be underestimated as it is part of a host of dynamics located within organ and tissue donation; it can be an incredible motivator to perform acts of kindness.[20]

Yet, living donation cases, particularly those involving children, are deeply nuanced and may be influenced by a host of factors too difficult to monitor and predict. These transactions involving child-donors certainly are not altruistic, but our limited vernacular for describing the processes born out of rapidly expanding biotechnology leaves us at a loss. You will note, a few pages hence, how courts reinforce the limited vernacular of the transplantation industry. Courts are not the best bodies to deal with these issues and legislative relief does not appear on the horizon. Congress has not spoken on the issue; there are no federal regulations or guidelines about appropriateness of age for child or incompetent donation. Courts are left to tangle with children gifting siblings and mostly in cases where hospitals or physicians have sought declaratory judgments (to avoid liability should mistakes occur during tissue or organ harvesting). The jurisprudence in this area must become more nuanced in light of the potential for coercion, confusion, manipulation, and conflicts of interest not only among physicians, but also parents. Indeed, each case of compelled organ donation involves competing interests among parents, physicians, courts, and children.

B. Obsessive Altruism – It's Not Really Altruism at All or Is It?

In 1994, organ donations in Italy tripled shortly after California tourists Maggie and Reg Green donated their 7-year-old son's organs following his murder during a family excursion.[21] In honor of their benevolence, hospitals, events, schools, and streets in Italy have been named for their son, Nicholas Green.[22] According to the family, they could never have anticipated what has become known in Italy as the "Nicholas Effect;" that their generosity would have such a tremendous effect on the public.[23] The Greens' blind giving, particularly after their incredible tragedy, is perhaps one of the best examples of donation as a selfless, noble act. The Greens' generosity extended altruism's reach beyond their home community.

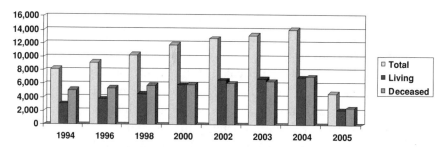

Figure 3.1. U.S. organ donors by organ donor type, 1994–2005.* * 2005 data as of July 30, 2005.

Altruism's successes however, may obscure the complicated or darker issues lurking within that framework. The lusts for power, to influence decision making, to be owed, remembered, desired, or simply to belong as a part of something, are the less desirable dynamics and passions of altruism.[24] According to Siminoff and Chillag, "altruism" in organ transplantation "carries complex and contradictory meanings that have had unexpected and detrimental effects on donor families, as well as on recipients and their caregivers."[25] These emotions complicate social giving in general, and particularly the living donor subrealm of tissue donation, wherein the psychological benefits, but also pressures are strongly connected to family relationship as the majority of these types of donations derive from family donations.[26]

Living Donations

The most dramatic increase in the altruistic pool, as shown in Figure 3.1, are living donations, which have steadily increased, whereas deceased donations have tapered. Living donations currently outpace deceased donations.[27] Compare, for example, in 1994, deceased donors represented 5,099 organ contributions whereas living individuals donated 3,102 organs.[28] By 2003, deceased donations had tapered at 6,455 and living donations reached 6,820.[29] Most living donors who contribute to the organ pool are relatives providing direct donations to sick family members. Siblings, followed by offspring, comprise the largest of those donor pools.[30]

To what can we attribute this trend and is it significant? Does it indicate anything about American law, ethics, and social values? We could

read the outpacing phenomenon as Americans' reluctance to participate in blind, anonymous altruistic processes where they help others
whom they do not know.[31] This may be less true outside the transplantation context. According to one court, "our society, contrary to
many others, has as its first principle, the respect for the individual,
and that society and government exist to protect the individual from
being invaded and hurt by another."[32] Thus, purely altruistic transfers
involving deceased donations are perhaps truly outside of our American
norms.[33] Such generosity may be inconsistent with the general framework of our daily lives; there is no duty to rescue someone in harm's way
even when doing so would pose minimal risks and be cost effective as
discussed later.[34]

The rise in living donors could also indicate that the psychological
bonds of family relationships carry over or may be intensified during
illnesses, thereby stimulating a sibling's willingness to undergo invasive,
potentially dangerous surgeries.[35] Perhaps also the spiritual and psychological benefits that inure may be long-lasting and indescribable.[36]
Courts have suggested that this psychological benefit is "grounded
firmly in the fact that the donor and recipient are known to each other
as family."[37] Beyond the psychological benefits experienced by donors,
might there be other factors motivating living donations?

Within the living donor context, wherein more donations are harvested than through the purely blind process, time and emotions are
pivotal issues; the imminence of death is part of that reality.[38] Indeed,
coercion, pressure, and feelings of entitlement may arise in these time-
sensitive, life-threatening situations from both family members and
doctors.[39] For the donee, the tyranny of the gift may be the oppression
of the debt itself, an inability to ever repay.[40] Consider the predicament
of cousins in *McFall v. Shimp*,[41] a noteworthy case because it addresses
emotions, expectations, and legal dilemmas involved with the "living
donor" subset of altruism.

The Cases

McFall v. Shimp

In *McFall v. Shimp*[42] the plaintiff, Robert McFall (39) suffered from a
rare bone marrow disease, aplastic anemia, and the prognosis for his

survival was unlikely absent a bone marrow transplant from a suitable donor. After an arduous search, including locating and testing six siblings split apart through his parents' divorce, it was determined that only the defendant, his cousin David Shimp (43), was a suitable donor. Although Shimp agreed to be tested, which involved minimally invasive blood tests, he later refused to provide bone marrow. What an incredible family predicament! The cousins were former camping buddies, and McFall recalled, "I used to buy gifts for his children when they were little. We werer [sic] good friends."[43] Even Shimp's children volunteered as donors, but none of the four were matches.

The stage was set for an incredibly unique case that tested the notion of compelled marrow donation; whether a person can be forced to be altruistic, which of course does not mean that he is altruistic, but that he has been forced to be a bone marrow donor. The case was not unique, in that it was not the first to address the question of donation, but all earlier cases involved persons who were legally incompetent.[44] In effect, those cases unlike McFall's where he was unwilling to accept "no" from a competent adult, involved incompetent minors. Judge Flaherty, the lone justice hearing the case, required Shimp to submit a brief to the court documenting why he should not be compelled to save his cousin's life. In submitting his brief, Shimp proved to the court's satisfaction that to force him to surrender his bone marrow to his cousin would violate U. S. legal norms. Shortly thereafter, the court denied McFall's injunction, although Judge Flaherty took the liberty to characterize Shimp's decision as "morally indefensible."[45]

What are we to understand from each of the parties' actions, Shimp, McFall, and the court? The McFall dilemma is significant not only for the study of transplant jurisprudence, but also the conflicts between autonomy, individualism, and altruism. Judge Flaherty's opinion is unambiguous; a dying person does not possess a special right to invade his cousin's body even to save his own life. *McFall v. Shimp* remains, however, an interesting test case, particularly because it involved bone marrow donation and not that of an organ. Bone marrow transplantation is considered far less invasive than the surgery required to harvest an organ.[46] Thus, although the court took notice of the potential for harm to result, its main emphasis was not so much about the process of donation, but rather on "respect for the individual."[47] The court made clear that altruism cannot be compelled, and indeed, donation cannot really be a gift if it is mandated.

The government, through its judiciary, is not in the position to "change every concept and principle upon which our society is founded."[48] And although cases like *Brown v. Board of Education* challenge that notion (i.e., the role of the judiciary to bring about social change), ultimately to compel an individual to submit to an invasion on her body is an incredibly dangerous legal construct.[49] Where would such a legal rule end? Could a husband have legal right to rape his wife? Could a domestic partner force her mate to undergo in vitro fertilization to harvest eggs for transplantation? Although media reports labeled Shimp a "Bad Samaritan," Flaherty's denial of an injunction was not an egregious error, but rather a demonstration of American jurisprudence in action. After all, we abjure rescue doctrine; the law does not require a duty to aid or rescue when a victim is in danger. In preserving such "no duty" rules, we are bound to cause harms, but they too must be weighed against the protecting principles and values of a just society, which in this case was protecting Shimp from the tyranny of McFall. Reconciling the case with international precedent, however, is a different matter.

McFall, having found no U.S. judicial authority support for his case, relied on a 700-year-old statute of King Edward I, 81 Westiminster 2, 13 Ed. I, c. 24, hoping the court would find that in order to preserve or save the life of another, a society has the right to impose on an individual's right to "bodily security."[50] According to Judge Flaherty,

The common law has consistently held to a rule which provides that one human being is under no legal compulsion to give aid or to take action to save another human being or to rescue. A great deal has been written regarding this rule which, on the surface, appears to be revolting in a moral sense. Introspection, however, will demonstrate that the rule is founded upon the very essence of our free society.[51]

Indeed, McFall's theory of compelled donation does not reflect the development of American jurisprudence, which contrary to others cited by McFall, "has as its first principle, the respect for the individual."[52] Great moral conflicts will result from strict interpretations of individual rights.[53] As biotechnology progresses, conflicts will often attend that progress. One month later, nearly to the day, Robert McFall died.

Individualism too, must have its limits, but where should such boundaries be drawn? As for Shimp, his indefensible immorality according to the court, was legally protected and furthermore, a reflection "of our free society."[54] Indeed, Shimp's immorality is likely found only in the context of his relationship to McFall. Were Shimp a stranger in McFall's neighborhood, would his refusal have been so immoral? McFall's invocation of moral authority, law, and courts to resolve his dilemma, which was truly a matter of life and death, although not persuasive to the court, does inform us about the underlying drama of tough choices family members make and the pressures to involuntarily participate in altruistic regimes.[55]

Curran v. Bosze

More recently, in *Curran v. Bosze*,[56] the Illinois Supreme Court followed the same line of jurisprudence extolled in *McFall*, opining that an individual's altruism cannot be legally compelled by a relative. Although this line of jurisprudence does not consider whether the legislature may legally do so, as in the cases involving presumed consent, we shall leave those questions for later. The *Curran* case is significant for three reasons. First it introduces and responds to a conceptual nuance not at issue in *Shimp*, specifically, compelled donations from minors for their siblings, but presumably other relatives too. Second, it introduces a framework involving a three-prong test for deciding whether a parent's decision to compel his children to donate against the wishes of the other parent will be legally enforced. Third, it speaks to the emotional and psychological issues involving blended families, highlighting special, presaging future dynamics in tissue transplantation.

The question before the court in *Curran* was whether a noncustodial parent, Mr. Tamas Bosze, could compel the production of his 3-year-old twins for blood testing and possible bone marrow harvesting in order to save the life of their 12-year-old half-brother, Jean Pierre, who would surely die without the transplant.[57] Their mother, Ms. Nancy Curran, the twins' legal guardian, refused to provide consent for the procedure, leaving the court to decide, not only a case of first impression, but one that would shape future jurisprudence on altruistic donations from minors.[58] Two decisions were issued by the Illinois Supreme Court; first a pronouncement from the court in September of 1990 and later a written ruling.

Days before Christmas, December 20, 1990, justices of the Illinois Supreme Court delivered their written opinion announcing why they refused to grant Tamas Bosze's request for an injunction to order Ms. Curran to produce the twins for blood testing and bone marrow harvesting. The court refused to invoke a more than century-old legal tenet to substitute its judgment for that of the children, instead upholding a lower court decision that the blood test and possible transplant would be an invasion of the twins' privacy.[59] Traditionally, a court may substitute judgment in cases where individuals lack capacity to make sound decisions for themselves, either due to youth, illness, or psychological and mental inability.[60] Had the court substituted its judgment for that of the twins, doing so, according to their guardian *ad litem*, would have set a dangerous precedent.[61]

However, that precedent was previously established by the Illinois Supreme Court in both the *Longeway*[62] and *Greenspan*[63] decisions, involving substituted judgment for incompetent adults. In both cases, the court permitted the substituted judgments of incompetent patients for the purpose of removing artificial nutrition and hydration, which would most certainly result in death. The court declined to adopt the best interest standard in both cases, opining instead that the record in both cases demonstrated the relevancy of substituted judgment theory.[64] Ultimately, the court avoided addressing perhaps a more troubling ethical issue presented by the best interest standard; namely, is the death that results from the discontinuance of hydration and nutrition in the best interest of a patient? Is it ever in the best interest of a patient, particularly one who is incompetent, to have hydration and nutrition withdrawn? In the case of a child donor, is the removal of healthy bone marrow or a vital organ ever in her best interest?

By the time the written opinion was issued, Jean Pierre had already died.[65] *Curran v. Bosze* is not an uncomplicated case nor is it free from moral doubt; it is emotionally compelling because a child would surely die and saving his life might require so little from his siblings.[66] Yet there are risks. During the procedure, the donor is anesthetized and harvesting can be painful. Subsequent pain can be treated through postoperative medication.[67]

However, Jean Pierre had no relationship with his half-brother and sister; they were in the eyes of the court practically strangers.[68] We are left to ponder whether social relationships should trump biological relationships as the court sets out. Families today are a blend of biological, legal, and social connections. Biological lines alone according to the court may be insufficiently narrow and other factors more relevant, but is the court right? Where is the pragmatic line to be drawn in familial altruism?[69] Ironically, in order to confirm paternity for child support, Ms. Curran previously had the twins appear for blood testing only a year before. It was on the basis of that test that Mr. Bosze's paternity was established. In whose best interest was the Illinois Supreme Court to consider, the twins, Jean Pierre, or the parents? The difficulty here is determining how a court should balance withholding life-saving transplantation from one child and the infliction of an invasive procedure on a healthy child. The court's three-prong analysis attempts to answer these questions.

The *Curran* court held that a parent or guardian may provide consent on behalf of minor children to donate bone marrow to a sibling only when to do so would have been in the minors' best interest.[70] The court addressed three critical factors necessary for a determination of that kind. First, the consenting parent must have been informed of the risks and the benefits of the procedure.[71] Second, there must have been emotional support available to the donor child from his or her caretakers.[72] Third, there must have been an existing, close relationship between the donor and recipient.[73]

Here, there was no existing, close relationship between the half-siblings who shared the same biological father but different mothers.[74] At the mother's request, the children were never informed that Jean Pierre was their brother.[75] Consequently, the court indicated, the limited time the siblings shared was insufficient to prove a close relationship.[76] As for altruism, the test seems to address the altruism of the parents and less so of the children.[77] Does the best interest of the twins shift according to their age, custodial parent's consent, quality of the relationship to the donor? Had the twins been 7 years old instead of 3 would that have made a difference in their ability to consent, thereby bypassing their mother's objection? According to the court, the answer would be no if the mother could not or refused to provide the psychological support necessary under the "caretaker" prong.[78] Commentators have since suggested that Curran may have been legally right, but morally wrong.

The *Curran* holding demonstrates the nascent qualities of this fluid jurisprudence. As discussed later, the law is incoherent with regard to compelled living donations; the underlying dynamics of each transaction may be ambiguous and troubling. Also, it seems apparent in the broader jurisprudence involving tough medical decisions that technology outpaces both legislative responses and judicial decision making, creating gaps in the rule of law.[79] Ergo, we have at least four by-products of this jurisprudence that together seem inconsistent and open for interpretation.

The first being the court's unequivocal position that it does not recognize and will not enforce a social, altruistic duty for potential donors to assist relatives, even siblings, by undergoing minimally invasive non-therapeutic procedures when the prospective donor cannot formulate consent.[80] In fact, the court relies on testimony from psychologists and pediatric surgeons urging the court to protect potential donors from invasive procedures even where the risk is minimal if a psychological benefit cannot be attained.[81]

Second, the court does not and will not assume that a psychological benefit naturally arises from bone marrow donation and arguably more invasive transplantations, seemingly dismissing any possible claims to the contrary, which can be inferred from federally supported public service announcements and state-sponsored advertisement campaigns encouraging organ donation.[82] Clear and convincing evidence must be demonstrated to the court that a potential donor will psychologically benefit from providing tissue, bone marrow, or an organ.[83] This can perhaps be accomplished through a showing of an "existing, close relationship" between the potential donor and recipient.[84] It seems possible, based on the ruling that as long as there is an existing, close relationship that will likely continue, the donor child will be psychologically benefited, thereby satisfying the third prong.

Third, the court makes subtle distinctions about nature of the family relationship, between potential donors and recipients, but fails to erect boundaries or give guidance. What weight should be given to biological status in familial relationships? In *Curran*, half-sibling rather than full blood status was emphasized, but what does it mean when considering "family"? Because the court recognized the biological status, but not the "family status" of the children, the twins were barred from donating their bone marrow. Thus, biological status would seem rather irrelevant, whether the potential donor was a half-brother, full sister, or a step-sister.[85] What will matter to the court is the "existing, close relationship," one of the prongs in its three-part analysis, which in the future may prove just as problematic.[86] After all, foster children can develop close relationships with each other or their host families and because some placements are semipermanent it may be possible to continue the relationship.[87] The court leaves open the possibility then for clever adults to apply the rule in cases where there is no biological relationship, but long-standing intimate social relationships, such as children in foster care. This slippery slope is not so unimaginable.

The *Curran* court declined the opportunity to address potential but likely parent or guardian conflicts of interest in such cases. Based on the court's analysis it is sufficient that the parent be aware of the risks, consent on behalf of the child, and give emotional support.[88] With such limited guidance, adopting the best interest standard might have less significance and meaning for children's interest in light of the test established.[89]

Finally, perhaps neither substituted judgment theory nor the best interest standard, as enforced by the court, are appropriate for organ donation involving children.[90] This is not to suggest that the ultimate decision would be different were a more nuanced theory applied. Rather, the jurisprudence might stretch and develop in ways that specifically address this new frontier of problems rather than relying on doctrines that did not anticipate our foray into transplantation regimes. Indeed, it would always seem against the best interest of a child to submit to nontherapeutic surgeries.[91] Such invasive procedures pose health risks, including the potential for complications with anesthesia, difficulties during the operation, the need for possible postoperative blood transfusions, and other problems unique to the particular type of harvesting.[92] Yet, the moral questions are not insignificant.

Substituting judgment may also pose difficulties as it requires assessing prior manifestations of intent.[93] For this reason, it is a legal fiction in these contexts. How does a 3-year-old manifest her intent to donate bone marrow or a kidney?[94] Children lack the capacity to engage in such decision making. As for evidence of intent, what should a guardian *ad litem* look for?[95] What gestures or actions indicate an intent to donate prior to your sibling's illness manifesting? What type of inquiry should be made to uncover evidence of intent? Can intent be influenced by parents, thereby undermining the court's scientific inquiry?

Let us conclude this section by addressing other tough dynamics that intersect with the legal limitations and nuances of altruism. Neither *Shimp* nor *Curran* represents exclusively the jurisprudence on living donations. Curiously, they are the exceptions and not the rule. In most cases judges side with parents and permit organ harvesting from minors. Rather, they represent one aspect of the coin. The other, equally nuanced aspect of this jurisprudence is alluded to in *Curran*. Within it are the judicial struggles involving conflicts of interest and mental incompetence. Within the gaps of legislative guidance and nascent jurisprudence further nuances are born.

Fluid Jurisprudence

Parents may be free to become martyrs themselves. But it does not follow they are free, in identical circumstances, to make martyrs of their children before they have reached the age of full and legal discretion when they can make that choice for themselves.[96]

Inconsistent case law vis-à-vis parental authority to remove kidneys from otherwise healthy minors and incompetent persons for implantation and benefit of their siblings illustrates the complexities involved with living donations, which are system by-products of altruism.[97] In absence of legislative pronouncements, parents and guardians have stretched the boundaries of consent within the altruistic model.[98] According to Cheyette, despite the absence of medical necessity or medical benefit, when confronted with petitions to harvest organs from incompetents, courts generally retreat behind presumptions of parental beneficence and give these procedures the blessing of judicial approval.[99] This highlights not only the fluidity of the jurisprudence in this area, but also complex questions about fiduciary responsibility, conflicting interests, and the roles of parents and the rule of law.[100] Some of these tensions and inconsistencies are illuminated in recent legislative enactments imposing criminal penalties on mothers whose possible drug use during pregnancy might undermine the health of their fetuses or children.[101] Such new enactments are designed to prospectively encourage healthy babies and punish mothers who

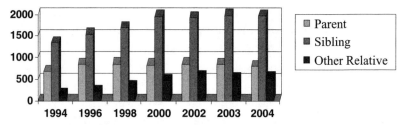

Figure 3.2. Living donor characteristics by relative, 1994–2003.

potentially compromise their children's health regardless of attendant circumstances.[102] Intent to harm is not a necessary element of such laws, as their foci rest exclusively on acts done to compromise children's health.[103] Such inconsistencies reflect a poorly developed legislative agenda about parents' legal roles with respect to their children's health.[104]

Siblings account for more living donations than any other group as shown in Figure 3.2.[105] This is in part due to optimal matching between relatives, particularly siblings, which diminishes the possibility of organ or tissue rejection.[106] Optimal matching results in fewer postoperative complications and, therefore, more efficient and effective transplantations. Of course, immunosuppressive pharmacology also reduces the likelihood of rejection, providing patients and their families broader options than previously possible. Thus, although siblings can provide a closer match, biotechnological advancements in pharmacology have enhanced consumer choice by expanding the donor pool from which patients can draw.

Fiduciary obligations between patient and physician are to run with the patient needing the operation. Yet, it is very likely that the same set of doctors will perform operations for both the donor and donee, leaving some parents and children to ask who is the primary patient? The answer to this question establishes both ethical and legal duties for the physician.[107] It is not always clear to patients undergoing harvesting for another that the physician interacting with her (as the donee) is primarily focused on the health and saving the life of her sister. Although it may seem insignificant to family members, if an accident were to occur during harvesting, the relevance of these questions becomes more significant.

When altruism is the exclusive legal forum for organ and tissue procurement, demand creates pressure within the limited pool, causing tissue and organ solicitation to spread into black markets and seep into less desirable altruistic subsystems.[108] Parents, patients, relatives, and friends are faced with tough, limited legal alternatives. The jurisprudence involving compelled donations from children[109] of siblings dying from terminal illnesses presages future dynamics where the biological lines of family may be less determinative and, therefore, more fluid.[110] The "existing, close relationship" standard adopted in *Curran* informs us less about biology and more about personality, compatibility, and friendship. The biology of family may be replaced by "family relationship," which would seem logical given the sometimes legally and socially arbitrary or ambiguous nature and definition of family.[111] Blended households, step-siblings, adopted siblings, siblings born of ova or sperm transactions, surrogate siblings, negotiated siblings (children of same-sex parents, born with the aid of an involved friend), and foster siblings all represent adaptations on the traditional nuclear family "child" model.[112] Yet, such a standard does not come without cost.

A few cases provide a glimpse of the fluid jurisprudence in this area, reaching back to *Strunk v. Strunk*,[113] a case involving a mother granting permission for her institutionalized 27-year-old son with the capacity of a 6-year-old to undergo an operation to remove his kidney for the benefit of his brother, and resting for now with reproductive altruism, which describes a subset of altruism, wherein parents conceive for the explicit purposes that their newborn will be harvestable. In those instances, parents genetically test or hope that the newborn will be the "right match" to provide the necessary bone marrow or organ to assist another child.

Strunk v. Strunk

Several courts have addressed whether consent from a parent, guardian, or court for the removal of a kidney or bone marrow for transplantation from a healthy child to a terminally ill sibling is legally effective.[114] Some have answered this question in the affirmative. The issues are complicated ultimately by the donor's lack of capacity to legally consent to invasive medical procedures, their unequal bargaining power, and by confused loyalties;[115] to whom does the physician[116] owe his loyalty and how can parents distinguish one child's best interest from the other if their collective fate is tied?

In 1969, the Kentucky Court of Appeals was the first jurisdiction in the United States to publish its opinion as to whether a parent could authorize removal of one child's kidney for procurement to another in a reported decision.[117] Ava Strunk petitioned the court for the removal of one of Jerry Strunk's kidneys for implantation in his brother, Tommy.[118] Jerry Strunk, a 27-year-old incompetent person with the capacity of a 6-year-old was confined to Frankfort State Hospital as a ward of the state.[119] His brother, Tommy, 28 years old, suffered from chronic glomerulus nephritis, a kidney disease, which most certainly would have caused his death without the transplant.[120]

Owing its authority to the doctrine of substituted judgment,[121] the court opined that the principles laid out over the centuries in the United States as well as abroad, were broad enough "not only to cover property but also to cover all matters touching on the well-being of [Strunk]."[122] With that authority, the court, in a split four-to-three decision, found it to be in the best interest of Jerry Strunk to provide a kidney to his older brother, Tom.[123] The court reasoned that Tom's life was more valuable to Jerry than his kidney, suggesting that "emotionally and psychologically . . . his well-being would be jeopardized more severely by the loss of his brother than by the removal of a kidney."[124] The majority found Jerry's happiness to be linked to Tom's survival.[125] Jerry's guardian *ad litem* strongly urged against the operation, but the court was not persuaded.[126]

Strunk is a unique case to launch this jurisprudence because it involves a distinctive set of circumstances at an interesting time in American history. That Jerry was mentally incompetent with an IQ of 35 may have been more revealing and probative for the court than the close bond between the brothers that the justices allude to but fail to substantiate with any clear evidence. America's unkind period toward the disabled reaches far back. One of the most notorious rulings involving incompetent persons was that of *Buck v. Bell*,[127] wherein Justice Holmes opined, "three generations of imbeciles is enough"[128] to give the state authority over their reproductive functions, particularly the fallopian tubes of women alleged to be mentally incompetent. His notorious eugenics cry heralded an era where thousands were sterilized in the United States based on the notion that they harbored bad genes.[129]

According to Holmes and other jurists for some time to come, the mentally disabled usurped significant state resources; they were burdens to society that never reciprocated social or economic generosity. His reasoning in *Buck v. Bell* illuminates this point:

it would be strange if it could not call upon those who already sap the strength of the State for these lesser sacrifices, often not felt to be such by those concerned, in order to prevent our being swamped with incompetence. It is better for all the world, if instead of waiting to execute degenerate offspring for crime, or to let them starve for their imbecility, society can prevent those who are manifestly unfit from continuing their kind.[130]

What we can learn in *Strunk*, beyond the seminal precedent set by the court, is that the mentally ill were compromised citizens and perhaps more easily at the disposal of courts for less sensitive treatment.[131] Consider, for example, that Jerry is referred to as "defective" throughout the amicus brief submitted by the Kentucky Department of Mental Health, which supported the removal of his kidney. Tom had a social value recognized not only by the court but also by society; the two brothers, however, were not socially or legally equals. Building toward its holding, the court observed that Tom was married, working, and going to college; undoubtedly he would benefit society.[132]

The ruling in *Strunk*, however, was not limited to "mentally deficient persons," but rather to persons who were incompetent to make those decisions independently.[133] Viewed in this way, the ruling was more about judicial authority to interpose its judgment when an appropriate situation involving a legally incompetent person was presented to the court. Indeed, it would appear inappropriate to explicitly and exclusively target the mentally ill as the unwitting participants in nontherapeutic surgeries as the U.S. Supreme Court permitted in *Buck v. Bell*. Nevertheless, given the social status of the mentally ill at the time,[134] the judges in *Strunk* may have been blinded to the external possibilities of the ruling.

For example, what is the appropriate legal remedy for a similarly situated family, save for the son who is not mentally ill, but possesses two healthy kidneys? According to *Strunk*, if that person is legally incompetent, such as a minor, the court's authority gives rise to decision making about his health as well as his property. The court's reliance on legal competence expanded the potential class of individuals for whom the court could substitute judgment. I should also mention the court's provocative evocation of arcane legal tenets such as substituted judgment (formerly used only for property disposition) to reach its conclusion in *Strunk* has attracted intense scrutiny over the years, although adopted by a number of courts. In failing to predict the robust technological developments, that would facilitate better diagnosis of diseases and make organ transplantation more accessible, the court may have been somewhat shortsighted.[135] Within a few years of *Strunk*, jurisdictions in Virginia,[136] Texas,[137] and Connecticut[138] would adopt its expanding jurisprudence.

Subsequent jurisprudence expanded the *Strunk* ruling to include living donors who are minors.[139] In *Hart v. Brown*,[140] Connecticut parents of 7-year-old twins sought a declaratory judgment to permit the removal of one daughter's kidney for implantation in her sister. The donee's physician refused to perform the operations and the hospital was unwilling to permit the use of its facilities unless the court declared the parents able to consent on behalf of Kathleen Hart, their daughter, to organ removal for procurement to her sister.[141] For the physicians, clear ethical problems existed; to whom would they owe a duty of loyalty? As for liability, could Kathleen later sue for battery, having been subjected to an unwanted or undesired medical procedure or conversion for the extraction of the organ and use by a third party?[142]

The Connecticut Superior Court found that it would be of "immense benefit"[143] for Kathleen to participate in the donation and that she would be happy if her family were happy, thus permitting her parents to substitute their legal judgment for her. *Strunk's* instructive posture proved helpful for the *Hart* court as it too reached beyond the original intent of substituted judgment theory by expanding its scope to children. Is "immense benefit" the appropriate standard of review? The longevity of happiness in a child or a family is difficult to predict. Families separate, divorce, and may be later reconstituted with different people. Placing responsibility on a child to promote that type of happiness through uninformed, invasive surgeries stretches the boundaries of pragmatic decision making. It may be the case that circumstances present an opportunity for family members, particularly children, to help in extraordinary ways, but the courts' analyses in these cases have yet to establish the pragmatic limitations and reconcile those with moral principles.[144]

C. Reproductive Altruism

Headlines refer to them as "designer babies" and modern-day "angels."[145] They are the children of *reproductive altruism*, specially conceived to save dying siblings.[146] Some are born with the help of genetic manipulation, as was Adam Nash, a test tube baby,[147] specially tested to have the exact cell type necessary for bone marrow transplantation to his sister who was diagnosed with Fanconi anemia.[148] The Nashes are thought to be America's first couple to screen their embryos before implanting in the mother's womb for the purpose of harvesting bone marrow.[149] However, 12 years before, Abe Ayala surgically reversed his vasectomy, hoping that his wife would become pregnant with a child who would save their daughter's life.[150] They were unabashed about "making" Marissa to save Anissa. According to doctors at the time, the Ayalas had a 25% chance that Marissa would be a match for her teenage sister. One reporter noted, they "won that gamble too."[151] Marissa Ayala was 14 months old when she underwent bone marrow harvesting for transplantation to her sister, Anissa, who was 17 years old.[152]

The couples were very different; one Hispanic and the other white, hailing from different regions in the United States. The Nash family lived in Colorado and the Ayalas in California. The couples, however, were motivated by similar desires. Both were unwilling to accept the inevitable deaths of their daughters. The Nash family followed the development of preimplantation genetic diagnosis; a process involving the removal of a single cell from embryos created through standard in vitro fertilization techniques and developed in a laboratory petri dish.[153] Before implantation in the uterus, the embryos were tested for Fanconi and those exhibiting no signs of the disease were implanted.

It was not love for their daughters that troubled ethicists, but rather the shared passion to create children strictly for the purpose of aiding siblings.[154] The psychological ramifications were unpredictable and continue to be; the Nashes eliminated the need for luck by employing science, but how will Adam adjust to the purpose of his birth? The Ayalas gambled on luck, but it seems possible that disappointment might have resulted from a mismatch.

As a society, we do not police parent motivations for having children. Whether we should do so is not a new question, but seemingly settled by the Supreme Court's analysis on the right to parent.[155] Years ago the country entered a slippery slope deciding that certain people were not "fit" for reproduction. Carrie Buck was one among thousands subjected to draconian procedures to ensure American society would not be overrun with those deemed less socially and culturally desirable.[156] The pendulum has swung, although pressures continue to exist to constrain the birthing of some mothers, as so eloquently addressed by Professor Dorothy Roberts' scholarship.[157] Today, heterosexual and homosexual couples can choose when and how to have children through a variety of means, including surrogacy, in vitro technology, or sperm and ova donation. The distinction, however, between the desire to parent and the aspiration to bear a child to save another is a matter of intent. Certainly less noble causes have inspired copulation and child making, whether to grow the family business, save a marriage, express ego, stimulate financial resources, or even the sublime romantic, sentimental reasons. Should parents espousing reproductive altruism be held to a different ethical standard than those with hidden, nonaltruistic motivations?

The births of Adam and Marissa raise serious doubts about the confluence of the rule of law, biotechnology, ethics, and parenting. Although an effort to ban "transplantation" parenting in England was recently overturned, U.S. legislators and courts have yet to address the issue of reproductive altruism, the practice of having children to save the lives of other children.[158] Although selling children is illegal,[159] U.S. law does not set limits on who can parent, nor on how many children couples may produce, or when or under what circumstances they may reproduce. Save for child sexual abuse, resulting in pregnancies and preterm illegal drug use, the right to parent is closely guarded and protected.[160]

Producing an additional child to supply an organ or bone marrow for a living offspring is certainly not an easy decision to come by.[161]

The predecision considerations may be endless; economic concerns, social adjustment, and even fertility doubts may be part of the decision-making process.[162] Can the family afford to raise another child? The potential for disharmony and anger between the children rather than romantic notions of unconditional love is possible. Balancing the risks, might the disease appear in the planned donor child?

For poorer parents, who cannot afford genetic testing to eliminate poor matching embryos, it will surely be the case that some newborns will not be viable bone marrow donors. Marissa Ayala for example, had only a 25% chance of being a compatible donor.[163] It is also possible that the mother's health will be compromised in the process. If a mother learns that a baby isn't the right match, is the child abortable? Legally, perhaps so depending on the trimester in which this is discovered, but morally, even for privacy and abortion proponents, aborting viable healthy fetuses simply because they are not the "right match" may expand the abortion battleground into murkier territory.[164] Such medical procedures may also be criminal, given recent state legislative enactments, which criminalize harm to viable fetuses, whether due to a mother's drug use or her unwillingness to undergo a cesarean birth operation to prevent the death of a fetus. The potential risks and legal ramifications remain incalculable.

Reproductive altruism creates natural hierarchies; one child is born a supplier or healer and the other special or sacred. Turned on its head, the supplier becomes a household miracle worker or savior, but both siblings are victims of unfortunate circumstances. In a recent study, researchers found that organ recipients who had received a donation from a living donor were less comfortable about the charitable act, feeling burdened by the "debt."

The children were depressed, complained of recurrent nightmares, had overdeveloped fears of hospitals and needles and had a constant sense of dread that the experience might be repeated. This was true for both siblings who donated and siblings who did not donate. The siblings who donated, however, were more withdrawn, anxious, depressed and had a lower sense of self-esteem, which the researchers attributed to a guilty fear that their tissue might not be "good enough." Other researchers have similarly warned that if the child turns out to be an incompatible donor or the transplant is unsuccessful, '[t]he . . . guilt which may follow in the wake of [that] failure could be transferred to the donor child with untoward effects, either in early bonding or later, as the child grows up under the shadow of having failed in an important task.[165]

Donors were particularly uneasy about transplants from children. Other studies reveal a connection between the donee's health and the psychological well-being of the donor. UCLA researchers discovered that donors were negatively affected by the recipients' postoperative quality of health. What the study could not reveal is whether donors would have suffered similar psychological distress had they not donated. Also, it would be useful to know from where the stress derives. For example, was donor stress linked to feelings of sympathy or guilt about the quality of the tissue donation?

What neither of the aforementioned studies nor any other has determined are the long-term psychological effects on child sibling donors. One that comes close, however, is a study conducted by researchers at the University of California at San Francisco who explored the psychological significance of donation among children who supplied bone marrow for another sibling. Most siblings, whether donors or not, according to their finding, experienced some form of stress and depression.[166] Some of the donors experienced nightmares connected with the bone marrow harvesting process, becoming fearful of hospitals and needles. According to researchers, 33% of the donors suffered posttraumatic stress disorder-type symptoms at some point after donating.[167] Sibling donors were also more likely to have a compromised sense of worth, suffer bouts of anxiety, and be withdrawn.[168]

Thus, the notion that children donors are psychologically benefited from donating organs deserves serious scrutiny. Psychological benefit for the child donor is not an absolute. The possibility that the children donors experience relief for their recovering sibling seems likely; that would also appear to be true for nonsibling donors and other family members. Parents are probably more likely to be psychologically benefited by their children receiving an organ or tissue donation, which in part explains parental motivation for reproductive altruism. The UCLA and UC–San Francisco studies offer a different view of posttransplant psychology and relationships. Their analyses highlight fault lines in jurisprudence on compelled donations, indicating that courts have misinterpreted immediate psychological relief, satisfaction, and possibly joy with long-term sibling relationships. The studies seem to refute the underlying message that strong, healthy, psychological relationships develop between donors and recipient siblings. The mistaken assumption could be explained by urgent desires to assist innocent children suffering from organ failure. Waterman at the Washington University School of Medicine suggests that more psychosocial interventions are necessary to address the tensions involved with living donations.[169]

CONCLUSION

I have provided a glimpse of the dynamics through reported law and media cases. These however, do not represent unpublished legal opinions, cases without reports, family conflicts that never appear before a judge, nor the genetic or natural births motivated by reproductive altruism, which are simply not adjudicated. With the precedent established by *Strunk* and its progeny, concerns about the legality of parental consent for minors to undergo nontherapeutic extractive surgeries for the benefit of their siblings is also reduced. Thus, we see a reduction in petitions requesting declaratory judgments seeking consent for bone marrow and kidney transplants.

After *Strunk* and its progeny, important questions remain unanswered as to the breadth of the ruling. These include the roles of doctors and medicine. Is the role of medicine to prolong life as long as possible? How do we manage potential conflicts of interests, including physician involvement in the decision-making processes, where they have pecuniary and research interests? Biotechnology transports us to types of medical research unforeseeable and uncharted 30 years ago. The human genome was yet to be mapped, and bioprospecting had relevance only for plants and wildlife, not human beings as we see now. Technology was less sophisticated and its robust economic potential was yet to be fully appreciated. From this perspective, *Curran, Strunk*, and *Hart* were possibly short-term solutions to problems on a much grander scale. We must also chart the rights of children and the disabled too, which have developed in more sophisticated ways over the past quarter century. With parental immunity challenged in some jurisdictions, the possibility to ward off subsequent privacy and tort lawsuits from children harmed psychologically or physically by nonconsensual organ, tissue, or cell removal may be less guaranteed.

Exclusive reliance on altruism to meet increasing demand for sophisticated, life-saving medical therapies forces strains on the system, and drives individuals to create unregulated, living-donor subsystems, some which are legal and others that are not. The altruism subsystems, including compelled living donations and reproductive altruism, operate on principles inapposite to the legal values associated with altruism. The subsystems lack voluntariness, informed consent, and mutual bargaining power, subverting the intention of altruism, with heightened possibilities for coercion, pressure, guilt, and unequal positioning. Thus, these systems are overshadowed by ethical, moral, and even legal doubts. As discussed earlier, this jurisprudence must become more nuanced in light of the potential for confusion, manipulation, and other cases to which this line of legal thought might be applied.

Currently, siblings account for more contributions to the living donor pool than any other groups.[170] Most sibling donors are adults; however minor siblings continue to be represented among living donors. OPTN does not indicate the relationship to the donee of child donors under 10 years old. Yet, as described earlier, the margins by which siblings contribute are substantially greater than all other relatives. Siblings' contributions to the altruistic pool are double that of parents. Nonetheless, the dynamics behind the donations are difficult to monitor.

I have emphasized before that a social contract functions only when mutual bargaining power and beneficial reciprocity exist. The benefits need not be equal, but should be of some tangible value to both parties. It also seems important that individuals be allowed to express their generosity and humanity in ways that at times may infringe on their liberties, including bodily integrity and privacy in the aid of another. Therefore, it would be unwise to prophylactically proscribe individuals from participating in living donation, even some children. There must, however, be a balance beyond the tests previously established.

First, it must be clearly understood that compelled living donations from children and incompetent persons are the least desired forms of donation. Donations from persons legally incompetent cannot easily fit under the umbrella of altruism; the heightened probability for compromising their humanity and dignity makes it so. We must consider alternatives for desperate parents and siblings beyond the reach of the most vulnerable members of their families. Currently, federally mandated altruism procurement constrains their ability to seek alternative, viable sources domestically. Again, the weaker, less desirable options become the exclusive options, quite unnecessarily. Conversely, those suspicious of the American transplantation system lack the confidence and motivation to participate in the current altruistic regime as donors, but it is possible other systems might prove more attractive to them. Let us remember that children and the mentally ill are not viable replacements for an incompetent, ineffective, organ procurement system. Their participation should be limited to the narrowest possibilities.

Second, minors younger than 13 years old should be proscribed from participating in living donation procedures. An age barrier would be no different that those imposed in labor or employment systems. Children under 13 lack the capacity to substantially appreciate the nuances of these transactions, including potential future health risks. This may also be true for teenagers; however, it is more likely that teenagers will be more literate, knowledgeable, educable, and aware than 7-year-olds. Their understanding of the transplantation process will be more substantive than symbolic, resulting in meaningful dialogues about risks and benefits of tissue and organ harvesting. Age should not be the only criteria, less it become an arbitrary element. Courts should borrow from the Tort common law by examining the child's experience and intelligence.

Third, a guardian *ad litem* should always be appointed. Fourth, family and independent counseling must be required to ensure that parents understand the dynamics of the depth of their actions and long-term consequences. Fifth, an independent physician must be appointed for the prospective donor to avoid conflicts of interest. Finally, a statement should be issued to the court from the donor as to why she desires to participate as an organ or tissue donor. Limiting the participation of children will reduce the pool of viable organs, and other solutions must be sought.

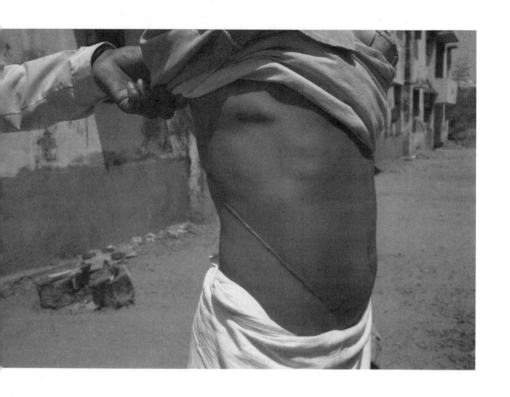

Man with harvesting scar in India. A man in India shows the scars left after his kidney was harvested and sold. (Corbis Images)

4 Getting the Organ You Want

Typically, in countries where there are waiting lists, people wait years for organs. With me it's immediate. Because I just get their medical records, forward them to the different hospitals I work with and they make a decision if they want to do it or not and within a few days the person is on a plane to another country in a day or two for testing and within a week they've got a new organ.[1]

INTRODUCTION

As of July 21, 2005, there were 89,012 candidates registered on organ waitlists in the United States.[2] This figure from OPTN does not include those removed from the waitlist, patients too sick to be placed on the waitlists due to cancer or some other illness, or the very unfortunate who never make it onto the list because their conditions have not been diagnosed or they simply have not been referred. Thousands of these candidates will die before the end of the year. For each loss, many more will come to wait in her place. Relatives will be tested to see if there is a blood match; some will be pressured to donate. Other waitlist candidates will take a gamble and turn to the black market and seek a living donor outside of the U.S. transplantation system, in Brazil or perhaps India. Still, others may call Jim Cohane, an "organ transplantation coordinator," who arranges for organ transplantations abroad. I interviewed Jim for this book. His fees are on the steep side, $125,000 for a kidney, but that includes transportation costs (airfare and local travel), a companion ticket, and an organ.[3] This is the status of organ transplantation for Americans.

This brief chapter closes Part I of *Black Markets* by describing the organ referral and allocation processes. It provides the reader an overview of the general dynamics of organ referral and also the criteria for organ allocation. Section A discusses the organ referral process. It becomes clear in this section that "there is no science to the referral process."[4] This section is informed by interviews with Joel D. Newman, Communication Liaison, United Network for Organ Sharing; Jack Lynch, Community Affairs Director for the Illinois organ procurement organization, Gift of Hope; and several others who helped to explain the referral process from their perspective or that of the organizations for which they work. This section scrutinizes allegations of racial discrimination in the organ referral process. Section B explains and analyzes the organ allocation process.

A. Organ Referral: Getting Onto the List

The organ referral process is so highly subjective that patients with similar conditions may be treated quite differently at evaluation centers, with one making it onto the list and the other turned away. Studies suggest that two significant factors may impede a patient's likelihood of referral onto a waitlist. First, for-profit dialysis clinics have less incentive to refer patients for transplant evaluation. Second, "green screening" or "social valuing" of Black and low-income patients may reduce their chances for referral.

Patients rely on their physicians' knowledge, care, and willingness (and ability) to share information. For purposes of this discussion we will primarily examine the kidney referral and waitlist process. Empirical data collected from UNOS and their research arm OPTN provide the most accurate data about donors and recipients. UNOS performs an incredible service for the public, researchers, and policymakers by providing very detailed data by region, states, race, gender, and other categories. In fact, critical examination of their data reveals stark racial disparities in transplantation waiting times, death rates, and need. Their data are accessible through annual reports and also on the Internet. Although UNOS is our most reliable data source for organ waitlists, their data do not tell us anything about the referral process. Indeed, the data cannot tell us much about the referral process because that data is not collected, nor are there standards, guidelines, or protocols regarding the referral process.

Commentators suggest that gaps in the organ referral process provide room for pernicious forms of rationing to occur.[5] For nearly a decade, UNOS has expressed concern about racial disparities in the transplantation system. However, the focus of UNOS activities and the data it collects is primarily directed at patients who make it onto the waitlists. Rather than follow that approach, we will start with the referral process and briefly describe the stages from diagnosis to dialysis and transplant referral. By following the path of organ referral, this chapter adds an overlooked perspective – that of many dialysis patients – to the story of organ transplantation.

Referral onto an organ waitlist requires diagnosis of a condition for which transplantation would be an appropriate treatment. The first step is seeing a doctor. Early diagnosis of illnesses that pose such health risks will vary by a number of factors, including whether a patient has insurance and regularly visits her physician (which can be influenced by work schedule, access to transportation, cultural factors, and the quality of the physician-patient relationship). Patients who regularly visit their physicians are more likely to have life-threatening illnesses diagnosed earlier and thus prepared for the possibility of a transplant. For a patient exhibiting early stages of end-stage renal disease (ESRD), her doctor can assist in the eventual transition to dialysis. With early diagnosis, a patient has more time for researching, self-advocacy, and preparation to make educated, informed decisions.

According to Jack Lynch, too often African Americans are diagnosed for end-stage renal disease too late.[6] They are diagnosed in emergency rooms after complaining of fatigue, calves becoming larger, and retaining water or the inability to urinate. Sometimes, Lynch says, fear, lack of knowledge, and even embarrassment might keep them from seeing a physician at an earlier stage in their illness, including not understanding the gravity of their condition and even fear that their disease is related to a sexual illness.[7] Jack Lynch calls this avoidance "the ostrich move" meaning "it's out of sight and out of mind."[8]

The assessment and diagnosis process is the next step for a patient with symptoms of kidney failure. The patient's physician performs the laboratory screenings, including checking blood and protein levels. As one experts explains, "if protein is spilling into the patient's urine, it is a sign of acute renal failure."[9] It is at this point where patient experiences may be dissimilar depending on whether a patient has been prepared for the eventual diagnosis of ESRD. For the patient who has an ongoing relationship with her physician, news of ESRD may be disappointing, but not surprising; she has been medically and psychologically prepared for this news. The informed patient understands the next step will include dialysis. Disproportionately, however, Black patients learn about their condition at the time that they are in acute renal failure.[10] Late diagnosis, as we shall discuss, can dramatically change a patient's life overnight.[11] Quite literally, with late diagnosis of ESRD, a patient's interest in treating "aches and pains" within hours after testing results in being catheterized for dialysis and hospitalization if she has medical insurance.[12] Her doctor will inform her that she now needs dialysis. The quality of this patient's life is dramatically changed within hours and there is no rehearsal for this moment. She will forever be on dialysis; 3 days per week, 4 hours per session. Imagine how work, parenting, and spheres of her life will forever be changed.

Not all patients even at this stage will qualify for referral onto an organ transplant waitlist and an uninformed patient may not understand any link between kidney failure and a kidney transplant. Dialysis clinics are to provide information about transplantation to their patients. However, there are no federal regulations as to how this information must be conveyed, how long a counseling session must be, or that patients sign off to any documents acknowledging that they understand anything about transplantation and that they have been fully informed about the process. Sometimes the information that they receive is simply a phone number and an address of an evaluation center, according to Jacqueline Dillard.[13] Clearly, for information to be meaningful, patients need more than a passing reference that organ transplantation exists and a phone number where to be assessed. It is at this stage that so many Black patients begin to fall through gaps. Without a meaningful reference or support as to the benefits of transplantation, a dialysis patient may not follow up and seek assessment at an organ evaluation center. Moreover, some clinics will not make a meaningful attempt to refer patients for transplantation because dialysis is a profitable business; what is the motivation for losing paying clients?[14]

Profit in Dialysis

Patients don't know this is forever unless you get a transplant . . . [15]

A study conducted by researchers at Johns Hopkins School of Public Health found that patients at for-profit dialysis clinics experienced less successful outcomes than those at not-for-profit and hospital-based dialysis clinics.[16] The mortality rate of patients at for-profit centers was 20% higher than at not-for-profit centers.[17] Not only do for-profit dialysis facilities have a higher mortality rate, they also have a significantly lower transplant referral rate than not-for-profit centers.[18] Authors of the study indicate "that the care of patients with end-stage renal disease may be compromised in for-profit dialysis centers, particularly in localities where not-for-profit facilities are absent."[19]

Indeed, one dialysis nurse interviewed for this book who works at a for-profit dialysis clinic in Chicago, which serves a large African American population, argued that there was no incentive for clinic owners to refer patients for organ transplantation. The objective is to keep the "chairs full." The John Hopkins study validates her concern; researchers noted that "treatment in for-profit centers was also associated with a 26 percent lower likelihood that a patient would be put on the waiting list for a kidney transplant."[20]

One reason cited for the higher death rates at for-profit dialysis centers, "is that administrators must spend 10 to 15 percent of all expenses satisfying shareholders and paying taxes," according to Dr. P. J. Devereaux who authored a study about poor outcomes at for-profit dialysis clinics.[21] Devereaux argues, "for-profit providers cut corners to ensure shareholders achieve their expected returns on investment."[22] Devereaux's study links an extra 2,500 deaths per year to for-profit dialysis facilities when compared to non-profit dialysis facilities.[23] Studies reveal that for-profit clinics are more likely to reduce costs by providing lower doses of dialysis and reusing dialyzers.[24] These practices are associated with poor patient survival, but also reducing costs. For-profit facilities are also more likely to staff their clinics at lower levels.[25] For example, in the chronic care unit at a typical facility in Chicago, for 175 patients there was only 1.5 social workers. These practices often reduce costs, but also affect the quality of care that patients receive. With less than ideal oversight about referral rates and instances of morbidity, for-profit dialysis facilities have no incentive to change their business practices. A patient's ability to change facilities may be limited by geography. Moreover, most will only know what they are told at clinics, and depending on the quality of that information, some will never be referred for a transplant.

Green Screening and Social Valuing

Commentators allege that equitable distribution of organs has been impeded by the equivalent of racial profiling. [26] They argue that social valuing overwhelms the organ referral process, influencing whether Blacks and Latinos are provided entrée to the transplantation allocation process.[27] Dr. Clive Callender, chairman of the Department of Surgery at Howard University Hospital, characterizes this process as another forum in which institutional racism occurs.[28] According to Callender, "[m]inorities in many cases are not offered the opportunity for transplants [although] they can be donors, they cannot be recipients."[29] UNOS has not investigated such claims, nor are there research studies specifically on point with Dr. Callender's observations. However, an investigative report conducted by the *New York Daily News* highlights the experiences of people of color in New York as they attempted to overcome racial bias in the organ referral process.[30]

In a study focusing on fairness in New York's organ allocation and referral process, covering 2 years, The *New York Daily News* uncovered significant racial disparities in patient referrals for organ transplants.[31] The study revealed that relatively few Blacks and Latinos "make" organ waitlists; the numbers of those who are placed pale in comparison to those excluded from the process.[32] The study compared the demographic residential listings of Whites, Blacks, and Hispanics in New York City and eight surrounding counties with the "racial breakdown of patients who received transplants in the region from 1996 through 1998."[33] Being placed on the waitlist, according to the study, "is an all-important step that has proved to be a major hurdle for minorities: They don't make it nearly as often as Whites."[34] According to McCoy, the lead investigator, Whites were disproportionately advantaged by being referred for organ transplantation.[35] Between 1996 and 1998, nearly 75% or three of four patients from the New York City area referred for organ transplantation were White.[36] Consider these disparities in light of the fact that Whites account for only 54% of that region's population.[37] McCoy's data highlights disparities in the referral and subsequent allocation processes. This type of data has been interpreted to mean that "Whites are nearly twice as likely to get transplanted."[38]

The referral process is overly subjective, inconsistent, and ambiguous.[39] As described earlier, doctors typically interview patients to diagnose the cause of their illnesses and determine appropriate treatment. McCoy's study concludes that non-Whites in New York City who demonstrate signs of organ failure and would otherwise qualify for transplantation are not provided adequate information or the option for organ transplantation.[40] Authors of the study insist that the reason why "[B]lacks and Hispanics [don't] make the waiting list . . . is that doctors don't refer them to transplant centers as often as they should."[41] This concern was echoed by Jack Lynch in our 2005 interview.

Authors of the *Daily News* study examined the incidence of diseases with a higher prevalence in non-White communities (based on death rates) and performed a computer study to analyze liver transplants from 1995 through 1997 in 18 zip codes in minority communities.[42] Their analysis revealed that although "Blacks nationally have a fifty percent higher death rate from major heart diseases than Whites, [and] Hispanics die from chronic liver disease and cirrhosis nearly twice as often as Whites, and suffer higher rates of hepatitis," the predominantly non-White zip codes received "less than 4% of the liver transplants."[43] The zip code analysis covered East Harlem and the South Bronx. The study was expanded to look at Borough Park, Brooklyn; Manhattan's Upper West Side; the Lower East Side; and the Westchester community in the Bronx, and reached similar results.

However, critics charge that African Americans largely contribute to their own deteriorative health as well as their poor transplantation status.[44] They suggest that the very health conditions experienced by Blacks and other people of color may also be what hinder their access to

the transplantation process.[45] For example, Blacks are thought generally to have poorer health due to increased stress and decreased access
to care and the effects of socioeconomic conditions on health habits.[46]
Accordingly, Blacks and other people of color are more likely to have secondary health problems that make them medically less attractive candidates for transplantation.[47] Critics also scrutinize the participation of
African Americans in the organ donation process, highlighting an iniq-
uitous corollary between contribution and consequence in the transplantation industry.[48] They caution that African Americans "underfeed"
the organ pool, resulting in fewer available organs to their communities. Such caution would seem to indicate that organ transplantation
criteria have certain genetic features and that race may be a more significant feature of organ referral and subsequent allocation than what
the public might understand. Some healthcare officials and bioethicists argue that non-Whites' lack of access to organ transplantation is
a direct result of their lack of participation in organ donation. In other
words, if Blacks and Latinos donated more often, more organs would
be available for successful transplantation.[49] The *New York Daily News*
investigation discredits that theory. McCoy's investigation revealed that
proportionately, people of color in New York, particularly Blacks and
Latinos, donated organs more often than Whites.[50]

The *Daily News* investigation also highlighted the personal experiences of Black and Latino New Yorkers whose cases collectively illustrate the referral disparities discussed in the article.[51] Debbie Delgado's
case is rather informative. At 29, Debbie was a broker's assistant on the
New York Commodities Exchange when "stricken in 1992 with chronic
autoimmune hepatitis," a disease that destroyed her liver.[52] Debbie
visited seven doctors, four of whom, according to her, failed to communicate the possibility of a liver transplant.[53] In 1995, she received a
liver transplant at the NYU Medical Center, but only after aggressively
crusading "to save her own life," which included filling the gap of information through self-education, using medical books, and going to two
hospitals.[54] Others were not so fortunate, or died while on the waitlists, only after "losing time" because doctors would not refer them for
organ transplantation. One wife commented, "You wonder is it because
you're Hispanic? I wouldn't say it. But my husband would have."[55] Her
husband died in 1997 while waiting for a donor liver, after having been

turned away because of financial considerations, and later placed on the list once the couple resolved to sell their house.[56]

In another case, the Mahones "bounced back and forth among hospitals in Brooklyn," but by the time an ill family member was "rushed" to the New York University Medical Center in Manhattan, "'she was in such a deep coma she was brain-dead,'" recalled Dr. Devon John, a transplant surgeon at the hospital.[57] Dr. John explained to the family that had Ms. Mahone arrived 6 months earlier she might have been saved through a liver transplant. Families interviewed in that study claimed they were never provided information about organ transplantation; they were unaware that transplantation was an option for them.[58]

According to Dr. Niloo Edwards, director of Heart Transplantation at New York Presbyterian Hospital, "[i]f patients never get into the bottom of the pyramid, they're never going to get here, at the top of the pyramid." [59] He observes that "[i]t is clear that medicine [today] is not a fair system."[60] Although not a process endorsed by UNOS,[61] doctors can use non medical considerations in determining whether a patient will receive information about organ transplantation,[62] have it presented as an option, [63] or be placed on transplantation waitlists. Such gaps provide opportunities for bias to creep into the referral and allocation processes. Biased systems lose institutional confidence and usually participation. Here, however, is a system that appears to preempt that option through exclusionary practices that limit participation.

Financial considerations are also involved. Medicaid, a health insurance program for the poor, covers transplantation and medication costs, however, a patient's monthly income cannot exceed $579 per month to qualify for the program.[64] Furthermore, Medicare, another option, is reserved for senior citizens unless the patient meets disability criteria. That process may take more than 2 years. Moreover, Medicare covers only 80% of the costs for immunosuppressant drugs – and only for 3 years after transplant surgery. [65]

Doctors consider whether a patient can afford the costly immunosuppressant medications that keep the body from rejecting a new organ.[66] Dr. Clive Callender argues "[t]his means if one does not have the fiscal resources one will never get on the transplant waiting list and therefore will never receive a transplant."[67] Others suggest that a lack of cultural competence or multicultural sensitivity influences physicians and has an impact on their relationship with Black patients and the care that the physicians offer.[68] Dr. Clyde Yancy, medical director of Baylor University Medical Center in Dallas, Texas, complains about reviewing "records over the years," and coming away "wondering why certain tests had not been given to certain patients."[69] And yet, some commentators describe a deeply disturbing form of rationing, where one's interaction with authority figures, criminal past, past drug usage, education level, and other nonmedical, personal histories are considered in the referral process.[70]

Laurie Abraham, an investigative health reporter, documented the difficulties experienced by an African American family living in Chicago attempting to obtain quality healthcare.[71] She spent 3 years moving "in and out" of the Banes family's lives, "in an attempt to discover what healthcare policies crafted in Washington, DC, or in the state capital at Springfield look like when they hit the street."[72] Abraham devotes an entire chapter of her book, aptly titled, *Mama Might Be Better Off Dead*, to chronicling "the transplant game" and Robert Banes' and other Black patients' difficulties moving through that maze.[73] Through a series of interviews and observations, she analyzes and details the practical, healthcare-in-action access issues, and general dilemmas experienced by Black patients experiencing organ failure.[74]

Abraham describes how placement on waiting lists may elude the poor because of rationing practices used by doctors to make sure that "precious kidneys" are not "waste[d] . . . on people too strung out on drugs to take immunosuppressants."[75] Abraham also chronicles the visits of Robert Banes to the Neomedica Dialysis Center and appointments with a transplant coordinator at the University of Illinois transplantation program. She describes his efforts to be pleasant and amenable to doctors, not wanting to seem like Isaiah, a brash, boisterous, dialysis patient who many believed would never make the waitlist. Abraham notes that "[a]ny expression of discontent . . . might diminish his chances of getting a kidney, Robert thought, or at least extend the waiting period."[76]

Most disturbing, as Abraham observes, transplant coordinators lack an "objective science" at determining who is placed on transplant waitlists.[77] Not having "rules to help . . . make that determination" of who gets a kidney or goes on dialysis can lead to doctors or transplant coordinators making decisions based on "ideas about family, work, and ... 'drug culture' of inner-city neighborhoods."[78] Leanne Rockly, a transplant coordinator at Northwestern Memorial Hospital's transplant center, also interviewed by Abraham, comments, "You can't tell me that like or dislike for a patient doesn't sometimes cloud judgment."[79]

The use of social criteria to evaluate patient fitness for medical treatment clearly undermines confidence in the allocation process and the transplantation system. Such illegitimate practices contribute to patient mistrust and disillusionment, which ultimately compromise reliability and predictability in the institutional process. Over the past two decades, scholars including Guido Calabresi, Gloria Banks, and others have scrutinized the value of such information in the evaluation process for determining organ waitlist placement, particularly for kidneys.[80] In John Kilner's study involving 453 dialysis and transplant center medical directors, he discovered a variety of nonmedical criteria used in the transplantation and dialysis referral or decision-making processes.[81] Kilner, a former ethicist at the Park Ridge Center for Study of Health, Faith, and Ethics in Chicago, observed that physician decisions were shaped by a variety of factors.[82] The criteria, according to his study, included the patient's psychological stability, his or her family's financial and emotional support, scientific knowledge gained by treating the patient, and even how much society benefits if the patient lives.[83]

The God Squad

Claims of racial and socioeconomic profiling in organ allocation recall the bygone practices of an infamous, all-White committee in Seattle, Washington, referred to as the "God Squad."[84] Appointed by the Seattle Artificial Kidney Center in the 1960s, the committee's mandate was to assist in the development of rationing criteria for potential dialysis patients.[85] The committee measured patients' social value to determine whether they were appropriate candidates for life-saving treatments.[86] Comprised "of a doctor, a lawyer, a housewife, a businessman, a labor leader, a state government official, and minister," the committee considered patients' mental acuity, family involvement, criminal history, occupation, educational background, employment record, transportation ability, and future potential.[87] Divorce, homo-sexuality, and unemployment were frowned on, whereas wealthier "patients who held good jobs" were thought to have greater social worth, and thus favored to receive dialysis treatments.[88]

Committees throughout the United States engage in similar rationing practices, although perhaps not as overtly discriminatory.[89] That patients lack proof or are unaware that their denial of service was due to racial or socioeconomic status does not lessen the perception that bias drives the allocation process.[90] Indeed, proving bias might be difficult. Rationing, by definition, involves apportioning precious resources among the many and ultimately deciding who can live and who dies. Critics suggest that for the Seattle committee, saving lives of educated, White men seemed to be the priority. The committee's activities illumined the subjectivity and cultural biases inherent in the rationing process as well as the significant consequences of social valu-ing for African Americans and others with "poor" social markers.[91] The Seattle rationing regime illustrates how race and other factors matter not only in the delivery of healthcare, but also in the distribution of biotechnology.[92]

Resolving racial disparities in the organ transplantation process will prove difficult as this issue has yet to be adequately acknowledged by physicians, policymakers, and bioethicists. Informal social con-siderations may not exclusively govern physician considerations for organ referral, however, their contemporary role may be significantly greater than what some realize. Laurie Abraham contends that although "a parochial God committee no longer lurks in the background, the same group that received preference for dialysis when it was a scarce, life-saving resource receives preference for the new scarce, life-saving resource: transplant."[93]

B. Distributive Justice and the Waiting List Game

Inequities in organ transplantation are exacerbated by demand that continually exceeds supply.[94] With regard to kidney transplantation, the waiting time for Black Americans is 74% longer than for Whites.[95] As of July 2005, there are 24,872 Whites and 21,794 Blacks waiting for kidneys.[96] Although OPTN offers several reasons why people of color, Blacks in particular, may have a longer waiting time for kidneys, critics express concern that the network's ranking system leads to an inequitable and unjustifiable result.[97] Kidney allocation, the one area where Blacks show the most disproportionate need to Whites, is the only organ allocation process based on matching rather than need and first-in-line status.[98] Jack Lynch suggests that although matching "is very important, we can make it less important by the effective use of anti-rejection drugs."[99] Section B argues that use of nonpredictive technology, human leukocyte antigen matching, significantly reduces the likelihood that Blacks will receive timely transplantations, if at all.

History

Hospitals must adhere to the ranking system in order to receive federal funding. Initially, OPTN membership and policies were voluntary. However, the enactment of the Omnibus Budget Reconciliation Act of 1986 adding Section 1138 of the Social Security Act required that hospitals performing transplants and all organ procurement organizations (OPOs) abide by the rules and requirements of the OPTN in order to receive Medicare and Medicaid reimbursement.[100] To streamline and regulate the altruistic donations and allocation policies, the Health and Human Services entered into a contract with the United Network for Organ Sharing (UNOS).[101]

UNOS determines national allocation policies, of which compliance is tied to funding for Medicaid and Medicare. Although UNOS policy proposals are subject to the approval of the Secretary of Health and Human Services prior to being accepted into law, the agency operates with broad discretion, establishing policies that determine how organs will be rationed or distributed and what criteria should be followed in that process. Because most American hospitals receive Medicare and Medicaid funding, they fall within the auspices of the statute. Their funding is contingent on compliance with federal policies regarding organ procurement and allocation.[102] Thus, a violation of the UNOS regulations could result in the loss of federal dollars connected with both Medicare and Medicaid funding.[103]

The UNOS organ distribution regulations, based on a point system, appear neutral and in some cases seem very reasonable. For example, in the kidney allocation system children are assigned extra points (giving them a priority status). Extra points are assigned the longer one is on the waitlist. In addition, prior donors are assigned extra points (i.e., if one was a living donor 20 years before and now has kidney failure, she would receive extra points).

UNOS assigns points for organ matching – the more successful match will determine who is served first.[104] Or as Dr. Dreis comments, "the more points you have you win."[105] However, the ranking system adopted by OPTN attracts criticism because of the increasing racial disparities on the UNOS waitlists. The ranking system presently used to determine organ "transplantability" causes disparities in the distribution of urgent care resources for people of color, particularly Blacks.[106] UNOS does not promote nor explicitly consider race in the allocation of organs, nonetheless the present point system, which places significant consideration on "matching," [107] results in stark racial disparities. Thus, regardless of criteria intent, HLA matching causes a racial impact in kidney allocation, which disadvantages Blacks.[108]

Matching and Politics

The UNOS kidney-matching criterion was originally based on the model used in Pittsburgh.[109] That model gave credit to candidates for "time waiting, antigen matching, antibody analyses, medical urgency, and logistic practicality."[110] That point system became the official criteria for organ allocation in November of 1987.[111] However, policy changes with the UNOS Board of Directors "subordinated all other factors of kidney allocation (including credit for time waiting) to HLA matching."[112] According to Thomas Starzl, "this was folly at the highest level."[113] The result was institutionalization of a process that is predictably biased against Black patients.[114] The HLA matching process was not the result of a scientific study commissioned by UNOS. Rather, it was the result of political lobbying by tissue matching advocates "who for the most part managed or supplied the histocompatability laboratories."[115] Surgeons, including Dr. Clive Callender and others, deemphasize the value of strict tissue matching, stressing that tissue matching does not accurately predict transplant outcomes.[116] Critics of strict matching criteria argue that restrictive matching guidelines cannot be justified in light of studies revealing that matching between parents and children "gave no better early or late results than kidneys from randomly matched living spouses or other nonrelatives."[117]

Even proponents of matching have delivered hammer blows to its credibility, such as Teraski et al.'s report that one-haplotype-matched (parent to offspring or offspring to parent) kidney allografts gave no better early or late results than kidneys from randomly matched living spouses or other nonrelatives. When the physiological quality of the mismatched unrelated organ was equivalent to that of the one-haplotype-identical related kidney, there was no matching advantage.[118]

Some commentators claim that HLA matching criteria is an effort to protect the tissue typing industry.[119] The inflammatory nature of such claims detracts attention from efforts to secure a more equitable kidney distribution system for Blacks. However, critiques of the political process in the distribution of organs by Guttmann and others should not be entirely dismissed. Drafting policies for medical procedures are hotly contested and incredibly political. My experience as an observer to the committee redrafting the Uniform Anatomical Gift Act confirms this all too well. As to the legitimacy of HLA matching for kidneys, its predictability for success is far too low to justify passing over thousands of Blacks each year.

In an interview with Dr. Michael Dreis, an administrator in the Health Resources and Services Administration, Office of Special Programs, Division of Transplantation, (HRSA/OSP/DOT), he expressed the importance of antigen matching, but conceded that with recent biotechnological advancements in immunosuppressant pharmaceuticals that organ rejection is more treatable than ever before. He noted that recent clinical studies revealed that Blacks simply required higher dosages of immunosuppressant medications than Whites.[120] According to Dr. Dreis, "Blacks have more immune reactive exposures."[121] He noted that this may be more of an environmental factor rather than biological. It is possible, he suggested, that Blacks have been exposed to more foreign antigens and at a higher rate than have Whites, thereby causing the development of antibodies that fight off foreign antigens.[122] His observation is supported by the fact that Black communities in the United States are disproportionately located near environmental hazards and waste sights. Another consideration offered by Jack Lynch is that African Americans' genetic pools are diluted, affected by infiltration and antebellum race mixing. These variations appear in skin pigmentation, which "are all over the spectrum."[123] Too many genetic variances, according to Lynch, "make it very difficult to find the six antigen match."[124]

UNOS transplant points are assigned based on the number of mismatches between the transplant candidate's antigens and the donor's antigens. The fewer conflicting antigens the waitlist patient has with the possible organ, the more points she acquires toward transplantability.[125] The more points one has, the more likely one will receive the organ available, with attention given to length of time on the waitlist and regional concerns.[126] For example, with regard to kidneys, points are assigned as follows:

- 7 points if there are no B or DR mismatches;
- 5 points if there is one B or DR mismatch; and
- 2 points if there is a total of 2 mismatches at the B and DR loci.
- Highly sensitized candidates who have a preliminary negative crossmatch with a donor are assigned 4 points.[127]

UNOS' goal, to find patients with the best genetic fit, significantly reduces the probability of Blacks receiving organs and causes thousands to be passed over. In addition, the point evaluation system may not be the most effective, equitable, or humanitarian rationing system for at least two reasons. First, blood matching is a good idea; it seems reasonable that donors and recipients with matching blood would be more compatible. However, the emphasis placed on matching three antigens (A, B, and DR), which UNOS bases its matching point system on, is arbitrary; there are hundreds of antigens located in the body. Why does one receive extra points based on compatibility with these three antigens rather than others?[128] A better matching approach could be based on DNA. UNOS could also ration based on lupus or other health conditions that more severely threaten the possibility of rejection.

Second, if it is true, as Dr. Dreis asserts and studies support, that Blacks have more antigens present in the population, they will always be less successful in a matching system that awards points based on fewer antigens present. This is based on the theory that with better matches, there is a reduced likelihood of organ rejection. Such a system is far less justifiable given advancements in antirejection drug development. Moreover, emphasis on this particular type of matching does not begin to address how to better allocate based on need in a manner that is morally prudent and equitable for people of color, particularly Blacks. In some ways it would be akin to denying points based on something genetically shared by a large group of people with immutable characteristics. By doing so, Blacks are institutionally shut out in an altruistic system based on genetic or biological criteria that they could not possibly overcome (i.e., skin pigmentation, eye color, etc).

Although the objective makes sense economically – wanting to reduce likelihood of organ rejection, which has financial as well as other costs attached – the UNOS matching process is effectively an inequitable rationing system. UNOS does not refer to its matching system as a form of rationing. However, the function and purpose of matching is to equitably ration because resources are limited. Is rationing a poor idea in organ allocation? Arguably no, because demand is extremely high, and limited resources constrain availability; a system of priorities could be essential to the orderly and equitable distribution of life-saving biological materials. Thus, rationing in the abstract makes sense. However, distributive justice concerns, including rectifying present injustice, should be balanced against the gross collective concerns of medical efficiency, and trump other rationing schemes based on moral theories. Can one have medical efficiency if a significant population within a pool is hindered by institutional procedures that ultimately result to exclude them? Perhaps such a system is medically efficient for one group, but not all.

Because Blacks are considered "highly sensitized" to organs from non-Blacks, (i.e., there is a greater chance of rejecting the organ), they are often assigned a lower point value. In essence, UNOS' attempts to match organs perfectly with recipients result in people of color being passed on waitlists, longer wait times, greater apprehension of death, and higher rates of being taken off of the lists or dying while on the waitlist for an organ.[129]

OPTN provides four reasons that account for the disparities in organ allocation to Blacks. They include allocating organs based on blood distribution grouping, attaining a good cross match through human leukocyte antigen matching, crossmatching, and low donation among Blacks.[130]

1. Blood Distribution Grouping

First, OPTN argues the blood group distribution among potential African American recipients differs from that of the predominantly White pool.[131] The allocation process outcomes suggest that because Whites comprise a larger pool of donors, the blood group distribution could have a detrimental impact on Blacks. Blood grouping in its simplest forms is not necessarily unfair. It is another form of rationing and possibly not the most morally offensive. It intersects with other rationing theories, including "most likely not to reject" and "best resulting quality of life."

Such theories are justified based on the belief that others will be less likely to reject the organs and more likely to have a better quality of life without the side effects of medications controlling the mismatch. However, critics have attacked such policies in light of biotechnological advances that could minimize biological differences possibly causing the rejection of organs. Rejection or alloreactivity "is the phenomenon whereby the immune system of the organ recipient recognizes the transplanted tissue as foreign and seeks to destroy it. Much the same process is at work when the body seeks out and destroys foreign bacteria viruses that threaten the health of the body."[132]

The alloreactivity process is minimized through proper medication and most if not all organ transplant recipients use immunosuppressant drugs. Therefore, is the difference between dosages (Blacks having to take a more aggressive medical therapy) enough to justify the lengthy waiting time and high death toll resulting from the present rationing scheme? Some patients, if presented the option, might choose more aggressive drug therapies in order to live. That pharmaceutical companies have come under fire for failure to incorporate African Americans in drug studies points to an inherent flaw within rationing systems determining patient access based on drug compatibility.[133]

2. Human Leukocyte Antigen Disparity

OPTN also argues that some human leukocyte antigens (HLA) are rarer among Blacks than Whites (who comprise the majority of those in the kidney donor pool).[134] UNOS has developed a process that prioritizes kidney transplants based on HLA matching between donor and recipient. A point value system is used to determine the compatibility or "matching" between a kidney donor and her potential recipient. The system strongly favors a perfect match over all other possible combinations, thereby limiting Black patient access to the larger pool of organs. Consequently, Black organ recipients receive a perfect match at only one-tenth the rate of White patients.[135]

Critics voice strong opposition to a system that allocates kidneys by a point system.[136] In this ambitious technological age, with significant advancements in antirejection treatment options, this particular system is seemingly arbitrary and unethical.[137] Such a preference system would seem unnecessary with cyclosporine, a "highly efficacious antirejection drug" commonly used with kidney and liver transplantation.[138] Steve Takemoto raises an interesting point regarding how life is valued or perhaps should be. Should individuals waiting on lists for over a year be passed over for a kidney if there is another individual new or newer to the list, even if the match would be perfect for the new person? Might this also pertain to how we value "years to live," although applying that value differently? Should life be valued primarily in years and longevity?[139]

What are the humanitarian values or utilitarian ethics preserved in light of policies that comprehensively offer relatively minimal gains?[140] It would seem that such narrow medical advances (the reduced likelihood of rejection) do not rise to a level of significance for the state to justify the disparate treatment of Blacks and other people of color routinely passed over to provide organs to Whites who might have better "matches." That rationing is based on potential longevity between patients rather than by need, placement priority (i.e., first in line), or other more rational criteria contributes to profound racial disparities.

Arguably, average Americans expecting average results are being routinely passed over for opportunities to create "super recipients." The "super recipient" patient ideally has the perfect match and outlives previous organ transplantation expectations. The problem with this approach is that it dehumanizes the process at the cost of Blacks regularly losing their lives on American organ transplant lists. Although problems are inherent in a pure equity-based or lottery-type program of first come-first served, the present allocation system does not equitably serve all people, particularly in light of the overwhelming number of those who will die while waiting for the perfect match. Moreover, the disparate impact of matching borne by a single group that appears most in need should raise the scrutiny and ire of all medical professionals.

Researchers disagree on the significance of matching based on the A, B, and DR antigens. In fact, Dr. Clive Callender argues that 80% of Blacks can take organs from the general population.[141] Yet, although race neutral on its face, antigen matching disfavors Blacks' transplantation of organs from Whites. Endorsing transplantations that rely on racial criteria has tremendous social and medical implications that become more difficult to justify over time. Is it a result of institutional racism, reminiscent of a bygone era or legitimate scientific practice?[142] Commentators question whether this policy is purely based on medical necessity or part of an older medical philosophy with regard to the Black body.[143]

Arthur Caplan, for example, questions the legitimacy of such rationing. Ironically, candidates suffering from lupus, diabetes, or who are retransplant participants are not penalized.[144] However, we know their conditions hasten organ rejection. Such inconsistencies demonstrate a flaw in the correlation between the policy and its ultimate goal. The disparate impact of matching can be clearly observed at the University of Alabama, where Gaston observed kidney waitlists were 65% Black, however only 1 in 33 kidneys matched perfectly and was slated for a Black patient.[145] Commentators suggest that UNOS could revise the point system, thereby allowing greater point accumulation by Blacks. Such a system would compensate Blacks "for points accumulated by Whites on the basis of HLA matching."[146]

3. Higher Crossmatch

OPTN also asserts that Blacks have a higher positive crossmatch rate than other racial groups.[147] In other words, Blacks have a higher sensitivity to donor antigens regardless of the donor's race.[148] Accordingly, Blacks are assumed to have the most difficulty accepting organs from most people, including other African Americans. Is there validity in theories pointing to biological race differences between African Americans and Whites, particularly those that negatively influence health outcomes and access? Again, skeptics question why, if the biotechnological revolution on one hand has led to tremendous advancements in organ transplantation, have African Americans been left on the margins? For one thing, until recently women and racial minorities were excluded or effectively so, from clinical trials and drug studies.[149] Prior to 1993, 90% of federal research dollars for drug experimentation used Whites, and mostly White males as subjects.[150] Secondly, OPTN was slow to recognize and develop strategies to address broad participation and access issues. Congress charged OPTN to allocate organs equitably among all potential transplant recipients; current rationing structures defeat the congressional mandate.

4. Low Donations among Blacks

OPTN attributes the donation rate by Black Americans to the disparity in organ transplantation.[151] For example, Blacks account for 34% of Americans suffering from end-stage renal disease (ESRD), but are only 12% of the U.S. population. Because of immunological differences between Whites and Blacks, and the possibility of organ rejection, Blacks are less often allocated organs from the larger donor pool.[152] However, Blacks donate at similar rates as Whites, and their participation in organ donation is growing, according to Dr. Dreis at the Department of Transplantation of HRSA.[153] Blacks consistently donated proportionately with their population in the United States. For example, among living donors, Blacks constitute 13% of all donors. Among cadaveric donors, African American donations now are upward of 12%.

Nevertheless, African American demand is greater relative to their population, particularly for kidneys.[154] Thus, even with donations from Blacks correlating to their population in the United States, they cannot accommodate the demand within their population. Therefore, until the demand decreases, Blacks will have a greater need for organs. It seems unlikely that demand will subside as the U.S. population increases, Baby Boomers become older, and information about possible health treatments becomes more accessible. Blacks may continue to exceed proportionately their need for kidneys, as they "constitute a disproportionately large percentage of ESRD patients."[155] Although this might explain some disparities in kidney allocation, it does little to justify the continued inequities in the allocation of vital organs. Organs are special, life-saving materials, distinguishable from other life-enhancing resources that are beneficial or even necessary such as employment, education, clothes, and even shelter. Whereas one will not die in the absence of an automobile, a malfunctioning organ is a different matter.

CONCLUSION

What does this discussion mean for capacity alternatives or the models themselves, that is, altruism and allocation? My thesis remains: Institutional options must be explored if we are to take seriously the question of human transplantation. The options necessarily include procurement alternatives that enhance allocation opportunities; the two are wedded. African Americans are central to this discussion given the dual institutional failure to accommodate both their need and mistrust of the contemporary procurement regime. Again, the alternatives seem obvious, although each presents with problems. The alternatives involve rethinking our relationship with the state if a conscription model is used; directed donations (i.e., African Americans exclusively donating to African Americans, a model similar to affirmative action, could be conceivable, but challengeable on equal protection grounds; prison donation; and incentives, which involves transparent negotiations for organs. For purposes here, only the questions involving incentives are explored. Such questions return us to the private and public negotiations involved in organ distribution.

Legal Frameworks and Alternatives

Given the obvious life-saving importance of the issue, the principal options available are to reduce demand, to increase supply, and/or to develop alternatives.

Jack Kress

Part II of this book examines existing legal frameworks for organ procurement and analyzes alternative transplantation mechanisms. This section describes the Uniform Anatomical Gift Act and the recent efforts by the National Conference of Commissioners on Uniform State Laws (NCCUSL) to retool the Act, which was last amended in 1987. This section also scrutinizes two methods for increasing the organ supply: presumed consent and commoditization of body parts. I analyze the relative value and drawbacks of both models, primarily focusing on the value of these models to vulnerable populations.

Blood for sale. After selling his plasma to help make ends meet, Keith Taylor leaves a blood donor center in downtown Gary, Indiana.

5 The Uniform Anatomical Gift Act

Only a small percentage of potential donors die under circumstances that permit transplantation, particularly for organs ... For organs, after the donor is declared brain-dead, the body must be kept on a respirator and life support until the organs are taken. The OPO and/or Eye/Tissue Banks are notified as required by federal law of a potential donor, and they begin developing a medical and family history to determine whether the dying or deceased person is a suitable donor.[1]

INTRODUCTION

In 2004, an effort was underway to respond to great medical demand for organs. The National Conference of Commissioners on Uniform State Laws (NCCUSL) convened a panel of commissioners, chaired by Carlyle C. Ring, to begin retooling the Uniform Anatomical Gift Act (UAGA). On December 3, 2004, at a small hotel in Chicago, Illinois, observers, advisers, and commissioners began the process of redrafting the UAGA. Commissioners invited participation from a broad pool of specialists and interest groups, including representatives from the tissue banking industry, organ procurement organizations, UNOS, the American Medical Association (AMA), the American Bar Association (ABA), the National Association of Medical Examiners, and even funeral directors. The committee was fortunate to have one of the original drafters participate and I was more than pleased to be part of a process that was at the core of much of my research. Redrafting the UAGA is not uncomplicated exactly because there are so many distinct interests in this process and some of those are competing interests. The original UAGA was drafted and passed over a summer. The current drafting process could take 2 years.

The committee's charge is to redraft the UAGA in light of organ demand, respect for donor and family autonomy, consistency with federal laws, and with attention to clarifying ambiguities found in prior versions. The committee is also challenged to draft adaptable legislation that can address future medical and biotechnological needs. Nearly 40 years ago when the original act was drafted, neither commissioners nor federal legislators foresaw the great demand for human biological resources, nor did they predict the multitude of ways in which body parts would be used. Human genome mapping, cloning, and aggressive stem cell study were off the radar even in 1987 when the last revisions of the UAGA were adopted. The UAGA draft currently in development will serve as the third revision of the act. Section A historicizes the Uniform Anatomical Gift Act, analyzing its early development and application.

A. 1968 UAGA

The National Conference of Commissioners on Uniform State Laws (NCCUSL) enacted the original UAGA in 1968. Promulgation of the original act immediately followed the first successful liver transplant performed in 1967,[2] and subsequent heart and pancreas transplants in 1968.[3] The UAGA's implementation signaled an urgent call for donation awareness and state action.[4] The act regulates the procurement of organs from cadaveric donors and establishes ethical and legal guidelines for organ transplantation.[5] Since its original implementation in 1968, the act has been revised with more liberal policies on organ and tissue procurement and greater clarity on ambiguous donation issues. By 1973 all states had adopted the main provision of the UAGA; revisions clarified ambiguities found in the original act. For example, the 1987 revisions made it clear that a donor's wish to provide her organs at death could be enforced by physicians, thereby overriding the possible objection of her next-of-kin. Although amended, the 1968 Act serves as the basic blueprint for organ donation in the United States.

The 1968 UAGA accomplished several goals. It established the scope of cadaveric donations, clarified the donation process, and categorized parts of the body for donation. Despite subsequent criticism, the 1968 UAGA was a proactive response to a lesser-known but burgeoning medical technology – organ transplantation. It also provided a legitimate, regulated means for university hospitals and research facilities to supply cadavers, which were needed for medical research purposes.[6] The 1968 Act provided a standardized method of donating organs and other body parts posthumously, defining parts as blood, organs, tissues, arteries, eyes, fluids, and "any other portions of a human body."[7]

Scope

The scope of the act is limited to cadaveric donors. The UAGA did not address living donations in 1968 (nor does it now), and it continues to draw a clear distinction between living and deceased donations. The 1968 Act provided for at least two types of donations upon a donor's death. First, a donor could predesignate her body or parts for transplantation. This was effectuated by a will or witnessed document. Today, this is most often accomplished at departments of motor vehicles with a statement on one's license. The second mode of cadaveric organ donation was designated to family members, who, in order of ranking, could donate the decedent's body or its parts (spouse, parents, and children) even over the preexisting objections of the deceased.

Some provisions of the 1968 Act were ambiguous and considered contradictory, particularly with regard to donation authority. For this reason, the act was not without controversy as family members had competing interests in bodies, particularly on religious grounds. For example, spouses and parents challenged the legality of donations based on religious beliefs that bodies must be buried whole or desecration of the body will affect the afterlife. Such objections effectively overturned their deceased relatives' donations, making some donations only symbolic because doctors could not collect the body parts for fear of litigation. Moreover, although a qualified donor (an individual of sound mind and age 18 or older) could bequeath her organs, and properly effectuate her interest through a will or other testamentary document, the act did not make clear whether family members were stopped from challenging the donation (i.e., whether donations were revocable by family members). These issues were further complicated by donations sometimes appearing surreptitious if the family members had not been apprised of the deceased's desire to donate until after his death.

Compensation

The 1968 UAGA did not foreclose financial compensation for organs or other body parts. In fact, E. B. Stason, chair of the UAGA Drafting Committee, suggested that "the matter [of compensation] should be left to the decency of intelligent human beings."[8] Stason's characterization is consistent with the notion that the 1968 UAGA may have had more immediate relevance for those performing medical research than those interested in pursuing transplantation, as organ transplantation was still a very new therapy, rejection rates were high, and antirejection medications were yet to be perfected. Cyclosporine, an antirejection medication, was not approved for general use until 1983; it reshaped the future of organ transplantation. Long before successful organ transplantation, however, dead bodies and body parts were needed for medical and scientific research. One can only speculate as to why there was no prohibition on compensating donors in the 1968 Act. My theory is that medical schools and early biotech industries were also in need of body parts (in a later chapter, these issues are discussed in greater detail). Stason's comment indicates that the question regarding payments for organs and other body parts was intentionally left open. Stason believed that not all payments would be unethical.[9]

Indeed, the more significant provisions of the act provide for express authorization of donations for medical, educational, and research purposes.[10] The UAGA provides for donations of any human body or body part to:

(1) any hospital, surgeon, or physician, for medical or dental education, research, advancement of medical or dental science, therapy, or transplantation;

(2) any accredited medical or dental school, college or university for education, research, advancement of medical or dental science, or therapy;

(3) any bank or storage facility, for medical or dental education, research, advancement of medical or dental science, therapy, or transplantation;

(4) any specified individual for therapy or transplantation needed by him.[11]

In relevant part, the act identified and ranked "next-of-kin" authorized to donate[12] (or by default object to donation);[13] and established a right for adults to donate their bodies or parts thereof. The next-of-kin was authorized to donate only in absence of the deceased's objection. Thus, relatives were provided authority to donate their kin's body if the decedent had not provided notice intending the contrary. This section authorized and ranked family members in order of greater "right" to donate:

(1) spouse
(2) an adult son or daughter
(3) either parent
(4) adult siblings (sister or brother)
(5) guardian
(6) any others authorized or obligated to dispose of the body (amended in 1987 Act §3(a).

Tensions

Two major events prompted both the 1987 UAGA amendment and the promulgation of the National Organ Transplant Act (NOTA) of 1984.[14] First, the original UAGA failed to increase organ supplies to keep pace with the demand.[15] In the advent of cyclosporine, organ transplantations became more common and demand grew. The act became viewed as a model for organ procurement and not simply organ donation regulation. Critics suggested that donations did not keep pace with medical need, and that the rate of donation compared to need had decreased with the act's passage.[16] This could possibly have been attributed to the number of living donors decreasing in critical areas like kidney donation. Perhaps relatives were relying on the altruism of others to meet the dying needs of their loved ones.

The 1968 UAGA was logistically problematic for procuring organs for transplantation. For example, it provided for donation through wills or nontestamentary documents, such as donor cards. Both methods were ineffective in procuring organs. Because organ donations require immediate harvest to procure and protect the vital parts while viable, wills posed significant delays. Viable organs must be retrieved immediately on death to ensure transplantability. Wills delayed the process owing to the very nature of that process, requiring that the document be found, read, and possibly probated. After the necessary measures are taken to execute the donor's will, her organs may no longer be viable for transplantation. Another significant drawback involved the donor card. Theoretically, donor cards would provide an effective means of effectuating one's intent to donate. However, a donor's failure to carry her card at all times was problematic. In addition, failure to notify a next-of-kin of her intent to donate would effectively void donation.

The second event prompting reform was the threat of organs becoming market commodities[17] with or without governmental regulation and monitoring. There was also the need to reconcile the act with federal regulations promulgated in 1984. Organ commodification became a growing concern, which ultimately prompted a less reasoned congressional response, intended more to ease immediate tensions rather than establishing a long-term vision for organ procurement.[18] Fears associated with slavery, child abductions, and body snatching for organ removal heightened tensions across the nation.[19] Organs were already being sold in other countries according to news reports in the 1980s.[20] Organ providers placed advertisements in newspapers to sell corneas and kidneys.[21] This information, combined with reports from the U.S. House Subcommittee on Health and the Environment reporting that it received letters from individuals desiring to sell their organs to finance college tuition or pay for medical treatment, created an atmosphere appropriate for congressional response.

B. The 1987 UAGA: Required Request and Presumed Consent

The 1987 UAGA was a significant departure from its predecessor.[22] The 1968 Act has been criticized by scholars and legislators for failure to generate a sufficient organ supply.[23] However, in fairness to the drafters, the act was intended to define the scope of donations; the UAGA by itself could not procure organs. The 1987 revision clarified issues left for broad interpretation and speculation in the 1968 UAGA. Indeed, much of the criticism directed at the original UAGA (1968) resulted from its ambiguities. Drafters in the 1968 version truly believed uncertainty would be eliminated.[24]

[U]ncertainty as to the applicable law will be eliminated and all parties will be protected. At the same time the Act will serve the needs of the several conflicting interests in a manner consistent with prevailing customs and desires in this country respecting dignified disposition of dead bodies.[25]

Yet, the early act failed to provide direction or take a position on several key issues. Among the critical areas left vague were: (1) whether organ donations could be and for what purposes the subject of sales;[26] (2) coroner or medical examiner authority to retrieve organs and under what circumstances or guidelines;[27] (3) requiring hospitals and physicians to request organ donation;[28] and (4) whether relatives could cancel the donor's effectuated gift.[29] These issues were given greater clarity in the amended UAGA (1987).

However, only 26 jurisdictions enacted the 1987 revision of the UAGA.[30] Thus, there continues to be "substantial non-uniformity not only between the 1968 Act states and the 1987 revision states, but also because of extensive federal statutes and regulations and state law changes promulgated since 1987."[31] The 1987 UAGA is not harmonized with federal law, which creates untenable gaps in the law. Greater uniformity would be desirable for donors (to create greater clarity), but also for recipients, who happen not only to be patients, but organ procurement organizations, tissue banks, hospitals, medical examiners, and others. Furthermore, state and federal legislation are inconsistent in their missions. According to Sheldon Kurtz, reporter for the third (current) revision process, "state anatomical gift laws (either the '68 or '87 version) largely governs the ability to procure organs through the donation process and federal law . . . largely controls how donated organs are donated to recipients."[32]

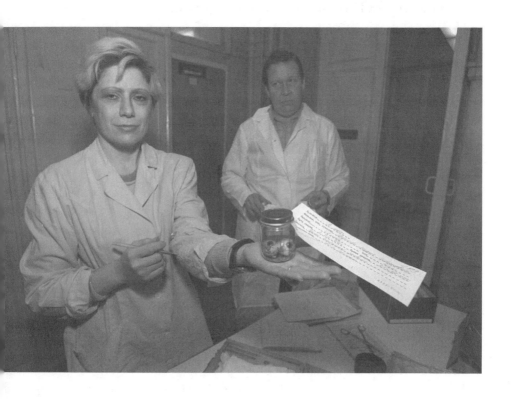

Eyes for sale. Eyes bound for the stream of international implantation. The Lefortovo Morgue was shut down for selling body parts. (Corbis Images)

6 Presumed Consent
The Unsuspecting Donor

INTRODUCTION

Carlos M. Gudino would appear twice in the *Los Angeles Times* news-paper.[1] The first time would be a kind of turning point or rebirth. He was only 19 years old when he worked on a mural with Jesse Rojas, another young, aspiring artist, trying desperately to move beyond the reach of Los Angeles gang life.[2] Their story, one of a possible triumph or at least a story of hope, would be captured by a bold headline: "*Praise for His Art Keeps Young Muralist from Being Walled in by Harsh Gang Life.*"[3] A photograph would memorialize Carlos' gaze of Jesse applying the final brush strokes to the mural of Madonna he helped to create.

The Community Youth Gang Services and the Los Angeles Police Department helped to underwrite the project in an effort to bring calm to a community riddled by gang violence, teen unemployment, and drug transactions.[4] The mural, located at a corner in Los Angeles, California, where Wilmington meets G Street, is considered a tough place, where drug transactions occur nightly and trouble awaits. The project was aimed at helping the community overcome despair and transforming the lives of talented young men with a sincere interest in leaving "gang-banging behind." Although the *L.A. Times* article would focus consid-erably on Jesse's artistic talents, Carlos' youthful gaze would forever be captured and give the vision of hope.

Five years later, in November 1997, almost to the very day, Carlos would again appear in the same daily newspaper that had previously captured him gazing at the Madonna.[5] His brutal death from 12 bullet wounds to the head and chest, which had occurred earlier in the year, ironically was not the focus of the second article. His death was less newsworthy; too many young men in Los Angeles met similar fates. Instead, the article exposed the surreptitious harvesting of corneas at the local morgue. None of the so-called donors or their families in the investigation provided consent to the local coroner who harvested over 1,000 corneas.[6] The article raised questions about the role race, socio-economic status, and consent in this controversial process known as presumed or legislative consent.[7] The *Los Angeles Times* contacted Carlos M. Gudino's family the second time as part of a study they were conducting to confirm whether families were aware that their deceased relatives' corneas had been harvested and later sold.

Like all the families in Ralph Frammolino's investigation, the Gudinos were uninformed about the cornea extractions.[8] Carlos' corneas were nonconsensually harvested pursuant to the presumed consent legislation.[9] The family expressed dismay that the Los Angeles coroner's office possessed legal authority to operate in what some have called a "clandestine" manner, referring to the legislation and process that presumes that one is willing to be a donor unless a prior refusal has been recorded or relatives have objected.[10] What made their situation somewhat unique and all the more troubling was that Maria, Carlos' sister, had registered the family's objection to any organ or tissue donation the morning after Carlos' death.[11] In fact, their objection, dutifully recorded by an investigator from the coroner's office, was quite specific and noted in a report: "Family is profoundly against ANY organ or tissue donation."[12]

The family's objection was too late; three hours earlier Carlos' corneas had been harvested by the Doheny Eye and Tissue Bank under authorization of the coroner.[13] Doheny and the coroner's office had an arrangement whereby corneas were harvested and the coroner's office was paid "an average of about $250 for a set of corneas, which are then sold to transplant institutions for a 'processing fee' of $3,400."[14] Carlos' family learned about the harvesting and financial transactions 8 months after his death.[15] Doheny's markup was more than 1,000%!

Frammolino's investigation involved reviewing 572 cases of cornea extraction and selling during a 12-month period.[16] The overwhelming majority of the donors, 72%, were young homicide victims. Accident victims, the next largest donor pool, accounted for only 16%.[17] Over 80% of the donors were of color (nearly 60% Latino and 21% African American).[18] Whites were only 16% of the donor pool.[19] Were it not for Frammolino's investigation, which was funded by the *Los Angeles Times*, families would never have known about legislative or presumed consent law or nonconsensual tissue harvesting.

Indeed, presumed consent operates on the principle of silence. It manipulates the notion of intent with regard to donations in the most dramatic death cases. Remember, the presumed consent laws operate pursuant to mandatory autopsy laws (i.e., cases of homicide and catastrophic deaths, such as drowning, poisoning, etc.). The law basically says, "we presume that you really wanted to donate your corneas and if you were not dead, you would manifest that intent. We are here to help you make that donation a reality." Yet, if left to Carlos' family, his corneas would never have been donated. Presumed consent is an illusory proposition. Given the social reluctance to donate body parts (without compensation), as discussed earlier, the wiser and most reliable presumption is that people will refuse to donate. That is one of the most significant factors in why only 20% of Americans carry donor cards. The Guidinos did in fact manifest their intent regarding donation, and it was a refusal.

A. Presumed Consent: Origins and Obstacles

This chapter analyzes the practicality and pitfalls of organ and body part procurement through presumed consent legislation (also known as medical examiner laws and legislative consent). It examines the value of consent in the donation process and evaluates the practicability of applying presumed consent measures to organ procurement. It begins by further explaining the implementation of presumed consent statutes in the United States. This chapter includes commentaries from eye bank officials whom I interviewed at the height of political crisis involving presumed consent. Because, as we discussed in Chapter 3, there is no duty to rescue found in American jurisprudence, the only way to justify compulsory donation would be through a theory of social contract. This chapter concludes by analyzing whether social contract theory actually justifies nonconsensual body parts appropriation by the state.

What Does Consent Have to Do with It?

The Uniform Anatomical Gift Act gave license for the passage of pre-sumed consent laws (also referred to as legislative consent laws) in 1987 through its most significant amendment.[20] That law, as discussed in Chapter 5, permits the nonconsensual harvesting of body parts. The leg-islative consent statutes operate through mandatory medical inquest or autopsy. Autopsies, although common, are mandatory only in cer-tain circumstances, most notably homicides. These statutes, however, refer to autopsy as the mandatory medical examiner investigation. It should, therefore, not be confused with routine autopsies that a private individual may request, but which the state is not investigating.

The UAGA does not limit nonconsensual harvesting to corneas, although most states have drawn the line with corneas.[21] Cornea extrac-tion may be perceived as less invasive, it certainly is less disfigur-ing, and thus less noticeable. Cornea extraction does not leave signs easily noticeable to laypeople; there are no bruises on the face and no scratches on the eyelids.[22] Thus, if the deceased is prepared for burial, particularly with her eyes closed, her family would be completely unaware of the medical intrusion.[23] For this reason, critics of presumed consent measures regard these laws as surreptitious and unethical and supporters argue that they are creative efforts to procure corneas.[24] Pro-ponents argue that compulsory donations require so little – and fami-lies hardly notice.[25]

Obtaining consent has always been a barrier in donations.[26] In her article *Organ Donation as National Service: A Proposed Federal Organ Donation Law*, Linda Fentiman argued that presumed consent helps to avoid the cumbersome task of asking permission for body parts: "Physi-cians would no longer need to confront a grieving family with the need to make a quick decision about organ donation."[27] Fentiman proposed that states move beyond presumed consent with corneas and apply the legislation to organs. At the time of her article, medical examiner laws were passed in 28 states, and most were promulgated during the 1980s, a time marked by a scourge of violence and death in urban communi-ties of color.[28] The urban landscape of the United States changed dra-matically during that time.[29] Homicide rates exponentially increased in

Midwest cities, such as Milwaukee and St. Louis.[30] Drug wars annually took the lives of more than a 1,000 young Black and Latino youths in California.[31] In the nation's capital, the drug violence was so acute that Nancy Reagan, former President Ronald Reagan's wife, created an advertising campaign, "Just say no to drugs."[32] Based on drug use data, homicide statistics, and arrest rates, Reagan's campaign was not successful.[33]

To the contrary, during this period of violence in the 1980s and into the 1990s came rising death tolls of young Blacks and Latinos and the promulgation of presumed consent laws.[34] These two overlapping occurrences were a tragic coincidence. It would be unjust to characterize the promulgation of presumed consent laws as an intentional effort to exploit Black communities or that Black deaths provided an opportunity for which tissue banks could capitalize. Some commentators claimed a conspiracy was underfoot and that dead Black boys were being used to supply body parts to White Americans.[35] Louis Farrakhan remarked to an audience of 6,000, mostly college students in 1994, "when you're killing each other, they can't wait for you to die ... [y]ou've become good for parts."[36] I am not suggesting that presumed consent laws were passed because Blacks and Latinos were dying in mass numbers due to causes that would require coroner investigations and autopsies. Yet, such unfortunate coincidences, especially if they violate medical trust, viscerally resonate in Black communities throughout the United States, particularly when reality (i.e., nonconsensual cornea harvesting and selling) connects so closely with myth: clandestine organ harvesting from Black homicide victims. Placed in context, it is not so difficult to understand why Blacks would perceive themselves as caught in a vicious cycle of violence, death, and exploitation. According to an African American commentator, Julienne Malveaux, the "unfinished business," meaning acknowledgment of historical harms to Black Americans, keeps them justifiably suspicious of medicine and other social interventions.[37]

Indeed, if it were ever thought inflammatory, the claim that more corneas (particularly from Blacks and Latinos) became available in California from gang and drug violence is irrefutable. Moreover, some eye bank officials, including those from California and Alabama, credited presumed consent laws for the increase in corneal tissues available for transplantation in their states.[38] Doyce Williams, one of the eye bank officials I interviewed in 2000, expressed that presumed consent legislation positively contributed to tissue procurement.[39] For Mr. Williams, presumed consent was about giving sight to those suffering with body parts (corneas) that would otherwise be wasted. Indeed, data from Alabama and California indicated that cornea availability increased, particularly as more tissues were available from victims of trauma and homicides.[40] At times, surpluses were created, which allowed tissue banks to sell "leftover" tissues to medical research laboratories, sometimes at tremendous markups.

However, whether or not presumed consent has always worked effectively and safely is debatable. Problems associated with presumed consent include harvesting tissue without consent, the possibility of transmitting communicable diseases where health or social histories have not been obtained, including Creutzfeldt-Jakob disease,[41] transplanting low-quality biological materials (from former convicts), and failure to obtain consent. Any policy that limits donor autonomy and ignores family consent warrants serious scrutiny.[42] Yet, presumed consent proponents remind us that saving the living and enhancing quality of life should be society's greatest concern and presumed consent is a method for doing just that.[43] They also point out that many of the legislative consent statutes offer a right for the donor to refuse the extraction. The "opt-out" provision, they say, actually allows for one to revoke consent.[44]

But how does a dead person opt out of cornea takings? The opt-out provision is misleading. Living persons are unaware of how exactly to opt out. The fact that there isn't a national or state registry, except in Iowa, where one can opt out of tissue donation, is a significant barrier. States that passed presumed consent laws failed to take secondary measures to give full meaning to an individual or her family's choice to decline extraction. Their failure to do so unquestionably contributes to legal and social backlash against presumed consent policies.[45] Such secondary measures would have included information about presumed consent through public service announcements; an opportunity for citizens to effectively opt out through state databases, driver licensing, or other method; and prohibition of extraction absent communication from a family member. In states where presumed consent has been litigated in the press, the policy is considered a public relations nightmare. Tissue banks are even reluctant for the policy to be extended, recalling the litigation and negative press after scandals in Los Angeles, Washington, DC, and Florida. Indeed, presumed consent undermines the very "gift of life" concept. Ultimately, the extractions in these instances are not "gifts," but rather "takings" that would otherwise require due process from the state. In instances where the state intends to remove or infringe on another's liberty or property, notice, hearings, and sometimes compensation is warranted.

Whether an increased supply of corneas and as a hypothetical extension, organs, should be the prime or sole focus of an ethical and equitable procurement policy seems a relevant and timely question.[46] Furthermore, it appears debatable whether other procurement methods, which are less intrusive with regard to privacy and autonomy, would not prove more successful at balancing the need for human body parts and protecting civil liberties. I interviewed eye bank officials in Kentucky, Vermont, Michigan, Illinois, Massachusetts, Wisconsin, Arkansas, northern Florida, northern Ohio, Indiana, New Hampshire, Rhode Island, New Orleans, New York, and Alabama. Some of these officials were skeptical about presumed consent policies, arguing in some instances that even though the volume of body parts such as corneas might increase, there was little control on safety.[47] They argue that eye banks using strict consent policies with effective educational programming also experience surpluses in donation.[48]

Too Much to Not Ask For...

In my recent survey of African Americans regarding organ transplantation, when asked whether it should be legal for the state to remove organs without consent, over 86% answered in the negative.[49] More than 500 of 588 participants believed that states should not have the authority to remove body parts without consent.[50] Survey participants articulated the importance of consent to their decision making and levels of trust. That is not surprising; fiduciary trust and informed consent in medicine have long been important principles protected by courts and international treaties.[51] Of the 15 eye bank directors or administrative staff interviewed for this study, only three shared the opinion that the benefits of legislative consent policies outweighed obtaining donor consent, or for that matter, collecting medical and social histories, which are impossible to do with a dead person.[52]

Indeed, the Nuremburg Code, which reinforces the value of informed consent, was born out of the unspeakable harms directly targeted at the Jewish communities in Germany and Poland. The same values, informed consent and trust, are essential ethical and legal principles in organ donation. Yet, as discussed earlier, obtaining consent for donation proves problematic. For this reason Linda Fentiman proposed in 1993 that consent could be circumvented through adoption of presumed consent measures.[53] However, the success of presumed consent relies on an unaware public, and it is for this reason that such policies will prove marginally successful in the long term. The policy relies on social ignorance.

However, because consent has become an obstacle in organ procurement, presumed consent is particularly attractive to some policymakers and the tissue lobby. Although their interests diverge, increasing tissue supply helps different institutions. For the commercial tissue lobby, their product supply increases at relatively low costs with such programs, creating windfalls and huge markups when their biological products go to the market. One eye bank official suggested to me during our second interview that donor registration is too bureaucratic and that lives could be saved with softened consent requirements, such as presumed consent. Others have proposed organ donation as a national service, and support legislative consent with the possibility of opting out.[54] States that have adopted this model are presented with significant moral and ethical problems, particularly because these laws operate through medical examiner inquiries into homicides, trauma, poisonings, and deaths that happen disproportionately in urban and poor communities.[55] Only a few courts have addressed the legality of these state statutes because so few cases have been brought to challenge such laws.[56] Mark Larson, the executive director of the Eyebank of Wisconsin, attributes this to people being generally unaware of presumed consent statutes in their states, and the fact that it is difficult to detect when corneas have been removed.[57]

B. Can Presumed Consent Work for Organs?

Presumed consent, developed initially in Maryland with the passage of its presumed consent law[58] and passed in 28 states[59] (with 9 states actively using the law),[60] operates in a shroud of secrecy; very few people are aware of these laws.[61] In practice, however, presumed consent has been problematic and may not be the best solution for increasing organ and tissue procurement.[62] According to Dr. Jim Martin, executive director of the Louisville Eye Bank in Kentucky, compulsory procurement was not successful in his state and annual deficits were experienced until the eye bank changed their procurement strategies and stopped operating under presumed consent.[63] Perhaps one reason for Kentucky's inability to meet demand under legislative consent was that the policy failed to earn the support of medical professionals and the eye bank community, and thus was not consistently or effectively applied.[64] Another reason could be the relatively low number of homicides in Kentucky counties.

Over the course of two interviews in Kentucky and in subsequent conversations, Dr. Martin explained that the presumed consent policy was simply morally unacceptable and fraught with ethical and potential legal problems.[65] An organized tissue lobby had a planned, strategic approach with various states, including Kentucky. According to Dr. Martin, Kentucky legislators adopted that state's measure in response to the enactment of similar provisions by other state legislatures and pressure from strong lobbying efforts at both the state and federal levels by eye banks supporting legislative consent measures. Ohio, Arkansas, and West Virginia, all bordering or region states with Kentucky, adopted similar statutes a year or two before Kentucky enacted its policy.

Dr. Martin cited an array of problems posed by presumed consent. However, most urgent for him were two issues: the poor quality of donor tissues and the possible overrepresentation of tissues harvested from young, poor Black kids.[66] Consequentially, the Kentucky medical community sought alternative solutions.[67] Other eye bank officials, including Mark Larson of Wisconsin;[68] Donica Davis, hospital division coordinator for the Tennessee Eye Bank; and Tom Buckley, executive director of the New England Eye and Tissue Transplant Bank,[69] voiced similar concerns. At an interview in his Madison, Wisconsin, office, Larson shared concerns quite similar to those addressed by Martin, including his perception that a sufficient supply "of transplantable corneas can only be obtained through effective hospital development and donor awareness programs"[70] and not through "shortcuts."[71] One misstep, such as transplanting contaminated tissue, could undue or overshadow the positive efforts in transplantation.

Consider, if you will, that social histories are usually not obtained for presumed consent donors. Several eye bank procurement officials cautioned about the quality of presumed consent tissue, noting that tissue and organs might not be high quality or safe because communicable diseases such as hepatitis B and C, rabies, and Creutzfeldt-Jakob syndrome (similar to mad cow disease) can be transmitted through corneas.[72] Social history could indicate a person's sexual history, any criminal history, including time as part of a prison population, any past diseases, infections or illnesses, or habits, including smoking, drinking or drug use. Because of consent problems, coroners have no incentive to interview immediate family members and friends may be difficult to trace and contact. How would they be found short of investigation? In an opinion paper, Larson indicated that in his experience, social history interviews provide necessary information normally not required under presumed consent policy.[73] Beyond the supply issue, consent, according to Larson, is simply "the right thing to do."[74]

Despite Martin's protestations to the contrary, Doyce Williams is quick to point out that legislative consent works when done consistently. For example, the state of Alabama experienced annual surpluses in the supply of transplantable corneas until lawmakers abandoned legislative consent laws.[75] Yet, newspaper headlines in Alabama conveyed a much different attitude about presumed consent laws: "*Cornea Controversy: Eye Banks Don't See Eye to Eye*" and "*Mother Feels Corneas Were Stolen*."[76] These front-page news items illustrate the drama lurking behind consent laws that operate in a vacuum, without donor or relative consent, or any communication for that matter. These headlines came after investigative reports revealed that corneas were being harvested in Alabama, pursuant to state statute, without consent from the decedents' relatives. In a case that made headlines and resulted in an out-of-court settlement, a mother, Patsy Burton, learned about the medical examiner's removal of her teenage son's corneas only after reading news reports about the nonconsensual harvesting of tissues in Alabama.[77] Angered at "not being given a chance" to give consent, Burton demanded, "What else can they do, or what do they do, when they have the chance?"[78] In a letter to the county commissioner, she asked, "did the coroner's office take my son's corneas because they were trying to help someone else see again or just because he was young and they thought nobody would care?"[79] According to Doyce Williams, the fallout from the negative publicity had a chilling effect on altruistic donations[80] and led to the abrupt abandonment of the legislative consent provision by lawmakers.[81]

Thus, at what cost to community trust and the long-term success of tissue procurement do such programs operate? Legislators seem quickly inclined to abandon the policies when confronted with an outraged public. Alabama abandoned its plans after several lawsuits. In California, they abandoned the program as well by forbidding nonconsensual cornea harvesting. The Los Angeles County coroner's office responded to an angry public by no longer "routinely permit[ting] a local eye bank to harvest corneas without the permission or knowledge of surviving family members."[82] Accordingly, organ and tissue procurement cannot be viewed as simply a numbers game.[83] Saving lives and restoring sight is important, but not at the cost of donor autonomy and community health.

How then is a sustainable system to be crafted? Certain realities must be squarely acknowledged – tissue and organ shortages result in deaths otherwise avoided. State legislatures are vulnerable to strong tissue lobbies that ultimately profit handsomely from donor tissue. Moreover, the presumed consent pool is woefully narrow; greater public attention to seatbelts, for example, has dramatically reduced potential accident victims as donors. Those who remain in the presumed consent pool are homicide victims – most disproportionately Blacks and Latinos. Mary Jane O'Neil, a legislative consent proponent, cautioned, "Ten years ago people who would have been donors have been saved by seatbelt laws, helmet requirements, and gun control."[84] However, most Americans would probably agree that saving lives by restricting certain behaviors that are known to cause injury or even death is a "good thing to do,"[85] even if there are other Americans who would benefit from their corneas, kidneys, and other potential body parts. Besides, why should people who engage in risky behavior be a primary target of tissue and organ procurement?

Religious Concerns

Still, deeply human factors shape our understanding of our bodies and of the divine image in which we are all created, and transplantation efforts must preserve the dignity and respect that God's creation demands.[86]

Other ethical problems are posed by the legislative authorization to waive consent to autopsy and tissue harvesting. Certain cultural expectations and religious doctrines emphasize human dignity, the sacredness of the body, and preservation of life, even when medically the body may be considered "dead."[87] For example, Orthodox Judaism has to be appreciated for the very complex way in which life and death are valued and evaluated; it is not so easy to simply conflate meanings and practice about dying within that religious tradition.[88] According to Elliot Dorff, a philosopher as well as a rabbi, Jewish law "requires that Jews take steps to preserve their life and health," even when secular law and medical practice might have determined death.[89] This is not to suggest that the Jewish community speaks with one voice regarding transplantation, nor that Dorff has appointed himself as the spokesperson of his faith. Rather, his comments indicate the complexity of tissue and organ harvesting in the Jewish community. Appreciating that perspective should cause some reflection on whether prophylactic use of compulsory harvesting would violate a sacred trust that extends beyond medicine and secular law.

Strong Judaic values associated with life pose difficulty for "agreeing to donate."[90] The connection to the spiritual afterlife, and the belief in the existence after death of "spirits who look like the embodied people they were in life," is attributed to making the more conservative members of the Jewish faith reluctant to grant consent to donate.[91] It stands to reason that Orthodox Jews and other persons of faith might find legislative consent offensive and religiously impractical.[92] Indeed, Mary Jane O'Neil alluded to as much when I interviewed her.[93]

According to O'Neil, "Jewish people would not donate and would fight [presumed consent]"[94] for the reasons suggested by Elliot Dorff and other commentators. Lawsuits brought by Laotians and other ethnic minorities based on religious violations of relatives' bodies indicate that presumed consent will prove problematic. African Americans share similar concerns based on their religious perspectives, although they cannot be grouped under one religious umbrella as they are Catholic, Baptist, Christian Methodist Episcopalian, African Methodist Episcopalian, Muslim, and Jewish. Nevertheless, Black people voice concerns about being buried "whole" for heaven and preserving what "God" gave them.[95]

Religious conflicts with presumed consent may have less to do with opposition to performing a loving and kind act that would benefit another, or even sharing human organs, but more to do with human dignity. The major obstacle is the perception of bodily harm or mutilation caused by the actual removal of organs. Philosophically, this view challenges the notion that a dead body is simply a corpse, no longer able to support feelings, emotions, thoughts and, therefore, lacking a certain integrity or humanity that is deemed exclusively for the living. Rather, a profound respect for the deceased seems to drive religious doctrines that oppose compulsory organ harvesting.

Cultural Concerns

African Americans interviewed for this book also strongly disapproved of mandatory organ donation. They were concerned about autonomy, privacy, and equitable distribution or allocation. Their concerns were articulated broadly. Some might read their comments as "scattered," but they speak to what Julienne Malveaux called the "unfinished business" discussed earlier in this chapter. In essence, their broad concerns reflect a different social understanding of medicine, law, and society in the United States. K.S., a resident physician, asked, "Who are they going to give the organs to? Is there going to be a signal – if someone knows the organ came from a Black woman or a Chinese woman or a Hispanic woman? Are people going to ask about races and classes? . . . And who is going to be at the top of the list?"[96] K.S. was also concerned about health status and lifestyles of donors. According to her, "so maybe not everyone will participate and, depending on the health status, maybe not every-body should donate…organs because not everyone lives a lifestyle where the organs would meet the health criteria to give to someone."[97] Others, such as D.J., suggested that the state could not account for individual personal and perhaps religious beliefs. According to him, "I think it is a choice that [an individual] should make. [Someone's] personal beliefs may be that they should not be dealt with physically after death, especially not for medical reasons, so no."[98]

Only 2 of 40 African Americans interviewed suggested that presumed consent is a legitimate method to procure organs. According to A. S., a 50-year-old nurse technician, "I don't think [dead people] should have any rights."[99] J.F. answered back, "what do you need them for [when you are dead]?"[100] Others were less optimistic, articulating notions of "freedom of choice" and noting that presumed consent does not speak to "distribution."[101] For example, J.F., a banker, recognized that privacy could be violated and that rights to the body followed individuals to their graves, offering, "You know you have the right to do what you want with your body even when you're dead."[102]

Others were skeptical about government distribution of organs. J.D., a 38-year-old police officer, posited, "You know how the government is, they might be giving African Americans' organs to people with a good deal of money – to the rich. Predominantly White Americans may get most of them. I think White America would benefit from that."[103] L.J., a 27-year-old medical records clerk, was alarmed by the idea, opining, "it's almost like having a dictatorship almost. One should still be able to decide – or one's family should be able to decide what they can do with their body."[104] When asked whether mandatory donation would resolve the organ crisis, her response was, "No. They would give them all to White people."[105]

L.L.B., a 28-year-old homemaker who is a registered donor, is none-theless opposed to presumed consent. When asked whether the gov-ernment should require all Americans to donate their organs, she responded:

No. Not at all. I mean some people may have religious reasons or just moral reasons or – I have a cousin who says that she would not do it because it is almost like you are not really whole or something, like they are not fully burying you. So, I mean people have all kinds of reasons why they wouldn't do it, just like people have all kinds of reasons why they would.[106]

Overwhelmingly, African Americans were ambivalent about the proposition of federal policies that would mandate organ donation among civilian or incarcerated populations. Their concerns included the desire for choice with regard to such decision making, and also a right to privacy. Mistrust, as discussed earlier, was a repeating theme. N.B., a schoolteacher, believes that donation is "a personal issue and also ... a religious issue."[107] He shared that fewer African Americans participate in the current system "because of the fear that if something is to severely happen to them, that they would not get their proper healthcare that they are looking for. Thus, people are ... actually the doctors are sort of like vultures and they are all standing around waiting for you to die."[108]

Ironically, many felt that even with mandatory donation, such would not resolve the organ crisis for African Americans. They were not convinced that African Americans would be the beneficiaries of organs even with such a system. They warned that the organs would be siphoned off to White Americans. Whether true or not, their concerns speak to mistrust and concern about being left out of the process. Choice was a concern repeatedly raised. For example, what if a person wanted to object?

Proponents of legislative consent argue that those with religious and cultural objections can opt out of consent, meaning that they can make known or register their refusal to donate.[109] Although opt outs might be available, they are often more illusory than real.[110] First, many people are not aware of the existence of presumed or legislative consent policies.[111] Second, even if people were made aware of their rights, many are skeptical as to whether and how the opt-out provisions would be enforced.[112]

Opt-Out Viability

In 2000, I conducted two surveys to determine the potential success of opt-out provisions. As reported in an earlier article, in one survey over 90% of survey participants in a state with presumed consent laws were unaware that the law existed.[113] One survey was administered to 15 local government officials in Lexington, Kentucky, with the assistance of Janet Givens, special assistant to former Mayor Pam Miller. The other survey was administered to 100 participants through phone interviews. The participants were randomly selected from lists of names obtained from community leaders, clergy, college students, and community advocates. Participants were from southern states: Kentucky, Arkansas, Maryland, Alabama, Tennessee, and North Carolina.

Only 1 of the 15 people (or 6.6%) surveyed in the Mayor's office was aware of presumed consent laws in Kentucky. Of the larger group surveyed, only 5 of the 100 people (5%) had ever heard of presumed consent laws. One of the groups surveyed consisted of administrators in the Mayor's office and members of the City Council of Lexington, Kentucky.[114] Only 1 of 15 people surveyed in this group had any knowledge about presumed consent, although Kentucky authorized the legislation over 10 years ago.[115]

Beyond the problems attendant to marginal public information, would opt-out provisions work? Because timing is critically important to organ and tissue harvesting, the necessity to transplant in a timely manner might supercede waiting for a possible objection, particularly when the most viable tissues require harvesting within 3 to 6 hours after death. James Nelson's commentary on presumed consent and opt-out measures illuminates important ethical concerns:

A simple reliance on our moral intuitions isn't enough. As the history of medical research in the nineteenth and even twentieth century reveals, we have been more than willing to subject those who were "clearly less valuable" to the rigors of research only then, the ones who were obviously less valuable were Jewish, or people of color. Our gut instincts simply aren't good enough as reliable moral guides when we're dealing with those whom we've pushed to the margin of moral discourse.[116]

You Vang Yang v. Sturner, the closest case on point, illustrates the difficulty with opting out of autopsies.[117] The Yangs, members of the Hmong community, adhere to an orthodox religious tradition, "which prohibits any mutilation of the body, including autopsies or the removal of organs during an autopsy."[118] The Yangs brought an action for damages after an autopsy was performed on their son, claiming that the Rhode Island autopsy statute, both facially and as applied by the medical examiner, violated their First Amendment right to exercise their religion freely, and their Fourteenth Amendment rights to due process and equal protection.[119] The court held that the couple's exercise of religious beliefs against mutilation of a body was clearly established, and denied Sturner's qualified immunity defense. In reaching its decision for the plaintiffs, the court opined that a medical examiner should know the law governing his conduct.[120]

Although the court initially granted relief, there is some question about whether or not its opinion would have been different were the autopsy performed and organs or tissue used for transplantation, which alters the case just slightly – as then there are competing interests. What are the interests of the dead or their families versus state interest in promoting health? Moreover, the case illustrates how one can find out too late to opt out, at which point a legal victory may pale in comparison to the family's perception that a son's or daughter's soul is doomed to hell. *Yang* and its progeny are instructive on this point. The Yang trial judge felt compelled to reverse himself after the U.S. Supreme Court handed down its decision in *Employment Div., Dept of Human Res. of Oregon v. Smith.*[121]

C. Compulsory Donation and a Duty to Rescue: Why Social Contract Theory Doesn't Apply

Presumed consent is perhaps best justified through the social contract theory, but even so, it does not add up for most Americans, particularly African Americans.[122] Viewed through a collective scheme of social justice, the procurement and allocation of scarce organs is a worthy social goal. In various ways our national healthcare system has demonstrated a commitment to promoting health and safety, and provides a safety net for the very poor through Medicaid and Medicare. This distribution is to address present health needs through societal obligation, and helps to correct past inequities that unfairly burden the disenfranchised and limit their opportunities. Although the quality, or perhaps the potential outcome, for the argument does not rise to the level necessary to justify its prophylactic implementation because it limits individual autonomy and removes donor consent (at least in my opinion), it is nonetheless worthy of consideration in this chapter.

Philosophers and scholars, among them Rousseau, Rawls, Hobbes, and Locke, carved out early thinking on social obligations, duties, and responsibilities for the nation-state. The social contract theory was their brainchild, and although not commonly invoked in judicial opinions, it may be the strongest argument for presumed consent. Ideally, presumed consent promotes the equitable distribution of scarce resources. As discussed earlier, presumed consent as with other organ procurement schemes poses ethical and legal challenges. Fentiman, Dukeminier, and Nelson argue, however, that these moral challenges are largely overcome by the tremendous social good that is done.[123] Annually, more than 90,000 people await new organs.[124] Some will die before a donor is found. Waitlists are long, and organs are neither distributed in the order in which recipients signed up, nor by an assessment of the sickest patients' medical needs (with regard to kidneys). Proponents suggest that presumed consent could ease the collective suffering and death of people awaiting organ transplants. Accordingly, presumed consent proponents argue that the policy maximizes a community good for the benefit of all people, with a relatively small collective burden.[125] However, significant problems must be acknowledged.

A Few Problems

First, legislative consent strips bare informed consent, leaving at best a tacit agreement to be construed as consent. Arguably, Black Americans and others tacitly agree to relinquish control, privacy, and any property interests if their bodies come before the coroner for an investigation because of risky or dangerous behavior. Second, this means that presumed consent would be tied to one's behavior, actions, or circumstance, such as living in a violent neighborhood. Behaviors such as reckless living or driving might accordingly hasten one's appearance before the coroner. Living in violent, poor neighborhoods and reckless behavior predetermines whether or not one will be a donor. Third, and most importantly, the people are left out of legislative consent. An opt-out scheme is not consent, and the true effect of the measure would be to circumvent bona fide consent, thereby sidestepping the involvement of involuntary donors. Moreover, the metaphorical presumption of consent from the legislature cannot override the importance of individual decision making and autonomy. It seems inappropriate and a bit absurd from a medical perspective that the state could speak about the intimate and personal spheres of death in a collective and distant manner. Finally, whether scholars or judges will ever agree who owns what in the body, it is nevertheless clear from the common law that possession is one of the most fundamental elements indicating property ownership.[126]

Perhaps one of the most important questions to be answered is whether or not body ownership or possession can or should be compromised to fulfill a state interest in organ procurement and donation. The *Brotherton* court, closely on point with this question, found that the state's interest was not so substantial as to burden one's property interests in her husband's body. However, in a passionate dissent, Judge Joiner parted ways with the majority, suggesting that much of the common law regarding dead bodies evolved from burial statutes, which were necessarily narrowly tailored to fit such an occasion, and perhaps not intended to address broader issues of property ownership.[127]

Early courts hearing presumed consent cases refused to address whether a property interest was at stake or not. They focused instead on the value provided to the greater society balanced by an abrogation of rights of the deceased or her kin. These courts insinuated that if a property right were burdened by the state's interest in preserving "the health of the living," such would be properly within the scope of the state's authority, pointing to a "social contract"[128] between the state and its citizens.

According to Professor Anita Allen, "[s]ocial contract theories seek to legitimate civil authority by appealing to notions of rational agreement."[129] Such rational agreement(s) referred to in early modern social contractarianism as the "state of nature," are encompassed by both hypothetical and actual circumstances dealing with politics, law, and morality.[130] For example, "social contract theories provide that rational individuals will agree by contract, compact, or covenant to give up the condition of unregulated freedom in exchange for the security of a civil society governed by a just, binding rule of law."[131]

Presumed consent derives part of its authority from notions of a social contract between the state and its citizens as related to public health.[132] In the past, the state has invoked the social compact to justify its authority in requiring certain obligations of its citizens. Indeed, the state has relied on the social contract to address public health concerns. In *Jacobson v. Massachusetts*,[133] a case involving compulsory vaccinations, the court referred to the Massachusetts Constitution, arguing that a fundamental principle of the social contract requires that citizens are governed according to a common good, and therefore must sacrifice, comply, and otherwise acquiesce to that "common good."[134]

Judge Joiner's dissent in *Brotherton* embraces traditional notions associated with social compact theory. Although he refused to acknowledge any property rights in the human body, thereby ignoring a mature body of case law indicating at least a "quasi-property right" interest in the body, his analysis can avoid addressing that issue. He relies on the community good that is performed through the act of organ donation. Throughout his dissent Judge Joiner reminds us that the state's nonconsensual appropriation of the decedent's eyes would "bring sight and health to the living disabled, and thus to society as a whole."[135] In fact, the community benefit argument may be one of the most salient and compelling arguments articulated by presumed consent supporters, and one of the more difficult to refute. Theoretically, presumed consent saves lives, and Americans have decided that saving lives is a worthy cause for the state. However, have Americans chosen to give up informed consent and autonomous decision making? Arguably they have not, and certainly the response to nonconsensual appropriation of body parts indicates that most Americans are unwilling to compromise on this point.

The arguments supporting presumed consent evoke images of bodies "on loan" to the state, available for whatever uses will best benefit the community.[136] Fentiman argues that presumed use of organs would be similar to a national service like that of the military, where individuals serve for the benefit of the "greater community." The difference, however, is that the flawed allocation system creates a disparity in terms of who in the greater community will be served by such sacrifices. Accordingly, some argue that a corpse cannot feel the emotional weight of the act, thus perhaps pointing to an inability to be denigrated, compromised, or betrayed by the act. The betrayal could be compared to Black enlisted soldiers returning from integrated armies to hostile segregated communities. Fentiman talks about presumed consent being a community service, or a duty, like military service.[137] In that context, young men and women surrender their bodies in ready preparedness for combat and possible death for the purpose of preserving the state. However, broad claims of a presumed contract between all citizens and the United States are not only potentially problematic, but they also lack legitimacy.[138]

Black Exclusion

What this compact means in modern negotiations and relationships may be more difficult to answer.[139] Whether the social compact works for those who have traditionally experienced the American legal, political, and health systems on the margins seems answered by their continued disenfranchisement.[140] Such an inquiry also points to whether the social compact obligates their involvement. These questions are not only provocative, but aim to point out America's historical inequities as related to certain groups, and ask whether more can be expected from them when they have traditionally received less.[141] Charles Mills, professor of philosophy, argues that the "Racial Contract" undercuts the evolution of the modern version of the contract. The social contract, he argues, "characterized by an antipatriarchalist Enlightenment liberalism, with its proclamations of the equal rights, autonomy, and freedom of all men, thus took place simultaneously with the massacre, expropriation, and subjection to hereditary slavery of men at least apparently human."[142] The contradiction or hypocrisy, Mills argues, needs to be reconciled, and it is best conceived or reconciled "through the Racial Contract, which essentially denies [Blacks] personhood and restricts the terms of the social contract to Whites."[143]

Accordingly, the early American social compacts excluded Blacks and other non-Whites, frequently finding them outside the American legal, political, and social agreement, and therefore not entitled to the privi-leges and immunities granted Whites.[144] According to Francis Jennings, "[t]o invade and dispossess the people of an unoffending civilized coun-try would violate morality and transgress the principles of international law;" however, he reconciled, "savages were exceptional. Being uncivi-lized by definition, they were outside the sanctions of both morality and law."[145] Whether contemporary policies or the application of laws and medical customs perpetuate that philosophy can be examined through case law, policies, and practices.[146] Thus, we must probe beyond the face of the law to the law as applied or in action.

My purpose in examining the notion of a social contract that justifies presumed consent is to illume what Allen calls the "seductive, malleable fiction" that there exists such a social policy wherein all parties subject to the agreement are treated equitably.[147] America's history with her social contract in many ways mirrors her history with healthcare.[148] Disparate and unequal treatment shadows American healthcare; history is far too replete with stories detailing the undignified treatment of Blacks and other people of color in sacrifice for a common good to which they were excluded.[149] Chapter 2 provided a brief but penetrating glance at that history. The legal protections and privileges born of American citizenship were most clearly granted to a narrow population of White, male land owners.[150] Others hoped to be considered in the contract, and thus bravely shared resources, life, taxes, materials, education, and skills. Some of America's first sons to die in battles for early American settlers to be free from European political tyranny were men of color.[151] It is America's history with social contract philosophy and its relation to the legal system that poses potentially problematic results for those who are disenfranchised and marginalized in the organ transplantation and donation systems.

A century after publication of W. E. B. Dubois' *Souls of Black Folks*, the color line continues to divide America in tangible, powerful ways.[152] Of course, as slaves, Blacks lacked political and legal standing in the United States; they were neither protected by nor recognized within the context of the law. Moreover, Blacks were deprived of social status, and were more often compared with field animals than human beings. Surely part of America's social contract relied on recognition and some form of citizenship that evidently aided in the contract's enforcement. Blacks, even those American-born, were forbidden citizenship, and thus kept out of the benefits of the law.[153] However, this is not to say that Blacks were not contributors to America's growth and development; indeed they were, as builders, agriculturists, subjects for scientific experimentation, and educators. They were contributors to a contract that America breached.

Although America's social contracts are based more on a normative view of law and nature and not on an actual physical agreement, the terms are basically similar. In the context of presumed consent organ-taking and transplantation plan, Americans would collectively suffer a detriment for an equitable community benefit.[154] Thus, all Americans would contribute to a pool for organs, and all Americans would equitably receive from that well.[155] In an optimal social contract, all Americans regardless of race, gender, and socioeconomic distinctions could withdraw from the pool of body parts made available, and progressive efforts would be made to minimize organ rejection, thereby achieving distributive justice. However, an equitable social compact for presumed organ-taking also requires the elimination of social valuing (the process by which some doctors subjectively engage in determining which patients should be referred for organ allocation), greater access to organ transplantations for Blacks, and all deaths to be subject to harvesting.[156] After all, economically disenfranchised Americans should not be forced to participate as organ donors and later suffer rejection or indefinite delays as organ recipients.

The social contract sounds ideal; indeed, it gives the impression that all Americans are treated equally and possess the same leverage to bargain for exchanges. However, social contract theory, what Allen refers to as a "metaphor," "can hide what is unpleasant and unwanted, and focus attention on what is pleasant and wanted."[157] In terms of presumed consent, social contract theory can operate to focus on the desired effect of maintaining public health, saving lives, and providing biological materials to aid research. However, hidden behind the social compact, or simply what is not acknowledged, is the racism and social valuing that occurs in the healthcare industry in general, and particularly in organ procurement and donation.[158] In this capacity the social compact avoids acknowledging painful racial realities and historical inequities that directly influence why people choose not to voluntarily donate, and why potential recipients of color face some-times insurmountable obstacles in the waitlist process.[159] The hidden reality for Black Americans is that they are less likely than Whites to be selected as organ recipients, are more likely to have longer stays on waitlists, and are more likely to die while waiting on organ lists.[160] In this way, the "coercive dimensions of law" can operate to require certain things from some and not others, all under the misleading heading of community benefit, "consensualism," and "rational self-interest."[161]

Commentators supporting presumed consent policies based on social compact theory must acknowledge that, were such a compact to exist, America's present transplantation system reveals a contract worthy of being voided because it lacks accountability and mutual benefit in response to detriment. Indeed, urban, poor Americans are more likely than all other groups to be subjects of presumed consent laws that are attached to autopsy statutes.[162] State-imposed autopsies, as explained earlier, are more likely to occur with certain kinds of deaths that may disproportionately affect economically disenfranchised urban Americans, including deaths by violence, unknown causes, poison, and suicide.[163]

Those more likely to be the subjects of autopsies would be under the control of the coroner or medical examiner who, empowered by statute, is permitted to delegate the removal of the deceased's organs. Other Americans, dying by other means, would avoid subjection to present presumed consent statutes, and as such, have no obligation to sup-ply organs because their deaths would fall outside of investigative or mandatory autopsy provisions. Therefore, coroners would not have the authority to invade their bodies and harvest organs. Presumed consent policies, in general, are discomforting because they disregard auton-omy, privacy, and a right to choose how one shall have her flesh used in the afterlife.[164] Furthermore, even those highly protected and regarded rights are increasingly threatened and potentially impinged on if, as in the case of presumed consent, one belongs to a vulnerable or "othered" community (such as Black, Latino, homeless, or poor White).[165] Con-sider how presumed consent worked in Los Angeles only a few years ago: Over 80% of the uniformed donors were Black and Latino, with Whites making up only 16% of the donor pool.[166]

Over the years, the state's involvement with bodies has necessarily influenced how others, namely those in the medical profession, will approach certain bodies.[167] Certainly, when Jefferies points to the amoral consequences of social valuing in organ allocation, he is focusing on practices that directly or indirectly result from a government-endorsed system.[168] Jefferies acknowledges that some form of rationing must occur when resources are limited and there is a social necessity to cure and heal. However, he writes, "due to the shortage of organs . . . physicians and other medical personnel make the choice by weighing the patients' social worth."[169] He argues that criteria could include "family-related considerations such as marital status and number of dependents; other criteria are income, educational background, employment record, relationship to authority figures, past irresponsible behavior," and intelligence.[170] Unfortunately, Jefferies' analysis of the inequities found within a "social worth" system end there. Nevertheless, the author does note that "[a] system that decides who lives and dies based on considerations such as income and education is unfortunate and may lead to inequitable results."[171]

Finally, if a social contract in the area of healthcare ever existed between Black Americans and the state, and especially with regard to organ transplantation, its compact was breached long ago. Evidence of a social compact in healthcare for Black Americans is difficult to muster, and ultimately may be impossible to prove. Although one might suggest that Medicaid and Medicare programs demonstrate a commitment to groups with an "othered" status, especially Blacks, such arguments ultimately are weakened by the fact that those government programs limit the types of services one might receive. For example, if a patient has Medicare only because of kidney failure, Medicare coverage ends 36 months after the transplant (for kidneys); however, if the patient had Medicare before the transplant was needed, Medicare will continue to provide immunosuppressant therapy with no time limit.[172] The natural consequences of life without immunosuppressant medication could mean rejecting an organ or living in severe discomfort.

Typically, Blacks that could benefit from organ transplantation have been kept alive through dialysis, a time-consuming and painful process.[173] Thus, for many of America's poorer citizens, organ transplantation was not a possibility, and certainly not one advanced by the state. Recent federal campaigns to end disparities are hopeful, but results remain to be seen. One could make a very sound argument that a healthcare compact could not exist, and certainly could not be universally applied when Americans lack access to universal healthcare coverage.

Autonomy and State Interference

Indeed, there are other circumstances of healthcare inequality that challenge the notion of a social compact existing between all Americans and the state. Certainly, America's poor have experienced extreme obstacles to obtaining services ranging from those addressing mental health needs to prenatal care. Political activists argue that a government reluctant to provide for its poorest and most vulnerable citizens cannot expect the disenfranchised to forego religious practice and sacrifice their bodies, as well as those of their deceased relatives, to satisfy an interest that disproportionately benefits a particularly privileged group.

A social contract, along with any legal transaction, should be granted legitimacy only according to its potential for equitable implementation and results. A compact lacking equitable outcomes for vulnerable populations resembles a coerced confession. In the law, we seek to recognize only those agreements obtained legitimately, outside the reach of duress and coercion. Ultimately, a social compact exists only when a real social relationship exists. In this way, the party subject to the state's compact must be valued, their contributions respected, and their communities honored and afforded the rights and privileges granted through the state's laws and policies.

CONCLUSION

Legislative consent is a policy characterized by mixed moral considerations and obligations. One obligation is for the state to preserve life and the health of its members. For this reason, Linda Fentiman proposed organ donation as a national service.[174] Another political obligation of a democratic society "is that the power of the state [be] circumscribed, even if what the state wants to do is a good thing."[175] Legislative consent creates a philosophical crossroad, where opposing interests must be weighed for ultimate action that will result in a justifiable and morally acceptable community benefit.

Politically and philosophically, presumed consent is perhaps best justified through the social contract. It demonstrates how we can live in what Rousseau referred to as the "chains" of civil society, but not compromising core values or principles, including freedom.[176] Through our relationships with the state are born obligations that are entered into involuntarily for the good of the common or whole.[177] Rousseau referred to these as general wills, in which the best interest of a group is considered collectively, rather than individually.[178] Why then would one choose to participate in the collective will if it means assuming a political, economic, or social burden?

People want to engage in the general will (as Americans have done), when the exchange, or what is placed in return, affirms and protects values such as freedom, political autonomy, and free expression and customs. In this way the social contract is the operational and functional equivalent of insurance – an investment in preserving financial, social, and political order. However, the social contract works only if those involved believe themselves to be members of that society and the society in return grants them the benefits of membership and distributes goods equitably.[179] Membership cannot be defined as simply physical placement. Slaves have historically been physically planted in foreign societies, but have lacked membership. The same is true of most foreigners; they are allowed physical space on foreign soil, however, the benefits of a society are not always bestowed on outsiders.

Does the social contract justify the use of present presumed consent laws? Could it support legislative consent for organ procurement? Although social contract theory is perhaps the most persuasive moral justification for taking a good from another for the benefit of the whole, it cannot reconcile the disparities existing in the present system. Arguably, the social contract works only when applied equitably and distributive justice is achieved. Rousseau suggests that the basis for the entire social system is a society's membership becoming "equal by convention and legal right."[180]

Social compact theory ultimately fails to support the cause of presumed consent, particularly in the case of those with an "othered" or "outsider" existence.[181] Arguably, for America's disenfranchised members, the social compact lacks legitimacy.[182] The existence of a social compact naturally depends on a demonstrable social contract, where allocation is equitable and proportionate to resources derived from a particular community. To this end, social compacts between the disenfranchised with an "othered" American experience and the greater community are legitimate only to the extent that the marginalized groups have equitable access to and distribution of the goods claimed by the larger community.

Consider, for example, that lawmakers do not require the wealthy to share wealth in order to eliminate poverty. Although it is true that estate taxes help to fund programs that benefit the general population, sometimes those benefits are kept close to home (e.g., schools, quality of streets, policing, etc.). We need only consider social policies to alleviate poverty. Recently, commentators have proposed that sound transportation policies could help poor mothers who cannot commute to work.[183] Such policies could include providing cars to these women.[184] If poverty and homelessness could be eliminated, or at least alleviated, by individuals having the ability to obtain jobs and commute to work, wouldn't that be a good social cause?

However, the state does not mandate that individuals with more than five cars (or homes for that matter) provide one to a capable but "transportationless" (or homeless) individual so that she might attend school, go to work, participate in a training program, or pick up her children from childcare. Having five cars seems a bit excessive; after all, how many cars does one really need? Clearly, automobiles are not needed after death. Thus, although the cars could be left to a beneficiary, such as the deceased person's son or daughter, would he or she need them? It is not inconceivable that one of the best social uses for multiple cars from an estate would be to provide one to the state for a campaign to eliminate poverty.

Would we dare shape a proposal that requires those who die with five cars to leave one to the state as part of an anti-poverty program? Probably not, although sharing one of five cars is hardly invasive when compared with removing one's organs for transplantation into a stranger. If an anti-poverty car policy worked as clandestinely as presumed consent presently does, the policy might seem all the more outrageous. The wealthy, who would be disproportionately affected by this plan, might rightfully charge that it is unfair to exploit the resources of those who earned their cars, homes, or other non-necessary goods through hard work. Why, they might wonder, should the burden of helping the underclass be disproportionately borne by them?

Let us apply that same reasoning to the economically disenfranchised. At one's death, the state does not transfer one's property to a stranger simply because it might benefit the person receiving the property. In theory, life tenancy in human flesh, although troubling, is nonetheless thought provoking. If Americans participated in a new social program that allowed the state to use their bodies as needed at death, perhaps more transplants would occur. The plan could occur with limited restrictions placed on the donor during life, thereby causing minimal interference in lifestyle, and the donor could perform the ultimate form of community service. Arguably, this type of service to the state is less invasive and risky than military service, or transporting nuclear waste. Indeed, in other capacities service to the state may alter one's lifestyle through injury, for example and emotional and physical health could become an issue. Hence, proponents like Fentiman and Dukeminier conclude that presumed consent at one's death allows one to serve the state while, unlike in military service, not being burdened with the obligation during life.

Nevertheless, there is something eerie about the State's ownership of bodies. America's precedent with treating the body as property, slavery, surely demonstrates the dangers of community ownership in the body or the ownership of anyone other than the possessor embodying the flesh. Although it might be equally eerie to think of self-ownership from the grave, somehow that seems less unconscionable than the state plucking body parts from certain communities.

Solutions are needed to properly and equitably address America's organ shortage. Those solutions, as Nelson argues, cannot be quick fixes that ignore the historical and contemporary racial dimensions of healthcare. Is it possible to develop solutions for our organ transplantation system without studying and understanding past inequities and injustices? I think not. Our present healthcare system and the relationships between White physicians and Black patients are largely informed by inescapable cultural realities. The cultural realities have, in part, helped to shape cultural attitudes and norms with regard to how some bodies are valued and treated. Whereas we would hope that the arms of medicine would operate beyond the reach of race, gender, and socioeconomic politics and realities, believing so would be naive, and in light of institutionalized racial oppression, perhaps would be expecting too much.

The central focus of organ procurement strategies should be distributive justice and equity. Those objectives may best be achieved through communication, education, and relationship building. These are not accomplished in a vacuum; rather medical schools must train doctors to be culturally competent so that they can communicate better with patients of color and thus serve their patients more effectively. Sadly, cultural competency is often misunderstood and stigmatized. Therefore training sessions are not always effective. Yet the value of strong communication skills between physicians and their patients cannot be overemphasized, particularly when informed consent is so very central to the physician/patient relationship. Where there may be language and socioeconomic barriers, cultural competence may help to overcome those barriers. Two practical ways to address this training issue is to place cultural competency components within medical school ethics training and to require a national ethics exam for medical students. Unlike law students, medical students are not required to take a national ethics exam. However, testing medical students' knowledge as to professional diligence, competency, communication, and professional responsibilities is overdue. Also, physicians of color are needed. It is a cultural imperative that the ranks of physicians achieve diversity. Achieving this goal means increasing enrollment and retention of students of color at American medical schools, where medical doctors of color continue to be the exception.[185]

Building trust in communities of color is crucial. Dr. Clive Callender and other medical scholars have recently expressed such sentiments before Congress and in the national media. More people of color are needed in the discussions about healthcare and the role of law, both as scholars and laypersons receiving services. Accountability from communities of color should not be overlooked (e.g., improving health habits); however, it seems that a moral obligation of fairness and access to healthcare services is due to communities that have historically experienced racial discrimination in the forms of medical and legal exploitation. Trust must be won. Finally, overcoming racial disparities can be achieved through a more equitable distribution of healthcare services in the physician's office. Patients need information, regular visits with physicians, and better communication about their options.

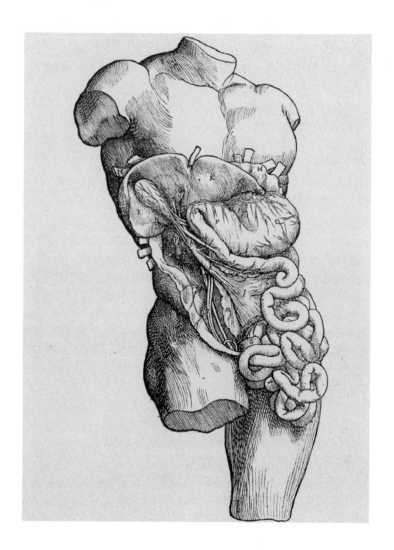

Body parts.

7 Commoditization

Incentives for Cadaveric Organ Harvesting

The federal government has long had rules governing the trade and use of blood and organs. But the extraction and use of things like bones, veins, corneas, ligaments, and sperm by nearly 150 companies have largely gone unregulated.[1]

INTRODUCTION

This chapter proposes a market solution to address organ demand. As described earlier in the book, a cadaveric market that coexists with altruistic procurement will reach potential organ "owners" who are otherwise skeptical and reluctant to participate in the altruistic system. This chapter argues that incentives for cadaveric organ donation would be *pareto superior* were a market to be legalized.[2] *Pareto superior* requires that in a market transaction for limited social goods, that at least one person be made better off and that no one be made worse off.[3] The application of this principle fits squarely within the debate about the efficient procurement and distribution of organs. Our challenge is to procure a sufficient supply of organs to make transplantation an efficient mode of saving lives and valuing autonomy, respecting individual (and collective rights) of everyone, but especially marginalized groups, and maximizing transplantation access.

It must be noted, however, that some scholars believe that *pareto superior* is a likable fiction and that no one can be made better off without making someone worse off (i.e., *pareto inferiority*).[4] In this context, opponents of a market might argue that such transactions are inferior because they coerce poor people to alienate family members and degrade personhood. It is also likely that they could suggest that organ purchasers are also "worse off" because they have degraded themselves in the process, like buying sex from a prostitute.[5] Such situations are said to violate the purchaser's dignity; he, the argument follows, is requiring that another (the prostitute) subordinate her autonomy and personhood to satisfy a prurient, selfish (sexual) desire.[6]

Yet, unlike *pareto inferior* transactions, which make someone worse off to make someone better, in these unique transactions the social resources distributed (organs from deceased persons) help to save sick patients' lives in an open transaction that promotes individual and collective autonomy. By collective autonomy, I am referring to cultural groups, such as Black Americans, who speak to broader, shared concerns.[7] The comparison between prostitution and organ alienation overstates the goals of organ transactions and undervalues the social good that results. Indeed, the dark assertion that the personhood of poor individuals, particularly Blacks, is violated by markets ignores the fact that Blacks can be market participants on both sides of those transactions.[8] We need only consider the fact that saving lives is found to be noble in all other contexts, even when payment is involved. We abjure the duty to rescue but commend firefighters, police officers, and others who are paid to rescue us in day-to-day, life-threatening situations. That they are paid is insignificant; it does not devalue their effort, time, and risk in saving lives. It would be ludicrous to suggest that White police officers should not be paid when saving the lives of Blacks and vice versa. Nor have payments to police, rescue teams, and firefighters compromised our understanding of their motivations for engaging in employment that poses high risks to themselves and their families. We would hardly consider their motivations to be spuriously philanthropic.

In this chapter, I contend that commoditization would achieve the primary goal of organ procurement, which is to increase the supply. Yet, unlike presumed consent, which accomplishes the same goal, a market in cadaveric organs values individual and collective liberty to refuse organ harvesting and promotes greater transparency. This book does not encourage nor support incentives for living donations; it draws a distinction between living and cadaveric donations and the motivations for each. This chapter urges greater dialogue about the benefits as well as limitations of a commoditization scheme for procuring organs from deceased persons. We must confront uncomfortable realities about altruistic organ procurement, including the inability of that system to procure an adequate supply of organs. Myths and misinformation about commoditization schemes reduce productive discussions about organ commoditization to social hysteria. Among the myths are that a market will drive down altruism and deter such donors from giving at all; children will murder their parents for organs; that dirty tissue will enter the organ pool; and commoditization will be "like slavery." The mythology of organ commoditization is seductive and safe; it distances us from the realities of organ shortages and the imperfections of altruistic procurement.

Change brings about discomfort; it naturally upsets social, political, and economic order. Yet change is exactly what the present procurement regime needs. Failure to effectively assess the system failures will only exacerbate an already staggering death toll and siphon away public support. This chapter argues that an organ market can efficiently coexist with the present altruistic procurement system. The development of such a system would reduce reliance on the limited altruistic pool and provide an incentive for reluctant and otherwise disinterested potential suppliers to participate in saving lives or enhancing the quality of life for others. The incompetence and ineffectiveness of the present procurement model has been addressed in prior chapters. Thus, this chapter shall focus on the nuances of a potential market of cadaver tissues and organs, how such a model could be regulated. This approach would be far more sensible and superior to targeted donations from children, coercing organs from third-world participants, and presumed consent models.

First, in Section A, I challenge the notion that Richard Titmuss was right in his seminal account of the blood market in *The Gift Relationship*, where he described a direct link between payment for blood with the introduction of infected blood in the blood supply. It compliments earlier discussion about Titmuss and is appropriate for this chapter as Titmuss' vehement opposition to markets in biological resources was based on his theory that insalubrious blood from sellers would infect the supply. In fact, when properly scrutinized the dangers in such an argument are revealed as it ignores the possibility of blood borne pathogens and diseases present in the altruistic donor pool. The answer, of course, is better screening for both pools rather than attacking either the market or altruistic procurement. Second, in Section B, I address otherwise distracting arguments based on inconsistently applied moral criticisms.

For example, the booming tissue industry, which profits shareholders, CEOs, and even hospitals, generates far less ethical scrutiny and criticism than do proposals to create deceased donor markets. In addition, ova and sperm sales and advertisements cannot escape this analysis as that marketplace is ubiquitous. Finally, in Section C, I address how a system might be structured. These are initial thoughts, which will hopefully serve as a starting point for future analysis and development. I leave my response to those who claim markets would be bad for people of color or resemble slavery to the next chapter.

A. Bad Blood

Blood markets and donor systems illuminate the false dichotomy that suggests that voluntary donation and compensation for biological resources cannot mutually coexist. Annually in the United States about 14 million units of blood are donated to not-for-profit hospitals, agencies, and blood banks.[9] The Red Cross recovers nearly 45% of donated blood, and blood banks another 42%.[10] Hospitals recover just under 12%. Their supplies are provided for free, but with a service fee attached.[11] Donations are grouped by plasma, blood, and clotting factors.

Supply, however, is also generated through a competitive, functional market.[12] At times the not-for-profit system closely mirrors the market. For example, the service fee associated with voluntary donation is increasingly indiscernible from payments in the market system according to some commentators. Richard D. Crowley, former executive director of the Central Illinois Blood Bank in Springfield, Illinois, is mystified by the hollow distinction: "It drives me crazy when the Red Cross says it doesn't sell blood. That's like the supermarket saying they're only charging you for the carton, not the milk."[13] He asks, "What else do you call it? We're in the blood-selling business."[14] Commercial plasma companies extract and sell over 13 million units of plasma in the United States through plasmapheresis, an uncomfortable process, which usually takes 2 hours.[15] Great benefits are derived from these products as they not only aid hemophiliacs, but help others to manage with unique, rare illnesses. Suppliers are protected by blood shield laws promulgated in the 1950s and 1960s, exempting companies from implied warranty and strict liability claims, thereby equally reducing risks of product litigation both by commercial providers and supply from the altruistic pool.[16]

As evidenced by Americans traveling abroad to procure organs, and numerous studies, the desire for an appropriate legal alternative organ procurement system, which addresses our tissue demand or shortage, is apparent.[17] Of the alternatives available, tissue commoditization offers tremendous possibilities worth acknowledging and pursuing just as we have with plasma. Other potential, but less desirable solutions include presumed consent (discussed earlier) and cloning, which has yet to become a real alternative. In June of 2002, the American Medical Association approved a controversial proposal to commence research on whether payments for organs would increase tissue supply.[18] The AMA decision caused considerable backlash within the medical community, attracting immediate criticism from those opposed to the commercialization of human biological material.[19] Concerns that commercialization of human tissues violates the sacredness and integrity of the body are not wholly unfamiliar, nor unique to organ supply.[20] Richard Titmuss raised those concerns almost 40 years ago about blood supply. Titmuss argued that procurement systems based on altruism are necessarily better than those involving compensation. His assertion that for medical and ethical reasons altruism is a more sensible approach is compelling, but not necessarily accurate. Nor are the fears that financial transactions in organ procurement might lead to further commoditization of the human body completely ungrounded; this is completely possible.

For example, an emergent supply of stem cells might result and could provide treatment options for thousands dying annually from cancer. Individuals might claim greater control over body parts usually left at hospitals, such as placentas, umbilical cords, even foreskins, and demand compensation. This could upset the applecart. Biological goods, such as those mentioned, are currently sold – hospital to tissue banks, but the individuals whose genetic blueprints are left behind are not compensated. These transactions are often outside of the line of scrutiny even though hospitals profit on human body parts.[21] Social and legal demand for economic inclusion might lead to a reorganization and clarification of body part supply systems. Thus, further commoditization is not necessarily a social evil. To the contrary, it would discourage imperfect and incomplete information and promote equitable compensation. Financial relationships between hospitals and tissue firms could also become more transparent as currently their transactions occur in the shadows of public scrutiny. Those are not bad by-products of a regulated market.

Considerable opposition is stirred by the possibility of financial transactions being used as an incentive to increase organ donations. Such financial interactions some say taint or contaminate the gift process. Opponents to a market system argue that altruism promotes ideal community relationships and that society inures an incomparable benefit from such generosity. Accordingly, they suggest legalization of organ sales would be akin to allowing commercial forces to dictate the value of human flesh, an unsettling thought to critics in medical and legal communities.[22] Even permitting funeral costs to be covered is a slippery slope and, according to Dr. Thomas R. Russell, should be avoided at all costs.[23] An open market in organ sales, they suggest, would lead to unpleasant collateral results, particularly in the culture of organ procurement.[24] Altruistic participation in organ procurement, for example, could suffer, inspiring otherwise sympathetic donors to seek financial compensation for their relatives' organs. Gratuitous donations might further decrease as potential donors seek to avoid a distasteful system.[25] Relatives might withhold consent for life-saving and sustaining treatments in avaricious pursuit of compensation for organs.

It is true that financial motivations could also entice economically vulnerable, unhealthy candidates, such as drug addicts and alcoholics, to participate in the market. However, it does not follow that those interested in participating would expose insalubrious tissues to critically ill patients.[26] This, in fact, was the crux of Titmuss' concern; he believed that "skidrow" indigents would place impure, unhealthy blood in the supply and, therefore, harm good people. However, most scholars ignore the racialized innuendo of his theory. If placed in proper context, serious scholars should be doubtful of Titmuss' claims – not on the social good of altruism – but his vitriolic denouncement of markets based on "public health" rationales. Titmuss' claims were based on "Negro," male part-time employees selling their blood as discussed in an earlier chapter and arguably infecting the blood supply.

Titmuss assumed all the Negro blood acquired through alienation was necessarily bad because they were poor. Titmuss never suggested that "Negro" blood was "bad" because paid donors were Black, but his overemphasis on race should cause us to more closely scrutinize his

presumption. Placed in context, Titmuss' claims reflect an era of segregation, social division, and eugenics thinking, and beyond that, he
was wrong; economic status does not predetermine whether one will
infect blood. Behavior is the most critical factor. Titmuss created a last-
ing, mistaken, negative presumption that labeled Negroes as skidrow
blood contaminators, while ignoring that the behaviors he catalogued –
drinking and drugs – were not exclusive social pastimes to Blacks. This
misstep in his analysis could be cited as a contributing factor to countries failing to adequately protect blood supplies from altruistic, but
unsafe wealthy White people. Where will we draw the socioeconomic
line between who is healthy or not? The current, dramatic organ shortage necessitates rethinking Titmuss' theories on the gift relationship
and altruism-based procurement programs.

Blood Crisis

Probably the most compelling arguments against promoting an even
more transparent and robust tissue market are the concerns about tissue safety. These were concerns raised by Richard Titmuss years ago
that led to blood procurement reforms in Europe and America. Titmuss
hailed from Europe, but had a surprising impact on the structuring of
blood supply in the United States. Shortly after the publication of *The
Gift Relationship*, then-president of the Red Cross George M. Elsey wrote
that paying for blood was "medically and morally unjustifiable."[27] He
pledged that the Red Cross would "never pay for blood."[28] Titmuss urged
that blood be procured exclusively through altruistic means, which he
thought would eliminate "bad blood" or "skidrow donors" from the
blood pool. He was only partially correct, although at the time, policy
makers were greatly influenced by his theory.

First, it is important to understand that a variety of blood resources
are always sought after and were during Titmuss' time. Healthy blood
could be used in transfusions and other medical procedures. Blood
with unique variants and also contaminated or unhealthy blood were
(and are) used for medical research. The commercial enterprise Titmuss
abhorred also brought about the discovery of blood products that rev-
olutionized methods to save people's lives. Within this context, we can
examine what Titmuss observed.

In the 1970s, plasma donation attracted prisoners (in fact they were sought after and provided the means to "donate"), the indigent, and others whose lifestyles may have indicated the potential for health risks.[29] The risks of contamination should those donations be included in the blood supply posed problems not only for transfusion recipients. During the 1970s, there were also risks for paid and altruist donors; methods to extract blood by-products were not closely regulated, nor was the frequency at which one might participate monitored.[30] Blood banking had become decentralized and a robust business was created. More than 6 million pints per year were collected in the United States. Blood banking was an important biotechnological enterprise and highly valuable. In fact, the value of the supply exceeded the comparative values of gold and oil per pound. The growth of blood harvesting led to the discovery of important blood products, such as albumin, gamma globulins, clotting factors for hemophiliacs, and blood-typing sera. Commercial success for certain doctors, brokers, and researchers accompanied the growth of blood product discoveries, which inevitably drew scrutiny from market detractors.[31] Titmuss' concerns about safety in the blood supply were sensible given procurement decentralization and the potential for diseases, including hepatitis, to be spread through blood. Yet, this was also an important issue for doctors and researchers who supported financial incentives in blood supply.

A decade later, during the 1980s with the rise of AIDS, health officials judged donated blood far safer than sold plasma.[32] Policy makers came to wrongly believe that problems with blood supply were primarily caused by blood markets and that market devices will always and only attract unhealthy participants.[33] Such was not true then and today, as we will see, it is even far less accurate.[34] For example, hospitals like the Mayo Clinic pay their suppliers for blood and continue to harness clean, healthy supplies of blood.[35] Yet, fears about selling blood revealed the deeply grounded moral values associated with giving versus the perceived avariciousness of selling an essential human good. Also grounded in this perspective is the fear of contamination that comes with poverty. Paul Lombardo writes quite eloquently on this point, highlighting America's troubling period with eugenics.[36] There is a personality associated with philanthropy and the ability to be generous. This moral attachment extends beyond the acts of shedding blood, but reaches to the personalities of giving – those who share with absence of financial interests are assumed to be healthier, spiritually, and physically, unlike their for-profit counterparts whose financial interest in blood supplying is less seductive and more suspect.

Titmuss advocated the reorganization of blood supply in the United States, suggesting that altruistic supply is not only morally superior to a commercial market, but avoids health risks associated with "skidrow"-type donors attracted to blood selling. In doing so, he conflated moral reasoning with science and health. Titmuss was wrong, and America's reorganization of blood supply and subsequent HIV scandal in the 1980s indicates the flaws in Titmuss' analysis.[37] The introduction of AIDS actually demonstrates flaws in Titmuss' analysis and detrimental reliance on the theory. Gay men – a population of responsible, financially stable, voluntary donors – happened to be "reliable givers" and "good volunteers."[38] They also happened to be the unsuspecting carriers of HIV.[39] Thus, the altruistic system attracted donors who unwittingly contaminated the supply, resulting in numerous deaths.[40] They, however, did not contaminate the supply because they were bad people, with perverted interests – any more than a prior generation of commercial donors with hepatitis. During the height of the AIDS crisis, in fact, commercial blood banks reacted far more swiftly than the altruistic industry.[41] They realized profitability, consumer confidence, and safety were otherwise at substantial risk.[42]

Kieren Healy examined blood procurement in the United States between 1981 and 1983 and suggests that Titmuss was not entirely correct that commercial interests had a direct and negative affect on the blood supply.[43] Among his theories was that financial incentives provide reasons and opportunities for individuals to lie about their health and contribute infected blood to the blood pool. It followed that those with a heightened incidence for disease and insalubrious tissues would disproportionately sell blood; whereas healthy, socially upstanding, morally minded individuals would donate. Once the two pools combined – as they did 40 years ago – healthy supply would become contaminated by "skidrow" blood. Thus, markets would be inefficient because they were dangerous. Economists who suggested that the problem was not paying for blood, but rather payment for contaminated blood, were ignored.[44] That human relationships were contaminated by financial exchanges appealed to an idealism otherwise absent from the organization of American medicine.

Healy points out two obvious flaws in the Titmuss argumentation; First, the fixed false dichotomous nature of how altruism and commercial blood supply are juxtaposed; a virtue-laden idea and practice on one hand, and the other, a pernicious, selfish, denigrating act. Second, the actions can never be contingent or changed based on social demands. The argument is essentialistic at its core; identities, social needs, and economic demands are no more fixed among blood donors than those who sell. Donors and commercial suppliers' health circumstances and interests may change over time. Titmuss' moral arguments were more persuasive at the time because technologies associated with blood supply were relatively nascent, and health and safety are important concerns; the purpose of blood donation is defeated if the recipients become ill and die. Lawsuits could and did result.[45] Furthermore, technology was yet to provide answers that would enhance and sustain both charitable donations and blood sales.

However, it is important to recognize that blood was not contaminated because providers were paid in the 1980s.[46] Rather, altruistic gay men helped to contaminate the blood supply.[47] Unhealthy blood was introduced to the blood supply due to unsafe administrative practices or an underdeveloped technology to appropriately determine specific risks in a case-by-case analysis of blood donations. I do not wish to reduce the complications involved with that period of blood supply; my analysis here is simply to identify the core concepts and arguments during that period, particularly as they continue to be posed with regard to human tissue and organ supply. Suffice to note that the risk for contaminated blood was no less reduced in unsuspecting, generous altruistic participant pools. Hepatitis was a significant problem when Titmuss researched *The Gift Relationship*. The technology was not yet available to detect the presence of certain communicable diseases in the blood supply, thus, equally affecting altruistic donations.

B. Costs

An organ market need not be cost-prohibitive for individuals, their insurance providers, or government-subsidized sources. For example, the cost of kidney dialysis averages $65,000 per year, per individual.[48] This figure represents only the financial costs, as the quality of life and independence for dialysis patients are significantly compromised by the procedure, which involves extracting and cleaning the blood. The process may involve up to four visits to a clinic per week for the procedure, which can take hours. For patients subsisting on dialysis, those costs never recede, but are compounded annually. Over the course of 7 years, an average life span of a patient on dialysis, the costs are at least $450,000 per patient. Much of this bill is absorbed by the federal government for indigent and low-income patients.

Once rationally considered, "market-based" organ transplantation is far less expensive and healthier than dialysis. The average cost for a kidney transplant is estimated at $90,000.[49] Subsequent expenses are for immunosuppressant medications totaling $16,000 per year for 2 years.[50] After 2 years, transplantation saves the patient and her financial provider on average $8,000 per year. Thus, not only would a market expand organ availability, it would ultimately reduce system costs. Among these patients, Blacks are disproportionately represented.

According to Alexander Tabarrok, a professor of economics, even at $10,000 in compensation to donors, with 9,000 supplying per year, the costs for financial compensation would be $90 million per year. However, the federal government would save almost $210 million per year by reducing the number of patients on dialysis, and the high yearly costs of providing treatment. One should also consider that with restored quality of life, individuals are better able to support themselves, their communities, and families. Thus, financial benefits and reduced costs are truly tangential to the more substantive benefits of saving lives and improving the quality of life for not only patients, but their families.

Ethicists unsatisfied with market analysis claim that there are costs that can never be reduced to financial terms and that saving money and lives means little if human dignity is sacrificed in the process. These are the moral costs of human commoditization – the denigration of spirit, body, and humanity. For them, once the body enters the realms of commerce, it loses its inviolability and dignity. Such moral consideration traditionally justified the prohibition of organ markets. However, social and cultural demands often presage change and a willingness to reach outside of traditional frameworks, which may be inconsistent with contemporary norms. The question of costs ultimately center on values and obligations. To whom do our moral obligations attach: the deceased woman or the dying man? Does giving value to his life automatically reduce the value of hers? Is the proper role of our society to prohibit the dying man from saving his life through sharing her organ? How does the law treat those who interfere with victims, causing harm that could result in death? How do we reconcile endorsement of organ transplantation only when the supplier is stripped bare, without compensation, and condemn those who are financially rewarded?

C. Subjective Ethics

How we socially organize tissue and organ procurement will ultimately reveal our level of commitment to saving the lives of those most vulnerable. Arguments, which seem to derive from principled or ethical beliefs, can be seductive and even enlightening, but they can also mask nefarious or at least unenlightened practices. The most repugnant practices often find justification based on some notion of injustice and legitimized by moral force. Religious intolerance is but one example of the slippery slope of moral superiority and ethical subterfuge. Medical experimentation without informed consent was practiced in Germany and the United States on vulnerable populations. These experiments were considered for the "social good." Armies sometimes refer to such atrocities as simply collateral damage. Thus, ethics, although usually a philosophical code to promote a better understanding of the way to live in harmony with fellow human beings, can also be a manipulated philosophy, trotted out when convenient and otherwise ignored. That we never engage in valuing the body, its constituent parts, or its potential is a malleable fiction.

Tissue and blood markets are thriving enterprises in America that not only save lives, but generate significant profits for entities otherwise perceived as not-for-profit.[51] In 1988, the plasma industry had sales that exceeded $2 billion per year.[52] The human tissue industry is estimated to be valued beyond $1 billion this year.[53] Consumers may not always be aware if their insurance providers pay for the bulk of their treatments.[54] Other financial transactions in the body are more transparent, and as such include those governing the most intimate spheres of the body, including ova and sperm.[55] Sperm and ova solicitations appear in magazines, college newspapers, and cleverly advertised on bus kiosks. Such gifts of life usually are attached to a "service fee."[56] The advertisements are direct, purposeful, and often descriptive (narrowing contenders by race, height, and SAT scores) – indicating that sperm and ova consumers are clearly attempting to pay for what they want.[57]

However, reproductive markets are far less criticized for promoting incentives by policy makers than other potential biological markets. Arguments that sperm and ova are regenerative and thus less risk-intensive extractions and more favorable overall are less than convincing when we narrow organ markets to the deceased – dead kidney suppliers have no use for multiple kidneys, and no physical risk of harm exists. Those who have religious objections will not alienate. Furthermore, it does not matter whether kidneys can regenerate or not; they will not benefit the dead. Such inconsistencies have much to do with cultural meanings and values associated with parenting versus simply extending life and also how we judge the ill.

Perhaps as a society we are more inclined to be flexible and forgiving to those who are perceived as being free from moral blame for the illnesses from which they suffer. Maybe we perpetuate sexist notions that all women were meant to become mothers, even when doing so is either biologically impossible or entails great risk and expense. According to such reflections, that a woman cannot produce a healthy supply of eggs is not her fault. In fact, some go so far as to argue that we must rescue her from the grasps of infertility. They claim that fertility is a right. However, a dried up and blackened liver in a man could be evidence of a sleazy and sordid lifestyle, which resulted in his poor health and need for a new liver.[58] Little of our sympathy is expended on cases such as his. Perhaps these types of considerations extend to kidney patients; to what degree could their diabetes have been controlled by proper diet, exercise, and healthy lifestyle? Such arguments are heard about obesity and other health conditions that result in blaming the patient.[59]

Furthermore, there are the issues of confidence and autonomy. Let's face it; people of color are needed to save the lives of other people of color – at least according to UNOS. If their lives are to be saved, their participation on the procurement side is crucial. Their present lack of confidence and faith in the procurement system are grounded in different spheres, but a theme does run through: the lack of control, independence, and autonomy within the procurement regime deters participation. These issues will not be resolved through presumed consent harvesting and seem best addressed through a market system, which could even be organized and supported within their communities.

Of course, acceptance of a market in organs would bring us a step closer to recognizing value or property interests in the body. In some ways, the law presently accommodates such thinking; movie stars often insure parts of their bodies for significant sums. Rock singer Tina Turner once insured her legs for more than $5 million. Property interest in the human body is not a new legal concept; it is a very old idea once protected by legal precedent. The law has not always stood in opposition to recognizing property interests in human body parts or cadavers. In fact, judicial opinions predate discussions about ova, sperm, and organ sales.

D. Life, Death, and Insurance

At the turn of the century, life insurance was better known as death insurance.[60] Its proponents were likened to criminals, allegedly promoting a nefarious practice that would result in murders and family disunity. Accordingly, it was presumed children would sacrifice their parents for quick gain and colleagues would murder their business partners. Criminal activity aside, placing a value or worth on the body was difficult to reconcile.[61] Prior to this time only animals and slaves were conceived of as having financial value. Although slaves were insured, particularly in the journey from Africa to the Americas,[62] White Americans were hesitant to insure themselves. Although a rich history here is worth exploring, my point is to suggest that insurance programs of the early 20th century closely resemble organ incentive proposals today. Equally, the tensions addressed a century before can adequately be scrutinized and addressed in much the same way as before. Both the insurance market and an organ market require placing value on the dead.

Murder does not cease to be illegal simply because a market in organs and other human tissues develops. Safeguards within criminal law to deter homicide already exist and would not need to be developed as a response to organ commoditization. Rather, with already established sanctions in the criminal law, there is a disincentive to harm family members for moderate or even significant compensation. Stiff Criminal penalties, including lifetime incarceration, serve to discourage those who might be tempted to injure or kill family members for compensation. Naturally organ commoditization promotes incentive-based procurement, which could attract poorer Americans. Yet it would be equally disturbing to hint that poorer Americans are more inclined than wealthier Americans to violate the law for pecuniary gain. Corporate scandals of the 1980s, 1990s, and 2000s give indication that the wealthy are just as motivated and perhaps far more capable to exploit financial opportunities. Scandals involving Tyco, Enron, and even Martha Stewart should help to disabuse us of the notion that only the poor violate the law for financial gain. Prosecutors and juries have equally shown intolerance for such criminality.

Finally, health insurance companies can treat organs just as any other health item; in many ways as it is treated today. If an HMO can pay for a knee, plastic surgery, or other treatments, why can't it pay for a heart, kidney, or liver? There seems no rational justification for eliminating the role of HMOs and other health insurance providers. Payments need not directly come from patients. Rather, just as any other health risk or condition requiring medical treatment, including cancer, reproductive services, or postoperative surgeries requiring prosthetics, insurance companies can help us to resolve the details of such financial transactions. Of course in reality, individuals are paying into their insurance programs, thus they are spending toward their health needs. For that reason, it is all the more sensible for individuals who suffer unique health risks that can be treated through organ transplantation to be serviced by their insurance plans. Government caps on costs would reduce the need for organ shopping, thereby eliminating the need to get the "best organ" for the "cheapest price."

Who would receive compensation for organs? Payments could be received by the estate of the deceased, in similar fashion to a life insurance policy or Social Security benefits. Currently, beneficiaries of life insurance policies receive a set amount negotiated and planned for by the deceased. The manner in which the estate would spend the proceeds need not be a question for policy makers any more than how college youths spend payments for blood or sperm.

E. System Components and Government Power

There is much to be learned from other market systems involving sensitive commodities, including blood, ova, and sperm. From health concerns to protecting individuals from coercive measures and exploitation, procurement systems (both altruistic and commercial) require effective protocols, regulation, and monitoring. Problems within supply pools can usually be attributed to mistakes in administering the programs rather than either pool simply attracting particularly unappealing participants.

The need for regulation is apparent even in the current tissue market. Of the 150 companies estimated to be engaged in tissue selling, only half are registered with the Food and Drug Administration (FDA).[63] The need for better oversight is clear as unhealthy tissue has entered the bone and knee transplantation industry resulting in the death of Brian Lykins after a knee transplant and many illnesses, and "scores of injuries."[64] For the organ commoditization industry, much is to be learned from existing markets and systems. How do we reduce the potential for loss, litigation, and mistrust in a commoditization system and ensure *pareto superior* transactions?

Pareto superior transactions in organ procurement will require government involvement. The government possesses powers that individuals and private entities do not. The government differs from private institutions because it can do things that market executives (in this case every family is essentially a market executive in organ supply) cannot. Stiglitz, for example, speaks to the government's power of compulsion.[65] Individuals normally cannot compel others to do a particular thing without the force of law, which is a branch of government. According to Stiglitz, "The government's power of compulsion (associated with its property or universal membership) gave it distinct advantages (and concern about abuses of those powers gave rise to constraints that resulted in distinct disadvantages)."[66]

First, the market system in organs from cadavers must be competent. A commercial market will only succeed if its participants have confidence in the transactions and find the system to be reliable. This means promoting and protecting the health and safety of all participants must be a primary goal of organ commoditization. How would this be accomplished? The FDA is the appropriate body to establish a special subunit, which exclusively addresses organ protocols, monitoring, and licensing. The FDA currently oversees the development and monitoring of medical products, drugs, foods, and most recently, sperm and tissue banks. In 2004, the FDA adopted long-awaited protocols on tissue procurement to screen and test for "all kinds of tissue."[67]

The FDA is also a proper monitoring force because it is recognized as the government's primary source for regulation of medical devices and services.

Funding for FDA monitoring of cadaveric kidney procurement could be generated through licensing for a sister industry, tissue banking, which also needs greater government oversight. To ensure appropriate oversight, industry participants would have to apply for and maintain a license as a prerequisite to tissue banking. Administrative costs could be absorbed through fees the companies must pay for their licensing and possibly through taxes – as Americans currently support federal agencies, their monitoring, litigation, and organizational expenditures across a broad social and political spectrum. The fees received by the FDA would increase its ability to provide better oversight in the existing tissue industry and also the cadaveric market. Presently, the FDA is stymied in its efforts to regulate the tissue industry. The slow action has resulted in over 150 tissue bank companies being unregulated and at least one death and dozens of injuries.[68] In 2002, after a routine knee surgery, Brian Lykins died because the transplanted bone and tissue were infected with virulent bacteria.[69] A subsequent investigation revealed that the tissue Lykins received had been unrefrigerated 19 hours. Over 60 people suffered tremendous injuries from similar operations.[70]

Horror stories from universities selling body parts to the unsafe treatment of human biological material serve as examples of poor industry oversight. However, such problems are avoidable. Horror stories are not an indication that the technology is bad or should not be pursued; helping people to walk again is a positive social agenda. However, the FDA must take a more proactive role in the development of emerging body part industries. Learning from prior mistakes should assist organ banking.

The finer points of licensing include limitations and expiration dates. Industry licenses would not be indefinite, nor should any entity that applies be granted a permit to establish an organ bank. Licenses should be renewable every 2 years and a cap should be established on the first round of licenses given. Fewer industry licenses means greater capacity for effective monitoring and oversight. Licensing standards will help keep track of the companies, their location, number of employees, and types of services offered. Licensing also works to discipline companies that breach their responsibilities to the public.

Second, regulations must be tied to meaningful policies, the violations of which lead to discipline. A useful tool in this regard would be the development of an industry code of ethics. Some professions, such as lawyers, have developed protocols to promote and establish a standard for appropriate conduct and behavior. Medical schools across the United States are now considering the mandatory teaching and testing of professional ethics. Ethics consultants have found a new niche among corporations in the United States looking to not only repair their images, but also understand how to properly engage with the public.

The rationales attached to ethical standards seem obvious. However, they are further extolled in court cases that speak to protecting the public from conflicts of interests, fraud and abuse, financial exploitation, professionalism, and confidentiality.[71] Such principles are designed to place the public interest ahead of pecuniary gain. As in the legal profession, failure to abide by professional standards and the industry code of ethics results in discipline, civil penalties, and possible criminal charges.

The Law

Implementing a market procurement model means repealing part of the National Organ Transplantation Act, which imposes fines up to $50,000 and a maximum of 5 years incarceration for buying organs. The repeal would require congressional action, but would not be unlike other federal reconsiderations of policies that have outlived their value. Once a market is introduced legal questions may arise about organ defects, undisclosed health risks, inappropriate handling of human tissue, and it seems industry malpractice or strict liability.

Blood shield laws of the 1950s and 1960s protected both commercial and nonprofit blood banks by exempting their products from strict liability claims. Whether such policies are applicable for a commercial organ and tissue industry is debatable. In a recent case against Cryolife, a U.S. tissue bank, for selling infected knees, the court held against the injured plaintiff, citing blood shield laws. Whether such claims move forward may in large part depend on federal and judicial conceptualization of what body parts mean in legal terms. Are body parts property? Or should they be described in other terms? If a kidney is stolen from an organ bank, would it not amount to larceny and theft? What should the legal remedies be for such actions?

Cases in this area give some indication about the law's treatment of such issues, but they provide only the historical roadmap. For example, historically, the law's primary property interaction with the body at death was to order its speedy and sanitary burial.[72] Despite its incoherence, the common law as related to corpses demonstrates more clearly a protection of the community from outrage and nuisance, rather than protecting or recognizing a state control or ownership of the dead. The law is unsettled in this area, with some courts recognizing property interests in the body, and others rejecting plaintiffs' claims, opining that it would denigrate the human body to place it on par with property. And yet, we still struggle with value and the body as the Special Master, appointed after the September 11th attacks, was assigned to do just that; place value on the persons who died.

CONCLUSION

Institutional choices involve great trade-offs. In making decisions about which institutions to participate with or select, competence and confidence are significant issues. Greater competence, however, is bartered or purchased through difficult trade-offs. In the case of a market regime, the trade-off could be our moral innocence as related to the body. We would like to believe that our bodies exist outside the domain of alienability at all times. If we are honest, we realize this is not true as wage for labor debunks that notion, corporations alienate tissues from cadavers, and university hospitals sell cadaver parts. Value is placed on our labor, skill, intellect, brawn, and beauty. Moreover, we are not free from coercion or pressure in the accepted patterns of daily alienation (i.e., doing work we would rather refuse). Moreover, we are sensitive to the distorted trade in prostitution that burdens women both as participants (sellers) and the criminal justice system, which punishes them as defendants.

However, body sales frequently occur in the United States, although our general ignorance of these transactions shields us from that reality. As discussed in subsequent chapters, individuals profit, although perhaps unknowingly, through stocks and incentives purchased with companies that trade in body parts or develop devices using human parts they have purchased. This too is alienation of the human body. The balance here, however, is that lives are saved and the quality of life improves for thousands of Americans. But is that enough?

Chinese whistle blower speaks to Congress. Harry Wu (right), Executive Director of the Laogai Research Foundation, waits with "Mr. X" (left, who is keeping his identity secret) to testify before the US House of Representatives International Relations Committee and the Government Reform and Oversight Committee on June 16, 1998. Wu and "Mr. X," a former Chinese prison official who witnessed the harvesting of organs from dead prisoners, testified on the sale of body parts by the People's Republic of China. (Luke Frazza/AFP/Getty Images)

8 Black Markets

The Supply of Body Parts

We in the United States cannot claim any high moral ground, given the number of U.S. transplant centers, public and private, with the idea of donated organs as a national and community resource. Dr. Michael Friedlander, chief nephrologist at Hadassah Hospital in Jerusalem, tired of reports about commercialization of kidneys in Israel, decided like Dr. Diflo, to speak out, and he says that among his recovering international transplant patients are several Israelis who have recently returned this year and last from the United States with kidneys purchased here from living donors.[1]

INTRODUCTION

Another method to address organ demand is to simply allow underground systems to independently flourish. This would ultimately be where we are now; altruistic procurement coexists with private, unregulated, or loosely regulated tissue and organ supply. Organ traffickers and the transplant tourism industry are secondary players in our national transplantation system. These players fill in the gaps of our procurement system, but are they safe alternatives? Unregulated, private organ procurement subsystems pose serious problems that extend far beyond our moral criticisms. These problems include an inability to properly monitor public health, which is not an individual problem. We learned from recent experiences with Severe Acute Respiratory Syndrome (SARS) how quickly a local health crisis can reach international epidemic proportions in a very short period. In a matter of weeks, populations were quarantined on three continents after the SARS outbreak.

Recent reports indicate rabies and other contagious diseases such as West Nile Virus spreading through organ transplants. Those were cases from the United States, which were easier to trace because they were in the public record, with data monitored by the Centers for Disease Control and Prevention (CDC). However, the CDC lacks monitoring capacity with underground transplantations in third-world countries. In addition, the role of physicians is complicated by these transplants; does a physician expose himself to liability for failure to treat a patient who obtained an organ abroad? If the physician provides postoperative care for her patient, does she expose herself to discipline from the hospital where she serves or federal penalties?

Our indifference to alternative solutions drives individuals to create procurement subsystems that operate in the shadows of law. This is the de facto mode of organ procurement; altruism mixed with black market transactions. These transactions are best categorized as *Pareto inferior*; that is, there is always one party that is worse off. The victims are third-world indigent men, women, and sometimes children who are exploited by organ tourism.[2] There is considerable economic pressure for indigent people of color (and those from Eastern Europe) to participate in organ tourism and no guaranteed medical follow-up for any illnesses that may result from harvesting. Organ trafficking has been the subject of congressional hearings,[3] the lead report in *The New York Times*,[4] *Christian Science Monitor*,[5] and broad international press.[6] Congressional reports, at least three in the past 7 years, include detailed testimony about the black market, international trade in organs. Often the testimony has been accompanied by video, photographs, and other compelling evidence. Yet, Americans are reluctant to acknowledge this growing international trade. However, recent evidence, including the personal testimonies of Americans who travel abroad for organs and interviews with transplant coordinators and brokers, confirm that a robust organ trade exists. Those who travel abroad for their surgeries cite the failure of our transplantation system to adequately procure organs as the reason why Americans pursue organs from living persons.

Black markets in general are unattractive systems, which result from poor information sharing, acute demand with limited legal alternatives, and of course the free will of desperate and sometimes "greedy" people who break norms. Yet black market participants in organ trades are not so easy to categorize. According to Jim Cohane, a coordinator for overseas transplants, his clients represent a diverse group of Americans; some are middle class, others are wealthy and from time to time, he is able to waive fees for poorer participants.[7] To the extent that we avoid dealing with serious inquiry about less normative alternatives, we will in the case of organ shortages avoid the people who are most desperate and willing to operate outside of the law. This chapter examines domestic and international black markets. It does not endorse black markets, nor am I recommending a free market system in living donations. To the contrary, this chapter argues that black markets and the people who turn to them deserve our attention.

Section A examines the early foray into the public and private in body shopping, which occurred centuries ago in both Europe and the United States. There are lessons to be learned from those models. Demand for cadavers, primarily for use in medical schools, impelled physicians to create underground markets in body parts, which resulted in widespread grave robbing. The underground and private procurement of cadavers involved negotiations and transactions quite literally in the dark. Top medical schools, including Johns Hopkins, the University of Michigan, the University of Maryland, and others, were involved in this nefarious affair. Those most compromised then too were people of color, particularly African Americans as discussed later. Section B scrutinizes and analyzes by comparison, the public and private financial transactions in tissue transplantation. Section C scrutinizes another public/private system, biotech parenting, involving payments to egg and sperm sellers, which operates more as a grey market. This chapter concludes by examining the private transactions in organ supplying.

A. Taking from the Dead: Robbing Black Cemeteries

On one hand, the law demands that the surgeon must possess the proper skill to practice his vocation, and that he be subject to monetary loss, in civil court, at the whim of a dissatisfied patient. On the other hand, the only mode of acquiring that skill is by the dissection of human bodies, which itself is a crime punishable by law.[8]   Dr. Ryno Smith circa 1830

Slavery gave Southern schools an edge in procuring bodies – masters could sell them – which schools used as a recruiting tool.[9]

The history of grave robbing in the United States and Europe demonstrates that when a public, legal system limits access or is unduly constrained, private systems will emerge. Often the private systems will be more pernicious than the avoided alternatives. By comparison, the experience with alcohol prohibition in the United States is a provocative and informative lesson on this point. Private systems that operate in the shadows of law are less attractive economically, socially, and legally. They are more difficult to monitor and police, thereby heightening the possibilities for abuse of vulnerable populations. Public health and safety are also more likely to be compromised by such systems as the institutions developed in these regimes are unregulated and operate in clandestine ways. Black markets may infringe on privacy and autonomy. Black markets may also operate in coercive ways and promote unethical conduct. Finally, black markets demand surreptitiousness. The secretive manner in which black markets operate conceals many of the problems and flaws associated with the underground activities. Thus information is always lacking about such systems and the individuals who engage with those institutions enter with compromised ideas of what the black market offers them. In an effort to protect our innocence, both in the past and today, we may indirectly promote black market private systems that we seek to avoid.

In 1890, the state of Maryland created a board of anatomy to provide bodies of "unclaimed" indigent individuals for medical use.[10] The board provided a legitimate or legal means for doctors and medical hospitals to procure dead bodies for dissection. The state's efforts were on the heels of rampant grave robbing, which helped to supply bodies to Johns Hopkins and the University of Maryland hospitals. Commentators at the time credited Baltimore with becoming a "first-class medical school town,"[11] as a result of surgical knowledge derived from anatomy research and dissection.[12] A University of Maryland circular claimed, "It is well known that in the city of Baltimore the materials for the pursuit of Practical Anatomy are most ample, and easy of acquisition. In no city in America is public sentiment so indulgent in this respect."[13] Although the circular did not highlight the infrequent public riots resulting in the storming of the dissection rooms, students flocked to Maryland as it was thought to provide the best training and technology of its time.[14]

The Hospital department of the University, in the immediate vicinity, and nearly opposite the Medical College, from its proximity, offers advantages for Clinical studies not to be found elsewhere. Here the student can, day by day, watch the progress of disease and the operation of remedies, and become familiar with the aspect of both acute and chronic complaints – can not only witness surgical operations, but also what is equally important, the nature and result after treatment – advantages not to be obtained, where the Hospital is at a distance and visited only at long intervals.[15]

Bodies were transported from Maryland to Maine during the high-point, or "Golden Age of grave robbing," according to Kercheval.[16] The University of Maryland was not alone in the practice of paying for cadavers procured illegally through grave robbing; the University of Michigan, the Medical College of Georgia (MCG), Johns Hopkins, Harvard, Yale, Jefferson Medical College, and the Medical College of Louisiana were all participants.[17] At the turn of the 19th century, laws permitted only the dissection of condemned murderers;[18] states could not execute enough inmates to adequate supply medical schools. States later permitted the dissection of unclaimed paupers, although those most commonly sacrificed were Black and poor; the exploitation of African American cemeteries continued into the 20th century.[19]

Grave robbing occurred in the shadows of the law. Despite being illegal, pillaging graves was tacitly permitted as well-known, successful surgeons procured bodies for their medical centers through such means and were rarely publicly censured. For example, the University of Michigan charged William Herdman, the Demonstrator of Anatomy at the University of Michigan Medical School, with keeping the medical school competitive by having an adequate supply of cadavers.[20] At the time, more than half of the University of Michigan's faculty were located in the medical school.[21] Herdman knew that grave robbing was rampant, but that it supplied bodies. In a letter to university officials, Herdman called resurrecting a "clandestine business." Indeed it was. Robbers would "go to the cemetery late at night, with only the moon watching... [and] quickly dig down to the upper end of the box, smash it with an ax, reach in there with his long and powerful arms and draw the subject out. He would put the subject in a big sack, place it in a cart and carry it to the school."[22]

Thus, the proscription on cadaver sales or grave robbing did not deter medical doctors from seeking sources on which to experiment. Rather, as in the case of organs and other body parts, it motivated a private industry. Demand for services and surgical knowledge increased, and bodies were procured. States had an interest in doctors being well trained to save lives, avoiding injuries to patients due to careless mistakes, limiting lawsuits, and reducing the strains on courts resulting from malpractice litigation. However, politicians were able to avoid making morally unpopular decisions or proposing creative alternatives, including open sales and altruism, if grave robbing was condemned. In the shadows of public proclamations, however, bodies continued to be procured by robbing cemeteries. Clinics were occasionally stormed, but that White doctors were rarely jailed for their complicity in such activities is very telling.

In 1989, construction workers "made a gruesome discovery," at the Medical College of Georgia; the remains of 400 cadavers were discovered beneath the 154-year-old building.[23] Most of the cadavers are believed to have been African Americans. According to one medical commentator, "[W]e concluded that the professors preferred the bodies of African Americans over whites, men over women and adults over children."[24] Indeed, African American cemeteries suffered the brunt of legislative indifference about cadaver procurement. Black cemeteries were disproportionately targeted by grave robbers and segregated medical schools, which benefited greatly from this open-secret type enterprise. This lack of attention to alternative procurement models contributed to the expansion of the black market in body parts. As a result, African American gravesites throughout the United States were pillaged and relatives of those whose bodies were snatched had limited legal recourse during the Jim Crow era. African Americans and their families suffered considerably as long as institutional alternatives for procuring body parts were limited. The compromised social status of African Americans undercut legal rights as well. Thus, African Americans were easy targets of grave robbing by Blacks and Whites. Blacks were hired too to pillage from Black cemeteries.

This history is informative for contemporary inquiries about procuring organs for transplantation. According to one commentator, the study of anatomy "laid bare an uncomfortable tension in 19th-century medicine."[25] Respect for the dead mattered, but also maintaining the health and safety of the living human body itself was important. These same concerns exist today. There was an urgent need; "[p]atients wanted to be treated by doctors who understood the body's inner workings, which could be learned only by studying a human corpse."[26] At the center of this conundrum was the law, which for a time forbade the creation of alternative institutional choices.

B. Public and Private Transactions in Tissue Procurement

Cadaver skin is used to enhance penis size, puff up lips or erase laugh lines. Plastic surgeons have reported no trouble obtaining skin for plastic surgery, but burn centers across the country are struggling to find skin to treat burn victims.[27]

Black market transactions are deeply imbedded in the transplantation scheme and will likely further expand. Thinking otherwise ignores a growing social phenomenon. Individuals and corporations interact in the public marketplace, including local and college newspapers, the Internet, and magazines for a range of human biological materials. Potential parents advertise for sperm and egg donors, often with very specific criteria for paid "donors." Tissue banks advertise their stock to the public.[28] Their executives are paid well, and even non-profit organ procurement agencies have significant ties to for-profit tissue firms. For example, "85 percent of the federally designated organ procurement organizations sell" hearts, veins, tendons, bones, and other human biological material directly to tissue banks.[29] These donated parts that organ procurement agencies receive generate significant revenue for corporations, their stock holders, and savvy chief executive officers.[30]

A 2001 article published by the *Orthopedic Technology Review* raised serious concerns about the loose regulation of companies producing tissue-based products.[31] Authors noted that annually, over a half million procedures involve donor tissue products. However, monitoring tissue banks that process these body parts has proved difficult. These companies operate outside of public scrutiny. Tissue banks and their operations are a well-kept secret. Even their trade organization, the American Association of Tissue Banks (AATB), a nonprofit organization, which monitors the industry reports that a significant number of tissue banks are not registered with the organization. However, the AATB does not require membership and companies can avoid following its guidelines by simply not registering. For consumers, this is problematic as there is little opportunity to monitor such organizations; where does the investigation begin to determine if the knee that you receive was processed by an AATB affiliate or not and whether the facility was inspected by the FDA? The FDA has no set schedule of inspection at the facilities. Most facilities, only about half, which have been inspected, were visited only once. Similar concerns were raised in a more recent article in the *American Journal of Sports Medicine*.

Nancy Scheper-Hughes and other scholars have written about these transactions. Investigative reporters, often highly scrutinized and their motivation for covering such stories questioned, help to fill in the information gaps about black markets in human tissues. According to Mark Katches, an investigative reporter with the *Orange County Register*, of the 59 organ procurement agencies in the United States, 40 "sell body parts directly to for-profit firms."[32] Katches' investigation found "no organ agencies in America tell donor families about their ties" to for-profit companies.[33] Katches' observations are echoed by Jim Cohane. For example, CryoLife procures its tissues from a variety of sources, including tissue banks and organ procurement organizations.[34] The fees associated with shipping, procurement, and preservation of the tissues are paid by the hospital in which the implanting physician is associated.[35] Tissues are stored at CryoLife until the implanting physician requests delivery. Indeed, NOTA does not proscribe generous transaction fees for shipping, processing, and preservation.

Transplantation negotiations occur in the shadows of law as well as in the public. Corporate transactions transpire in the shadows, with no advertising or public service announcements to encourage participation from unsuspecting laypersons. As I discuss later, their activities are geared toward informing potential stockholders of the benefits of the body parts industry. Those most excluded from profit sharing in the shadows are the family members and estates of the deceased as they are the most unaware and unacknowledged in the black market transactions. Hundreds of tissue banks throughout the United States, with very little oversight, buy, retrieve, store, experiment with, and broker human tissues and body parts. For over a decade, these companies collected eyes, human skin, bones, and other body parts before the Food and Drug Administration was called to action in 2001 to implement registration requirements and an inspection plan.[36] Until the FDA registration requirements were implemented, it was unknown exactly how many for-profit tissue banks were operating in the United States.[37] It was quite clear, however, that a multimillion dollar industry had emerged that had powerful financial backing from hospitals, pharmaceutical companies, investors, and venture capital firms. Their success could in part be attributed to a rise in tissue donations, from about "6,000 in 1994 to about 20,000 by 1999."[38] The source of the donations, however seems somewhat unclear as those who believe that they are participating in an altruistic system are unaware that their loved one's body or her parts might become recycled products by CryoLife, Hybrid Organ, Islet Technology, Ixion Inc, VitaGen, Inc., or Regeneration Technologies, which although for-profit is affiliated with a hospital. Likewise, aborted fetuses, placenta, and other postbirth biological tissues are passed on or sold to companies that research and develop new technologies or products, often without the consent of the "donor."

Several transactions usually occur before bodies reach the biotech-processing company, which "turns the material into usable body parts."[39] Along the way, financial transactions govern each exchange from the agency or organization involved in harvesting the materials to the company that packages and sells the body part. Moreover, whereas for-profit tissue banks and biotechnology firms fill a void in the health industry, providing products such as knees, hips, skin, cardiac conduits, femoral veins, arteries, bone cells, and other body parts for eager consumers, their operations are not altruistically motivated. To the contrary, their express institutional purpose is financial. Their business objectives are to make profits and thereby generate revenue for their stockholders. In fact, some of these companies, including Olympus; Regeneration Technologies, and CryoLife, trade on national stock exchanges and provide hyperlinks to stock information on their Web pages.[40] In researching this book, my students and I uncovered an additional 50 such companies and visited their Websites. Although 10 years ago this industry was worth only 20 million dollars, in 2003 the tissue bank industry is reported to be an over 1 billion dollar niche in the marketplace.[41] A recent report investigating Regeneration Technologies claims that a single cadaver can yield more than $220,000 in products.[42]

Like any other business publicly traded, tissue banks' objective is not to lose money, but rather to aggressively stimulate profit for its shareholders. Olympus, for example, projects that it will generate annual sales of 10 billion yen from tissue-engineered bone by 2013.[43] Regeneration Technologies (RTI), a Florida-based firm, announced recently that it has secured a $15.1 million credit agreement with Bank of America.[44] Thomas F. Rose, the chief financial officer for the firm, informed investors that the credit line will help the company to focus on its "core business of developing innovative technologies and products."[45] RTI processes allograft tissue into shaped implants used for orthopedic, urologic, craniofacial, and cardiovascular surgeries from donated tissues, which are later sold to increase revenue for the company.[46]

Although several hundred companies have now registered with the Food and Drug Administration, according to one report, over 100 of these tissue banks are yet to be inspected by health officials.[47] The expanding human tissue processing and harvesting industry became a newsworthy topic and federal concern primarily due to fears arising out of unsanitary practices at some tissue banks, including the commingling of body parts from different cadavers and the mishandling of bodies after removal of bones, skin, and other tissues. Health officials feared that these practices could lead to diseases, and in 2002 several deaths occurred after implantation of processed body parts that were infected. That human body parts were purchased, modified, and sold, was not the primary concern of the FDA, which focused attention on the potential for diseases to spread through unsafe medical practices. Nor has there been significant public outcry about the nonaltruistic nature of this industry, although the Associated Press, *New York Times*, *Wall Street Journal*, and other news organizations have raised concerns about tissue companies and their products.

RTI and other biotechnology firms rely on the nonprofit industry and unsuspecting donors to supply the tissues that ultimately become reprocessed body parts sold to doctors and hospitals. In a recent investigation conducted by William Heisel and Mark Katches in 2000, they found that almost 70% of the 59 organ procurement agencies regulated by the federal government sell body parts directly to for-profit firms.[48] Another 18% sell body parts to other nonprofit tissue banks that "act as middlemen," who then ship the tissues to for-profit companies.[49] Over 20% of those selling directly to for-profit companies have expanded their cadaver and tissue recovery programs, arguably to meet the growing demand from corporate clients, which in turn increases their revenues.[50]

In the private negotiation process, transactions are difficult to trace as they occur outside the boundaries of regulation. They tend to lack clear regulation or standards and are driven exclusively by pecuniary interests. Perhaps most disturbing about the clandestine nature of black market negotiations is the incapacity to accommodate informed consent. Indeed, were the private to become more public or transparent, individual compensation might be demanded, thereby breaking the profit monopoly held by chief executive officers and their shareholders.

Additionally, protections such as informed consent are necessarily removed from this process, as they would drive down "donations." How many Americans would knowingly and willingly participate in a scheme that uses their unique and precious resources for others' private gain without any compensation or charitable relief?[51] Without informed consent, family members are divested of the protections governed by international human rights accords, such as the Nuremberg Treaty, and autonomy is pilfered. Private negotiations in the black market context can be extremely problematic and arguably more detrimental to patients' and their families' economic and moral rights absent transparency. Yet, black market transactions will continue to occur, absent strong oversight – both by consumer groups and government agencies.

C. The Private and the Public: A New Right to Choose in Sperm and Ova Sales

To imagine that not compensating the egg provider will prevent ova from being transformed into a commodity is to misunderstand the extent of commercial activity in fertility treatments.[52]

Sperm and ova sales are examples of the blended public and private financial exchanges in the body.[53] On the one hand, they are incredibly public; proponents and future parents advertise in college and local newspapers for willing contributors. Yet, there are also private dimensions or aspects that are more removed from public scrutiny; the negotiations for specific types of donors with the hope of creating custom babies. These transactions are generated by individual demand and have less to do with corporate negotiations as discussed earlier. To the extent that very private negotiations and transactions occur in this industry (i.e., sperm donations and transactions outside of an agency), they too are removed from public view. Nevertheless, there is general acceptance of ova and sperm sales – an industry far less diverse than the organ regime. Are we more willing to permit financial exchanges at the beginning of life rather than at the end?

Sperm and ova purchased from fertity clinics and private parties help infertile couples throughout the United States to achieve reproduction. In this process, doctors, lawyers, and a robust fertility industry exchange contracts and fees for services. Their participation, although critical in the exchange between donors and recipients, largely depends on the willingness of donors to engage in a "baby-making" market. Nationally, advertisements appear in college newspapers and now in *Newsweek* magazine directly targeting young men and women to share their sperm or eggs.[54] The ads are often very descriptive, usually requesting White, blond, tall, and intellectually gifted persons to respond.[55] However, these advertisements also include an incentive: The "donors" receive compensation for their services.[56] Ironically, although referred to as donors, those targeted to participate are provided compensation, and thus are not donors in the traditional altruistic sense.

The transparency of financial transactions associated with sperm, eggs, and ova has become more obvious over time as newspaper and magazine investigations scrutinize the practices behind these growing industries.[57] Some charge that the financial exchanges involved are simply for costs incurred in donating, and not for the actual sperm or eggs. They claim that payment is strictly intended to compensate for the donor's "time, inconvenience, and discomfort."[58] These claims, however, disguise the commercialism present in the infertility industry, which is largely unregulated. Longtime fashion photographer Ron

Harris in 1999 created a Website advertising the availability of models' eggs for the highest bidders.[59] Reports indicate the models would pay a 20% commission fee to Harris for his services.[60] According to Harris, they received serious bids. Only months before, a couple advertised that they would pay a tall, athletic, college student $50,000 for her eggs.[61] Although federal law forbids organ selling, it does not proscribe ova and sperm sales, nor does it regulate Websites or newspapers advertising such services.[62] American couples are not alone in the quest for human eggs. The British Broadcasting Company reported the "dramatic rise in the number of infertile British couples buying human eggs over the Internet from the U.S."[63]

Commentators claim that the lack of regulation in the fertility industry has led to elements of price fixing in some states and matching programs in others that resemble end-of-year solicitations by charitable organizations.[64] For example, several years ago, clinics in New York tacitly agreed to lower compensation for egg donors.[65] Sharon Lerner reported in *Ms. Magazine* that donors in the New York metropolitan area were rarely paid more than $2,500 for egg donations.[66] Two years later, however, a clinic in New Jersey offered double the compensation provided by New York fertility clinics, giving way not only to price wars, but also fundamental reconsideration about the process and whether human eggs should be a market item at all.[67]

The process involved with generating eggs for donation is complicated, painful, and invasive.[68] Drugs are administered to maximize the number of eggs produced by the donor.[69] Donors receive a series of hormone shots, which cause ovarian hyperstimulation, resulting in production of one or two dozen eggs (instead of one).[70] Once the ovaries are properly stimulated, eggs are removed with a needle and implanted in the womb of a woman attempting to conceive. The process poses health risks as well as potential psychological side effects. Donors complain of nausea, bloating, and depression.[71] The long-term side effects are unknown as most studies focus on the side effects experienced by infertile women who seek drug therapies to stimulate egg production. Given the risks involved for the egg donor, is it reasonable to expect that young women should voluntarily undergo such a highly complex regimen of drug therapies to help an anonymous couple conceive?

Market systems in this instance coexist with altruism. The market in this context has greater capacity to accommodate family demand than with exclusive reliance on altruism. Would foreclosing financial incentives and payment for services increase altruistic ova and sperm donations? Probably not. Indeed, it is unknown whether altruism would become a stronger, more efficient system if the market systems presently available were eliminated. It seems unlikely that greater charitable contributions would increase, as those who are motivated to donate altruistically are not prohibited from doing so presently. More than likely, the number of participants would dwindle significantly. With fewer donations, waitlists and wait times increase, and the altruistic system is further burdened by participants' frustration, lack of confidence, and disappointment. The system might be further complicated by inequitable rationing schemes, which seem unavoidable in most instances where demand outpaces supply. How would we choose who is first in line for ova? Would race matter? Would a couple be forced to accept ova from a different ethnic group or otherwise lose their place in line? Are these matters left better for the government to handle or individuals?

Technological advancements that now help couples that otherwise might never conceive also conflict with traditional notions of child conception, which usually did not involve payment. However, the right to parent and the privacy protecting it has been somewhat free from government intervention. Yet, there appears to be growing social acceptance of in-vitro fertilization as a viable method for nontraditional couples wishing to conceive, including single parents, gay couples, and unmarried heterosexual couples. This could be attributed to greater public awareness; over the past decade magazine reports, newspaper articles, and television specials have helped to educate a largely uninformed public about infertility and how it affects couples attempting to conceive.

The prospect of raising a child that shares the biological material of another woman or man is perhaps not very different than adoption. In both cases, couples and a rising number of single individuals strongly desire to have children and are prepared to devote energy to a process that they hope will result in a baby coming into their lives. Similar to the case of egg sales, couples seeking to adopt are prepared to spend fees in the tens of thousands to lawyers, agencies, and sometimes to the young woman offering her child.[72] Perhaps eased tensions about in-vitro fertilization also can be attributed to greater social acceptance and legal protections of gay parents who experience fewer problems with adoptions and obtaining custody of their own children than ever before.[73] For alternative couples, sperm and egg availability has enhanced the possibility of having a family with some genetic connection.

Attempts by some couples to create the "ideal" child, and their willingness to pay large sums, may be a thornier issue in in-vitro fertilization than mere payments to donors. This disturbing reality naturally raises concerns. Critics argue that because of the selective criteria at some fertility clinics, the human egg market "encourages couples to engineer the perfect baby."[74] They suggest that couples are paying for beauty rather than compensating a young woman for her time and inconvenience.[75] Perhaps they are right. Both critics and proponents question whether the federal government should step in to proscribe or regulate the family-making industry. Essentially, couples can pick and choose the qualities or characteristics they most desire in the donor providing eggs or sperm.[76] Traditionally, American courts have been reluctant to interfere with one's right to spend his or her money, particularly if it does not interfere with the liberties or rights of another. For this reason the sale of sperm, which predates the more expansive ova market, has been accepted or tolerated for some time. It is not likely that proscribing ova sales would actually achieve its intended goals, which include increasing altruistic donations and eliminating financial transactions in sperm and egg donations.

Finally, although the FDA has recently promulgated regulations for sperm donations, their concerns have only loosely to do with safety and not the commercialization of reproductive services. To explicate, the most recent regulatory step taken by the FDA limits the involvement of gay men in sperm donation.[77] New rules released during the spring of 2004 proscribe sperm donations from sexually active homosexual men. The regulations stipulate that gay men who have been sexually active with other men within the past 5 years can no longer donate sperm. Gay advocacy organizations, such as the National Gay and Lesbian Task

Force, denounce the recent rules, suggesting that the FDA has misplaced its concern because HIV tests are fast and effective. Some sperm bank officials disagree. Ultimately, where the agency has acted in regulation of this industry, its efforts pertain to health and safety, giving tacit approval of the reproductive grey market.

D. Black Markets and Organs

It's illegal to traffic organs . . . and so, a lot of people think that I do that and that's one of the problems I have speaking with this . . . So, every day people call me who want to sell their organs and because they read that like I do that. But, I've never had [sic] been involved in that. There's no reason to because the people that I send, the clients, the [patients] that I send to their countries, the hospitals in those other countries are the ones that arrange to do all that. I have nothing to do with that.   Jim Cohane, Transplant Coordinator[78]

In 2004, I was able to interview Jim Cohane twice about international organ coordination, trading, and brokering. Other coordinators, brokers, and middlemen whom I was able to locate were unwilling to be interviewed on tape, including organ finders at Glauhaus, another private organization that assists Americans with finding organs. For the most part, brokers are not terribly difficult to find; quite a few are located in the United States. They can be found on the Internet using search engines such as Google. Glauhaus, one of the companies I discovered during a search for kidney brokers, for example, has an office in Pennsylvania and Jim is located in California. Officials at Glauhaus were unwilling to provide a taped interview after consulting with their attorneys. Jim, however, shared his time and provided insight about this complex industry. He describes his services as "transplant coordination" and gave me his personal insight into his practice. According to Mr. Cohane, a typical kidney transplant through his services will cost "about $125,000 and that includes another person going with him and being with him during that time. Usually it's a friend."[79] According to Jim, he tries to keep some distance from the transactions. For example, he does not fly to the locations with buyers when they receive their organs. When asked about that he demurred, "I'm just the coordinator, another person . . . I coordinate everything from here."[80]

The Tale of an Organ

The black markets in organ supply are a mix of desperation, greed, avarice, support, generosity, exploitation, entrepreneurialism, conspiracy, and mourning. Suppliers range from those with no informed consent (Chinese inmates) to those living in incredibly compromised living conditions, where consent may be substantively meaningless, given economic desperation and an opportunity to alleviate poverty. The World Health Organization (WHO) issued nonbinding regulations in 1991 in an effort to stem exploitation and black market practices in organ procurement. Their protocols were adopted by 192 countries, including the United States. However, the guidelines have no force or power. Since the WHO protocols went into effect, organ sales have only increased. This, in part, is due to the fact that the WHO antitrafficking protocols are nonbinding, with no enforcement powers or funding to help smaller nations track illegal organ sales. Placing this economic burden on smaller countries to monitor, regulate, and prosecute cases of organ buying and selling creates a disincentive.

For poor countries that rely on tourism, using government funds to enforce a nonbinding WHO protocol may be perceived as poor economic policy. Transplant tourism stimulates local economies and this must have some political value to some politicians. Often, buying an organ is a "package deal," which includes travel for a companion or nurse, excursions, and fine accommodations.[81] In these instances, buying an organ comes with a vacation. Thus there may be little incentive for nations such as Iran and Pakistan, which are unabashed in directly or indirectly tolerating black markets, to adhere to WHO antiorgan trafficking protocols. Moreover, countries more committed to banning organ sales do little to support their political efforts when enforcement and sanctioning protocols are not in place. Monitoring outside of their borders is far more difficult and expensive than the internal regulation of organ transplantation.

Organ suppliers hail from primarily Pakistan, India, South Africa, Peru, Romania, Bolivia, and Brazil.[82] These individuals submit themselves to live organ harvesting, which may or may not take place at a clean hospital or clinic and that usually does not involve medical follow-up. The sellers help to supply kidneys, lungs, and liver lobes to

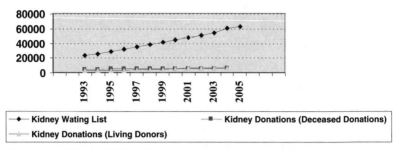

Figure 8.1. Kidney Waiting List (1993–7/2005)

individuals they may never see or come to know in any way.[83] American middlemen often secretly broker these arrangements, negotiating fees, payments to hospitals and surgeons abroad. The operations take place abroad and in the United States.[84] One commentator reports that this private, black market industry in organ sales is so vast and complex that foreigners arrive in the United States for the transplantation of organs purchased in other countries.[85] No longer is there a question as to the reality of organ sales or organ tourism; my interviews with Jim Cohane along with reports from Nancy Scheper-Hughes, testimony to Congress, and narratives from suppliers, provide a comprehensive picture that the black market not only exists, but thrives off of American, Canadian, and British dollars. The best point of inquiry is determining whether this subsystem or institutional response to poor altruistic organ procurement is any better or worse than other models, including presumed consent and a regulated market in cadaveric organ sales.

Figure 8.1 provides some perspective as to kidney demand and supply in the United States. The figures are daunting. By midyear 2005, over 62,000 Americans were waiting for kidney transplants.[86] By April of 2005 (the last data set available), only 4,600 donors *for all organs* recovered were made available for transplantation.[87] These figures are unambiguous; transplant candidates realize the odds of receiving an organ transplant in the United States are slim. The waiting time could be years and their health could deteriorate to the point where they are no longer suitable candidates for organ transplantation. These concerns, according to Cohane, motivate people from the United States to work through black markets for organs.

Buying an Organ

They never want you to see the donor... But I kept insisting that we meet because I know that he is now part of my being. I have a piece of him inside of me, so who wouldn't want that bond?[88]

Jane Doe, an American kidney buyer

In recent years, the demand for organs has spilled beyond the borders of the United States and now is part of an international dynamic. The demand for organs from the United States contributes to the global black market in organs. Once dismissed as myth, stories of body snatching, testimonials from participants, photographs, video footage, and interviews with brokers give evidence of an underground organ market. Much of the evidence of these industries has been collected by an organization located at the University of California named Organs Watch, which is directed by Nancy Scheper-Hughes. Other investigations have been sponsored by major news organizations, including the *New York Times* and the *London Guardian*. Yet, other reports have been gathered by political insiders and local governments in China, Pakistan, India, Brazil, South Africa, and other countries.

Jane Doe, age 49, is one of a growing group of Americans who bought an organ abroad. She describes herself as a deeply spiritual woman who is concerned about ethics in organ transplantation, but also felt trapped in the waiting game for an organ. Jane lives in Brooklyn, New York, in a simple one-bedroom apartment. She informed interviewers from the *New York Times* that she had been on dialysis for 15 years and on two transplant lists for 7 of those years.[89] She told reporters, "Nothing was happening, and my health was getting worse and worse."[90] She recalled that her doctors told her "get a kidney any way" she could or plan to die.[91] Jane had seen others die while waiting for kidney transplants in the United States. It was, in part, this experience that led Jane and her husband to find an organ for her on the black market. Jane and her husband found an organ through contacts in Israel.

Israel has emerged as a nuanced player in international kidney brokering.[92] Very strict protocols in Israel limit organ donations to altruistic procurement. The waitlist for kidneys grows by roughly 20% each year in Israel, yet donations are considerably low. In observance of more orthodox religious traditions, donation rates tend to be lower in Israel, owing in part to the belief by some that Jewish religious law forbids any desecration of the body, including for organ donations. Thus, according to one commentator, "organ donation rates in Israel are among the lowest in the developed world."[93] To help Israelis find organs, a health ministry directive allows "Israelis who go abroad for transplants to be reimbursed as much as $80,000."[94] This policy helps to relieve internal demand for organs, but on the other hand, economically supports the exportation of kidney demand. For Israel, providing a medical insurance that covers the costs of transplantations is not necessarily a bad policy; it helps to serve the medical needs of its citizens. The policy does not, however, police how the organs are procured, nor does it inquire as to from whom the organs have come.

Some brokers "advertise openly in Israeli newspapers and on radio stations, soliciting recipients and donors."[95] In 2003, Jane Doe and her husband were able to utilize an underground network through Israel to procure a kidney, which saved her life.[96] Jane's kidney did not, however, come from an Israeli. Rather, according to reports, it was an Israeli broker who assisted her in finding a kidney from Alberty Jose da Silva, then a 37-year-old Brazilian man, who sold his kidney to a middleman for $6,000. The middleman who coordinated the organ purchase was part of an international organ trafficking ring that spanned four continents.[97] The organ traffickers flew da Silva to South Africa, which bans organ selling, where he signed documents stating that he and Jane Doe were cousins.[98] He stayed at a safe house until going to St. Augustine Hospital where his kidney and a rib were removed.

The transactions were in cash, with brokers covering da Silva's travel and transportation costs from Brazil to Durban, South Africa. To da Silva, one of 25 children from a poor family, "six grand is a lot of money, especially when you don't have any."[99] Da Silva, however, was paid only one-tenth of what Jane Doe was charged. Jane Doe paid 60 thousand dollars for her kidney, which experts say is less than half of typical transplant costs. According to Jane's husband, "helping her get that kidney was the best thing that I have ever done for anyone in my entire life."[100] Three days after the operation, da Silva was flown back to Brazil more than likely never to see Jane Doe or the brokers again. In fact, shortly after selling his kidney, the organ trafficking ring was investigated and its members arrested by South African law enforcement. That one ring, officials suggest (based on confiscated records), supplied nearly 200 organs.

Costs

Figures are difficult to come by to provide a real estimate as to the size of the international black market organ industry. Jim Cohane stated that he alone has coordinated over 400 organ transplantations. Nor are there any uniform procedures between transplant coordinators, brokers, or the countries in which they operate. Each is his own marketer and spokesperson. Nancy Scheper-Hughes' group, Organs Watch, which has performed the most extensive inventory of underground markets does estimate organ asking prices and income data. Organs Watch estimates the average annual income of an organ seller is about $480 (based on figures from the Philippines).[101] According to the organization, organs are sold for as little as $750 in Iraq (prewar) to $30,000 in the United States.[102] Such payments represent only a fraction of buyer's costs, which include fees for surgeons, middlemen, hospital stay, luxury accommodations, and travel.

The costs, however, must be measured beyond the financial as in each procurement model from altruism to presumed consent, cadaveric selling, and this too, black markets. In the black market, business risk is dealt broadly. Coordinators, if caught, face criminal charges in some countries and fines. If the coordinators are physicians they stand to lose their license to practice. Sellers risk becoming sick, needing additional medical attention, and not being able to afford the medical treatments that they will need. Or, in the case of Jane Doe's seller, da Silva, he was robbed in Sao Paolo on his way back home, losing the $6,000 he had earned for selling his kidney. Moreover, there are no guarantees that life will be better for the man or woman who sells a kidney. For the buyers, there are no warranties of function, health, or longevity for organs that are purchased. It is truly a dynamic of buyer beware or "buy at your own risk."

The risks described here are unique to black market organ transfers. Other systems too have risks. This book has described in some detail the risks associated with an exclusive altruistic policy. Presumed consent also has known risks, those which have been documented by a few scholars. Given the very nature of black markets, follow-up with patients is bound to be discouraged. Jim Cohane informed me that he does hear from some patients long after they receive their new organs, but in most instances patients and their coordinators will desire anonymity to avoid prosecution.

CONCLUSION

The black market organ industry will continue to thrive until it is replaced with a viable alternative. Bans will be ineffective because most will not address the root problem; altruism is a good, but incomplete source for procuring kidneys and other organs. To fill in the tremendous gap between organ demand and organ supply, alternative procurement models such as black markets will emerge. Not all the actors in those markets will necessarily be nefarious. Doctors will emerge as organ brokers to save their patients' lives. Individuals like da Silva will attempt to better their lives, even if it means placing their physical health at risk and possibly breaking the law. And over 60,000 people like Jane Doe will be on our kidney waitlists facing similar dilemmas. Buying an organ might be illegal, but it saved her life. Ultimately, banning organ sales requires a comprehensive effort from the local medical and hospital associations, government, and enforcement agencies. For some countries, there is no incentive to police organ purchases outside of their borders. Maybe that is where we are in the United States, willing to export our organ shortages elsewhere so long as we can officially call organs "gifts" and turn a blind eye.

Critiquing the Slavery and Black Body Market Comparison

Part III scrutinizes the notion that a market in cadaveric organs is necessarily harmful to Blacks. Chapters in this section debunk that notion. Chapter 9 directly addresses this comparison, which although overgeneralized is ubiquitous in scholarly literature and popular media. Ironically, despite its prevalence in literature about markets in organs and other human supplies, no one has bothered to challenge the well-established theory that a market in organs is similar to slavery. Chapter 10 concludes by examining how organ sales might benefit African Americans and what pitfalls to avoid.

AUCTION

Having sold my farm and am leaving for Oregon territory by ox team, I will offer at public sale at my home 2 Miles South of Versailles, Kentucky, on McConn Ferry Pike, on

MARCH 1st, 1849

all my personal property, to wit :

ALL MY OX TEAMS

EXCEPT TWO TEAMS – BUCK and BEN, and TOM and JERRY

2 Milk Cows, one Gray Mare and colt, 1 pair of oxen and yoke, one baby yoke, two ox carts 1500 feet of poplar weather boards, plow with wooden moldboards, 800 to 1000 feet of clapboards, 1000 ten-foot fence rails, One 60-gallon soap kettle, 85 sugar troughs, made of white ash timber; ten gallons of maple syrup; two spinning wheels; 30 pounds of mutton tallow; 1 large loom, made by Jerry Wilson; 300 poles; 100 split hoops, 100 empty barrels: one 32-gallon barrel of Johnson-Miller whiskey, 7 years old; 20 gallons of apple brandy; 40-gal. copper still; 1 doz. real books, two handle hooks; 3 scythes and cradles, 1 dozen wooden spiles; bullet mold and powder horn; rifle made by Ben Miller; 50 gals. of soft soap, hams, bacon, lard, 40 gals. of sorghum molasses'

SIX HEAD OF FOX HOUNDS   All Soft Mouthed
Except One

At the Same Time I Will Sell My

6 NEGRO SLAVES

Two men 35 years and 50 years old; two boys 12 and 18 years old; two mulato wenches, 40 and 30 years old. We will sell all together to same party but will not SEPARATE them.

TERMS OF SALE---Cash in hand or note to draw 4 per cent interest with Bob McConnell as security.

PLENTY to drink and eat !

J.F. SCHWEER   J.L. MESS

Slave Auction advertisement from a Kentucky plantation.

9 Critiquing the Slavery and Black Body Market Comparison

INTRODUCTION

A more persuasive race-based challenge to markets in organs might be that given the current practices of discrimination in society and levels of poverty, which disproportionately affect African Americans, private and public decision makers might be more sensitive to the health concerns of Whites and less so to Blacks. In this, commentators might be right; numerous studies reveal racial disparities in healthcare.[1] Markets then might further correlate to that, but would not be causal, as discussed in Chapter 7. A market in cadaveric body parts will not be the cause of racial discrimination in America although it might reveal patterns of discrimination, which currently exists. Creating a transplantation system that promotes equity for all Americans is critically important. For this reason, I propose a hybrid model, which engages both altruism and a limited market in cadaveric organs, to increase the supply of organs. Such a model increases individual and collective autonomy, promotes greater organ awareness (there is an incentive in simply learning about whether organ donation is a worthwhile activity), and provides access for wealthy and poor individuals. Wealthier individuals can engage directly with markets and the altruistic pool can be utilized by the economically disenfranchised.

Relying exclusively on altruistic procurement, we avoid questions of property and ownership in the human body that obviously arise in market systems. The time has come where we must deal squarely with these issues. As discussed earlier, Richard Titmuss warned the West about devaluing human relationships through blood sales, cautioning that altruistic blood supplies could diminish, but more importantly that our humanity would slowly be bartered away.[2] American slave images quite often attend these theories and are poor comparisons to a well-designed market system. By no means am I suggesting that altruism has exceeded its usefulness. To the contrary, by relying on altruistic procurement, organ transplantation as a medical model gained social and legal acceptance and credibility, but avoiding questions of human ownership and payments, both of which might have reduced the act itself to a purely contested political point in the 1980s.

In Chapter 8, I suggested that organ commoditization would not possess the exact dimensions and power relationships that once existed with slavery. This position stands contrary to the opinions of some bioethicists, and is perhaps considered radical by others. Again, fears about organ alienation fail to take into account that financial arrangements govern many transactions with the body as Americans demonstrate a willingness to engage the market for healthcare and cosmetic medical technology. Failure to study African American involvement in market regimes has an unfortunate dual effect. First, it limits critical dialogue and the flow of information on organ sales to African Americans. Second, it further marginalizes the community that it sometimes seeks to protect by leaving African Americans out of the dialogue about organ sales. In an effort to protect African Americans from potentially poor decision making, some ethicists have strongly urged against commoditization, suggesting it would erode personhood and bring about the devaluation of donor participants much as slavery did.

Chapter 9 scrutinizes this oversimplified connection between slavery and markets. It bothers to spell out that which on one hand may be perceived as "not needing documentation." Yet, the glaring absence of any response as to this characterization deserves to be remedied because the myth has the power of reproduction. Indeed, popular commentaries as well as accounts from bioethicists have contributed over time to the ubiquitous spread of this notion. Let us examine it to see whether it has merit.

Black Bodies and Property

Our oldest and perhaps most profound, lingering memories of human bodies as commodified objects involve enslaved Africans toiling on domestic plantations. This image of subordinated Black slaves was firmly established in the precedents established by Justice Taney in *Dred Scott v. Sandford*[3] and other antebellum-era litigation and described by prolific scholars, John H. Franklin,[4] E. Franklin Frazier,[5] Winthrop Jordan,[6] Thomas Gossett,[7] Mary E. Goodman,[8] Fogel and Engerman,[9] and Phillip Curtain.[10] Popular accounts of slavery were romanticized in films like "Gone With the Wind", based on a novel by Margaret Mitchell, retold in Alex Haley's *Roots,* or otherwise examined in the turn-of-the-century classic, *Uncle Tom's Cabin* by Harriet Beecher Stowe. Such novels and films depicted Black Americans as powerless individuals, bought and sold at will, without any autonomy, legal rights, or protection of the law. Although of different genres, each fictional, biographical or autobiographical account captures the sociolegal status of Black Americans as second-class citizens within the law. Unborn children were considered the property of their mothers' owners, thus denying enslaved Black women or their families any rights associated with their progeny.[11]

Slavery is perhaps the clearest and most crude example of "body ownership." Robert William Fogel and Stanley L. Engerman chronicle slavery's corrosive effects on the Black community in *Time on the Cross: The Economics of American Negro Slavery*.[12] Of course, the institution of slavery extends beyond American involvement; its roots can be found in religious literature, dating back hundreds if not thousands of years, such as the Bible, Torah, and Koran, with roots in Africa and Europe. Other, but perhaps less well-known, examples of the commoditization of human body parts involved doctors and medical hospitals purchasing corpses for research purposes and use in anatomy classes. Even Leonardo daVinci is said to have hired grave diggers to support his mapping of the human body.

Thus, the market in human biological materials is not a new phenomenon, nor is the struggle between scientific advancement and ethical practice.[13] The two, in fact, are intimately wedded together as doctors and patients throughout time have sought human biological materials to treat illnesses and save lives.[14] Dissection of the dead to study the human organism predates modern medicine and has been critically important to the development of anatomical studies and the evolution of medicine.

Moreover, achieving positive medical outcomes for the living accomplishes positive social goals. In this way, medical advancement may be construed as social advancement. Nevertheless, advancing scientific knowledge and even saving lives can conflict with moral understanding and ethical practice.[15] At the heart of such conflicts are the tensions between the categories of supply and demand and that of individual rights, particularly the rights of the uninformed, coerced, defrauded, and incompetent. Therein, issues of informed consent, privacy, property, and autonomy help us to understand the legal evolution of bioethics as well as rights in the body.

Viewed as property or "private" objects, the human body is not unfamiliar to the market domain or commercial analysis.[16] For centuries the body and its constituent parts have been traded, bonded, and insured, both within the realm of the law's recognition and protection, but also outside of it. Within this context there is a distinction between those transactions involving uninformed consent (or none at all) versus those where the participants have mutual bargaining power and autonomous decision making. Consider for example, slavery, scientific patenting, and selling of nonconsensually harvested biological information and materials, and cadavers harvested and sold by grave robbers to medical institutions.[17] Clearly in these instances, the participants lacked consent, and yet a substantial social benefit was nevertheless gained. The relevant question then, is whether social benefit can ever justify limited human commoditization? How do we reconcile the tensions between remuneration in the body to achieve a medical goal and our moral anxieties over human alienation? If mutual bargaining power exists, are those financial transactions inherently better? Should all financial engagements with the human body be discouraged, and if so, how do we reconstruct America's medical model, which in many ways is organized around financial principles?

Opponents of organ commoditization warn that the human body would be degraded and devalued in the marketplace, likening it to more commonly traded goods and materials, creating as Margaret Radin observes, "an inferior conception of personhood."[18] Banks argues that the unique qualities that distinguish the human body from other market items might become indistinct.[19] Mahoney suggests that the risks of devaluing the human body extend "beyond actual transactions in human body components."[20] The use of market language and characterizations, for example, might be inappropriately applied.[21] Critics such as Gold, Kass, and Murray suggest that it would be a mistake, for example, to apply the language of property to the human body.[22] Others caution that applying the concept of property to the human body would be as morally reprehensible as slavery, sharing according to their view, many of the same characteristics.[23] According to such arguments, the most vulnerable would suffer, ostensibly coerced or forced into participating.[24] Commentators are also skeptical about who would benefit from organ commoditization, casting an eerie picture that African Americans would be the majority of those alienating their organs, with wealthy, White Americans being the recipients.[25] Such fears have been voiced over time by a number of scholars and bioethicists virtually bringing the discourse on organ commoditization to a halt.[26]

Whether evoking the grotesque images of slavery in the United States, or the purchasing of organs from death-row inmates in China,[27] the discourse about human alienation polarizes various groups, leaving questions about medical efficacy and social paradigm shifts largely ignored.[28] The horrors of slavery consume the discourse about human tissue alienation, particularly when race stands at the intersection of the discourse.[29] Commentators stress the need to avoid involvement with procurement systems and strategies reminiscent of an era involving human bondage. They compare contemporary interest in organ alienation with past rhetorical justifications for slavery. Quite rightfully, they highlight the disordered system of values, coercion, and economic greed intimately wedded to American slavery.[30] Indeed, it might seem all the more plausible that with any African American participation in compensation-based transplantation models implicit coercion or exploitation might govern such transactions. These concerns remind us that compassion, respect, and human dignity must collectively operate as the ethos by which transplantation occurs. Whereas slavery in American history should stand as a marker against which politically, legally, and morally we dare not trespass, to what extent, however, does its evocation obscure the realities of preexisting market transactions in the domain of organ transplantation? Most lacking in this discourse is the inclusion of African Americans.

Slavery's pernicious effect is not exclusively derived from a market evaluation in the human body. Indeed, many slaves were given away as gifts.[31] Harriet Jacobs in a most moving autobiographical account of slavery describes in penetrating detail the horror of being exchanged as a "gift" rather than being freed on her "mistresses" death.[32] Jacobs, at 11, was bequeathed to a 3-year-old.[33] Clearly, the gift relationship can be marked by the very injustices altruists and Marxists abhor. The gift relationship fails to account for preexisting injustices, which are not solved by altruism. The villainy of slavery is best characterized by the creation of a chattel system wherein Black men, women, and children were explicitly and exclusively exploited; stripped of their humanity, tortured, bred, denied legal protection, forbidden educational instruction and religious expression.[34] Race-based analysis, at least in connection to slavery and organ commoditization, may be less persuasive than socioeconomic arguments that squarely address poverty and acknowledge the ongoing economic disparities between African Americans (and people of color in general) and Whites.

Today, market transactions involving biological materials occur daily in cities throughout the United States.[35] These transactions reach beyond color lines, involving all ethnic groups, including African Americans.[36] Although disconcerting, lives are saved and critically important research is performed.[37] Whether African Americans experience those benefits seems one of the more relevant social and legal questions to be pursued, but too often overshadowed in the controversial debate about organ commoditization and slavery.[38] Concerns about the welfare of African Americans should clearly extend beyond whether they might be compensated for donating organs, or how such funds would be spent. Claims that African Americans would only be victims in a commoditization process detract attention from the possibility that African Americans might benefit from a market-based system.[39]

1. Saving Lives

Herein are several significant distinctions between antebellum slavery and African American involvement in a contemporary compensation-based organ procurement program. The most obvious distinction being that slavery involved the living and posthumous harvesting involves cadavers. First, African American organ donors might likely save the lives of African American patients in a compensation-based program. Commentators echo the position of organ transplantation officials, suggesting over the past decade that African American organ donors are desperately needed to save the lives of other African Americans.[40] They suggest positive blood and antigen matching, criteria used in kidney transplantation, will more frequently occur in intragroup donation.[41] In other words, African Americans are critical in the fight to save the lives of African Americans. Direct beneficiaries of such a system, unlike with slavery, could be African Americans, who at present represent the most disenfranchised sufferers on the kidney transplantation waitlists because they wait longer than all other patients and experience the highest rate of death while on the list.[42]

Slavery, by contrast, was not a life-saving system, at least not for African Americans. Noncompensated African American labor improved the quality of life for wealthy, White plantation owners, but did not ease a medical condition or actually save their lives.[43] Indeed, even if slavery were an expedient medical system explicitly designed to save the lives of Whites, it would not have been *pareto superior*, because one group gained as the other party was made worse off. A medicine-based slave system, similar to James Marion Sims' experimentations on slave women,[44] would have violated ethical, medical, and legal principles; informed consent and decision making are standard values and expectations in transparent medical transactions. Adherence to such principles and values are necessary in a regulated organ market. This distinction is significant. Instead, slavery was purely exploitative, motivated by economic expediency, and justified through racism.[45] The economic gains from slavery were intended for Whites and did not flow to African Americans, including the Black offspring of wealthy White plantation owners.[46] Legally, African American children of White farmers were disinherited according to state laws; they could only assume the legal and therefore social status of their slave mothers.[47]

Indeed, slavery was a compulsory system that largely benefited White Americans, although some Black farmers owned slaves or hired indentured servants.[48] The number of Black farmers with slaves was negligible in comparison to their White counterparts. However, had American slavery benefited more than the relatively few African Americans, would it somehow have been less pernicious and more in line with proposals for compensation-based organ donation? Arguably not, as such a system would be financially exploitative by failing to provide compensation for the labor exchange.

2. Compensation

A second distinction between slavery and organ alienation is that slavery failed to provide compensation to African Americans. This distinction, although obvious, is crucial to our understanding of the relative legal and economic differences between the two institutions (slavery and organ incentives). Slavery is, as we know it to have been, and by its very definition, a system of uncompensated economic exploitation.[49] Indeed, the shameful and exploitative legacy of slavery is in part due to African Americans being dispossessed of legal and economic rights. These rights would have included the right to contract, bargain for exchanges, enter legal agreements, own property, be compensated, and pursue legal remedies when contracts or other agreements were breached. African Americans lacked legal standing during America's antebellum era and therefore were barred from bringing causes of action against those responsible for their economic injuries. Without the right to engage in the marketplace, African Americans were effectively denied the opportunity to pursue the "American dream" of economic independence and growth. That some commentators might treat these distinctions as trivial is unfortunate and unwise, as later possession of such rights transformed the collective status of African Americans from enslavement to citizenship.[50] Economic freedom and the ability to engage in the marketplace is the cornerstone of American liberty.[51]

Therefore, in part, slavery's inhumanity could be attributed not only to extreme economic subordination, but also to the undignified legal and social status in which African Americans were then cast to justify noncompensation.[52] African Americans were deemed legally incompetent and intellectually inferior, therefore ill equipped (or unworthy) to possess economic rights.[53] In one of the most respected studies about slavery, John Blassingame shares how masters first attempted to demonstrate their moral and intellectual superiority over Blacks:

Many masters tried first to demonstrate their own authority over the slave and then the superiority of all Whites over Blacks. They continually told the slave he was unfit for freedom, that every slave who attempted to escape was captured and sold further South, and that the Black man must conform to the White man's every wish. The penalties for nonconformity were severe; the lessons uniformly pointed to one idea: the slave was a thing to be used by the "superior" race.[54]

It was perhaps considered wasteful to permit African Americans to receive compensation for labor, after all, according to social reasoning at the time, Blacks were inherently infantile and irresponsible.[55] This perpetual childlike status was a significant moral, social, and legal indignity to African Americans. Clearly, if African Americans were compensated for volunteering their organs to save the lives of others, such transactions would be far different from antebellum slavery, which was marked by forced labor, economic exploitation, and a lack of bargaining power.

3. Voluntary Participation

Third, slavery was compulsory for African Americans in slave states. It was not a system wherein African Americans could opt out by choice or whim.[56] Instead, African Americans were forced participants, unable to avoid the chattel system. By contrast, participation in organ donation is not compulsory, nor would a compensation-based system require African Americans to participate.[57] African Americans could choose not to engage in the marketplace. Of course, such a system provides an incentive for participation. Critics charge that such incentives are inherently coercive and would necessarily pressure African Americans to alienate body parts. Indeed, the goal of organ compensation, just as with other forms of tissue alienation, is to interest potential donors to participate in the organ donation process and African Americans are critically needed. However, African Americans would not be the exclusive targets of such a system, as incentives might appeal to Whites, Asians, Latinos, and others.

4. Physicality

Fourth, over the past two centuries, scholars have documented the physically abusive nature of slavery in the United States.[58] In one of the more famous exegeses, Thomas Bacon reminds slaves that disobedience to masters is equal to sinning against God:

Poor creatures! You little consider, when you are vile and neglectful of your master's business, – when you steal, and waste, and hurt any of their substance – when you are saucy and impudent – when you are telling them lies, and deceiving them . . . [that] what faults you are guilty of towards your masters and mistresses, are faults done against God himself, who hat set your masters and mistresses over you in His own stead, and expects that you will do for them just as you would do for Him. And pray do not think that I want to deceive you when I tell you that your masters and mistresses are God's Overseers, and that, if you are faulty towards them, God himself will punish you severely for it in the next world . . . for God himself hath declared the same.[59]

Whippings were not uncommon, and were perhaps best illuminated in the famous Civil War era photograph of Gordon, the slave who escaped from slavery to join the ranks of soldiers fighting on behalf of the Union. On his back the gruesome story of slavery was told through mazelike lacerations that had been scarred over by keloids.[60] The physical toll of slavery was experienced not only through excessive manual labor, but also through punishment in the form of whippings for those considered insubordinate.[61] Attempts to avoid enslavement often resulted in torture, disfigurement, and abuse.[62] Thus, the very physicality of slavery distinguishes it from market-based procurement proposals. African Americans would not be threatened with risk of bodily injury were they to decline participation in the organ procurement process, as was the harsh reality in the slave system. Moreover, the health of African Americans was not protected nor safeguarded by the law during the antebellum era.

Finally, whereas America has clearly been in a struggle to overcome a past scarred by racism, legal as well as social progress has been made.

Admittedly, some of this progress has been less than encouraging or so long overdue that the patience of our nation has been tested. For example, African Americans continue to disproportionately experience poverty,[63] inequitable schooling,[64] barriers to equitable healthcare,[65] and inadequate housing.[66] The challenge to overcome these plights deserves the highest attention. However, scholars should be careful not to conflate those incredibly legitimate and urgent concerns with African American participation in a compensation-based organ procurement program.[67] In fact, African American participation could help reduce one of the barriers in healthcare – death due to organ failure. Ironically, denying African Americans the opportunity to participate in an active, transparent marketplace would likely be justified through outdated rationales that hearken back to slavery and perpetuate stereotypes, most notably that African Americans would irresponsibly manage potentially large sums of money. Such notions also inflate the possible compensation donors might receive.

Both in concept and in practice, compensation for tissues commonly occurs in the United States.[68] Participants are solicited in newspaper advertisements, targeted by private contractors and third parties, as well as by agencies and universities. The industry in tissue exchanges might possibly be larger than what most Americans imagine. Of course, this raises the question of whether financial compensation should ever be involved with the body or where lines should be drawn.

CONCLUSION

Less frequently explored, but absolutely central to the present debate on organ sales, are the issues involving race and culture. Ironically, race, although ubiquitous in other discourses, has been conspicuously absent from the dialogue on organ commodification, with the exception of observations comparing organ sales to African American enslavement in the United States. Arguments suggesting that lifting the federal ban on organ sales is an act paramount to endorsing a system of neo-millennial slavery are political lightning rods. Potentially, sensational commentaries could reduce intelligent debates about organ procurement to rhetoric, while masking critical issues and avoiding relevant questions. For example, could organ sales benefit African

Americans? How would African Americans participate in a market regime? Would transfers be limited to postmortem harvests? How would such a system be regulated? Are all market schemes necessarily coercive to African Americans? Could equitable, noncoercive transfers result from informed decision making? What protocols might be necessary to ensure informed decision making?

Efforts to rely exclusively on gratuitous transfers veil the existence of a thriving, current market in human tissues and organs. The consequences of ignoring the possible advantages of organ sales for curing organ deficits and thereby enhancing the health opportunities for all Americans, especially Black Americans, are extreme. Although organ donating by African Americans has increased in recent years, demand dramatically exceeds supply. High blood pressure, diabetes, hypertension, and stress, conditions disproportionately affecting African Americans, contribute to widespread organ failure. A disproportionate number of these patients are Black Americans desperately in need of kidney transplantation. They are caught in a strange confluence of inadequate supply and overwhelming demand, as Black Americans account for more than one-third of patients on kidney waitlists. African Americans, however, wait longer than all other racial and ethnic groups while on the transplantation list. Moreover, they experience the highest rates of death on kidney transplantation lists. Some commentators attribute these dramatic disparities to the antigen distribution matching requirement, which is deemed essential and ascribed critical importance in the rationing process.[69] The unfortunate result has only recently been acknowledged as inequitable and biologically disadvantaging African Americans.[70] Although some scholars criticize the organ distribution system in the United States, calling it illogical and even pernicious, because of its inequitable results in the health care of African Americans, few have recognized the role and potential advantages of a market analysis to address the problem.

Black patients will continue to experience the longest waits while on America's transplantation waitlists until more organs become available for transplantation. Because they suffer the highest rate of mortality while on the transplantation waitlists this issue deserves urgent address.

Finally, other health, political, and legal risks will undoubtedly continue to emerge as desperate Americans in greater numbers seek life-saving transplantations outside the United States from death row inmates and others in India, China, and Brazil, and follow-up care from their local doctors and hospitals.

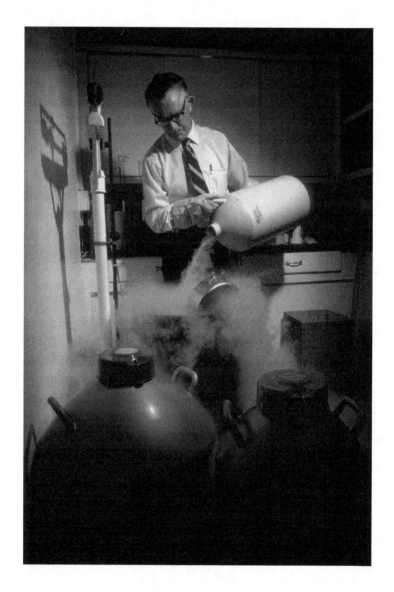

Selling genius sperm. Dr. Robert Graham, founder of the Genius Sperm Bank in San Diego pouring liquid nitrogen into tanks that contain frozen sperm. (Photo by Paul Harris/Liaison)

10 Conclusion

Competent systems are not lacking in controversy or bias.[1] Controversies as well as unattractive trade-offs are the natural outgrowths of change. Each procurement option discussed in this book is burdened by an undesirable aspect. This is a reality from which we cannot hide. Altruism too, when scrutinized, reveals unattractive flaws. Yet, change is often justified by a compelling government interest in the safety and health of its citizenry or even to correct past harmful behavior. For example, presumed consent, which permits involuntary donations absent refusal, requires forgoing autonomy, consent, privacy, and possibly accepting or mildly tolerating the possibility that religious freedom may be violated.

Presumed consent statutes were passed in 29 states, permitting cornea removal without donor or family consent so long as families have not objected. Naturally, the irony is that the dead cannot raise an objection, nor would a person know to whom he or she should object. Most Americans are unaware of these legislative procurement tools and strategies. Most statutes require a reasonable effort to contact families. These efforts are not enforced and may in fact be more delusive than real as homeless people, the poor, and those more likely to be uninformed participants may not have phones – the method most often used to contact relatives.

However, an adequate supply of organs could be harvested through that institutional choice. Presumed consent, as an institutional choice, would not be difficult to implement; however, it would pose significant legal, moral, religious, and social challenges. It is one of the more difficult choices because it compromises the most intimate spheres of our relationship with the state, not to mention our bodies. For these reasons and more, presumed consent is a burdened alternative. The risks are very high in comparison to what might be gained for the individual or her family supplying the organ. Indeed, a policy that requires a waiver of constitutional rights in order to save the life of others is a burdened choice. Would opting out really work? Because timing is critically important to organ and tissue harvesting, the necessity to transplant in a timely manner might supercede waiting for a possible objection, particularly with the most viable tissues requiring harvesting within 3 to 6 hours after death. James Nelson's commentary on presumed consent and opt-out measures illuminates important ethical concerns:

A simple reliance on our moral intuitions isn't enough. As the history of medical research in the nineteenth and even twentieth century reveals, we have been more than willing to subject those who were "clearly less valuable" to the rigors of research – only then, the ones who were obviously less valuable were Jewish, or people of color. Our gut instincts simply aren't good enough as reliable moral guides when we're dealing with those whom we've pushed to the margin of moral discourse.[2]

Trade-offs are also obvious in a cadaveric, market-based approach. The potential for pressure and conflicts within families over appropriate treatment of the dead may become more apparent. In addition, acknowledging financial interests or incentives associated with the body requires social adaptation. In both cases, however, these very pressures already exist although we may be more reluctant to acknowledge them as such. The constraints on the size of an altruistic market are obvious and more dramatic than comparable constraints on the size of the posthumous market.[3] However, markets are not boundless nor should we aim for them to operate as such. The desire for markets to replace altruism would be misplaced and irresponsive to the needs of indigent patients. By comparison, although the purchase of alcohol and tobacco are permissible and within the regulation of state and federal law, constraints are nevertheless placed on the age at which one may purchase. Thus, whereas a market in cadaveric organs could significantly alleviate the demand that depletes the altruism pool, it should not exist absent restraints, regulation, and monitoring. With such controls in place, markets reduce reliance on altruism and allow greater independence and expedience for the patient and incentive for the potential donor to participate.

When compared, both the cadaveric market and nonconsensual tak-ings promise significant supply, but with different moral, social, and legal risks. For example, whereas we might accept controversy and discontent as by-products of new systems, we may not be willing to sacrifice fundamental rights for greater access to organs. Both institu-tional options involve posthumous harvesting. Presumed consent has been characterized as a clandestine practice. Family members are often uninformed until after the harvesting has occurred. Tissues may be harvested absent consent, and sometimes after family refusal as in the *Brotherton v. Cleveland* case.[4] Tissues are sometimes sold with organ procurement organizations, tissue banks, and private commercial firms benefiting. Furthermore, grave racial disparities have been reported and documented in presumed consent transfers. On balance, markets are morally troubling to different groups, including some clergy, feminist legal theorists, and others. Feminist legal theorists express discontent over conceptualizing the body as property.[5] Fears suggesting that organ commodification resembles slavery appear in both popular and medi-cal literature. However, groups are unaware or unwilling to admit that altruism disguises the reality that trading already occurs in the body, sometimes between altruistic organizations and private for-profit com-panies. A balance must be struck between what we demand – life-saving technology and organs – and the means of achieving or supplying those goals.

Those mainly concerned about the most vulnerable are least aware of an existent market in human tissues. Julia Mahoney addresses this issue, observing, "The fact that human tissue is rarely advertised and is not traded on exchanges should not lead to the conclusion that com-mercial activity is absent."[6] Mahoney was nearly correct; tissue banks and biotech firms, which create new uses for human tissue, do trade on exchanges. Indeed, financial exchanges occur at each stage in the organ transplantation process, with the exception of the most crucial step: the donor providing the valued human organ.[7] The organ recipi-ent "pay[s] to receive [the] organ," procurement specialists are paid to recruit donors, organ procurement organizations are compensated for providing their services, and doctors are paid to transplant the organ.[8]

Efforts to rely exclusively on gratuitous transfers veil the existence of a thriving current market in human tissues and organs.[9] Financial exchanges occur regularly in the human biological transplantation community, involving the transfer of organs, blood, ova, sperm, and human cells for often-significant sums.[10] Except for the domestic proscription on organ sales (which seems to target individual transfers), these exchanges occur in view of the law, without clear regulation, language, or standards. For organ transfers, consumers turn to the Internet, newspapers, and sometimes clandestine organizations (and foreign governments) to purchase these human supplies, whereas biopharmaceutical companies are involved with a broad array of business partnerships, the scope of which includes collaborations with university hospitals, coroners' offices, abortion clinics, and morgues.

At the center of these exchanges is the tremendous demand for human biological materials to save the terminally ill or enhance the quality of life for transplant recipients. The fight against a pronounced tissue and organ market obscures a sad reality: Thousands of Americans unnecessarily die each year from treatable illnesses because organs are not available. Currently, there are more than 90,000 Americans in need of organs.[11] A disproportionate number of these patients are Black Americans desperately in need of kidney transplantation. They are caught in a strange confluence of inadequate supply and overwhelming demand, as Black Americans account for more than one-third of kidney waitlist patients.[12] African Americans wait longer than all other racial and ethnic groups while on the transplantation list.[13] Moreover, they experience the highest rate of death on transplantation lists.[14] These dramatic disparities can be linked to the antigen distribution matching requirement, which is deemed essential and ascribed critical importance in the rationing process.[15] The unfortunate result has only recently been acknowledged as inequitable and biologically disadvantaging African Americans.[16] Although some scholars criticize the organ distribution system in the United States, calling it illogical and even pernicious because of its inequitable results in the healthcare of African Americans, few have recognized the role and potential advantages of a cadaveric market analysis to address the problem.

The consequences of ignoring the possible advantages of cadaveric sales for curing organ deficits and thereby enhancing the health opportunities for all Americans, especially Black Americans, are extreme. Although organ donating by African Americans has increased in recent years, demand dramatically exceeds supply. High blood pressure, diabetes, hypertension, and stress, conditions disproportionately affecting African Americans, contribute to widespread organ failure. Black patients will continue to experience the longest waits while on America's transplantation waitlists until more organs become available for transplantation. Because they suffer the highest rate of mortality while on the transplantation waitlists, this issue deserves urgent address. Finally, other health, political, and legal risks will undoubtedly emerge as desperate Americans in greater numbers seek life-saving transplantations outside of the United States from death-row inmates in China and others in India, Brazil, Pakistan, and other countries. How they receive their follow-up care may indeed become a political as well as a medical issue.

Failure to acknowledge the possibility of implicit coercion in organ alienation would be irresponsible. Incentive programs are, by design, meant to lure individuals into considering options that might normally be passed over or rejected. Incentives can be viewed as tools of persuasion. This hardly means that incentives are **always** negative or that they **always** promote negative behaviors. Nor should acceptance of incentives imply that activities associated with the incentive are immoral or are unethical. For example, scholarships are incentives often used to attract the most competitive college, medical, and law school candidates by providing financial resources. The United States armed forces use incentives to attract young men and women to join the military through the use of financial and educational incentives. Physicians use incentives to recruit individuals for medical studies, which develop cures for diseases. Pharmaceutical companies likewise use incentives for drug trials. Incentives are used to attract traditionally disenfranchised students to elite universities and academic programs. Thus, not all incentives should be viewed as bad. If saving terminally ill patients is the ultimate goal in organ transplantation, there may be limited virtue in foreclosing compensation alternatives for cadaveric organ donations.

Notes

1. Nancy Scheper-Hughes, "The Organ of Last Resort," *UNESCO Courier*, July/Aug. 2001, at 51.

Preface

1. Dean Nelson and Mohammad Shehzad, *Police Arrest Kidney Thieves In Quake Zone* Times (London), October 30, 2005; available: http://www.timesonline.co.uk/article/0,2089-1849110,00.html (last searched December 22, 2005).

2. Id.

3. The terms "African American" and "Black" are used interchangeably throughout this work in order to recognize an existing international dynamic implicated through their use and so as to not overlook Black individuals who are not American.

4. *Moore v. Regents of University of California*, 499 U.S. 936 (1991).

5. *Carney v. Knollwood Cemetary Ass'n*, 514 N.E. 2d 430 (Ohio Ct. App. 1986).

6. *See, e.g., Davis v. United States Dept. of Army*, 602 F. Supp 355 (D.C. Md. 1985).

7. *See, e.g., Doodeward v. Spence*, 6 C.L.R. 406 (Australia 1908) (Although rejecting notion of property interest in a corpse, the majority articulated that because of the labor, attention, and investment in the corpse that a pecuniary interest did exist for the plaintiff).

8. *State v. Powell*, 497 So. 2d 1188 (Fla. 1986), *cert. denied*, 481 U.S. 1059 (1987) (holding parents had no property right in their son and therefore no constitutional violation had occurred when their deceased son's corneas were nonconsensually removed).

9. *See, e.g., State v. Bradbury*, 9 A.2d 657 (Me. 1939) (holding it improper to dispose of one's sister in a hot furnace; defendant was liable for breaching a common-law duty to properly dispose of a dead body).

1. Introduction

1. Quoted in Dale Russakoff, "The Heart That Didn't Die: One Evening, Mike Lucas Lay Beaten on the Ground. A Week Later, the Governor Was Saved," *The Washington Post*, Aug. 9, 1993, at B1.

2. *See* Joe Grata, "Beating Victim is Organ Donor," *Pittsburgh Post-Gazette*, June 15, 1993, at A6 (quoting Yvonne Lucas, William "Michael" Lucas' sister).

3. *See* Susan Stamberg, National Public Radio, Morning Edition, "Pennsylvania Governor Casey Recovering While in Office," Transcript #1243-14, Dec. 22, 1993 (Governor Casey in an interview).

4. Grata, *supra* note 10.

5. Russakoff, *supra* note 9.

6. *Id.*

7. *Id.*

8. *See* Russakoff, *supra* note 9.

9. *See* Grata, *supra* note 10.

10. Russakoff, *supra* note 9.

11. *See* Grata, *supra* note 10 (reporting "Monessen Police Chief John Bachinski blamed the attack on five carloads of 'gang members from Pittsburgh' and two men from Monessen who were with them").

12. *Id.* In April 1972, a White bar owner in their small town was charged with the fatal shooting of Michael's older brother Eugene Lucas, who died at 21. The "tavern owner emptied his gun into Eugene Lucas's back on a downtown street following an argument at a bar." Russakoff, *supra* note 9. The tavern owner was convicted of second-degree murder later that year. *Id.*

13. *See* Russakoff, *supra* note 9. Russakoff further describes Michael as one who "once found opportunity in Washington, D.C., but succumbed to crack cocaine, and came home to struggle free of it." *Id.*

14. Charles Dickens, *A Tale of Two Cities* (Wordsworth Editions Limited, 1999) (1859).

15. *See* Russakoff, *supra* note 9.

16. *Id.*

17. *Id.*

18. *Id.* (quoting Eric Tansmore, Michael Lucas's half-brother).

19. Sadly, Michael's nephew was the target of the drug gang. The nephew stole drugs and paraphernalia from a local dealer and although Michael was not involved, the payback was his death. *Id.*

20. *See* Russakoff, *supra* note 9. He notes:

[Casey's] transportation department built highways giving dying steel towns better links to Pittsburgh. He increased expansion grants to businesses in hard-hit regions. He and his labor secretary, Harris Wofford, beefed up services to the unemployed, and created a crisis-response team, activated when jobs were threatened. *Id.*

21. *See* Grata, *supra* note 10.

22. *See* Russakoff, *supra* note 9.

23. The officer who finally responded so happened to be "the only Black officer on the force, usually detailed on calls from the Black community." *See* Russakoff, *supra* note 9.

24. *Id.*

25. *See* Grata, *supra* note 10.

26. *See* Russakoff, *supra* note 9.

27. In 1993, according to United Network for Organ Sharing data, over 3,785 Americans were new registrants to receive hearts. *See* UNOS, *1998 Annual Report* at 258.

28. Russakoff, *supra* note 9.

29. Interview with J.D. (name withheld to protect confidentiality) Lexington, Ky. (May 4, 1998, Mar. 10, 1999, Mar. 18, 1999, and July 12, 1999).

30. Ashwini Sehgal, "The Net Transfer of Transplant Organs Across Race, Sex, and Income," Vol. 117, Issue 9 *American Journal of Medicine 670*, 673 (2004).

31. *Id.*

32. *Id.*

33. *See* United Network for Organ Sharing, *Fact Sheet*, at http://www.unos.org. UNOS is an incorporated, independent, nonprofit organization, which contracts with the federal government to develop policy, monitor, and oversee the Organ Procurement and Transplantation Network (OPTN). OPTN emanated from congressional enactment of the National Organ Transplantation Act, which requires it to facilitate the recovery and placement of organs. UNOS originated in 1977 "as an initiative of the South-Eastern Organ Procurement Foundation" (SEOPF). SEOPF was the first organization to develop a computerized system to use medical information to match organ donors with transplant candidates. "In 1984, UNOS was formally incorporated as an independent, non-profit organization." *Id.*

34. *See, e.g.*, Laurie Kaye Abraham, *Mama Might Be Better Off Dead: The Failure of Health Care in Urban America* (1993); John P. Merrill et al., "Successful Homotransplantation of the Human Kidney Between Identical Twins," 160 *JAMA* 277 (1956); Barbara A. Noah, "Racial Disparities in the Delivery of Health Care," 35 *San Diego L. Rev.* 135, 142–47 (1998).

35. The Organ Procurement and Transplantation Network at http://www.optn.org. There are 66,805 Americans currently on the list awaiting kidneys. Of those, slightly over 23,000 are African American.

36. *Id.*

37. The Organ Procurement and Transplantation Network, at http://www.optn.org (data indicates that in 2004, 1,681 African American individuals died while awaiting new organs. In comparison, 4,105 White individuals died while awaiting new organs.).

38. *Id.*

39. Data from the Organ Procurement and Transplantation Network indicates, for example, that Whites waiting for a kidney will wait nearly 600 fewer days than their Black counterparts (based on available data from 1997–1998). Blacks awaiting a liver will wait over 300 days longer than their White counterparts; those waiting for a lung will wait over 500 days longer than their White counterparts (based on available data from 2000–2002). *Id.*

40. *Id.*

41. *See, e.g.*, Marty Rosen, "Bangladeshi Woman Dies Waiting for Liver," *New York Daily News*, Jan. 8, 1999, at 36; Denise Grady, "Tubes, Pumps and Fragile Hope Keep a Baby's Heart Beating," *New York Times*, Aug. 22, 2004, at 1; Jeff Gottlieb, "4 Hearts, 1 Loving Marriage," *Los Angeles Times*, Dec. 1, 2004, at A1; Abraham, *supra* note 42.

42. *See* United Network for Organ Sharing Website at http://www.unos.org.

43. *Id.*

44. *Id.* Charts tallying the total number of candidates on waitlists are available at http://www.unos.org.

45. *See, e.g., 2004 Annual Report of the U.S. Organ Procurement and Transplantation Network and the Scientific Registry of Transplant Recipients*: Transplant Data 1994–2003. Department of Health and Human Services, Health Resources and Services Administration, Healthcare Systems Bureau, Division of Transplantation (2004). This data reflects the total number of candidates who entered the kidney waitlists in the United States. The figure may seem slightly higher than snapshot figures, which represent those taken off lists or those who have died.

46. *See, e.g.*, The Uniform Anatomical Gift Act (1968); *rev.* 1986; currently under reconsideration and amendment.

47. *See* 42 U.S.C. §274(e). NOTA prohibits the sale of any human organ for transplantation. The act specifies, however, that valuable consideration does not include reasonable payments that are associated with the removal, transportation, implantation, processing, preservation, quality control, or storage of a human organ or the reasonable expenses incurred by the donor in connection with the donation.

48. *See Richard Titmuss, The Gift Relationship: From Human Blood to Social Policy* (Ann Oakley & John Ashton, eds., New Press 1997) (1971).

49. *Id* at 167, 168–71.

50. *Id.* at 166.

51. My intention is not to dismiss a very valid point that underscores the Titmuss thesis involving the human bond resulting from non–self-interested giving in blood donation. Rather, by illuminating the limitations in his analysis, which are based in some part on racial characteristics and flaws of blood donors, the hope is that we can encourage a more complete dialog.

52. Titmuss found that "proportionately more blood [was] being supplied by the poor, the unskilled, the unemployed, Negroes, and other low income groups." *Id.* at 172.

53. *See, e.g.*, George Boehmer, "German Blood Crisis Worries U.S. Troops," *Chicago Sun-Times*, Nov. 7, 1993, at 43; Kieran Healy, "The Emergence of HIV in the U.S. Blood Supply: Organizations, Obligations, and the Management of Uncertainty," 28 *Theory and Society 529* (1999); Howard Schneider, "Canada Rebukes Red Cross: Agency Loses Authority over Nation's Blood Supply in Wake of 1980s HIV, Hepatitis Infections," *Austin American-Statesman* (Texas), Sept. 12, 1996, at A6; "Test Set for AIDS antibodies in Recipients of Tainted Blood," *The New York Times*, Nov. 5, 1987, at A30.

54. *See, e.g.*, Telephone interview with Joel D. Newman, Communication Liaison, United Network for Organ Sharing (July 7, 2005) (Mr. Newman described an initiative that at least nine organ procurement organizations are considering; the initiative would allow kidney patients not previously on a transplant waitlist to be placed on the waitlist, backdated to the point at which their dialysis treatments began.); *OPTN/UNOS Minority Affairs Committee Report*, at http://www.unos.org/members/pdfs/report_19.pdf.

55. *See, e.g.*, Neil Komesar, *Law's Limits: Rule of Law and the Supply and Demand of Rights* (2003).

56. *See generally*, Telephone interview with Jim Cohan, self-described "organ transplant coordinator" (March 30, 2004 and May 5, 2004); Scheper-Hughes, *supra* note 1.

57. *See, e.g.*, Christopher Drew, "U.S. Says 2 Chinese Offered Organs From the Executed," *The New York Times*, Feb. 24, 1998, at A1; Craig S. Smith, "Quandary in U.S. Over Use of Organs of Chinese Inmates," *The New York Times*, Nov. 11, 2001, at 1A; Greg Smith, "Human Organs Offered for Sale," *The Daily Telegraph* (Sydney, Australia), Feb. 25, 1998, at 36.

58. *See, e.g.*, Abantika Ghosh, "Organ Donation: Madness in the Method?," *The Economic Times of India*, Nov. 29, 2004; "In the City of Taj Mahal, a Major Eye Selling Racket is Busted," *Hindustan Times*, May 2, 2005; Chidanand Rajghatta, "Heart for Sale@USD100,000," *The Times of India*, Oct. 20, 2004; "Want a Kidney, Head for Pakistan, the New Organ Tourism Capital!," *Hindustan Times*, Apr. 9, 2005.

59. Abraham McLaughlin, Ilene R. Prusher, and Andrew Downie, "What is a Kidney Worth?," *Christian Science Monitor* (Boston, MA), June 9, 2004, at 1; Jim Warren, "Financial Support for Live Donors, Organ Trafficking, Stem Cell Research among Major News Events of 2004," 24(14) *Transplant News*, Dec. 31, 2004.

60. *See Sale of Human Organs in China: Hearings Before the Subcomm. on Int'l Operations and Human Rights of the House Comm. on Int'l Relations*, 107th Cong. (2001) [hereinafter *Hearings*] (testimony of Professor Nancy Scheper-Hughes) (testifying that "the traffic in human organs, tissues, and body parts" is extensive, occurring in China, India, Brazil, and other countries).

61. Saleh Al Jibouri and Colin Freeman, "Black Market Organ Trade is Baghdad's New Growth Industry: Cash-strapped Iraqis Driven to Sell Kidneys for as Little as $700," *Sunday Telegraph* (London), May 22, 2005, at 24.

62. *Hearings, supra* note 68 (testifying that executed Chinese prisoners supplied organs to Americans).

63. *Id.*

64. *Id.*

65. *Id.*

66. *Id.*

67. *Id.*

68. *See The New Oxford American Dictionary*, 47 (2001).

69. *See, e.g.*, Deborah L. Shelton, "Who Looks Out for the Donors?," *St. Louis Post-Dispatch* (MO), May 11, 2005, at A1 (noting that family members especially are pressured into donation when another member of their family becomes sick. The belief that individuals with two kidneys have a "spare" is becoming more common as kidney transplants become more routine.).

70. *See, e.g.*, Vanessa McCausland, "Bigger Better Babies by Design," *Daily Telegraph* (Sydney, Australia), June 17, 2005, at 2 (describing a family that "created" a new child in order to cure an older sibling's serious illness).

71. *See* Laura A. Siminoff and Kata Chillag, "The Fallacy of the 'Gift of Life'," 29 *The Hastings Report 34* (1999).

72. *See, e.g.*, Cara Cheyette, "Organ Harvests from the Legally Incompetent: An Argument Against Compelled Altruism," 41 *B.C. L. Rev.* 465, 477–78. Cheyette describes the physical and psychological traumas associated with living donations from children, noting that they were depressed, anxious, fearful of needles, and withdrawn.

73. *Id.*

74. *See 2003 Annual Report*; OPTN/SRTR data as of August 1, 2003. In the sibling pool, both full and half siblings are included.

75. *Hart v. Brown*, 289 A.2d 386 (Conn. Super. Ct. 1972) (ruling that the parents of twin girls, one of whom required a kidney transplant, could consent to the removal of a kidney from the healthy twin and donate it to the twin in need).

76. *See, e.g.*, Michael T. Morley, "Proxy Consent to Organ Donation by Incompetents," 111 *Yale L.J.* 1215 (2002); Sally Ann Stewart, "Toddler May be Sister's Lifesaver," *USA Today*, June 4, 1991, at 3A (the Ayala family decided to conceive another child in order for that child to become a donor for their older daughter who was dying of leukemia).

77. See notes accompanying Chapter 3.

78. Timothy B. Wheeler, "Miracle Molecule," *Baltimore Sun* (MD), Feb. 24, 2003, at 8A.

79. *Id.*

80. The Organ Procurement and Transplantation Network, *supra* note 46 (in 2004, 1,681 African American individuals died while awaiting new organs, whereas 4,105 White individuals died while awaiting new organs).

81. *See* U.S. Department of Justice, "UIC Medical Center Pays $2 Million to United States and State of Illinois to Settle Liver Transplant Fraud Suit," November 17, 2003, 1 (Press Brief).

82. *Id.*

83. *Id.* at 3.

84. *Id.*

85. *Id.*

86. *Id.* at 2.

87. *See* Telephone interview with Joel Newman, (July 7, 2005); Telephone interview with Jack Lynch (July 7, 2005).

88. U.S. Department of Justice, *supra* note 89 at 3.

89. The cornea is the outermost layer of the eye and is described as a "highly organized group of cells and proteins." The cornea both protects the eye from foreign objects and focuses the entry of light into the eye. National Eye Institute, "Facts About the Cornea and Corneal Disease," at http://www.nei.nih.gov/health.

90. Michele Goodwin, "Commerce in Cadavers is an Open Secret," *Los Angeles Times*, March 11, 2004, at B15.

91. For an example of a presumed consent or "medical examiner" or "legislative consent" statute, see Maryland Statute § 4-509.1 "When Chief Medical Examiner or his Deputy or Assistant May Provide Cornea for Transplant". *Md. Code Ann. Est. & Trusts* § 4-509 (1998).

92. *See, e.g., Md. Code Ann. Health-Gen.* § 5-309 (1999). The Maryland statute requires that a medical examiner must investigate deaths that occurred by violence, suicide, or casualty.

93. *See* Goodwin, *supra* note 98.

94. *See* Arthur Caplan, *"Am I My Brother's Keeper?,"* 125 (1997).

95. *See, e.g., Newman v. Sathyavagls-waran*, 287 F.3d 786 (9th Cir., 2002) (holding that the parents had exclusive and legitimate claims of entitlement to possess, control, dispose, and prevent the violation of corneas and other parts of the bodies of their deceased children); *Brotherton v. Cleveland*, 173 F.3d 552 (6th Cir., 1999) (holding that neither the Eye Bank Association nor the Coroner were acting as agents of the state and, therefore, were not entitled to Eleventh Amendment Immunity); *Whaley v. County of Tuscola*, 58 F.3d 1111, (6th Cir., 1995) (holding that the survivors had a constitutionally protected property interest in the bodies of the deceased relatives).

96. See Michele Goodwin, "Deconstructing Legislative Consent Law: Organ Taking, Racial Profiling, & Distributive Justice," 6 *Va. J.L. &. Tech.* 2 (2001).

97. *See Id.* at 27.

98. In an interview with Doyce Williams, Executive Director of the Alabama Eye Bank, he expressed his great support for presumed consent legislation. Mr. Williams asserted that legislative consent had a very positive influence on the number of corneas that were

made available for transplantation. Interview with Doyce Williams, Executive Director, Alabama Eye Bank (Feb. 23, 2000, on file with author). *See also*, Goodwin, *supra* note 98; Ralph Frammolino, "Harvest of Corneas at Morgue Questioned," *Los Angeles Times*, Nov. 2, 1997, at A1.

99. *See* interview with Doyce Williams, *supra* note 106.

100. *See* Frammolino, *supra* note 106.

101. *Id.*

102. *Id.* The Doheny Eye & Tissue Transplant Bank paid more than one million dollars over a 5-year period (1992–1997) to the Los Angeles County coroner's office. They "harvested without the permission or knowledge of the families of the dead," according to the *Times* investigation. Doheny's "markup" was more than 1,200% of the purchase price – or gift provided to the coroner's office, which by even industry standards was higher than usual.

103. *See, e.g.* Ralph Frammolino, "L.A. Coroner Alters Policy on Corneas," *Los Angeles Times*, Nov. 4, 1997, at A1. In highlighting the controversy involving cornea transplantation and presumed consent legislation, Frammolino draws our attention to the potential for abuse and racial discrimination in this process.

104. According to a Website run by the United States Department of Health and Human Services, OPOs "coordinate organ procurement" in a given geographical area, "evaluate potential donors," and "preserve organs and arrange for their distribution" at http://www.organdonor.gov.

105. *See* Appendix A for chart of biotechnological firms engaged in these processes that trade publicly.

106. *See* Jim Warren, "UCLA Suspends Willed Body Program Following Charges Body Parts Were Sold Illegally," *Transplant News*, March 29, 2004; Amy Ling, "Recent Developments in Health Law: UCLA Willed Body Program Comes under Scrutiny as Companies Sued for the Purchase of Body Parts," 32 *J.L. Med. & Ethics 532* (2004).

107. *Id.*

108. *See, e.g.*, "UCLA Apologizes for Apparent Sale of Body Parts: Donor Families Sue School," March 8, 2004, at http://www.CNN.com (last searched July 13, 2005).

109. *See, e.g.*, Jeffrey Kluger et al., "The Body Snatchers," *Time*, March 22, 2004, at 49.

110. *Id.*

111. *See, e.g., University of Texas Medical Branch v. Harrison*, No. 14-02-01276-CV, 2003 Tex. App. LEXIS 6768 (Houston [14th Dist.] Aug. 7, 2003) (in which the University of Texas is alleged to have sold bodies to private companies and failed to return the ashes to the appropriate family members).

112. The FDA does not currently identify which tissue banks are for-profit enterprises, and which are nonprofit enterprises. Telephone interview with Chris Middendorf, (Consumer Safety Officer), Food and Drug Administration (July 14, 2005); Jerome Groopman, "Do You Know Where that Cartilage Came From?," *New York Times*, May 17, 2003, at A17 (indicating that even after a young man died as a result of an infection from a knee surgery in which he received tissue from a cadaver, the Food and Drug Administration only investigated 100 or so tissue banks. That inspection yielded results that indicate safety procedures are not always followed.).

113. *See, e.g.*, "Donated Bodies Used in Land Mine Tests," *New York Times*, March 11, 2004, at A1.

114. *See, e.g.*, David B. Ottaway & Warren Brown, "From Life Saver to Fatal Threat," *The Washington Post*, June 1, 1997, at A01; Alice Fleury Kearns, "Better to Lay It Out on the Table than Do It Behind the Curtain," 13 *J. Contemp. Health L. & Pol'y 581* (1997).

115. Centers for Disease Control and Prevention, 50:48 *Morbidity and Mortality Weekly Report* 1077, 1081 (Dec. 7, 2001), at http://www.cdc.gov/mmwr/PDF/wk/mm5048.pdf ("In the United States, approximately 50,000 knee surgeries are performed each year for repairing...ACL injuries. Tissue allografts [from cadavers] frequently are used....").

116. *See, e.g.*, Ronald Bailey, "Warning: Bioethics May Be Hazardous to Your Health," 31 *Reason 24*, 31 (Aug.–Sept. 1999) (maintaining the importance of patient choice as central to the debate on altruism versus commoditization); Stephen Ceccoli, "Open Purse to Boost Organ Donations," *Commercial Appeal* (Memphis, TN), July 12, 2002, at B5 (discussing why altruism as the exclusive basis for organ procurement does not work). Some commentators have suggested that alternative procurement strategies should be pursued. *See, e.g.*, Mark F. Anderson, "The Future of Organ Transplantation: From Where Will New Donors Come, to Whom Will Their Organs Go?," 5 *Health Matrix* 249, 279 (1995) (highlighting the discrepancy between African American donors and recipients in organ transplantation); Lori B. Andrews, "Is There a Right to Clone? Constitutional Challenges to Bans on Human Cloning," 11 *Harv. J.L. & Tech.* 643, 648 (1998) (discussing cloning as a procurement strategy); Phyllis Coleman, "Brother Can You Spare a Liver?" Five Ways to Increase Organ Donation, 31 *Val. U.L. Rev.* 1, 19–20 (1996) (offering conscription as a procurement alternative); Michele Goodwin, *supra* note 104 (comparatively analyzing presumed consent procurement measures with corneas to that proposed by some lawmakers with organs, suggesting that significant harms could result); J. Steven Justice, "Personhood and Death – The Proper Treatment of Anencephalic Organ Donors Under The Law". T.A.C.P., 62 *U. Cin. L. Rev.* 1227 (1994) (critiquing and analyzing the standard of care owed to anencephalic organ donors); Christian Williams, Note, "Combating the Problems of Human Rights Abuses and Inadequate Supply Through Presumed Donative Consent," 26 *Case W. Res. J. Int'l L.* 315 (1994) (discussing the limitations of presumed consent models).

117. This new technology would allow the body to "regrow" organs rather than have a foreign organ transplanted into the body.

118. *See, e.g.*, Jack M. Kress, "Xenotransplantation: Ethics and Economics," 53 *Food Drug L.J. 353* (1998). Kress discusses xenotransplantation, noting that:

> For DHHS, "xenotransplantation" refers to any procedure that involves the use of live cells, tissues, or organs from a nonhuman animal source, that are injected, implanted, or transplanted into a human being. *Id.* at 354.

119. *See* Coleman, *supra* note 124, at 18 (commenting that "presumed consent represents a more extreme proposal than required request"); Linda Fentiman, "Organ Donation as National Service: A Proposed Federal Organ Donation Law," 27 *Suffolk U.L. Rev.* 1593, 1598–99 (proposing a presumed consent system that would avoid delay); James Lindemann Nelson, "Transplantation Through a Glass Darkly," 22:5 *Hastings Center Rep.* 6 (Sept.–Oct. 1992); Mackenzie Carpenter, "Presumed Donor Bill Aired," *Pittsburgh Post-Gazette*, July 14, 1993, at A10 (raising questions about the constitutionality of proposed presumed consent measures); Elliot Pinsley, "Routine Donation of Organs Pushed: Ethics Group Seeks 'Presumed Consent,'" *Record*, Dec. 22, 1992, at A1 (noting fear among Orthodox Jews that presumed consent measures would be problematic and "that a government bureaucracy cannot be trusted to maintain proper records"). *See generally* Goodwin, *supra* note 104.

120. *See, e.g.*, Goodwin, *supra* note 104; Pinsley, *supra* note 127.

121. *See, e.g.*, Gloria J. Banks, "Legal and Ethical Safeguards: Protection of Society's Most Vulnerable Participants in a Commercialized Organ Transplantation System," 21 *Am. J.L. & Med.* 45 (1995) (analyzing various market approaches, including from living providers, a futures market for posthumous collection, a combined donation/market approach, and a voucher system); Michael B. Gill & Robert M. Sade, "Paying for Kidneys: The Case Against Prohibition," 12 *Kennedy Inst. Ethics J.* 17 (2002) (proposing a market system controlled by public-interest agencies); Radhika Rao, "Property, Privacy,

and the Human Body," 80 *B.U.L. Rev. 359* (2000) (exploring human body "property" in applicable laws); Gregory S. Crespi, "Overcoming the Legal Obstacles to the Creation of a Futures Market in Bodily Organs," 55 *Ohio St. L.J. 1* (1994) (suggesting that alternatives to altruism might decrease the number of avoidable deaths each year).

122. *See, e.g.,* 42 U.S.C. § 274(e) (2000).

123. *See* Larry Rohter, "Tracking the Sale of a Kidney on a Path of Poverty and Hope," *N.Y. Times,* May 23, 2004, at A1 (documenting the purchase of a Brazilian man's kidney by a 48-year-old Brooklyn woman).

124. *See, e.g.,* The Organ Procurement and Transplantation Network, *supra* note 46.

125. Jonathan Kahn, "Controlling Identity: Plessy, Privacy, and Racial Defamation," 54 *DePaul L.Rev. 755,* 758 (2005).

126. *Id.*

127. *See, e.g., Wright v. Gray,* 2 S.C.L. 464 (1802) (where a master was compensated for the value of a slave that was killed while riding the defendant's horse).

128. *See, e.g.,* Alexander Glennie, *Sermons Preached on Plantations to Congregations of Negroes* (1844); J. M. Balkin, "Group Conflict and the Constitution: Race, Sexuality, and Religion: The Constitution of Status," 106 *Yale L.J.* 2313, 2324 (1997) (arguing that "obviously, a system of subordination cannot be stable if it is too easy to exit from the criteria of subordination status. That is why biological traits can be such useful markers of cultural differentiation. The advantage of immutability lies in its guarantee of stability – it helps ensure that social hierarchy can be reproduced effectively.").

129. *See, e.g.,* Mark A. Graber, "Dred Scott as a Centrist Decision," 83 *N.C. L. Rev.* 1229, 1232 (2005) ("Southern politicians running for national office competed over who best protected slavery.").

130. Justice Taney's opinion in the Dred Scott case is informative on this point. The Chief Justice concluded that Blacks, freed or not, "had no rights Whites were bound to respect." Taney opined, "the Negro might justly and lawfully be reduced to slavery for his benefit." *See, e.g., Dred Scott v. Sandford,* 60 U.S. 393 (1856).

131. George Washington, Thomas Jefferson, and other presidents owned slaves. *See, e.g.,* Thomas Jefferson, "Notes on the State of Virginia" (1781–82), at http://etext.lib.virginia.edu/modeng/modengJ.browse.html. Jefferson espoused eugenic-like considerations in his explanation of differences between Blacks and Whites. Consider the following exegesis from Thomas Jefferson:

> [Slaves] secrete less by the kidneys, and more by the glands of the skin, which gives them a very strong and disagreeable odour... Perhaps too a difference of structure in the pulmonary apparatus, which a late ingenious experimentalist has discovered to be the principal regulator of animal heat, may have disabled them from extricating, in the act of inspiration, so much of that fluid from the outer air, or obliged them in expiration, to part with more of it. They seem to require less sleep. A black, after hard labour through the day, will be induced by the slightest amusements to sit up till midnight, or later, though knowing he must be out with the first dawn of the morning... But this may perhaps proceed from a want of forethought, which prevents their seeing a danger till it be present. When present, they do not go through it with more coolness or steadiness than the whites. They are more ardent after their female: but love seems with them to be more an eager desire, than a tender delicate mixture of sentiment and sensation. Their griefs [sic] are transient. Those numberless afflictions, which render it doubtful whether heaven has given life to us in mercy or in wrath, are less felt, and sooner forgotten with them. In general, their existence appears to participate more of sensation than reflection. *Id.* at 265.

132. Indeed, there are a number of race and property metaphors applicable to organ transplantation: colonization (invading Black bodies), reverse colonization (Black body parts entering White bodies), squatting, etc. But are these metaphors useful?

133. *See, e.g.,* Guido Calabresi, "An Introduction to Legal Thought: Four Approaches to Law and the Allocation of Body Parts," 55 *Stanford L. Rev.* 2113 (2003).

134. *See, e.g.*, Herbert Hill, "Race and the Steelworkers Union: White Privilege and Black Struggles," 32 *New Politics* (Winter 2002); James E. Jones, Jr., "The Genesis and Present Status of Affirmative Action in Employment: Economic, Legal, and Political Realities," 70 *Iowa L. Rev.* 901 (1985); James E. Jones, Jr., "'Reverse Discrimination' in Employment: Judicial Treatment of Affirmative Action Programs in the United States," 25 *How. L.J.* 217 (1982). *See also*, Lewis Wickes Hine, *Lewis Hine: Passionate Journey: Photographs 1905–1937* (Karl Steinorth, ed., 1997); Lewis Wickes Hine, *Men at Work: Photographic Studies of Modern Men and Machines* (1977).

135. *See, e.g.*, E. Franklin Frazier, *The Negro in the United States* (1957); Winthrop Jordann, *White Over Black* (1968); Franz Fanon, *Black Skin, White Masks* (1967).

136. *See, e.g.*, Amii Larkin Barnard, "The Application of Critical Race Feminism to the Anti-Lynching Movement: Black Women's Fight Against Race and Gender Ideology," 3 *UCLA Women's L.J.* 1, (discussing the work of Ida B. Wells); Mary Wollstonecraft, *Vindication of the Rights of Women* (1792).

137. *See, e.g.*, Ruquaiijah A. Yearby, "Racial Disparities in Nursing Homes: Building on a Corrupted Foundation of Inequality," *DePaul J. Health Care L.* (forthcoming in 2006); Ruquaiijah A. Yearby, "Civil Rights in Nursing Homes: The Unfilled Promise of Equal Quality," *Loy. Consumer L. Rev.* (forthcoming in 2006); Ruquaiijah A. Yearby & Matt Murer, "Medicare's New Underclass," *RT Imaging*, Vol. 1d, R. 13 (July 1999).

138. *See, e.g.*, David B. Cruz, "Disestablishing Sex and Gender," 90 *Cal. L. Rev.* 997 (2002); David B. Cruz, "The New "Marital Property": Civil Marriage and the Right to Exclude?," 30 *Cap. U.L. Rev.* 279 (2001); David B. Cruz, "'Just Don't Call it Marriage': The First Amendment and Marriage as an Expressive Resource," 74 S.*Cal. L. Rev.* 925 (2001); Pamela D. Bridgewater, "Reproductive Freedom as Civil Freedom," 3 J. *Gender Race & Just.* 401 (2000); Pamela D. Bridgewater, "Connectedness and Closeted Ques-

tions," 11 *Wisc. Women's L.J.* 351 (1997); Adele M. Morrison, "Queering Domestic Violence to "Straighten Out" Criminal Law," 13 *S. Cal. Rev. L. & Women's Stud. 81* (2003); Kenji Yoshino, "The Epistemic Contract of Bisexual Erasure," 52 *Stan. L. Rev.* 353 (2000); Kenji Yoshino, "Assimilationist Bias in Equal Protection," 108 *Yale L.J.* 485 (1998); Kenji Yoshino, "Suspect Symbols: The Literary Argument for Heightened Scrutiny for Gays," 96 *Colum. L. Rev.* 1753 (1996).

Part I. Understanding the Strain on Altruism

1. David E. Rosenbaum, "Senate Panel Votes Organ Transplant Policy," *N.Y. Times*, April 13, 2000, at A24 (quoting Senator Frist).

2. Institutional Supply, Demand, and Legitimacy

1. *See* Laura A. Siminoff & Kata Chillag, "The Fallacy of the 'Gift of Life,'" 29 *Hastings Center Report* 34 (1999).

2. *See Id.* Siminoff and Chillag write: "[e]ducation campaigns identifying organ donation as the gift of life were designed to make the public aware of the good that comes from transplantation and to encourage people to become donors." *Id.* at 34.

3. *Id.*

4. *See, e.g.*, Todd L. Savitt, "The Use of Blacks for Medical Experimentation and Demonstration in the Old South," XLVIII *J. of Southern History* 331 (1982).

5. *See, e.g., Hearings Before the House Appropriations Comm. Subcomm on Labor, Health and Human Services, and Education.* 105th Cong., 2d Sess. (1998) (testimony of Benjamin, F. Payton) [hereinafter *Payton Testimony*].

6. *Id. See also*, Savitt, *supra* note 5; Katherine Olukemi Bankole, "A Critical Inquiry of Enslaved African Females and the Antebellum Hospital Experience," 31 *J. of Black Studies* 517 (2001); Katherine Olukemi Bankole, *Slavery and Medicine: Enslavement and Medical Practices in Antebellum Louisiana* (1998).

7. *See* Michele Goodwin, "Deconstructing Legislative Consent Law: Organ Taking, Racial Profiling & Distributive Justice," 6 *Va. J.L. & Tech.* 2 (2001).

8. Ta-Nehisi Paul Coates & Sora Song, "Suspicious Minds," *Time Magazine*, July 4, 2005, at 36; Holly Auer, "Clinical Trials Seek More Minorities," *The Post and Courier* (Charleston, SC), Apr. 25, 2005, at 1A.

9. *See, e.g.*, Jonathan Kahn, "How a Drug Becomes "Ethnic": Law, Commerce, and the Production of Racial Categories in Medicine," 4 *Yale J. Health Pol'y, L. & Ethics* 1 (2004).

10. *See, e.g.*, Rene Bowser, "Race as a Proxy for Drug Response: The Dangers and Challenges of Ethnic Drugs," 53 *DePaul L. Rev.* 1111 (2004); Ruqaiijah Yearby, "Good Enough to Use for Research, But Not Good Enough to Benefit from the Results of that Research: Are the Clinical HIV Vaccine Trials in Africa Unjust?," 53 *DePaul L. Rev.* 1127 (2004). To be clear, the African American experience only illumes further the Native American experience with radiation studies, or the use of mentally disabled persons in other government-sponsored medical research projects.

11. *See* Savitt, *supra* note 5, at 331. Savitt writes, "[f]urther investigation into this subject indicates that southern white medical educators and researchers relied greatly on the availability of Negro patients for various purposes."

12. *See* Rebecca Sinderbrand, "A Shameful Little Secret: North Carolina Confronts Its History of Forced Sterilization," *Newsweek*, March 28, 2005, at 33. Sinderbrand describes the psychological trauma and continuing legal battle of African American women sterilized in North Carolina. For one victim, she reports:

> She soon learned that the operation had been performed by state order in North Carolina in 1968 when she was just 14, and had given birth to a baby after being raped. At the time, she'd assumed doctors were just performing a routine post-birth procedure. The sterilization-consent form had been signed by her neglect-
ful father and illiterate grandmother, who had marked her assent with an X.

See also, Paul A. Lombardo, "Taking Eugenics Seriously," 30 *Fla. St. U.L. Rev.* 191 (2003). *See* Dorothy Roberts, *Killing The Black Body: Race, Reproduction, and the Meaning of Liberty* (1997). Thousands of African American women were sterilized during the 20th century. Many were considered feeble minded or dirges to society. Postslavery African American women's once exploited reproductive abilities were of little value and rather a "social" threat. State-sponsored sterilizations occurred in more than half of the United States, again long after the Nazis' horrible regime of experimental medicine had been exposed. *See also*, Michele Goodwin, "The Black Woman in the Attic: Law, Metaphor and Literature," 30 *Rutgers L.J.* 597 (1999).

13. *See* Ralph Frammolino, "Harvest of Corneas at Morgue Questioned," Los Angeles Times, Nov. 2, 1997, at A1 (hereinafter *Frammolino, Harvest of Corneas*); Ralph Frammolino, "L.A. Coroner Alters Policy on Corneas," *Los Angeles Times*, Nov. 4, 1997, at A1.

14. *See generally, Tuskegee's Truths: Rethinking the Tuskegee Syphilis Study* (Susan M. Reverby, ed., 2000).

15. Fred D. Gray, *The Tuskegee Syphilis Study: An Insiders Account of the Shocking Medical Experiment Conducted by Government Doctors Against African American Men* (1998) (condemning the government-led program that studied the effects of untreated syphilis in Black men); James H. Jones, *Bad Blood: The Tuskegee Syphilis Experiment* (1981).

16. "The White House: Remarks by the President in Apology for Study Done in Tuskegee," *M2 Presswire*, May 19, 1997.

17. Caroline M. de Costa, "James Marion Sims: Some Speculations and a New Position," 178:16 *Medical Journal of Australia* 660 (2003).

18. Payton Testimony, *supra* note 8.

19. *Id.*

20. A strong body of literature in the field of critical race scholarship, ethnic studies, and women's studies, as well as empirical studies, document disparities and inequality. This scholarship further underscores America's race problem. *See, e.g.,* Cara A. Fauci, "Racism and Health Care in America: Legal Responses to Racial Disparities in the Allocation of Kidneys," 21 *B.C. Third World L.J.* 35, 35 (2001) (asserting that African Americans have "long been subjected to racism within the health care system"); Sidney Watson, "Race, Ethnicity and Quality of Care: Inequalities and Incentives," 27 *Am. J.L. & Med.* 203 (2001) (urging adoption of a systemic approach to reducing race-based treatment disparities that uses reporting systems and financial incentives to produce structural change); Lindsey Tanner, "Blacks' Mental Care Lags that of Whites," *Chi. Sun Times,* Mar. 13, 2002, at 33.

21. *See* Martia Graham Goodson, "Enslaved Africans and Doctors in South Carolina," 95 *JAMA* 225 (2003).

22. *Id.* at 226.

23. *Id* at 229.

24. *Id.*

25. *Id.* Three statues honor Sims' legacy, the most famous is in Central Park in New York City "where Sims achieved national and international fame as a pioneer gynecologist."

26. *See, e.g.,* J. Marion Sims, *The Story of My Life* (Da Capo Press, 1968) (1884).

27. *Id.* at 243.

28. *Id.* at 246.

29. *See McKnight v. South Carolina,* 576 S.E.2d 168 (S.C. 2003), *cert. denied,* 540 U.S. 819 (2003). Regina McKnight was convicted of homicide by child abuse when she gave birth to a child whose gestational age was estimated between 34 and 37 weeks (an age at which the child would otherwise have been viable). An autopsy revealed the presence of benzoylecgonine, a substance that indicates the presence of cocaine.

30. The Organ Donation and Recovery Improvement Act, 42 U.S.C.A. §273f-2 (2004), provides grants to hospitals and organ procurement organizations for "hospital organ donation coordinators" designed to increase the rate of organ donations in eligible hospitals.

31. Neil Komesar, *Law's Limits: The Rule of Law and the Supply and Demand of Rights* (2001).

32. *Id.* at 35 (comparing the adjudicative process to a "tiny engine" confronted by "increasing strains on both its substantive abilities and physical capacity").

33. *Id.* at 37.

34. *Id.* at 23.

35. *See, e.g., id.* at 3 (insisting that to truly understand what the law is, one "must consider both supply and demand" focusing primarily on legal rights and court-made law).

36. *See* OPTN, "Deceased Donors Recovered in the U.S. by State of OPO Headquarters," available at http://optn.org/data/annualreport.asp (reporting for donors recovered January 1, 1988, to November 30, 2002) (last visited January 3, 2003) (hereinafter *OPTN, Deceased Donors*).

37. *Id.*

38. *Id.*

39. The graph, developed using statistics from the Organ Procurement and Transplantation Network and the United Network for Organ Sharing, illustrates the number of donations over a 6-year period and the causes of death for the cadaveric donors.

40. *See* OPTN, *Deceased Donors, supra* note 37; Data for 2003 from *OPTN/SRTR 2004 Annual Report,* available at http://www.optn.org/AR2004/default.htm (last visited July 16, 2005) (hereinafter *2004 Annual Report*).

41. *Id.*

42. *Id.*

43. *Id.*

44. *Id.*

45. *Id.*

46. *Id.*

47. Consider, for example, that in organ transplantation many donors are actually family members of patients. *See, e.g.,* Michael B. Gill & Robert M. Sade, "Paying for Kidneys: The Case against Prohibition," 12.1 *Kennedy*

Institute Ethics J. 17 (2002) (suggesting that a living donor market could alleviate the strain on altruism, although not interfering with altruistic donations as family members represent the most significant class of donors).

48. See, e.g., Michael J. Lysaght, "Maintenance Dialysis Population Dynamics," 13 *J. Am. Soc. Nephrol.* S37, S37 (2002).

49. *See, e.g., McFall v. Shimp*, 10 Pa. D. & C.3d 90 (Ch. Ct. 1978) (denying injunction to force Shimp to donate bone marrow to his dying cousin in need of a bone marrow transplant though the procedure is relatively safe, but painful); S*ee also Curran v. Bosze*, 566 N.E.2d 1319 (Ill. 1990) (refusing to grant a biological father's request for an injunction to force a mother to produce her twins to undergo blood testing and possible bone marrow transplantation to save their half-brother's life).

50. *See* Gloria J. Banks, "Legal and Ethical Safeguards," 21 *Am. J.L. & Med.* 45 (1995) (suggesting a mixed altruistic and market system that would benefit the indigent).

51. *See OPTN/SRTR* 2000 *Annual Report*, at 20–21.

52. *Id.*

53. *2004 Annual Report, supra* note 41, at Table 1.1.

54. *2003 OPTN/SRTR Annual Report*, Table 1.1 (hereinafter *2003 Annual Report*).

55. *See Id.*, at Table 9.4a. Noncholestatic cirrhosis was, according to OPTN, the primary liver diagnosis in 2002. The *Annual Report* shows that the illness accounted for 57.6% of all "primary diagnosis," marking an increase from 39% in 1988.

56. According to OPTN, the distribution of primary diagnosis among kidney recipients fluctuated over the past 10 years: "The frequency of glomerular diseases decreased while renovascular and other vascular diseases increased. The percentage of retransplants also increased. Among living donor recipients, glomerular diseases decreased while hypertensive nephrosclerosis, polycystic kidneys, and vascular diseases appeared to be on the rise." *Id.*

57. *See Id.*, at Table 1.8. Lung transplants increased dramatically over the past 14 years.

For example, in 1988 there were only 33 lung transplants; however, by 2002 that number grew to 1,041. Emphysema and cystic fibrosis, the primary diagnosis for lung transplantation, increased over the past 10 years, whereas "alph-1-antitryspin deficiency and idiopathic pulmonary fibrosis decreased." *Id.*

58. *Id.*, at 10. Among heart-lung transplants, congenital disease and primary pulmonary hypertension were the two most frequent diagnoses.

59. *2004 Annual Report, supra* note 41, at Table 1.7.

60. *Id.*

61. *Id.*

62. *Id.*, at Table 2.1, 2.8.

63. Barbara A. Noah, "Racial Disparities in the Delivery of Health Care," 35 *San Diego L. Rev.* 135, 142 (1998).

64. Laurie Kaye Abraham, *Mama Might Be Better Off Dead: The Failure of Health Care in Urban America* 185–87 (1993) (detailing racial disparities found in several studies and systems).

65. *Id.*

66. *Id.*

67. *2003 Annual Report, supra* note 55, at Table 1.1., 5.1, 6.1, and 9.1 and *2004 Annual Report, supra* note 41, at Table 1.1 and Table 1.3.

68. *See* Telephone interview with Dr. Mary D. Ellison, United Network for Organ Sharing Representative (July 1999 and Aug. 17, 1999); Telephone interview with Scott Helm, United Network for Organ Sharing Spokesperson (Apr. 20, 2000) (hereinafter *Helm Interview*).

69. *See* Helm Interview, *supra* note 69.

70. *See 2004 Ann. Rep., supra* note 41, at Table 1.3 (noting that this number reflects the number of registrations and not the number of persons on the waiting list; the total number of patients is less than a 2% difference from the number of registrants).

71. *See 2003 Annual Report, supra* note 55, at Table 1.7.

72. *Id. See also* Mark F. Anderson, "The Future of Organ Transplantation: From Where Will New Donors Come, to Whom Will Their Organs Go," 5 *Health Matrix*

249, 253 (1995); Phyllis Coleman, 'Brother Can You Spare a Liver?' Five Ways to Increase Organ Donation, 31 *Val. U.L. Rev.* 1, 2–3 (1996) (stating that the number of individuals in need of organs exceeds the number of organs available); Jack M. Kress, "Xenotransplantation: Ethics and Economics," 53 *Food Drug L.J.* 353, 356 (1998) (discussing the possibility of increasing organ supply through xenotransplantation).

73. *See, e.g.*, Coleman, *supra* note 73, at 26–41 (offering several ways to address the demand for organs, including nationalization, use of pediatric donors, and market systems); David E. Jefferies, "The Body as Commodity: The Use of Markets to Cure the Organ Deficit," 5 *Ind. J. Global Legal Stud.* 621, 644–57 (1998) (proposing the use of a market-based system to alleviate the organ shortage and meet demand); Kress, *supra* note 73, at 379–81 (recommending xenotransplantation to increase organ supply); Noah, *supra* note 64, at 169–77 (offering solutions to end the racial disparities in the delivery of health care services, with attention given to organ transplantation).

74. *See* Jefferies, *supra* note 74, at 622. Jefferies highlights the widening gap in his recent article, pointing out that although a variety of systems have been proposed, and many implemented, their results have been less than positive, or as he says, "they have failed." *Id.* Failure is the one uniform characteristic shared by the various state and federal proposals and mandates. *Id.; See* Coleman, *supra* note 73, at 3 (characterizing the shortage as "severe and tragic").

75. Organ Procurement Transplant Network, "Death Removals by Ethnicity by Year: Removed from Waiting List," January 1995–April 30, 2005, at http://www.optn.org/latestData/rptData.asp (hereinafter *OPTN Death Removals*). According to the *2003 Annual Report*, there were 111,716 reported deaths on the waiting list in 2002. *2003 Annual Report, supra* note 55. That number represents an increase from the 50,944 deaths reported in 1993. *Id.* The number of patients on the waiting list during each year

also increased substantially, according to the report. *Id.* For example, in 1988 there were 27,803 people who had been on the list at any time during that year; by 1997 that figure increased to 82,749 patients who had ever been on the list during 2002. *Id.*

76. *2003 Annual Report, supra* note 55, at Table 1.7.

77. *See* Helm Interview, *supra* note 69.

78. *See* OPTN, *Death Removals, supra* note 76.

79. *Id.*

80. *Id.*

81. *See* Coleman, *supra* note 73, at 3.

82. OPTN Data by Candidate Registered by Organ.

83. Based on OPTN data as of July 17, 2005.

84. *See 2004 Annual Report, supra* note 41, at Table 5.1.

85. *Id.* The number of women on the waitlist went from 11,021 to 23,035 during the period discussed. *Id.* For men also, the waitlist increased dramatically. Note that in 1994 there were 14,806 men on the waitlist, making up 57.3% of those on the list. *Id.* Although the male-to-female ratio remained constant, the overall number of men on the waitlist increased to 31,196. *Id.*

86. *Id.*, at Table 1.5.

87. *Id.*

88. *2003 Annual Report, supra* note 55.

89. *2004 Annual Report, supra* note 41, at Table 5.1.

90. *Id.*

91. *Id.* (noting that approximately 80% of kidney registrants of color were African American).

92. *Id.*

93. *Id.*, at Table 5.2.

94. *Id.*

95. *Id.*, at Table 5.2.

96. *2003 Annual Report, supra* note 55, at 13 (noting that "[t]he same trend among racial groups was observed for those awaiting their first transplant. The median waiting time in 1995 for White registrants was 638 days, while it was 991 days for Hispanic registrants, 1,244 days for Black registrants, and 1,112 days (in 1994) for Asian registrants").

97. *2004 Annual Report, supra* note 41, at Table 5.2.

98. OPTN Data, "Organ by Waiting Time," as of July 8, 2005, at http://www.optn.org/latestData/rptData.asp.

99. *2003 Annual Report, supra* note 55, at Table 5.4c (stating that among recipients of living donor kidneys, people of color rose from 17.1% in 1993 to 18.8% in 2002).

100. Based on OPTN data as of July 8, 2005.

101. *See 2003 Annual Report, supra* note 55, at Table 9.2.

102. *Id.*

103. *See 2004 Annual Report, supra* note 41, at Table 1.3.

104. *Id.*at Table 9.3 and OPTN Death Removals, *supra* note 76.

105. *See 2003 Annual Report, supra* note 55, at Table 9.2.

106. *Id.*, at Table 9.3.

107. *Id.*, at Table 9.2.

108. *See 2004 Annual Report, supra* note 41, at Table 1.6.

109. *2003 Annual Report, supra* note 55, at Table 11.2. OPTN Data, Current U.S. Waiting List, Overall by Organ, July 8, 2005, at http://www.optn.org/latestData/rptData.asp (as of July 8, 2005, 3,134 patients were registered to receive a new heart). *See also* Helm Interview, *supra* note 69.

110. *2003 Annual Report, supra* note 55, at Table 11.2.

111. *2004 Annual Report, supra* note 41, at Table 11.1.

112. *Id.*

113. *2003 Annual Report, supra* note 55, at Table 11.3, *See also* the death rates among those on the heart waiting lists. Asians, Latinos, and Blacks have a substantially higher death rate than Whites on the Incidence Cohort on the Waiting list. *Id.* For example, Asians have a 326.2 rate per thousand compared to Whites at 132.0. *Id.* Blacks and Latinos also have substantially higher death rates than do Whites, at 189.4 and 199.6 per thousand, respectively. *Id.* The figures provided are for 2002. *Id.*

114. *Id.*

115. *See, e.g.,* Noah, *supra* note 64, at 142–47.

116. *Id.*

117. AAOTS II, Interview with D.W.

118. Chicago was an ideal site for this research. Not only is it one of the largest health-resource–rich cities in the United States, but it also serves as the national headquarters for the American Medical Association, American Hospital Association, American Pediatric Association, as well as numerous other health and medical organizations. Another advantage is its diverse population of residents who, because of housing patterns, continue to live in rather segregated ways. Thus, African Americans across economic strata live within certain zip codes and are less assimilated throughout the city.

119. Students from DePaul University College of Law assisted in the distribution of surveys.

120. AAOTS II, Interview with K.S.

121. AAOTS II, Interview Q.

122. AAOTS II, Interview with J.M.

123. AAOTS II, Interview with N.H.

124. AAOTS II, Interview with P.W.

125. AAOTSII, Interview with H.C.

126. RAVE II, Interview with K.

127. AAOTS II, Interview with M.M.

128. AAOTS II, Interview with D.W.

129. Institute of Medicine, *Unequal Treatment: Confronting Racial and Ethnic Disparities in Health Care* 74 (2003).

130. *Id.*

131. AAOTS II, Interview with U.J.

132. AAOTS II, Interview with D.J.

133. AAOTS II, Interview with N.

134. AAOTS II, Interview with J.F.

135. AAOTSII, Interview with Y.W.

136. AAOTS II, Interview with D.W. II.

137. *See* Stephen Ceccoli, "Open Purse to Boost Organ Donations," *Commercial Appeal* (Memphis, TN), July 12, 2002, at B5 (noting that half of the patients who die while waiting for the "gift" of life are of color).

138. *See generally,* Jim Warren, "Financial Support for Live Donors, Organ Trafficking, Stem Cell Research among Major News Events of 2004," 24(14) *Transplant News,* Dec. 31, 2004.

139. *See, e.g.,* Khiara M. Bridges, Note, "On the Commodification of the Black Female

Body: The Critical Implications of the Alienability of Fetal Tissue," 102 *Colum. L. Rev.* 123 (2002) (arguing that the Black body would be devalued and Black participants would be exploited if there were a fetal tissue market).

140. A proliferation of literature in the field of critical race scholarship, ethnic studies, and women's studies, as well as empirical studies, documenting disparities and inequality, further underscores America's race problem. *See, e.g.,* Fauci, *supra* note 21, at 35 (asserting that African Americans have "long been subjected to racism within the health care system"); Watson, *supra* note 21 (urging adoption of a systemic approach to reducing race-based treatment disparities that uses reporting systems and financial incentives to produce structural change); Tanner, *supra* note 21; *see also* Derrick Bell, *Faces at the Bottom of the Well: The Permanence of Racism* 7 (1992) (stating that African Americans will continue to be "disadvantaged unless whites perceive that nondiscriminatory treatment for [African Americans] will be a benefit for them"); Dorothy Roberts, *supra* note 13 (discussing the lack of reproductive freedom for African American women); Marc Mauer, *Race to Incarcerate* (1999) (exploring the reasons for high incarceration rates in the African American community); *The House that Race Built: Black Americans, U.S. Terrain* (Wahneema Lubiano ed., 1997) (providing a collection of thoughtful scholarship from leading scholars on issues of race, culture, and society); Deborah Kenn, "Institutionalized, Legal Racism: Housing Segregation and Beyond," 11 *B.U. Pub. Int. L.J.* 35, 52 (2001) (suggesting that "deep patterns" of contemporary social and economic disparities are vestiges of past racial discrimination); Maurice E.R. Munroe, "Unamerican Tail: Of Segregation and Multicultural Education," 64 *Alb. L. Rev.* 241 (2000) (discussing a confluence of discriminatory practices and consequential racial disparities, which collectively undermine aspirations for racial equality).

141. *See* Lisa Belkin, "Fairness Debated in Quick Transplant," *New York Times,* June 16, 1993, at A16 (reporting that "the organs

[Governor] Casey received came from the body of 34-year-old William Michael Lucas, who police said was savagely beaten with clubs and guns ... on the steps of his family's home"); Dale Russakoff, "The Heart That Didn't Die: One Evening, Mike Lucas Lay Beaten on the Ground. A Week Later, the Governor Was Saved," *Wash. Post,* August 9, 1993, at B1 (remarking on the irony that a young, poor Black man, "marked by every scourge of his times – violence, drugs, joblessness, racism – saved the life of the governor of Pennsylvania"); *cf.* Janet L. Dolgin, "Personhood, Discrimination, and the New Genetics," 66 *Brook. L. Rev.* 755 (2001) (discussing the potential for discriminatory repercussions resulting from "decoding the human genome"); Benjamin Mason Meier, "International Protection of Persons Undergoing Medical Experimentation: Protecting the Right of Informed Consent," 20 *Berkeley J. Int'l L.* 513 (2002) (analyzing the "right of informed consent to medical experimentation"); Frammolino, *Harvest of Corneas, supra* note 14 (questioning the mortality of the resale of corneas taken without permission).

3. Nuances, Judicial Authority, and the Legal Limits of Altruism

1. *See* Laura A. Siminoff & Kata Chillag, The Fallacy of the "Gift of Life," 29 *Hastings Center Report* 34 (1999). Siminoff and Chillag write: "[e]ducation campaigns identifying organ donation as the gift of life were designed to make the public aware of the good that comes from transplantation and to encourage people to become donors." *Id.* at 34.

2. *Id.*

3. *Id.* at 40.

4. *John Rawls, A Theory of Justice,* 28–32 (1972).

5. *See* Duncan Kennedy, *A Critique of Adjudication: Fin de Siècle 1719* (1997) (writing that the basic legal institutions, such as the Social Security system, do have an obvious altruistic basis, and are viewed as

"after-the-fact adjustments to a pre-existing legal structure that has its own, individualist, logical coherence.").

6. *See* Charles R. Beitz, *Political Theory and International Relations*, 131 (1979) (suggesting that "decision-making focuses on the requirements of justice and applies to institutions and practices (whether or not they are genuinely cooperative) in which social activity produces relative or absolute benefits that would not exist if the social activity did not take place").

7. *See* Dorothy Brown, "The Marriage Bonus/Penalty in Black and White," 65 *U. Cin. L. Rev.* 787 (1997) (arguing that African American families are more likely to pay a marriage penalty than White families because Black women tend to contribute a larger portion of their households' income than White women, which results in a more significant "penalty" for Black families); *See also* Patricia Hill Collins, "African-American Women and Economic Justice: A Preliminary Analysis of Wealth, Family, and African-American Social Class," 65 *U. Cin. L. Rev.* 825 (1997) (arguing that "criteria for 1930s Social Security programs illustrate how institutionalized racism combines with gender-specific" to undermine the purpose that utilitarian programs serve by rewarding or punishing individuals based on marital status).

8. *See* Thomas Nagel, *The Possibility of Altruism* 3, 19, 82, 88, 100, 144 (1970) (altruism arises from the human capacity to view oneself simultaneously from both the personal and the impersonal standpoints. This capacity is premised on "a recognition of the reality of other persons, and on the equivalent capacity to regard oneself as merely one individual among many") *Id.; See also* George P. Fletcher, *Loyalty: An Essay on the Morality of Relationships* 18 (1993) (arguing that altruism can be explained in communitarian terms); *See* Eric A. Posner, "Altruism, Status, and Trust in the Law of Gifts and Gratuitous Promises," 1997 Wis. L. Rev., 567, 585 (1997) (suggesting that "altruistic gifts make the beneficiary better off, because the beneficiary prefers the gift to nothing; and they

make the donor better off because the donor derives utility from the donee's increase in utility").

9. *See, e.g.,* Martha E. Ertman, "What's Wrong with a Parenthood Market," 82 *N.C.L. Rev.* 1, 18 (2003) (declaring that sperm donor anonymity "is crucial because family law often links biology to parental rights and responsibilities").

10. *See* Michele Goodwin, "Deconstructing Legislative Consent Law: Organ Taking, Racial Profiling and Distributive Justice," 6 *Va. J.L. & Tech.* 2 (2001) (critiquing the moral and legal legitimacy of "presumed consent" statutes that allow for the nonconsensual removal of tissues from cadavers and their disparate impact on communities of color).

11. *See* Siminoff & Chillag, *supra* note 1.

12. Posner, *supra* note 8, at 567 (postulating that gift-giving's social value is derived from "its role in nonlegal relationships, and therefore efforts to regulate it with the law would reduce its value").

13. *See* Andre Jacob, "On Silencing and Slicing: Presumed Consent to Post-Mortem Organ "Donation" in Diversified Societies," 11 *Tulsa J. Comp. & Int'l L.*, 239, 242 (2003) (articulating a communitarian perspective on organ giving, suggesting that when individuals die, their legacy is best served by organ donations). Jacob's perspective is grounded in communitarian thinking. Accordingly, his position that sharing "has a higher value" than bodies buried intact is not surprising. What is worthy of scrutiny, however, are the answers as to who benefits (i.e., who receives the organs) from such arrangements.

14. Anne Freud critiques altruism as the secondhand derivative of "forbidden fruits." Her skepticism about altruistic motivations comes through quite clearly. According to her, individuals vicariously identify "prohibited" instinctual impulses with another, and thereby project their desires onto the "nonself, not out of an understanding of the other's needs, but as a neurotic form of self-gratification." *See* Anne Freud, *The Ego and the Mechanisms of Defense* 125–126 (1936)

(Cecil Baines trans., International Universities Press, 1966) (challenging broad assumptions about selflessness and altruism). *But see* Posner, *supra* note 8 (suggesting that reciprocity naturally inures from altruistic processes). *See* Carl H. Fellner & Shalom H. Schwartz, "Altruism in Disrepute," 284 *New Eng. J. Med.* 582, 582 (1971).

15. *See* Julia D. Mahoney, "The Market for Human Tissue," 86 *Va. L. Rev.* 163, 175 (2000). Mahoney writes about the chains of altruism and bargaining. Although individuals are strongly pursued to be altruistic in their dispensation of body parts, those involved in the asking may be motivated by other impulses, including commercialism and greed. She warns:

> Although the initial transferors (e.g., donors of solid organs, patients who agree to provide tissue to be used in medical research) may be spurred solely by beneficence, subsequent transferors (e.g., transplant programs, pharmaceutical companies) often are not. In consequence, human tissue that enters the chain of distribution as a gift is frequently transformed into a commercial product – one that is sold, not donated, to its ultimate recipient). *Id.*

16. *See* Joseph Bankman & Thomas Griffith, "Social Welfare and the Rate Structure: A New Look at Progressive Taxation," 75 *Calif. L. Rev.* 1905, 1940 (1987) (relating the tax favorable consequences of nonprofit donations and other investments that are thought to be desirable for society and are thus encouraged by the tax code); Frederick R. Parker, et al., "Organ Procurement and Tax Policy," 2 *Hous. J. Health L. & Pol'y* 173, 175 (2002) (speaking to how financial incentives might encourage greater "altruism" in organ donation).

17. *See* Cynthia E. Garabedian, "Tax Breaks for Higher Education: Tax Policy or Tax Pandering?" 18 *Va. Tax Rev.* 217, 218 (1998) (analyzing tax schemes and their impact on education financing).

18. *See* Posner, *supra* note 8 (comparing and contrasting good altruist from the "bad," arguing that "pure" altruism is based exclusively on the care of the "other").

19. *See* "Organ Donation Miracles Come From Tragedy," at http://www.medmag.org/miracle.html.

20. Although, there are other motivating factors contributing to organ donation. For example, some scholars have suggested that payments could be capped or in the form of tax incentives. *See* Fred H. Cate, "Human Organ Transplantation: The Role of Law," 20 *Iowa J. Corp. L.* 69, 86 (1994) (arguing that compensation could be a motivator for organ donation).

21. Reg Green, "A Child's Legacy of Love," *L.A. Times*, May 15, 2002, Part 5, at 2. *See* Jennifer M. Krueger, "Life Coming Bravely Out of Death: Organ Donation Legislation Across European Countries," 18 *Wis. Int'l L.J.* 321, 322 (2000) (recalling that "Nicholas was well-traveled for a boy of seven. He had seen the sights of Canada, the United States and several European countries, but Italy would be his greatest adventure yet, or so he thought. The Green family was traveling to their next destination on September 29, 1994, when tragedy stuck: a car of bandits drove up next to their car and fired several shots. Sadly, one of those bullets struck Nicholas. The bullet became lodged deep in Nicholas' brain stem. Doctors were helpless. Two days later, Nicholas, once full of life and energy, was declared brain dead.").

22. *See* The Nicholas Effect, at http://www.nicholasgreen.org/chapter15.html.

23. *Id. See* Green, *supra* note 21.

24. *See* Stephanie Strom, "An Organ Donor's Generosity Raises the Question of How Much Is Too Much," *NY Times*, August 17, 2003, at 14 (reporting on a wealthy donor considering giving his second kidney away, characterizing Zell Kravinsky's altruism as bordering on the obsessive).

25. *See* Siminoff et al., *supra* note 1, at 40.

26. *See OPTN/SRTR 2003 Annual Report*, Living Donor Characteristics, 1993 to 2002, Table 2.8 (hereinafter *2003 Annual Report*); *OPTN/SRTR 2004 Annual Report*, Living Donor Characteristics, 1994 to 2003, Table 2.8 (hereinafter *2004 Annual Report*); *See also* Arthur A. Caplan, "Biomedical Technology, Ethics, Public Policy, and the Law: Am I My

Brother's Keeper?," 27 *Suffolk U.L. Rev.* 1195, 1200 (1993) (arguing that volunteerism is more illusory than real in the context of organ donation. Emotions factor significantly in the process, causing feelings of guilt, obligation, to have a significant presence in the decision making.).

27. *2003 Annual Report, supra* note 26, at Table 1.1; *2004 Annual Report, supra* note 26, at Table 1.1.

28. *2003 Annual Report, supra* note 26, at Table 1.1.

29. *2004 Annual Report, supra* note 26, at Table 1.1.

30. *Id.* at Table 2.8.

31. *See* Peter Agulnik & Heidi Rivkin, "Criminal Liability for Failure to Rescue: A Brief Survey of French and American Law," 8 *Touro Int'l L.R.* 93, 96–7 (1998) (arguing that "deeply ingrained in the American psyche is the individual's desire to live free from governmental interference. American law has long respected the autonomy of the individual and has been reluctant to punish for failure to rescue.").

32. *See, e.g., McFall v. Shimp*, 10 Pa. D. & C.3d 90 (Ch. Ct. 1978) (hereinafter *McFall v. Shimp*).

33. *See* Adam J. Kogler, "A Matter of Priority: Transplanting Organs Preferentially to Registered Donors," 55 *Rutgers L. Rev.* 671, 697 (2003) (arguing that the altruistic motivation to donate has proved itself woefully insufficient, and although commentators urge that it should be sufficient, people on organ waiting lists are dying at an average rate of 16 per day in the United States).

34. *See* Robert Justin Lipkin, "Beyond Good Samaritans and Moral Monsters: An Individualistic Justification of the General Legal Duty to Rescue,"31 *UCLA L. Rev.* 252, 254 (1983) (positing that there is no general legal duty to rescue in most Anglo-American jurisdictions). There are special relationships in which the law requires a duty to rescue. For example, a carrier has a legal duty to take reasonable steps to rescue a passenger (*Middleton v. Whitridge*, 108 N.E. 192 (N.Y. 1915)) and an innkeeper must aid a

guest in case of fire (*West v. Spratling*, 86 So. 32 (Ala. 1920)).

35. *See* Howard S. Schwartz, "Bioethical and Legal Considerations in Increasing the Supply of Transplantable Organs: From UAGA to Baby Fae,"10 *Am. J.L. and Med.* 397, 423–424 (1985) (commenting on intra-family reluctance to participate in organ donation, finding "not infrequently, related potential donors ask the physician to inform the family that he or she is not a 'good match' in order to relieve these pressures"). *See also, Strunk v. Strunk*, 445 S.W.2d 145 (Ky. 1969); *Little v. Little*, 576 S.W.2d 493 (Tex. Civ. App. 1979).

36. *See* Michael T. Morley, "Proxy Consent to Organ Donation by Incompetents,"111 *Yale L.J.* 1215, 1223 (2002) (pointing out that, in a study of 451 living kidney donors with a 92% response rate, "[a]lmost all of them felt that the donation affected their lives in a positive way.... Of particular interest was that only three (0.8%) of the donors regretted the donation, two were undecided (0.5%), and thus almost 99% reported that they did not regret their decision").

37. *See Curran v. Bosze*, 566 N.E.2d 1319, 1343 (Ill. 1990) (hereinafter *Curran v. Bosze*).

38. *See* Schwartz, *supra* note 35, at 429 (arguing that whereas it is conceivable that a mother, father, or sibling may have sound psychological reasons to become volunteer donors, experience indicates that individuals who write to a transplant center in order to donate a kidney to a prospective recipient to whom they are not connected by any kind of emotional tie are frequently pathologic by psychiatric criteria).

39. *See* Joel D. Kallich & Jon F. Merz, "Transplant Imperative: Protecting Living Donors from the Pressure to Donate,"20 *Iowa J. Corp. L.* 139, 144 (1994).

40. Anderson argues that "we should not subject the families of potential cadaveric organ donors to this kind of emotional upheaval against their will. Instead, we should protect the emotional health of those who survive and not focus completely on the desires of those who no longer have emotions to experience." Mark F. Anderson,

"The Future of Organ Transplantation: From Where Will New Donors Come, to Whom Will Their Organs Go?" 5 *Health Matrix* 249, 268 (1995).

41. *McFall v. Shimp, supra* note 32.

42. *Id.*

43. *See* Dennis Williams, "Bad Samaritan," *Newsweek*, August 7, 1978, at 35.

44. *See Curran v. Bosze, supra* note 37; *See also In re Estate of Longeway*, 133 Ill. 2d 33 (1989); *In re Estate of Greenspan*, 137 Ill. 2d 1 (1990).

45. *McFall v. Shimp, supra* note 32, at 91.

46. National Marrow Donor Program, "ABCs of Marrow or Blood Cell Donation," at http://www.marrow.org/DONOR/abcs_of_donation.html (noting that "[m]ost donors are back to their usual routine in a few days.").

47. *McFall v. Shimp, supra* note 32, at 91.

48. *Id.*

49. This concept would resemble slavery far more than cadaveric organ incentives.

50. *McFall v. Shimp, supra* note 32, at 91.

51. *Id.*

52. *Id.*

53. *Id.*

54. *Id.*

55. Some commentators argue that our individualism should be protected by the law. For them, the law should guarantee a "moral sphere" of life that is unpolluted by human interference. In this sphere, each individual should possess the right to independently determine her own desire to engage with the "other." *See, e.g.,* Hanoch Dogan, "In Defense of the Good Samaritan," 97 *Mich. L. Rev.* 1152, 1162 (1999) [arguing that "because each individual is distinct and unique, each should be able to choose her goals voluntarily (as well as the means of achieving such goals)"].

56. *Curran v. Bosze, supra* note 37.

57. *Id.* at 1321.

58. *Id.*

59. *Id.* at 1339.

60. *Id.* at 1331.

61. *See* Andrew Fegelman, "Guardian Allowed to Talk to Twins," *Chicago Tribune*, August 24, 1990, at C4.

62. *In re Estate of Longeway, supra* note 44.

63. *In re Estate of Greenspan, supra* note 44.

64. *Curran v. Bosze, supra* note 37, at 1326.

65. *See* "Boy at Center of Suit for a Marrow Donor is Dead of Leukemia," *N.Y. Times*, Nov. 20, 1990, at B9.

66. *See* Janet B. Korins, "*Curran v. Bosze:* Toward a Clear Standard for Authorizing Kidney and Bone Marrow Transplants Between Minor Siblings," 16 *Vt. L. Rev.* 499, 502 (1992).

67. Id.

68. Bryan Shartle, "Proposed Legislation for Safely Regulating the Increasing Number of Living Organ and Tissue Donations by Minors," 61 *La. L. Rev.* 433, 458 (2001).

69. Curran and Bosze were paramours with a conflicted relationship; at once engaged and later feuding over paternity, which ironically was settled through the twins being subjected to a blood test when they were one year old at the behest of Curran.

70. *Curran v. Bosze, supra* note 37, at 1343–44.

71. *Id.* at 1343.

72. *Id.*

73. *Id.*

74. *See* "Boy at Center of Suit for a Marrow Donor is Dead of Leukemia," *supra* note 65.

75. *Curran v. Bosze, supra* note 37, at 1326.

76. *Id.* at 1334.

77. *See* Barbara Redman, "Rethinking the Progressive Estate and Gift Tax," 15 *Akron Tax J.* 35, 48–9 (2000). Redman argues that altruistic concerns for children's well-being springs from an extension of a "household production model." In that model, parental utility encompassed the utility of children. She writes:

> This model's predictions include bequests to children by such 'altruistic' parents, even if the children behave selfishly. In fact, the 'rotten kid' of this theorem finds it in his/her own self-interest to help the altruistic parent maximize family income, though only if the parent retains the last word (that is, the ability to make bequests). Soon, however,

researchers presented an alternative explanation for bequests to children, that of exchange for services rendered. *Id.*

78. *Curran v. Bosze, supra* note 37, at 1335.

79. *See* Rebecca C. Morgan, "How to Decide: Decisions on Life-Prolonging Procedures," 20 *Stetson L. Rev.* 77, 102 (1990) (arguing that statues cannot anticipate every situation or factual pattern, and medical technology advances faster than law).

80. *See* Robert W. Griner, "Live Organ Donations Between Siblings and the Best Interest Standard: Time for Stricted Judicial Intervention," 10 *Ga. St. U.L. Rev.* 589, 599 (1994) (distinguishing rights and duties involving rescue doctrine, arguing that "the right of an adult to refuse medical treatment includes the right to refuse to become an organ donor. There is no affirmative duty to come to the rescue of a stranger. However, a special relationship, such as a family relationship, may impose a duty to rescue. The courts have not imposed this duty on collateral family members when the need for an organ transplant has arisen.").

81. *Id.* at 589 (arguing that "the requirements of informing the consenting parent of risks and benefits and ensuring that emotional support is available to the donor child, allows psychological benefits to the donor to be assessed. The existing and future sibling relationships are examined to determine whether the donor's best interest is served by the procedure"); *See also* Shartle, *supra* note 68, at 467 (arguing for the use of child testimony, oral or otherwise, to determine the consent of minors to organ and tissue donation).

82. *See* Gloria J. Banks, "Legal and Ethical Safeguards: Protection of Society's Most Vulnerable Participants in a Commercialized Organ Transplantation System," 21 *Am. J.L. & Med.* 45, 90 (1995).

83. *See* Maria M. Morelli, "Organ Trafficking: Legislative Proposals to Protect Minors," 10 *Am. U.J. Int'l L. & Pol'y* 917, 942 (1995) (courts undergo a balancing process in order to ascertain whether the donation serves the donor's best interests);

Cara Cheyette, "Organ Harvests from the Legally Incompetent: An Argument Against Compelled Altruism," 41 *B.C. L. Rev* 465, 493–4 (2000) (arguing that some courts seek to balance the relative harms to which donors and recipients will be subjected, or alternatively, the relative benefits donors and recipients will realize).

84. *See* Sheila R. Kirschenbaum, "Banking on Discord: Property Conflicts in the Transplantation of Umbilical Cord Stem Cells," 39 *Ariz. L. Rev.* 1391, 1411–2 (1997) (finding "the similarities between kidney or bone marrow transplants and umbilical cord blood transplants are multiple and obvious").

85. *See Curran v. Bosze, supra* note 37, at 1343–3. *See also* Jennifer K. Robbenholt et al., "Advancing the Rights of Children and Adolescents to be Altruistic Bone Marrow Donation by Minors," 9. *J.L. & Health* 213, 231 (1994).

86. *See* Banks, *supra* note 82, at 89.

87. *See* Shannon H. Smith, "Ignorance is Not Bliss: Why a Ban on Human Cloning is Unacceptable," 9 *Health Matrix* 311, 328–9 (1999) (critiquing the Curran court's use of "existing close relationship" with the "substantial benefit" to the donor notion in determining what is in the donor's best interests) Smith asserts that in order to find "an existing close relationship," there must necessarily be an existing donor, who has had the opportunity (and time) to form a close bond with the recipient."

88. *See* Shartle, *supra* note 68, at 458–9.

89. *See* Elizabeth Price Foley, "The Constitutional Implications of Human Cloning," 42 *Ariz. L. Rev.* 647, 660–1 (2000).

90. *See* Deborah K. McKnight & Maureen Bellis, "Foregoing Life-Sustaining Treatment for Adult, Developmentally Disabled, Public Wards: A Proposed Statute," *Am. J.L. and Med.* 203, 223 (1992) (arguing against the substituted judgment standard because it lacked objective content).

91. *See* Dwight Newman, "An Examination of Saskatchewan Law on the Sterilization of Persons with Mental Disabilities," 62 *Sask. L. Rev.* 329, 332 (1999) (suggesting that nontherapeutic surgeries can never be in the best

interest of the patient, even when parents and guardians are involved).

92. *See* Jennifer L. Rosato, "Using Bioethics Discourse to Determine When Parents Should Make Health Care Decisions for Their Children: Is Deference Justified?," 73 *Temp. L. Rev.* 1, 57 (2000) (according to Rosato's organ donation is always, by definition, nontherapeutic, and therefore, even with parental consent, such operations must be strictly scrutinized by courts).

93. *See* Thomas J. Brindisi, "Right to Die – Court Requires Clear and Convincing Evidence of Persistent Vegetative Patient's Intent to Terminate Life-Sustaining Procedures," 23 *U. Balt. L. Rev.* 619, 623 (1994).

94. Or, how does a mentally incompetent manifest intent? *See In re Moe*, 432 N.E.2d 712, 720 (Mass. 1982) (acknowledging the potential slippery slope in pursuing substituted judgment.).

We are aware of the difficulties of utilizing the substitute judgment doctrine in a case where the incompetent has been mentally retarded since birth. The inability, however, of an incompetent to choose, should not result in a loss of the person's constitutional interests . . . We admit that in this case we are unable to draw upon prior stated preferences the individual may have expressed. An expression of intent by an incompetent person while competent, however, is not essential . . . While it may thus be necessary to rely to a greater degree on objective criteria . . . the effort to bring the substituted judgment into step with the values and desires of the affected individual must not, and need not, be abandoned. *Id.*

95. In the case of a guardian *ad litem* declining whether to terminate life support, *see* Anne Marie Gaudin, "Cruzan v. Director, Missouri Department of Health: To Die or Not to Die: That is the Question – But Who Decides?" 51 *La. L. Rev.* 1307, 1322 (1991) (arguing that if clear and convincing evidence is lacking, the court might look to a conversation between the patient and another); *Cruzan v. Director, Missouri Dept. of Health*, 110 S. Ct. 2841(1990). Cruzan is perhaps one of the seminal cases involving evidence of consent from a third party. In the case, the court considered a testimony of a conversation between Nancy Cruzan and her roommate. In the conversation, Nancy is said to have communicated her desires as to treatment options were she to become vegetative.

96. *See Prince v. Massachusetts*, 321 U.S. 158 (1945).

97. *See* Kallich, *supra* note 39, at 139, 144–45.

98. *See* Cheyette, *supra* note 83, 467–8.

99. *Id.*

100. *See* Shartle, *supra* note 68, at 461–2 (arguing that the presumption that parents will act in the best interests of their minor children is not always reasonable). Shartle scrutinizes parental motivations in organ transferring, finding that an inherent conflict of interest exists between the parents and each child. Shartle writes:

The desperation of parents faced with this conflict is best illustrated by reports of parents who have conceived a child for the purpose of donating that child's bone marrow to a sibling, a phenomena termed 'parity for donation.' And while medical consultation may provide some clarity to the decision-making process, the medical professional providing the advice may be the donee-recipient's physician; thus, the advising physician may also face a conflict of interest because he must seek to aid his patient but also provide accurate medical advice. *Id.*

101. *See* Nancy K. Schiff, "Legislation Punishing Drug Use During Pregnancy: Attack on Women's Rights in the Name of Fetal Protection," 19 *Hastings Const. L. Q.* 197, 197–8 (1991).

102. *See* South Carolina's Homicide by Child Abuse Statute, S.C. Code Ann. § 16–3–85 (2002); Utah Code Ann § 75-5-109 (2000) (child criminal abuse statute) and Utah Code Ann § 76-5-208 (criminal child abuse homicide statute); KY. Rev. Stat. Ann. § 508.110 (Michie 2002) (defining abuse as "torture, cruel confinement or cruel punishment; to a person under twelve (12) years of age or less, or who is physically helpless or mentally helpless"). *See also State v. McKnight*, 576 S.E.3d 168 (2003). Regina McKnight is

currently serving a 20-year prison term, which has been reduced to 12 years for ingesting cocaine while pregnant.

103. *See Michigan v. Moye*, 491 N.W. 2d 232 (Mich., 1992) (reinstating manslaughter conviction of mother whose drug use resulted in death of prematurely born child. This decision overturned the Appellate Court's reversal of the Trial Court decision, wherein they opined the mother did not have intent to kill or inflict bodily harm.).

104. *See* Shellie K. Park, "Severing the Bond of Life: When Conflicts of Interest Fail to Recognize the Value of Two Lives," 25 *U. Haw. L. Rev.* 157, 168–9 (2002) (noting that the law must recognize two lives involved in compelled donations cases).

105. *See* Laura J. Hilmert, "Cloning Human Organs: Potential Sources and Property Implications," 77 *Ind. L. J.* 363, 368 (2002) (arguing that the closer the match between the tissue of the donor and the tissue of the recipient, the better the chances are for success. Identical twins are ideal donors).

106. *See* Patricia Huna, "Infants as Organ Transplant Donors: Should it Happen," 6-*SUM Health Law* 24 (1992) (critiquing the new frontiers in transplantation, noting that because siblings of donees are the most compatible donors, some parents are creating a new child in order to provide a donor to the older sibling).

107. *See* Georgetta Glaves-Innis, "Organ Donation and Incompetents: Can They Consent? Comparative Analysis of American and Canadian Laws of Consent and Brain Death Determination," 10 *Touro Int'l L. Rev.* 155, 178 (2000) (arguing that with regard to organ donation, the patient becomes dependent on the physician's disclosure of diagnosis, prognosis, and treatment options).

108. *See* John Lawrence Hill, "Exploitation," 79 *Cornell L. Rev.* 631, 645 (1994) (suggesting that the most controversial alternatives in organ transplantation would be to create markets wherein living donations are solicited).

109. *See* Cheyette, *supra* note 83 (cautioning the use of incompetent persons as organ donors, declaring "organ harvests from chil-

dren and mentally disabled adults should be categorically prohibited.... [U]sing the most vulnerable members of society to shield us from the pain of a loved one's illness or imminent death is unfair").

110. *Id.* at 505–6.

111. Note, "Looking for a Family Resemblance: The Limits of the Functional Approach to the Legal Definition of Family," 104 *Harv. L. Rev.* 1640 (1991) (offering a different legal view of what family means in the United States, calling it a rapidly changing "anachronism").

112. *See* Larry V. Starcher, "The Family of 2003," 2003 Nov. *W.V. Law* 8 (2003) (pointing out that "we have now moved into the twenty-first century, and the percentage of American children living in "traditional" married nuclear families is well below a majority. Single parents are raising 30% of our nation's children. In some urban areas, 30 to 60% of children are being raised by neither biological parent.").

113. *Strunk v. Strunk, supra* note 35.

114. *See Strunk v. Strunk, supra* note 35; *Hart v. Brown*, 289 A.2d 386 (Super. 1972); *Bonner v. Moran*, 126 F.2d 121 (D.C. Cir. 1941); *Little v. Little*, 576 S.W. 2d 493 (Tex. Civ. 1979); *Hurdle v. Currier*, 5 Va. Cir. 509 (1977); *In re Guardianship of Pescinski*, N.W.2d 180 (1975) and *In re Richardson*, 284 So.2d. 185 (LA. App. 1973).

115. *See* Caplan, *supra* note 26, at 1200.

116. *See* Donny J. Perales, "Rethinking the Prohibition of Death Row Prisoners as Organ Donors: A Possible Lifeline to Those on Organ Donor Waiting Lists," 34 *St. Mary's L. J.* 687, 725 (2003) (pointing out that the "AMA's Principles of Medical Ethics asserts a duty that" "a physician shall recognize a responsibility to participate in activities contributing to an improved community").

117. Three nonreported decisions in Massachusetts dealt with parental authority to consent to similar medical procedures involving twins. These cases however were not reported, and thus not readily accessible to judges and law clerks in other jurisdictions. The *Strunk* court as well as other courts may have been unaware of their existence at the

time. *See Masden v. Harrison*, No. 68651, Eq. Mass. Sup. Jud. Ct. (June 12, 1957); *Hushey v. Harrison*, No. 68666, Eq. Mass. Sup. Jud. Ct. (Aug. 30, 1957); *Foster v. Harrison*, No. 68674, Eq. Mass. Sup. Jud. Ct. (Nov. 20, 1957).

118. *Strunk v. Strunk, supra* note 35, at 146.

119. *Id.* at 147.

120. *Id.* at 145.

121. Substituted judgment arises from English case law, which permitted courts of equity to intercede on behalf of employers suffering from "lunacy" to provide a pension for retiring servants. *See Ex parte Whitebread* (1816) 2 Meriv 99, 35 Eng Reprint 878 (Ch); *Re Earl of Carysfort* (1840) Craig & Ph 76, 41 Eng Reprint 418.

122. *Strunk v. Strunk, supra* note 35, at 148.

123. *Id.* at 149.

124. *Id.* at 146.

125. *Id.*

126. *Id.* at 147.

127. *See Buck v. Bell*, 274 US 200 (1927) (ruling, "the principle that sustains compulsory vaccination is broad enough to cover cutting the Fallopian tubes.").

128. *Id.* at 207.

129. *See* Dorothy Roberts, *Killing The Black Body: Race, Reproduction, and the Meaning of Liberty* (1997); *See also* Paul Lombardo, "The American Breed': Nazi Eugenics and the Origins of the Pioneer Fund," 65 *Alb. L. Rev.* 743 (2002) (documenting the early economic, political, and social ties to eugenics in the United States).

130. *Buck v. Bell, supra* note 127, at 201.

131. Shortly after *Strunk*, two cases with similar facts were brought to sister jurisdictions, one in Wisconsin and the other, Louisiana. Those courts departed from *Strunk*, holding that it would not be in the best interest of mentally disabled siblings to have parents or courts substitute their consent for nontherapeutic surgeries to procure their organs for the benefit of a sibling. *See In re Guardianship of Pescinski, supra* note 114; *In re Richardson, supra* note 114.

132. *Strunk v. Strunk, supra* note 35, at 145–46.

133. *See* Jeffery M. Shaman, "The Evolution of Equality in State Constitutional Law," 34 *RU. L.J.* 1013, 1078 (2003) (arguing that both the elderly and physically and mentally deficient have been subjected to arbitrary discrimination in court rulings).

134. During the mid-1800s, in England and the United States, mentally disabled women lacked due process and judicial recourse with regard to confinement and the conditions they suffered as a result of that detainment. Due process was an elusive concept unknown to the poor mentally ill. One's unchangeable social, psychological, economic, or genetic condition unfairly determined whether she had standing before the law. Biased laws, conveniently used by magistrates, husbands, and roaming overseers, dictated the process by which the poor were to be removed from the streets. Women, unlike propertied men, were without the protection or recognition of the law; they could have no hearings or jury trials to defend their sanity. Laws were biased against their gender and economic status. *See, e.g.,* Michele Goodwin, "The Black Woman in the Attic: Law, Metaphor and Madness in *Jane Eyre*," 30 RU. *L.J.* 597, 643–4 (1999).

135. *See* Emily Denham Morris, "The Organ Trail: Express versus Presumed Consent as Paths to Blaze in Solving a Critical Shortage," 90 *KY. L.J.* 1125, 1149 (2001) (arguing that "one problem with most of the regulations passed and common law rules set out by courts regarding organ and tissue donation has been short-sightedness when dealing with future technological advances. Courts do not have crystal balls that can predict the future" of technological advancements).

136. *See Hurdle v. Currier, supra* note 114.

137. *See Little v. Little, supra* note 114.

138. *See Hart v. Brown, supra* note 114.

139. *See also Little v. Little, supra* note 114 (holding a parent of an incompetent daughter could legally substitute her judgment for that of her daughter to permit the procurement of her organ for benefit of a younger brother).

140. *See Hart v. Brown, supra* note 114.

141. *Id.* at 369.

142. *See Bonner v. Moran, supra* note 114 (opining that a doctor must obtain consent before performing surgery on a minor in a case where minor's skin was removed on two occasions for grafting onto his cousin).

143. *Hart v. Brown, supra* note 114, at 374.

144. *See* Morley, *supra* note 36 (arguing that guilt often influences organ donation decisions).

145. *See* Jo Anna Kowalski, "Blow for Couple in Designer Baby Bid," *Nottingham Evening Post,* Dec. 11, 2003, at 13; Lance Morrow, "When One Body Can Save Another; A Family's Act of Lifesaving Conception Was on the Side of Angels, but Hovering in the Wings is the Devilish Ghost of Dr. Mengele," *Time Magazine,* June 17, 1992, at 54.

146. *See* Kowalski, *supra* note 145.

147. Paul C. Redman II & Lauren Fielder Redman, "Seeking a Better Solution for the Disposition of Frozen Embryos: Is Embryo Adoption the Answer?," 35 *Tulsa L.J.* 583, 584 (2000).

148. *See* Rick Weiss, "Test Tube Baby Born to Save Ill Sister," *Washington Post,* Oct. 3, 2000, at A1.

149. See Jeffrey P. Kahn, "Making Lives to Save Lives," at http://www.cnn.com/2000/HEALTH/10/16/ethics.matters/index.html (Oct. 16, 2000); CNN.com, "Birth of a U.S. Boy as Donor Raises Ethical Question," at http:// www.cnn.com/2000/HEALTH/10/03/genetics.ethics.reut/ (Oct. 3, 2000) (writing that "in the event the stem cell transplant did not prove successful, the Nashes would have been faced with the difficult decision of harvesting bone marrow from Adam, which is by no means a risk-free procedure").

150. *See* Mary B. Mahowald, "Genes, Clones, and Gender Equality," 3 *DePaul J. Health Care L.* 495, 513 (2000) (discussing the story of the Ayalas).

151. *See* Morley, *supra* note 145.

152. *See id.* at 514.

153. *See* Donrich W. Joordan, "Preimplantation Genetic Screening and Selection: An Ethical Analysis," 22 *Biotechnology L. Rep.* 586, 586 (2003).

154. *See* Kahn, *supra* note 149; CNN.com, *supra* note 149.

155. *See Skinner v. Oklahoma,* 316 U.S. 535 (1942) (where the Supreme Court prevented the sterilization of a recidivist on equal protection grounds).

156. *See Buck v. Bell, supra* note 127 (where the Supreme Court approved sterilization of a mentally retarded woman).

157. *See Roberts, supra* note 129.

158. In April 2003, a three-judge panel comprised of senior justices of the Court of Appeal in London overturned a ban proscribing parents from reproducing to aid a dying child.

159. Although, Susan A. Munson argues that the restrictions currently in place may not be entirely effective in preventing the buying and selling of children. *See* Susan A. Munson, "Independent Adoption: In Whose Best Interest?," 26 *Seton Hall L. Rev.* 803, 814 (1996).

160. *See* Martin Guggenheim, "Minor Rights: The Adolescent Abortion Cases," 30 *Hofstra L. Rev.* 589, 603–4 (2002) (arguing that the right to parent has been recognized as a fundamental right in the Supreme Court).

161. *See* Susan Wolf & Jeffrey Kahn, "Using Preimplantation Genetic Diagnosis to Create a Stem Cell Donor: Issues, Guidelines, and Limits," 31 *J.L. Med. & Ethics* 327, 332 (2003) (considering whether creating a donor child transforms the nature of intra-familial relationships).

162. *See* Morrow, *supra* note 145.

163. "Marissa Ayala: Bonded by Bone Marrow, Two Sisters Live Happily Ever After," *People Weekly,* Mar. 15, 1999, at 78.

164. Additionally, the doctor who performs the abortion of a healthy viable fetus may face legal issues. *See* Jane F. Friedman, "Legal Implications of Amniocentesis," 123 *U. Pa. L. Rev.* 92, 143–6 (1974).

165. Cheyette, *supra* note 83, at 477–8.

166. *Id.* at 477–8. Cheyette reveals compelling data from a study involving children organ donors.

167. *Id.*

168. *Id.*

169. *See* Washington University School of Medicine Kidney Study, *supra* note 165.

170. *See 2003 Annual Report, supra* note 26; OPTN/SRTR Data as of August 1, 2003. In the sibling pool, both full and half siblings are included.

4. Getting the Organ You Want

1. *See* Telephone interview with Jim Cohane, Organ Transplant Coordinator (May 4, 2004) (on file with author).

2. Organ Procurement Transplantation Network, Data, at http://www.optn.org/ (hereinafter *OPTN Data*).

3. *Id.*

4. *See* Telephone interview with Jack Lynch, Community Affairs Director, Gift of Hope (July 7, 2005) (hereinafter *Jack Lynch Interview*).

5. *See, e.g.*, Barbara A. Noah, "Racial Disparities in the Delivery of Health Care," 35 San Diego L. Rev. 135, 142–47 (1998).

6. Jack Lynch Interview, *supra* note 4.

7. *Id.*

8. *Id.*

9. *Id.*

10. Kraig S. Kinchen, et al., "The Timing of Specialist Evaluation in Chronic Kidney Disease and Mortality," 137:6 *Annals of Internal Medicine* 479, 482 (2002) (indicating that Black men and women had later diagnoses than White men and women).

11. *Id.*

12. *Id.*

13. Telephone interview with Jacqueline Dillard, Director of Dialysis Services, Chicago-Area Dialysis Clinic (July 7, 2005) (hereinafter *Jacqueline Dillard Interview*).

14. Medicare and Medicaid, two government insurance programs for the poor, subsidize costs associated with dialysis treatment.

15. Jacqueline Dillard Interview, *supra* note 13.

16. Pushkal P. Garg, M.D. et al., "Effect of the Ownership of Dialysis Facilities on Patients' Survival and Referral for Transplantation," *New England Journal of Medicine*, Vol 341, 1653–1660, Nov. 25, 1999.

17. *Id.*

18. *Id.*

19. *See* Robert Wood Johnson, "For-Profit Dialysis Facilities Have Higher Mortality Rates and Lower Transplant Referral Rates than Not-For-Profit Facilities," John Hopkins Bloomberg School of Public Health, *Public Health News*, Nov. 24, 1999, available at http://www.jhsph.edu/publichealthnews/ press_releases/PR_1999/dialysis.html.

20. *Id.*

21. *See* P.J. Devereaux, et al., "Comparison of Mortality between Private For-Profit and Private Not-For-Profit Hemodialysis: A Systematic Review and Meta-Analysis," 288 *Journal of American Medical Association* 2449 (2002).

22. *Id.*

23. *Id.*

24. Pushkal P. Garg, M.D. et al., *supra* note 16.

25. *Id.*

26. *See, e.g., Putting Patients First – Allocation of Transplant Organ: Hearings Before the House Commerce Comm. Subcomm. on Health and the Environment and the Senate Labor and Human Resources Comm.*, 105th Cong., 2d Sess. 215 (1998) (testimony of Dr. Clive O. Callender) [hereinafter *Callender Testimony*] (commenting on institutional racism being "alive and well and thriving" in American healthcare and "the green screen," which he asserts is the financial barrier to Blacks receiving organ transplantation); Kevin McCoy, "Deadly Disparity in Transplants: Blacks and Hispanics Deprived," *Daily News* (New York), Aug. 8, 1999, at 6 (commenting that Blacks and Hispanics are not placed on organ waiting lists because their doctors tend not to refer them); Brigid Schulte, "Minorities Left Behind in American Health Care: Statistics Show Blacks Suffering at Greater Rate," *Akron Beacon Journal* (OH), Aug. 16, 1998, at A1 (commenting that doctors are less likely to both perform "high-tech" diagnostic treatments on Blacks and make extreme efforts to save their lives).

27. *See, e.g., Callender Testimony, supra* note 26; McCoy, *supra* note 26; Schulte, *supra* note 26.

28. *See* McCoy, *supra* note 26 (quoting Dr. Clive Callender).

29. *Id.* "National Public Radio Weekend Saturday: Race Relations" (NPR radio broadcast, Oct. 31, 1998) (transcript on file with author) [hereinafter *NPR: Race Relations*]. Dr. Callender commented on NPR about race in medicine, noting:

[T]he problem is that institutional organizational racism is here to stay, and wherever you go, you find organizational and institutional racism. For example, in the old days, okay, they castrated and decapitated us. Now, they just ignore us. We're invisible. I say something and you don't hear me, but if a Caucasian person says the same thing, brilliant idea! Okay? So that's how racism plays out today. *Id.*

30. McCoy, *supra* note 26.

31. *Id.*

32. *Id.*

33. *Id.*

34. *Id.; see also* Laurie Kaye Abraham, *Mama Might Be Better Off Dead: The Failure of Health Care in Urban America* 179–185 (1993) (discussing situations that contribute to minorities being less likely to get on transplant waiting lists).

35. *See* McCoy, *supra* note 26 (using population data and referral records to demonstrate racial bias in the physician referral process).

36. *Id.* (highlighting the racial disparity of transplantation referral based on population studies, revealing that Whites, in essence, are overrepresented in the referral stage for organs, whereas Blacks and Latinos are underrepresented).

37. *Id.*

38. *Id.* quoting Ashwani Sehgal.

39. *See* Abraham, *supra* note 34, at 184 (describing patient characteristics that can influence a doctor's selection of patients for transplants).

40. McCoy, *supra* note 26.

41. *Id.*

42. *Id.*

43. *Id.*

44. Donna E. Shalala, "Message from the Secretary," 1 *Healthy People* 2010 18 (2000) [hereinafter *Healthy People 2010*], available at http://www.healthypeople.gov/document/html/uih/message.htm; *Social Determinants of Health* (M.G. Marmot & Richard G. Wilkinson eds., 1999) (discussing environmental and behavioral aspects of health).

45. *See, e.g.*, Institute of medicine (Committee on Using Performance Monitoring to Improve Community Health), *Improving Health in the Community: A Role for Performance Monitoring* 40–58 (Jane S. Burch et al. eds., 1997).

46. *See e.g.*, Helen Epstein, "The New Ghetto Miasma," *New York Times Magazine*, Oct. 12, 2003, at 75.

47. *See* McCoy, *supra* note 26.

48. *See* Jodie Snyder, "Race Disparity in Transplants Questioned: Time Not on Minorities' Side," *Ariz. Republic*, May 11, 1999, at A1.

49. *See, e.g.*, Joyce Howard Price, "Organ Donations Aren't Keeping Up; Serious Shortage Has Experts Searching for Solutions," *Wash. Times* (Washington, D.C.), May 17, 1999, at A9; Snyder, *supra* note 48 (indicating that "inevitably, ... cultural reasons will be mentioned ... as reasons for the gap"); *See also* Abraham, *supra* note 34, at 185 (commenting that transplant professionals often blame the longer waits on the combined fact of "biological makeups of Blacks and Whites ... with the fact that Whites donate more organs than Blacks"). Other commentators argue that blaming the patient is ultimately counterproductive, particularly when the criticism is socioeconomically based.

50. *See, e.g.*, McCoy, *supra* note 26 (noting that disparities persist, "even though minorities are comparatively generous in donating organs so others might live. Proportionally, Blacks and Hispanics donate organs slightly more often than Whites.").

51. *Id.*

52. *Id.*

53. *Id.*

54. *Id.* Since her healthcare fiasco, Debbie Delgado has founded the Latino

Organization for Liver Awareness, a group based in the Bronx, aimed at supporting and educating members of the Latino community about liver transplantation.

55. *Id.*

56. *Id.*

57. *Id.*

58. *Id.*

59. *Id.* (internal quotations omitted).

60. *Id.*

61. Noah, *supra* note 5, at 144–45 (highlighting institutional bias in the organ allocation process, urging reconsideration of dispensation guidelines).

62. McCoy, *supra* note 26. McCoy notes that "[t]he screening includes medical and psychological tests. It also entails a review of a patient's health insurance and ability to pay for the surgery and the constant medication required afterward to block the body's natural rejection of a donated organ." *Id.*

63. *Id.*

64. *See* Centers for Medicare and Medicaid Services, "Medicaid Eligibility Groups and Less Restrictive Methods of Determining Countable Income and Resources: Questions and Answers" at http://www.cms.hhs.gov/medicaid/eligibility/elig0501.pdf ("[A] person with income below the SSI level gets Medicaid automatically...."); *See also* Centers for Medicare and Medicaid Services at http://www.cms.hhs.gov/medicaid/eligibility/ssi0105.asp.

65. *See* Abraham, *supra* note 34, at 183.

66. McCoy, *supra* note 26; *see* Callender Testimony, *supra* note 26.

67. Callender Testimony, *supra* note 26, at 218. Dr. Callender also notes that "some states do not pay for extra renal transplantation" and that patients who lack insurance or are underinsured "will never even be placed on the extra renal transplant waiting list." *Id.*

68. See Abraham, *supra* note 34, at 185; Carl M. Kjellstrand, "Age, Sex, and Race Inequality in Renal Transplantation," 148 *Archives of Internal Med.* 1305, 1309 (1988) (commenting that "the most favored recipient of a transplant is similar to the physicians who make the final decision: a young, White man"); *see also* Tom Corwin, "Doctors Face Culture Issues with Patients," *Augusta Chron.* (Georgia), Feb. 9, 2000, at C6 (noting that "[t]he success of the doctor-patient, the provider-client relationship is all about communication") (quoting Dr. Nathan, Jr., Stinson, Deputy Assistant Secretary for Minority Health in the U.S. Department of Health and Human Services); Jay Greene, "More Med Students Bone Up on Diversity Issues," *San Diego Union-Trib.*, Nov. 22, 1999, at E3 (noting the importance of cultural competency training for physicians because of the diverse and often critical healthcare needs of non-White communities); Jeffrey Weiss, "Doctors Soul-Searching After Bias Study; Unconscious Sexism and Racism May Be Killing Patients," *Hous. Chron.*, June 6, 1999, at A19 (reporting that "some doctors are unknowingly afflicted with a dangerous combination of racism and sexism that may be killing some of their patients").

69. *See* Weiss, *supra* note 68.

70. *See* Abraham, *supra* note 33, at 182.

71. *Id.*

72. *Id.* at 2.

73. *Id.* at 179–197.

74. *See generally* Abraham, *supra* note 34.

75. *Id.* at 184.

76. *Id.* at 182.

77. *Id.* at 184.

78. *Id.*

79. *Id.*

80. *Id.* at 145. *See also* John F. Kilner, "Selecting Patients when Resources are Limited: A Study of U.S. Medical Directors of Kidney Dialysis and Transplantation Facilities," 78 *Am. J. of Pub. Health* 144, 144–47 (1988); Gloria J. Banks, "Legal and Ethical Safeguards: Protection of Society's Most Vulnerable Participants in a Commercialized Organ Transplantation System," 21 *Am. J.L. & Med.* 45, 63 (1995) (discussing social criteria in transplantation policies); Guido Calabresi & Philip Bobbitt, *Tragic Choices*, 186–89 (1978) (criticizing the use of arbitrary criteria to exclude participation and access by groups to medical technologies).

81. *See* Kilner, *supra* note 80 *at* 144–47.

82. Abraham, *supra* note 34, at 184.

83. *Id.* at 145–46. *See also* Calabresi & Bobbit, *supra* note 80 at 186–89.

84. *See* David Sanders & Jesse Dukeminier Jr., "Medical Advance and Legal Lag: Hemodialysis and Kidney Transplantation," 15 *UCLA L. Rev.* 357, 378 (1968) (observing that because of the conservative decision making of the Seattle dialysis committee, "[t]he Pacific Northwest is no place for a Henry David Thoreau with bad kidneys"); Jessica Dunsay Silver, "From Baby Doe to Grandpa Doe: The Impact of the Federal Age Discrimination Act on the "Hidden" Rationing of Medical Care," 37 *Cath. U.L. Rev.* 993, 998–99 (1988) (noting that expenses relating to the purchase of dialysis equipment and the employment of hospital personnel necessary to "operate a dialysis program resulted in a shortage of treatment facilities," which ultimately led to dialysis being provided to few patients and "various means of rationing . . . employed").

85. Silver, *supra* note 84, at 998; Sanders & Dukeminier, *supra* note 84, at 377–78.

86. *Id.*

87. *Id.*

88. *See* Abraham, *supra* note 34, at 184.

89. *Id.*

90. *See* McCoy, *supra* note 26, at 6.

91. See Abraham, *supra* note 34, at 185.

92. *See id.* at 184. One member of the committee reflected on how "the choices were hard." He commented:

I voted against a young man who had been a ne'er-do-well, a real playboy, until he learned he had renal failure. He promised he would reform his character, go back to school, and so on, if only he were selected for treatment. But I felt I'd lived long enough to know that a person like that won't really do what he was promising. *Id.* at 184–85.

93. *Id.* at 185. *See* Sanders & Dukeminier, *supra* note 84, at 379.

94. Abraham, *supra* note 34, at 185; *see also* Arthur A. Caplan, "Biomedical Technology, Ethics, Public Policy, and the Law: Am I My Brother's Keeper?," 27 *Suffolk U.L. Rev.* 1195, 1200 (1993) (suggesting that equity stand as a top priority in any allocation plan); Mark F. Anderson, "The Future of Organ Transplantation: From Where Will New Donors Come, to Whom Will Their Organs Go?" 5 *Health Matrix* 249, 253 (1995) (stating that "there are many more candidates for organ transplantation than there are donors"); Ian Ayres et al., "Unequal Racial Access to Kidney Transplantation," 46 *Vand. L. Rev.* 805 (1993) (discussing the disparities in kidney transplantations among various racial groups); Phyllis Coleman, "Brother Can You Spare a Liver? Five Ways to Increase Organ Donation," 31 *Val. U.L. Rev.* 1, 3–5 (1996) (discussing the problem of an overwhelming demand for organs that cannot be met under the current organ procurement system); Jack M. Kress, "Xenotransplantation: Ethics and Economics," 53 *Food Drug L.J.* 353, 356–60 (1998) (discussing how equitable access to transplantation could come from a futures market).

95. *See* Institute Of Med. Comm. on Xenograft Transplantation, *Xenotransplantation: Science, Ethics and Public Policy* 66 (Nat'l Acad. Press, 1996) (hereinafter *IOM Comm.*).

96. *See* "The Organ Procurement Transplantation Network, Current U.S. Waiting List by Ethnicity," at http://www.optn.org/latestData/rptData.asp (last visited July 21, 2005) (hereinafter *OPTN Waiting List*). These numbers are current as of July 21, 2005. However, the reader should note that these numbers do not remain static and may change daily.

97. *See, e.g.*, Thomas E. Starzl & John J. Fung, "The Politics of Grafting Cadaver Kidneys," 348 *Lancet* 454 (1996).

98. *See* Telephone interview with Joel D. Newman, Communication Liaison, United Network for Organ Sharing (July 7, 2005) (hereinafter *Joel Newman Interview*).

99. Jack Lynch Interview, *supra* note 4.

100. *See also* United Network for Organ Sharing, "Fact Sheet," at http://www.unos.org.

101. *See OPTN/SRTR 2000 Annual Report,* iii (hereinafter *2000 Annual Report*).

102. *See* Letter from Claude E. Fox, Administrator of Health Resources and Services Administration to L.G. Hunsicker (on file with author) (hereinafter *Fox Letter*) (regarding the 1998 revisions for improving the fairness and effectiveness in allocating organs for transplantation). "Under conditions of participation regulations for hospitals . . . [they] will be required to engage in activities to increase organ donation, or risk losing eligibility for Medicare and Medicaid.") *Id.*

103. *See, e.g.,* Angela T. Whitehead, "Rejecting Organs: The Organ Allocation Process and the Americans with Disabilities Act," 24 *Am. J.L. & Med.* 481, 485 (1998).

104. *Id.*

105. *Id.*

106. *See* Noah, *supra* note 5, at 144. *See also* Fox Letter, *supra* note 102, at 5.

107. *See, e.g., 2000 Annual Report, supra* note 101. According to the 1998 *Annual Report:*

> When a donor organ becomes available, the match process begins. Matching uses donor information entered by UNOS members at the time of the match and existing potential recipient data from the UNOS waiting list. Using an allocation algorithm, the matching process generates a list of potential recipients for each available organ. *OPTN/SRTR 1998 Annual Report,* 445 (hereinafter *1998 Annual Report*).

108. Telephone interview with Dr. Michael Dreis, Administrator, Health Resources and Services Administration, Office of Special Programs, Division of Transplantation (Apr. 21, 2000) (hereinafter *Dr. Michael Dreis Interview*).

109. *See* Starzl & Fung, *supra* note 97.

110. *Id. See also,* Thomas E. Starzl et al., "A Multifactorial System for Equitable Selection of Cadaveric Kidney Recipients," 257 *JAMA* 3073 (1987).

111. *See* Starzl & Fung, *supra* note 97, at 454–55.

112. *Id.*

113. *Id.*

114. *Id.*

115. *Id.*

116. *See, e.g.,* Callender Testimony; P.I. Terasaki et al., "High Survival Rates of Kidney Transplants from Spousal and Living Unrelated Donors," 333 *NEMJ* 333 (1995).

117. Starzl & Fung, *supra* note 97.

118. *Id.*

119. *See* RD Guttmann, *The Graft Survival Curve: Ideology and Rhetoric in Organ Shortage: The Solutions* 235 (Touraine, ed).

120. See Interview with Dr. Dreis, *supra* note 108.

121. *Id.*

122. *Id.*

123. *Id.*

124. *Id.*

125. *Id.*

126. *See, e.g., 2000 Annual Report, supra* note 107, at 445.

127. *Id.* at 436.

128. United Network for Organ Sharing, "Who We Are: Membership: Histocompatibility Labs," at http://www.unos.org/whoweare/histoLabs.asp (noting that "There are many different HLA antigens, but the ones that seem to be most important for transplantation are HLA-A, HLA-B, and HLA-DR.").

129. *See* Fox Letter, *supra* note 102, at 5. Arguing in support of the 1998 revisions to UNOS's and OPTN's mandate, Dr. Claude Fox states:

> Our regulation does not disadvantage minorities or the poor, though the current system does. A 1991 HHS Inspector General report, as well as soon to be released UNOS data, show that minorities wait longer under the current system. The UNOS data show that women wait longer as well. And, at our 1996 public hearings, several witnesses testified to the prohibitive costs to poor people should they need to travel to or list at several hospitals in order to get needed organs. *Id.*

130. *See* Telephone interview with Scott Helm, United Network for Organ Sharing Spokesperson (Apr. 20, 2000) (hereinafter *Helm Interview*).

131. *See 2000 Annual Report, supra* note 101, at 13.

132. Anderson, *supra* note 94, at 251 n.10. *See* Kress, *supra* note 94, at 354 (discussing the possibility of xenotransplantation, and comparing progress in human transplantation).

133. "Clinical Trial Trends: Mistrust Limits Minority Representation in U.S. Biomedical Research," *Drug Week*, March 5, 2004, at 81.

134. *See 2000 Annual Report, supra* note 101, at 13.

135. *See also* Robert S. Gaston et al., "Racial Equity in Renal Transplantation: The Disparate Impact of HLA-Based Allocation," 270 *JAMA* 1352, 1353 (1993); J. Michael Soucie et al., "Race and Sex Differences in the Identification of Candidates for Renal Transplantation," 19 *Am. J. Kidney Disease* 414 (1992).

136. See Callender Testimony, *supra* note 26.

137. *See* Starzl & Fung, *supra* note 97; Benjamin Mintz, Note, "Analyzing the OPTN Under State Action Doctrine – Can UNOS's Organ Allocation Criteria Survive Strict Scrutiny?," 28 *Colum. J.L. & Soc. Probs.* 339, 340–41 n.9 (1995) (noting that anti-rejection drugs "increased kidney transplant recipients' one-year survival rates from 50% to 80% and liver patients' one-year survival rates from 35% to 70%"); Howard S. Schwartz, "Bioethical and Legal Considerations in Increasing the Supply of Transplantable Organs: From UAGA to 'Baby Fae,'" 10 *Am. J.L. & Med.* 397, 400 (1985) (commenting that Prednisone with cyclosporine were quite successful as anti-rejection agents used in organ transplantation, noting "[a]t the University of Pittsburgh, the one-year survival rate for liver transplants" had more than doubled in first year using the drugs).

138. *See* Noah, *supra* note 5, at 145.

139. Steve Takemoto et al., "Equitable Allocation of HLA-Compatible Kidneys for Local Pools and for Minorities," 331 *New Eng. J. Med* 760, 760 (1994) (discussing the longer life expectancies among those with perfect matching antigens).

140. *See* Abraham, *supra* note 34, at 185–87; Snyder, *supra* note 48 ("In 80% of the Black patient populations, it doesn't matter who they get a kidney from.").

141. *See* Snyder, *supra* note 48.

142. Anita Srikameswaran, "A Great Divide; Institutional Racism on One Side, Misinformation on the Other means Minorities Lag in Receiving Transplants and Heart Surgeries," *Pittsburgh Post-Gazette* (Pennsylvania), July 23, 2002, at F1.

143. Rod Watson, "In Blacks, Tragic Mistrust of Medicine," *Buffalo News* (New York), Feb. 22, 2001, at 1B. Skeptics of the medical necessity theory point to the vestiges of racism and theories of genetic superiority found in other antiquated American policies. They suggest that in other areas such as education, marriage, housing, shopping, dining, and many others, that interracial contact was scorned and often superficially connected to health and safety (i.e., water fountains, swimming pools, eugenics, etc.). *Id.*

144. Caplan, *supra* note 94.

145. *See* Gaston et al., *supra* note 135, at 1353.

146. *See* Noah, *supra* note 5, at 146.

147. *Id.* at 145–46.

148. *Id.*

149. *See* Schulte, *supra* note 26. *See also* Carol Rados, "Inside Clinical Trials: Testing Medical Products in People," *FDA Consumer*, Sept. 9, 2003 available at http://www.fda.gov/fdsc/features/2003/503_trial.html (reporting the exclusion of racial minorities and women in clinical drug studies).

150. *See* Schulte, *supra* note 26.

151. *See 2000 Annual Report, supra* note 107.

152. *See id.* at 13.

153. Dr. Michael Dreis Interview, *supra* note 108.

154. *See* Helm Interview, *supra* note 130; See OPTN Website *at* www.optn.org (providing demographic data by race, gender, and other demographic variants) (last visited July 21, 2005).

155. *See* Noah, *supra* note 5, at 145.

5. The Uniform Anatomical Gift Act

1. Sheldon Kurtz, Report to the Committee of the Whole, Revised Uniform Anatomical Gift Act (200_), July 21, 2005, available at http://www.law.upenn.edu/bll/ulc/uaga/2005AMAnatomicalReport.htm (hereinafter *Kurtz Report*).

2. *See, e.g.*, UNOS, "Timeline of Key Events in U.S. Transplantation and UNOS History," *at* http://www.Unos.org/whoWeAre/history.asp.

3. *See, e.g.*, Kurtz Report, *supra* note 1.

4. *See e.g.* Unif. Anatomical Gift Act § 5(b), 8A U.L.A. 47 (amended 1987).

5. *Id.*

6. *See generally*, Michele Goodwin, "Altruism's Limits: Law, Capacity, and Organ Commodification," 56 *Rutgers L. Rev.* 305, 376 (2004).

7. Unif. Anatomical Gift Act § 1(e) (1968).

8. E.B. Stason, *The Uniform Anatomical Gift Act*, 23 Bus. Law. 919, 927 (1968).

9. *Id.*

10. Unif. Anatomical Gift Act § 3 (1968).

11. *Id.*

12. Unif. Anatomical Gift Act § 2(b) (1968).

13. A common criticism of the act was its ambiguity regarding what have become essential issues. The act failed to make explicitly clear that one's next of kin could not revoke donor's "gift."

14. *See* Ann McIntosh, Comment, "Regulating The "Gift of Life" – The 1987 Uniform Anatomical Gift Act," 65 *Wash. L. Rev.* 171, 174 (1990).

15. *See* Erik S. Jaffe, Note, "'She's Got Bette Davis['s] Eyes': Assessing the Nonconsensual Removal of Cadaver Organs Under the Takings and Due Process Clauses," 90 *Colum. L. Rev.* 528, 535 (1990).

16. *See* Bay & Herbert, "The Living Donor in Kidney Transplantation," *in Organ Transplantation and Replacement* 273 (G. Cerilli ed., 1988).

17. Harry Schwartz, "Providing Incentives for Organ Donations," Wall Street Journal, July 25, 1983, at 10.

18. Virginia was the first state to ban the sale of organs from living or dead donors. *See* Va. Code § 32.1–289.1 (1985). *But see* Act of June 12 1967, ch. 353, 1967 Mass. Acts 202, 202 (repealed 1971) (prohibiting the sale of organs, body parts, tissues after death). Prior to adoption of the 1968 UAGA proscribed individuals from selling their bodies (or parts thereof) after death. However, on the passage of the UAGA and its ratification in their legislatures, they repealed their prior statutes. Law of Aug. 1, 1968, ch. 429, § 7, 56 Del. Laws, 1773, 1773 (1967) (repealed 1970); Law of May 20, 1967, ch. 94, § 1, 1967 Hawaii Laws 91, 91 (repealed 1969) (prohibiting the sale of bodies after death); Law of April 24, 1961, ch. 315, § 1, 11961 Md. Laws 397, 398 (repealed 1968); Law of April 22, 1964, ch. 702, § 1, 1964 N.Y. Laws 1827, 1828 (repealed 1971) (foregoing statutes cited in Susan Hankin Denise, Note, "Regulating the Sale of Human Organs," 71 *Va. L. Rev.* 1015, 1022–23). Most states banning posthumous sales of organs did not expressly ban the posthumous sale of organs by an individual's relative: Massachusetts was an exception. Denis Collins, "'Harvest of Dead' Bill Advances in Richmond," *Washington Post*, Jan. 23, 1981, at C1. The state, however, was motivated to act by the untimely proposal of H.B. Jacobs, and the increasing demand for life-sustainable body parts that would otherwise be "wasted." *See, e.g.*, Howard S. Schwartz, "Bioethical and Legal Considerations in Increasing the Supply of Transplantable Organs: From UAGA to 'Baby Fae'," 10 *Am. J.L. & Med.* 397, 409 n.79 (1985). Other states followed Virginia with presumed consent laws.

19. *See, e.g.*, Christian Williams, "Combating the Problems of Human Rights Abuses and Inadequate Organ Supply through Presumed Donative Consent," 26 *Case W. Res. J. Int'l L.* 315, 345–46 (1994).

20. *See, e.g.*, "News Conference by the Right-To-Life Committee," *Federal News Service*, Jan. 23, 1989 ("We have all kinds of fetal manipulation, the killing of babies now to get their organs...."); John Carey, "There Just Aren't 'Enough Hearts To Go

Around,'" *Business Week*, Nov. 27, 1989, at 94 (expressing fear of appearing to be "organ snatchers"); B.D. Colen, "Desperate Measures: Solving the Organ-Donor Shortage," *Health*, Apr. 1989, at 84 (expressing fear that life-supporting measures would be prematurely terminated to procure organs for transplantation).

21. *See, e.g.*, Gareth Parry, "Kidney Donor Tells of Pain," The Guardian (London), Dec. 13, 1989; Michael Kinsley, "Take My Kidney," *Please*," *Time Magazine*, March 13, 1989, at 88; Bjorn Edlund, "'Courage Isn't Up to Bank Heist?' Sell a Kidney; Cash Offered for Live Donors' Organs," *L.A. Times*, Nov. 13, 1988, at 12; Fern Schumer Chapman, "The Life-and-Death Question of an Organ Market," *Fortune*, June 11, 1984, at 108; "Kidney for Sale: $20,000," *United Press International*, July 17, 1981.

22. *See* McIntosh, *supra* note 14, at 176 (commenting that "[u]nlike the 1968 UAGA, which was swiftly embraced by state legislatures, the 1987 UAGA . . . met significant opposition.").

23. *See, e.g.*, Julian S. Moore, "The Gift of Life: New Laws, Old Dilemmas, and the Future of Organ Procurement," 21 *Akron L. Rev.* 443, 455 (1988); David E. Jefferies, Note, "The Body as Commodity: The Use of Markets to Cure the Organ Deficit," 5 *Ind. J. Global Legal Stud.* 621, 628 (1998).

24. *See* Preface, Unif. Anatomical Gift Act (1968); Georgetta Glaves-Innis, "Organ Donation and Incompetents: Can They Consent?," 10 *Touro Int'l L. Rev.* 155, 175–176 (2000).

25. *Id.*

26. *But see* Unif. Anatomical Gift Act § 10 (1987) (prohibiting the posthumous sale of organs).

27. *Id.* at § 4. *See also* McIntosh, *supra* note 14, at 176 (discussing provisions of the new act allowing "medical examiners to release any useable organ for transplantation according to procedures established by state law").

28. *See* Unif. Anatomical Gift Act § 5 (1987) (requiring hospitals to routinely inquire

about organ donation at or before hospital admission). *See also* 42 U.S.C. § 1320b-8 (requiring under federal law that among other things, families be made aware of option to donate and organ procurement agencies be notified of potential donors).

29. *See, e.g.*, Unif. Anatomical Gift Act § 2(h) (1987) (prioritizing donor's wishes over family objection).

30. *See* Kurtz Report, *supra* note 1.

31. *Id.*

32. *Id.*

6. Presumed Consent: The Unsuspecting Donor

1. *See* Lisa Richardson, "Praise for his Art Keeps Young Muralist from Being Walled in by Harsh Gang Life," *Los Angeles Times*, Nov. 27, 1992, at B1; Ralph Frammolino, "Harvest of Corneas at Morgue Questioned," *Los Angeles Times*, Nov. 2, 1997, at A1 [hereinafter Frammolino, *Harvest of Corneas*].

2. *See* Richardson, *supra* note 1.

3. *Id.*

4. *Id.*

5. *See* Frammolino, *Harvest of Corneas*, *supra* note 1.

6. *Id.*

7. *Id.*

8. *Id.* Frammolino, author of the study involving over 570 cases where corneas were removed without consent from donors or their next of kin during a 12-month period, comments in his article that all the families "were shocked that they had not been asked or told." *Id.*

9. *Id.*

10. *See infra* Chapters IV and V.

11. *See* Frammolino, *Harvest of Corneas*, *supra* note 1. Carlos, then age 24, died shortly before nine o'clock in the evening on March 26, 1997, from head and chest wounds. The next day his sister called the morgue. She recalls "[m]y parents told me to let them know they didn't want any organs donated or anything." *Id.*

12. *Id.*

13. *Id.*

14. *Id.* The Doheny Eye and Tissue Transplant Bank, which paid more than one million dollars over a 5-year period (1992–1997) to the Los Angeles County coroner's office, "harvested without the permission or knowledge of the families of the dead," according to the *Times* investigation. Doheny's "markup" was more than 1,200% of the purchase price – or gift provided to the coroner's office, which by even industry standards was higher than usual.

15. Carlos Gudino died March 26, 1997. However it was later that year in November, when Frammolino's story ran that the family became aware of the nonconsensual cornea removal.

16. *Id.*

17. *Id.*

18. *Id.*

19. *Id.*

20. Unif. Anatomical Gift Act § 4 (1987).

21. *Id.* (stating "[t]he [coroner] [medical examiner] may release and permit the removal of a part from a body within that official's custody...").

22. *See, e.g.,* Frammolino, *Harvest of Corneas, supra* note 1; S. Gregory Boyd, Comment, "Considering a Market in Human Organs," 4 *N.C. J.L. & Tech.* 417, 441 (2003).

23. *See, e.g.,* Frammolino, *Harvest of Corneas, supra* note 1; Boyd, *supra* note 22.

24. Marie-Andree Jacob, "On Silencing and Slicing: Presumed Consent to Post-Mortem Organ "Donation" in Diversified Societies," 11 *Tulsa J. Comp. & Int'l L.* 239, 254–55 (2003) (describing the criticism that presumed consent is unethical); Maryellen Liddy, "The 'New Body Snatchers': Analyzing the Effect of Presumed Consent Organ Donation Laws on Privacy, Autonomy, and Liberty," 28 *Fordham Urb. L.J.* 815, 819 (2001) (describing that many supporters believe presumed consent will increase the supply of organs available for transplant).

25. Linda C. Fentiman, "Organ Donation as National Service: A Proposed Federal Organ Donation Law," 27 *Suffolk U.L. Rev.* 1593 (1993); Boyd, *supra* note 22.

26. Erik S. Jaffe, "'She's Got Bette Davis['s] Eyes': Assessing the Nonconsensual Removal of Cadaver Organs under the Takings and Due Process Clauses," 90 *Colum. L. Rev.* 528, 535 (1990).

27. Fentiman, *supra* note 25, at 1599.

28. *See* DeWayne Wickham, "America's Smaller Communities Getting Taste of Urban Violence," *Gannett News Service,* May 25, (citation omitted) (noting rise in violence in the 1980s); Gabriel Escobar, "Deaths Pose Continuing D.C. Mystery; City Carries Hundreds of Undetermined Cases, Muddying Vital Statistics," *Washington Post,* Dec. 22, 1997, at A1 (commenting on the rise in urban violence in the 1980s and that many of the deaths of Black urban Americans from that era remain unsolved); Glen Loury, "The Impossible Dilemma," *The New Republic,* Jan. 1, 1996, at 21 (noting that the murder rate among Black youths (persons under age 20), which was already three times that of White youths in 1986, doubled in the five years between 1986 and 1991, but the White rate remained unchanged). *See also* Darryl Fears, "Urban Spotlight: Is Atlanta the Next Detroit?," *The Atlanta Journal and Constitution,* Dec. 18, 1994, at D1 (pointing out that in the early 1980s, the homicide rate soared). Fears reports that between 1983 and 1987, more than 700 people were slain each year. On No Crime Day in Detroit – a 1986 event sponsored by basketball star Isaiah Thomas to prove his city was still safe – a police officer was shot dead. *Id.*

29. *See* Keith Aoki, "Space Invaders: Critical Geography, The 'Third World' in International Law and Critical Race Theory," 45 *Vill. L. Rev.* 913, 920 (2000).

30. *See, e.g.,* John M. Hagedorn, "Gang Violence in the Postindustrial Era," 24 *Crime & Just.* 365 (1998); Richard Rosenfeld & Scott H. Decker, "Consent to Search and Seize: Evaluating an Innovative Youth Firearm Suppression Program," 59-*WTR Law & Contemp. Probs.* 197 (1996).

31. *See, e.g.,* CNN, "Crime in the U.S. is Discussed," The Late Edition, Oct. 24, 1993 (Transcript #4-2); Eric Lichtblau, "Reporter's

Notebook: Going beyond Line Scores of Gang Carnage," *Los Angeles Times*, Nov. 25, 1990, at B3 (noting that during a one-month time span there were over 300 gang-related killings in Los Angeles County); "Spying on Neighbors – The New Drug-War Strategy," *Larry King Live*, Aug. 15, 1990 (Transcript # 108-2).

32. Bob Barr et al., "Debate: The War on Drugs: Fighting Crime or Wasting Time?," 38 *Am. Crim. L. Rev.* 1537, 1539 (2001).

33. *Id.* at 1539–40.

34. *See, e.g.*, Frammolino, *Harvest of Corneas, supra* note 1.

35. "Farrakhan Links Race to Transplants," *The New York Times*, May 2, 1994, at A18.

36. "Farrakhan: Whites Want Black Donors," *Pittsburgh Post-Gazette* (PA), May 2, 1994, at A6.

37. CNN, "Farrakhan and Race Relations," *CNN & Company*, Transcript # 347-3, May 2, 1994.

38. Telephone interview with Doyce Williams, Executive Director, Alabama Eye Bank (Feb. 21, 2000) [hereinafter *Williams Interview I*]. Mr. Williams expressed his great support for presumed consent legislation, and asserted that legislative consent had a very positive influence on the number of corneas that were made available for transplantation. *See also* Ralph Frammolino, "L.A. Coroner Alters Policy on Corneas," *Los Angeles Times*, Nov. 4, 1997, at A1 [hereinafter Frammolino, *L.A. Coroner*].

39. Williams Interview I, *supra* note 38.

40. Telephone interview with Doyce Williams, Executive Director, Alabama Eye Bank (Feb. 23, 2000) [hereinafter *Williams Interview II*].

41. *See, e.g.*, Ronald N. Robin, "Elderly Heart Surgery Candidate with Concerns about Transfusion," *Consultant*, July 1, 2003 (noting that "prior infections, such as ... Creutzfeldt-Jakob disease, have been transmitted by donation of contaminated tissue, such as dura or cornea ... ").

42. *See, e.g.*, Interview with Mark Larson, Executive Director, Eyebank of Wisconsin, in Madison, Wis. (Feb. 21, 2000) [hereinafter *Larson Interview*]; Interview with Dr. Jim Martin, Executive Director, Louisville Eye Bank, in Louisville, Kentucky (Mar. 1999 and Aug. 1999) [hereinafter *Martin Interview*].

43. *See* Williams Interview I, *supra* note 38.

44. Michele Goodwin, "Deconstructing Legislative Consent Law: Organ Taking, Racial Profiling, & Distributive Justice," 6 *Va. J.L. and Tech.* 2, 18 (2001).

45. *Brotherton v. Cleveland*, 923 F.2d 477, 481 (6th Cir. 1991); *Newman v. Sathyavaglswaran*, 287 F.3d 786 (9th Cir. 2002).

46. Tissue Banks International (TBI) and the Doheny Eye Bank, which serve Los Angeles, have been criticized by former employees, ethicists, and investigative news programs like *20/20* and the *L.A. Times* for their eagerness to increase supply of cornea tissue, sometimes without regard for family consent, health factors, or social criteria that would restrict certain corneas from entering the stream of supply. Frammolino, *Harvest of Corneas, supra* note 1.

47. *See* Cornea Research Interview Notes and Transcripts (on file with author). Interviews were conducted with directors of eye banks representing Wisconsin, Kentucky, Arkansas, northern Florida, Michigan, Illinois, northern Ohio, Indiana, Massachusetts, New Hampshire, Rhode Island, Vermont, and New Orleans. Attempts were made to interview eye bank representatives or directors representing Georgia, California, Maryland, Texas, and Minnesota. *But see* Williams Interview I, *supra* note 40; Interview with Mary Jane O'Neil, Executive Director, Eye Bank Sight Restoration, in New York, N.Y. (Feb. 21, 2000) [hereinafter *O'Neil Interview*]. Both O'Neil and Williams support presumed consent laws and believe that it would greatly benefit their states. Neither state presently uses legislative consent to procure eye tissues.

48. *See* Cornea Research Interview Notes and Transcripts, *supra* note 47.

49. AAOTS I.

50. *Id.*

51. Charles M. Key & Gary D. Miller, "The Tennessee Health Care Decisions Act a Major

Advance in the Law of Critical Care Decision Making," 40-*Aug Tenn. B.J.* 25, 26 (2004); *Ostojic v. Brueckmann*, 405 F.2d 302, 304 (7th Cir. 1968)

52. Those interviewed include: Mary Jane O'Neil, Executive Director, Eye Bank Sight Restoration (New York, N.Y.); Florence Johnston, President and CEO, Midwest Eye Bank (Mich.); Tom Buckley, Executive Director, New England Eye and Tissue Transplant Bank (Boston, Mass.); Donica Davis, Hospital Development Coordinator, Tennessee Eye Bank; Mark Larson, Executive Director, The Eyebank of Wisconsin (Madison, Wis.); Dr. Jim Martin, Executive Director of Louisville Eye Bank (Louisville, Ky.); Gene Reynolds, Technical Director, Alabama Eye Bank; Kristen McCoy, Laboratory Director Illinois Eye Bank; Maurice Van Zance, Executive Director, Indiana Transplant Program; Chey Greiger, Administrator, Southern Eye Bank (New Orleans, La.); Doyce Williams, Executive Director, Alabama Eye Bank; David Sierra, Hospital Development Technical Director, North Florida Lions Eye Bank (Jacksonville, Fla.). Interviews were also conducted with representatives from Tissue Banks International (Md.) and The Eye Bank Association of America. Attempts were made to interview eye bank officials in California and Washington, D.C.; however, calls made in February and March (2000) were not returned. A concerted effort was made to interview officials from states with legislative consent provisions.

53. Fentiman, *supra* note 25, at 1599 (proposing presumed consent system that would avoid consent, and arguing that "[p]hysicians would no longer need to confront a grieving family with the need to make a quick decision about organ donation"); Jaffe, *supra* note 26, at 535 (stating that "[o]ne significant barrier was perceived to be the difficulty of obtaining consent for organ donation").

54. Fentiman, *supra* note 25.

55. Mark F. Anderson, "The Future of Organ Transplantation: From Where Will New Donors Come, to Whom Will Their

Organs Go?" 5 *Health Matrix* 249, 268 (1995) (discussing the purpose of autopsies to investigate the purpose of death and that state statutes authorize medical examiners to perform such inquiries without consent for "non-homicidal traumatic death" and "suspected homicides"). However, relatively little scholarly attention has been given to presumed consent and its impact on fragile communities (the poor, urban, of color, homeless, etc.).

56. Jaffe, *supra* note 26, at 538.

57. Larson Interview, *supra* note 42.

58. *See* Md. Code Ann., Est. & Trusts § 4-509.1 (2005). Titled: When Chief Medical Examiner or his deputy or assistant may provide cornea transplant, describes the statutory requirements and provisions for legislative consent:

> (a) Requirements – In any case where a patient is in need of corneal tissue for a transplant, the Chief Medical Examiner, the deputy chief medical examiner, or an assistant medical examiner may provide the cornea upon the request of the Medical Eye Bank of Maryland, Incorporated under the following conditions:
>
> > (1) The medical examiner has charge of a decedent who may provide a suitable cornea for transplant;
> > (2) An autopsy will be required;
> > (3) No objection by the next of kin is known by the medical examiner; and
> > (4) Removal of the cornea for transplant will not interfere with the subsequent course of an investigation or autopsy or alter the postmortem facial appearance.
>
> (b) Liability of Medical Examiner - The Chief Medical Examiner, the deputy chief medical examiner, an assistant medical examiner, and the Medical Eye Bank of Maryland, Incorporated are not liable for civil action if the next of kin subsequently contends that authorization of that kin was required.

59. Ariz. Rev. Stat. Ann. § 36-851 to -852 (1986 & Supp. 1989); Ark. Code Ann. § 12-12-320 (1987); Cal. Gov't Code § 27491.46-.47 (West 1988); Colo. Rev. Stat. § 30-10-621 (1986); Conn. Gen. Stat. Ann. § 19a-281 (West 1986); Del. Code Ann. tit. 29, § 4712

(Supp.1988); Fla. Stat. Ann. § 732.9185 (West Supp. 1989); Ga. Code Ann. § 31-23-6 (1985); Haw. Rev. Stat. Ann. § 327-4 (1988); Idaho Code § 39-3405 (Supp. 1989); Ill. Ann. Stat. § ch. 110 1/2, 351–354 (Smith-Hurd Supp. 1989); Ky. Rev. Stat. Ann. § 311.187 (Michie Supp. 1988); La. Rev. Stat. Ann. § 17:2354.1-3, 33:1565 (West 1982, 1988 & Supp. 1989); Md. Est. & Trusts Code Ann. § 4-509.1 (Supp. 1989); Mass. Ann. Laws ch. 113, § 14 (Law. Co-op. Supp. 1989); Mich. Comp. Laws Ann. § 333.10202 (1989); Miss. Code Ann. § 41-61-71 (Supp. 1989); Mo. Ann. Stat. § 58.770 (Vernon 1989); Mont. Code Ann. § 72-17-215 (1989); N.C. Gen. Stat. § 130A- 391 (1989); N.D. Cent. Code § 23-06.2-04 (Supp. 1989); Ohio Rev. Code Ann. § 2108.60 (Baldwin 1987); Okla. Stat. Ann. tit. 63, § 944.1 (West Supp. 1990); R.I. Gen. Laws § 23-18.6-4 (1989); Tenn. Code Ann. § 68-30-204 (Supp. 1989); Tex. Health & Safety Code Ann. § 693.012 (Vernon pamphlet 1990); Utah Code Ann. § 26-4-23 (1989); Wash. Rev. Code Ann. § 68.50.280 (Supp. 1989); Wis. Laws § 157.06 (1989); W.Va. Code § 16-19-3a (1985).

60. California, Florida, Hawaii, Kentucky, Louisiana, Maryland, Michigan, North Carolina, and Wisconsin.

61. *See* Betsy Butgereit, *Plan Would Require Conrnea Removal*, Birmingham News (Alabama), Feb. 17, 1998, at 1A [hereinafter *Cornea Removal*]; Betsy Butgereit, *Cornea Controversy: Eye Banks Don't See Eye-to-Eye on Laws*, Birmingham News (Alabama), Feb. 16, 1998, at 1A [hereinafter *Controversy*]; (commenting that "Jefferson County [Alabama] isn't alone in wrestling over whether medical examiners should be allowed to remove corneas of dead people without their families' permission or knowledge"); Frammolino, *L.A. Coroner*, *supra* note 38 (citation omitted) (reporting that eye bank employees "say they were discouraged from seeking family permission so corneas could be harvested under state law").

62. Martin Interview, *supra* note 42; Larson Interview, *supra* note 42; Telephone interview with David Sierra, Hospital Devel-

opment Technical Director, North Florida Lions Eye Bank (Feb. 23, 2000) [hereinafter *Sierra Interview*] (commenting that legislative consent "can't tell you what a person was doing at 4:00 am the morning prior"); Telephone interview with Kristen McCoy, Laboratory Director, Illinois Eye Bank (Feb. 21, 2000) [hereinafter *McCoy Interview*] (commenting that they do not use the Illinois legislative consent statute because of a fear of lawsuits and ethical considerations).

63. Martin Interview, *supra* note 42.

64. *Id.*

65. *Id. Compare* Ky. Rev. Stat. Ann. § 311.187 (1988); *Ohio Rev. Code Ann.* § 2108.60 (1987); *Ark. Code Ann.* § 12-12-320 (1987); *W.Va. Code* § 16-19-3a (1985).

66. Martin Interview, *supra* note 42.

67. *Id.*

68. Larson Interview, *supra* note 42 (stating that "not having consent is a bad thing. One bad thing can undue many things"); Telephone interview with Donica Davis, Hospital Development Coordinator, Tennessee Eye Bank (Apr. 5, 2000) [hereinafter *Davis Interview*] (commenting that "we also want consent from the family"); Telephone interview with Tom Buckley, Executive Director of New England Eye and Tissue Transplant Bank (Apr. 6, 2000) [hereinafter *Buckley Interview*] (stating that, "philosophically, we have felt that, isn't it better to contact the families? for courtesy if nothing else?").

69. Buckley Interview, *supra* note 69; Larson Interview, *supra* note 42; Davis Interview, *supra* note 68.

70. Larson Interview, *supra* note 42.

71. *Id.*

72. *Id.*

73. Mark E. Larson, *Use of Tissue Recovered Using Medical Examiner/Coroner Laws* (Mar. 5, 1998) (unpublished manuscript, on file with the author).

74. *Id.*

75. Williams Interview II, *supra* note 40. Mr. Williams proffered that more people had their vision restored under legislative consent laws, and they were able to export excess

corneal tissue. However, the state has suffered a dramatic decrease in the amount of tissues available since the abandonment of legislative consent laws, the emergence of bad publicity, and lawsuits. *Id.*

76. Butgereit, *Controversy, supra* note 61; Betsy Butgereit, "Mother Feels Corneas Were Stolen," *Birmingham News* (Ala.), Feb. 16, 1998, at A1 [hereinafter *Mother Feels*].

77. *See* Butgereit, *Mother Feels, supra* note 76.

78. *Id.*

79. *Id.*

80. Williams Interview II, *supra* note 40 (commenting on the effect of negative publicity on cornea procurement).

81. Karin Meadows, "Cornea Policy OK by Commissioners," *Birmingham News* (Ala.), Feb. 19, 1998, at B1. (noting that "the matter became the subject of controversy after commissioners discovered the coroner's office wasn't obtaining permission to remove the dime-sized clear tissue for transplants"). After the series of news articles chronicling Patsy Burton's misfortune, the Jefferson County Commissioner's office now requires that the Alabama Eye Bank make efforts to contact the next of kin. *See* Williams Interview II, *supra* note 40.

82. Frammolino, *L.A. Coroner, supra* note 38 (citation omitted).

83. *But see* O'Neil Interview, *supra* note 47. Reconciling the need to restore sight and promote life by violating a dead body can be a clear-cut case for some. O'Neil lobbied for a medical examiner statute in New York, believing that it would increase the number of corneas available for transplantation, and that eventually "80% of people would care less." *Id.*

84. *Id. See also* Fentiman, *supra* note 25, at 1594 n.6 (citing *End Stage Renal Disease Foundation Health Care Financing Research Report* (1990)) (commenting that "recent changes in both the law and public attitudes toward seat belt use and drinking and driving, along with broad demographic trends, have combined to decrease the pool of available donors").

85. Erica Noonan, "Sprinkler Bill Stirs Some Debate," *Boston Globe*, Feb. 25, 2001, at 3 (commenting that "safety prevention efforts save lives, noting it's no different than saying it costs money to install seat belts and air bags and baby car seats.... There are things we spend money on, and saving lives seems like a pretty good thing to spend money on"). *See also* Charles Wheelen, "Lives Changed in a Split Second," *N.Y. Times*, Jan. 10, 2001, at A19; Licia Corbella, "Don't Put Children Near Front Air Bags," *The Calgary Sun*, March 16, 2001, at 4; Lori Shontz, "Healing Rock: Process of Moving on after Earnhardt's Death Begins," *N.C., Pittsburgh Post-Gazette*, Feb. 25, 2001, at D1; Meredith Fischer & Will Jones, "Some Roads are Deadly: Deficient Design, Driver Inattention Can Be Fatal Mix," *Richmond Times Dispatch* (Va), at A1.

86. Elliot N. Dorff, "Choosing Life: Aspects of Judaism Affecting Organ Transplantation," *in* Organ Transplantation: Meanings and Realities" 169 (Stewart J. Younger et al., eds. 1996).

87. *Id.* at 168–93.

88. *Id.* at 177. Elliot Dorff comments that, "[f]rom [his] own perspective, the value of saving lives ultimately overcomes objections to organ transplantation per se." *Id.* at 169. Dorff acknowledges, however, that organ donation is a complicated issue in Judaism because death is perceived as "extended over several phases, and [Judaism] has a basic diffidence with regard to our ability to define the moment of death exactly." *Id.* at 177.

89. *Id.* at 177.

90. *Id.* at 177–78.

91. *Id.* at 178.

92. Mackenzie Carpenter, "'Presumed' Donor Bill Aired," *Pittsburgh Post-Gazette*, July 14, 1999, at A10 (raising questions about the constitutionality of proposed presumed consent measures because for "Native Americans, Orthodox Jews, and most Asian religions, disemboweling the body is a sacrilege"); James Lindemann Nelson, "Transplantation Through a Glass Darkly," 22 *Hastings Center Rep.* No. 5, 6 (1992);

Elliot Pinsley, "Routine Donation of Organs Pushed; Ethics Group Seeks Presumed Consent," *The Record*, Dec. 22, 1992 at A1 (noting the fear among Orthodox Jews that presumed consent measures would be problematic and "that a government bureaucracy cannot be trusted to maintain proper records").

93. O'Neil Interview, *supra* note 47.

94. *Id.* O'Neil argued that the Jewish community organized and fought against legislative consent in New York and her organization, which lobbied to support a medical examiner statute, withdrew their proposal. *Id.*

95. *See, e.g.,* E. Guadagnoli, et al., "The Public's Willingness to Discuss their Preference for Organ Donation with Family Members," 13:4 *Clinical Transplantation* 342 (1999) (a study of three ethnic groups, including African Americans).

96. AAOTS II, K.S. Interview.

97. *Id.*

98. AAOTS II, D.J. Interview.

99. AAOTS II, A.S. Interview.

100. AAOTS II, J.F. Interview.

101. AAOTS II, Interview with A.A., a federal investigator. Such perceptions were shared among the overwhelming majority of participants who spoke to "choice."

102. *Id.*

103. AAOTS II, J.D. Interview.

104. AAOTS II, L.J. Interview.

105. *Id.*

106. AAOTS II, L.L.B. Interview.

107. AAOTS II, N.B. Interview.

108. *Id.*

109. Pinsley, *supra* note 92 (commenting on James Nelson's presumed consent proposal, which "specified that people could opt not to have their organs removed if they objected on religious or philosophical grounds").

110. *See* Frammolino, *Harvest of Corneas, supra* note 1.

111. *Id.*

112. *See* Frammolino, *L.A. Corner, supra* note 38.

113. *See* Goodwin, *supra* note 44. The surveys were conducted over the phone in late January and February 2000. The author asked 11 questions of each participant. Of the initial 100 surveys analyzed, the race groupings were 86% African American and 14% White. Participants ranged in age from 18–70 years old. Sixty-five percent (65%) of the participants were 18–25 years old.

114. *Id.*

115. *Id. See also* Ky. Rev. Stat. Ann. § 311.187 (1988).

116. Nelson, *supra* note 92, at 7–8 (proposing a presumed consent measure with opt-out provisions the same year his article was published).

117. *You Vang Yang v. Sturner*, 728 F.Supp. 845 (D.R.I. 1990).

118. *Id.* at 846.

119. *Id.* at 847. The Yang's 23-year-old son died from a seizure, but physicians involved with the case were unaware of what caused the seizure, and thus an autopsy was recommended and performed. *Id.* at 846.

120. *Id.* at 853.

121. 494 U.S. 872 (1990).

122. For an overview of social contract theory, *see* Jean-Jacques Rousseau, *The Social Contract or Principles of Political Right* 5 (Wordsworth Classics, 1998) (1762); Ernest Barker, *Introduction to Social Contract: Essays by Locke, Hume, and Rousseau* (1947); John Rawls, *A Theory of Justice* (1971); Michael Lessnoff, *Social Contract* (1986); Will Kymlicka, "The Social Contract Tradition, in" *A Companion to Ethics* (1991); Jean Hampton, "Contract and Content," *A Companion to Contemporary Political Philosophy* (Goodin & Pettit eds., 1993). Other justifications for presumed consent can be made, including: (a) presumed consent avoids families having to be approached about organ donation – and the negative consequences possibly experienced by grieving family members who now must be asked for authorization; (b) presumed consents are real, not illusory consents. One truly has a choice of whether to donate. The opt-out provisions provide protections for the potential donor and her family who may decide to change their minds.

123. Fentiman, *supra* note 25; *See also* Dukeminier, "Suppllying Organs for Transplantation," 68 *Mich. L. Rev.* 811 (1970); Dukeminier & Sanders, "Organ Transplantation: A Proposal for Routine Salvaging of Cadaver Organs," 279 *New Eng. J. Med.* 413 (1968); Pinsley, *supra* note 92 (discussing James Nelson's presumed consent proposal).

124. Telephone interview with Scott Helm, United Network for Organ Sharing Spokesperson (Apr. 20, 2000) (providing recent figures for organ waitlists); Telephone interviews with Dr. Ellison, Representative, United Network of Organ Sharing (July, 1999 and August, 1999).

125. *See* Fentiman, *supra* note 25.

126. *See Brotherton v. Cleveland*, 923 F.2d 477, 481 (6th Cir. 1991).

127. *Id.* at 483 (Joiner, J., dissenting) (rejecting the theory of property ownership in dead bodies).

128. Anita Allen, "Social Contract Theory in American Case Law," 51 *Fla. L. Rev.* 1, 10 (1999) (noting that "like 'state of nature,' the expression 'social contract' has multiple meanings in the law").

129. *Id.* at 2.

130. *Id.*

131. *Id.*

132. Fentiman, *supra* note 25, at 1598.

133. *Jacobson v. Massachusetts*, 197 U.S. 11 (1905).

134. *Id.* at 27.

135. *Brotherton v. Cleveland*, 923 F.2d 477, 483 (6th Cir. 1991) (Joiner, J., dissenting).

136. Fentiman, *supra* note 25, at 1598–1602.

137. *Id.*

138. Charles W. Mills, *The Racial Contract* 73 (1997).

139. *See id.* at 62–75 ("arguing that [t]he Racial Contract underwrites the modern social contract and is continually being rewritten.").

140. Dalton Conley, *Being Black, Living in the Red: Race, Wealth, and Social Policy in America*, 61–62 (1999) (speaking to Blacks' continued economic disenfranchisement).

141. *See* Mills, *supra* note 138, at 64; *Dred Scott v. Sanford, 1856, in Race, Class, and Gender in the United States* 401 (Paula S. Rothenberg, ed., 4th ed. 1998); David E. Stannard, *American Holocaust: Columbus and the Conquest of the New Worlds* (1992).

142. Mills, *supra* note 138, at 63–64.

143. *Id.* at 64.

144. *See, e.g.*, C. Vann Woodward, *The Strange Career of Jim Crow* (1955); W.E.B. Du Bois, *Black Reconstruction in America* (1935).

145. Francis Jennings, *The Invasion of America: Indians, Colonialism, and the Cant of Conquest* 60 (1975).

146. *See* Dorothy Roberts, *Killing The Black Body: Race, Reproduction, and the Meaning of Liberty* (1997); Laurie Kaye Abraham, *Mama Might Be Better Off Dead: The Failure of Health Care in Urban America* (1993); Barbara A. Noah, "Racial Disparities in the Delivery of Health Care," 35 *San Diego L. Rev.* 135 (1998). For a critique of American racial policy or the law in action on education, housing, wealth, and employment *see, e.g.*, Derrick Bell, *Faces at The Bottom of The Well: The Permanence of Racism* (1992); Stephen Steinberg, *Turning Back: The Retreat from Racial Justice in American Thought and Policy* (1995); Tom Wicker, *Tragic Failure: Racial Integration in America* (1996); Melvin L. Oliver & Thomas M. Shapiro, *Black Wealth/ White Wealth: A New Perspective on Racial Inequality*; Conley, *supra* note 140.

147. Allen, *supra* note 128, at 13.

148. *See* Fred D. Gray, *The Tuskegee Syphilis Study: An Insiders Account of The Shocking Medical Experiment Conducted by Government Doctors Against African American Men* (1998); James H. Jones, *Bad Blood: The Tuskegee Syphilis Experiment* (1981).

149. Abraham, *supra* note 146, at 4–5; Denise Grady, "Discrimination is Painful, It Can Also be Agonizing," N.Y. Times, Apr. 9, 2000, at 2; Brigid Schulte, "Minorities Face Unequal Health in U.S.: Statistics Show Ethnicities Encounter Higher Illness Rates," *Ft. Worth Star-Telegram*, Aug. 2, 1998, at 1; Editorial, "Institutionalized Racism In Health

Care," *The Lancet,* Mar. 6, 1999, No. 9155, Vol. 353, at 765; Ismail Turay, Jr., "Reps Press Minority Health Research," *Dayton Daily News* (Ohio), Feb. 3, 2000, at 3A; Editorial, "Accepted for Too Long the Disparity in Health of White and Black Won't Disappear by Itself," Des Moines Register (Iowa), Feb. 25, 2000, at 12.

150. *See* Mills, *supra* note 138.

151. Mayor Sharon Pratt Kelly, "Thurgood Marshall Commemorative Issue: Keynote Address," 35 *How. L.J.* 61 (1991) (noting that "African Americans, have been in America for four centuries. We have defended America in every war and revolution since Crispus Attucks. We have contributed to her growth, enriched her culture, served her well. It's time for us to claim ownership, to own a piece of the American rock. This is our country and we need to embrace her as such; for we are Americans"); Daniel H. Pollitt, "Reflection on the Bicentennial of the Bill of Rights: The Flag Burning Controversy: A Chronology," 70 *N.C.L. Rev* 553 (1992) (commenting on observations that "the first American to fall in the Revolutionary War was Crispus Attucks . . . an African-American who died for freedom a century before our Nation ended slavery"); Constance Baker Motley, "Thurgood Marshall," 68 *N.Y.U. L. Rev* 208 (1993) (noting the symbol of heroism and loyalty found in those like Crispus Attucks, commenting that "it was not until Thurgood Marshall's funeral in January 1993 that I came to the full realization that in death he has become an authentic American Hero, a Crispus Attucks, a Patrick Henry, a Thomas Jefferson, a George Washington, an Abraham Lincoln, a Martin Luther King.").

152. *See* Anthony Paul Farley, "The Black Body as Fetish Object," 76 *Ore. L.Rev.* 457 (1997).

153. *See Race, Class, and Gender in the United States, supra* note 141.

154. Fentiman, *supra* note 25, at 1598.

155. *Id.* But note that Fentiman does not address in any depth how racial disparities would be overcome in her proposal. Neither are the historical racial disparities in healthcare discussed, which seem relevant to a discussion about legislative consent and the presumed donation of organs. One reason for this oversight could be that substantive race discussions in healthcare law, and disparities discussed in the context of civil rights and various other obligations are only recently emerging.

156. David E. Jefferies, Note, "The Body as Commodity: The Use of Markets to Cure the Organ Deficit," 5 *Ind. J. Global Legal Stud.* 621, 628 (1998).

157. Allen, *supra* note 128, at 14.

158. *Putting Patients First – Allocation of Transplant Organ: Hearings Before the House Commerce Comm. Subcomm. on Health and The Environment and the Senate Labor and Human Resources Comm.,* 106th Cong., 2nd Sess. (1998) [hereinafter Callender Testimony] (testifying before a congressional subcommittee about institutionalized racism in healthcare, and particularly in organ allocation).

159. Gabriella Boston, "Emory Addresses Reluctance of Black Organ Donors," *Atlanta J. and Constitution,* May 6, 1999, at 9JA (identifying why Blacks are more reluctant to donate, including distrust of the medical community and racism); Roger Campbell, "Too Many Blacks Await Lifesaving Donations," *Essence,* Apr. 1999, at 45.

160. Campbell, *supra* note 160.

161. Allen, *supra* note 128, at 15.

162. *See, e.g.,* Frammolino, *Harvest of Corneas, supra* note 1.

163. *Id.*

164. Jaffe, *supra* note 26, (arguing in general that presumed consent laws impinge on liberty, autonomy, and the right to exclude); Phyllis Coleman, "'Brother Can You Spare a Liver?' Five Ways to Increase Organ Donation," 31 *Val. U.L. Rev.* 1, 19 (1996) (commenting that "[p]resumed consent implicates the substantive rights to bodily integrity and to privacy in intimate decisions concerning a person's body") (footnotes omitted); Anderson, *supra* note 55, at 258–63 (arguing that presumed consent supporters ignore the "interests from the donor side of the equation which deserve the most protection").

165. Frammolino, *Harvest of Corneas*, *supra* note 1.

166. *Id.*

167. Gray, *supra* note 148 (condemning the government-led program which studied the effects of untreated syphilis in Black men); Jones, *supra* note 149.

168. Jefferies, *supra* note 156.

169. *Id.* at 626.

170. *Id.*

171. *Id.*

172. Abraham, *supra* note 146, at 183; Centers for Medicare and Medicaid Service, "Medicare Coverage of Kidney Dialysis and Kidney Transplant Services" 35, at http://www.medicare.gov/Publications/Pubs/pdf/10128.pdf.

173. *Id.* Abraham followed Robert Banes through what she refers to as the "transplant game." In this game, Black kidney patients are kept alive on dialysis, most hoping for transplants, but some not realizing that they are not on organ transplantation waitlists. *Id.* at 179–97.

174. Fentiman, *supra* note 25.

175. Pinsley, *supra* note 92 (quoting ethicist Robert Royal).

176. Rousseau, *supra* note 122.

177. *Id.*

178. *Id.* at 14–16.

179. *Id.* at 15. Rousseau reduced the notion of the social contract to the idea that "[e]ach of us puts in common his person and his whole power under the supreme direction of the general will; and in return we receive every member as an indivisible part of the whole." *Id.*

180. *Id.* at 23.

181. *See* Mills, *supra* note 138; Robin D.G. Kelley, "Playing for Keeps: Pleasure and Profit on the Postindustrial Playground," in *The House That Race Built* 195 (Wahneema Lubiano, ed. 1997) (arguing that America has a racial contract, which leaves Blacks out and causes their exploitation).

182. *See* Mills, *supra* note 138; Kelly, *supra* note 151.

183. *See, e.g.,* Catherine Blake, "Survey to Deal with Transportation Needs," *L.A. Times*, Mar. 9, 2000, at 3; Jean Hopfensperger, "Study

Offers a Hand on Welfare-to-Work," *Star Tribune*, March 17, 2000, at 1A.

184. *See* Pat Harper, "Savoring a Role in Workplace," *Chicago Trib.*, May 11, 1999, at 3; Blake, *supra* note 183; Hopfensperger, *supra* note 183.

185. Minority populations grew 18.5% between 1975 and 1990, but minority medical school enrollment rose only 7%. Dennis P. Andrulis, The National Public Health and Hospital Institute, "New Dimensions and Directions in Inner-City Health Care," *at* http://www.acponline.org/hpp/pospaper/andrulis.htm, at 270 (citing Satcher Rivo & D. Satcher, "Improving Access to Health Care Through Physician Workforce Reform," 270:9 *Jama* 1074 (1993)).

7. Commoditization: Incentives for Cadaveric Organ Harvesting

1. *See* Gardiner Harris, "New Rules on Sperm Donation by Gays," *New York Times*, May 20, 2004, at A16.

2. Adam J. Kolber, "A Matter of Priority: Transplanting Organs Preferentially to Registered Donors," 55 *Rutgers L. Rev.* 671, 704 (2005) (for a definition of *pareto superior* in relation to organ donation).

3. *Id.*

4. *See,* Joseph E. Stiglitz, *Whither Socialism* (1994); Jeffrey L. Harrison, "Piercing Pareto Superiority: Real People and the Obligations of Legal Theory," 39 *Ariz. L. Rev.* 1 (1997).

5. *See* Margaret Jane Radin, "Market-Inalienability," 100 *Harv. L. Rev.* 1849 (1987).

6. *See, e.g.,* Catherine McKinnon; *Sexual Harassment of Working Women* (1979); Catherine McKinnon, "Feminism, Marxism, Method, and the State: An Agenda for Theory," 7 *Signs* 541 (1982).

7. Geoffrey C. Hazard, Jr., "Communitarian Ethics and Legal Justification," 59 *U. Colo. L. Rev.* 721 (1988).

8. *See, e.g.,* S. Gregory Boyd, Comment, "Considering a Market in Human Organs," 4 *N.C.J.L. & Tech.* 417, 465 (2003) ("When considering market discrimination and the exploitation of the poor, one should first

consider that the current organ system has been accused of discriminating against the poor and minority racial groups.").

9. *See* America's Blood Centers, at http://www.americasblood.org (last visited June 26, 2004).

10. *See* Red Cross, at http://www.redcross.org.

11. *See* Gilbert M. Gaul, "The Blood Brokers: Red Cross – From Disaster Relief to Blood," *Philadelphia Inquirer*, Sept. 27, 1989 (part of a 6-part investigative series on the blood supply) [hereinafter *Gaul, Red Cross*].

12. *Id.*

13. *See* Gaul, *Red Cross, supra* note 11.

14. *Id.*

15. *See* Gilbert M. Gaul, "The Blood Brokers: How Blood, The "Gift of Life," Became a Billion-Dollar Business," *Philadelphia Inquirer*, Sept. 24, 1989, [hereinafter *Gaul, Gift of Life*].

16. *See, e.g., Doe v. Travenol Laboratories, Inc.*, 698 F. Supp. 780 (D. Minn., 1988) (dismissing a hemophiliac's strict liability and breach of warranty claims because of state blood shield laws); *Doe v. Cutter Biological*, 852 F. Supp. 909 (D. Ida. 1994) (denying hemophiliac's claim of strict liability based on Idaho's blood shield statute).

17. *See, e.g.,* Larry Rohter, "Desperation and Sympathy Impel the Illegal Purchase of a Kidney," *International Herald Tribune*, May 24, 2004, at 6 (describing an American woman who obtained [and paid for] a kidney abroad); Francis L. Delmarco et al., "Ethical Incentives – not Payment – for Organ Donation," *New Eng. J. Med.*, June 20, 2002 (noting that "patients with sufficient means can travel to distant locations in order to purchase kidneys for transplantation.").

18. *See* Tammie Smith, "Payment for Organs Weighed: Agency Seeking Way to Motivate Donors," *Rich. Times Dispatch*, June 24, 2002, at A1 (noting the medical community's interest in testing the incentive-based framework).

19. *See, e.g.,* "The Transplantation Society Reiterates Position at International Congress against Selling Organs," *PR Newswire*, Aug. 30, 2002 (discussing the Transplantation Society's position against payment for organs); "Surgeons Say Paying for Organ Donations Should not be Pursued," *PR Newswire*, June 28, 2002, available at http://www.facs.org/news/organdonation.html [hereinafter *Surgeons*] (suggesting that we find solutions to the organ donation problem outside of compensation); Jim Warren, "As Support Grows for Studying Financial Incentives to Increase Donation, Top Surgeon's Group Not Buying In," *Transplant News*, June 30, 2002, at 1 (reporting dissent in the medical community about organ commoditization).

20. *See, e.g.,* Guido Calabresi & A. Douglas Melamed, "Property Rules, Liability Rules, and Inalienability: One View of the Cathedral," 85 *Harv. L. Rev.* 1089 (1972) (asserting that the external costs of alienability outweigh certain other social benefits).

21. *See, e.g.,* Stephen J. Hedges & William Gaines, "Donor Bodies Milled into Growing Profits," *Chicago Tribune*, May 21, 2000, at C1.

22. *See, e.g,.* Arthur L. Caplan, *If I Were a Rich Man Could I Buy a Pancreas? and Other Essays on the Ethics of Health Care* 158 (1992); World Health Org., "Guiding Principles on Human Organ Transplantation," 337 *Lancet* 1470, 1470 (1991) (arguing that the financial exchanges for human biological materials should be prohibited).

23. *Surgeons, supra* note 19 (quoting Dr. Thomas R. Russell, Executive Director of the American College of Surgeons).

24. *See* Mark F. Anderson, "The Future of Organ Transplantation: From Where Will New Donors Come, to Whom Will Their Organs Go?" 5 *Health Matrix* 249, 299 (1995) (noting that citizens help to "improve our community" through voluntary organ donations); *See also* Radin, *supra* note 5 (analyzing personhood through market concepts and concluding that organ commoditization should be avoided); Leon R. Kass, "Organs for Sale? Propriety, Property, and the Price of Progress," in *Politics and the Human Body:*

Assault on Dignity 153, 171 (Jean Bethke Elshtain & J. Timothy Cloyd eds., 1995) (arguing that human dignity is compromised by treating the body in market terms).

25. *See, e.g.*, Arthur L. Caplan, "Organ Procurement: It's Not in the Cards," 14:5 *Hastings Ctr. Rep.* 9 (1984) (addressing the moral and ethical implications of organ sales); Lloyd R. Cohen, "Increasing the Supply of Transplant Organs: The Virtues of a Futures Market," 58 *Geo. Wash. L. Rev.* 1 (1989) (commenting on the particularly repugnant character of marketing organs, but ultimately underscoring the benefit of a futures market in human biological materials); Gregory S. Crespi, "Overcoming the Legal Obstacles to the Creation of a Futures Market in Bodily Organs," 55 *Ohio St. L.J.* 1 (1994) (discussing various proposals for a futures market for organs); Richard Titmuss, *The Gift Relationship: From Human Blood to Social Policy* 245 (Ann Oakley & John Ashton, eds., New Press, 1997) (1971) (warning that the introduction of commercial concepts into blood procurement could have a detrimental effect on altruism).

26. *See* Titmuss, *supra* note 25, at 245–46.

27. *See* Gaul, *Red Cross, supra* note 11 (quoting George Elsey's communication to the Comptroller General of the United States).

28. *Id.*

29. *See* Douglas Starr, *Blood: An Epic History of Medicine and Commerce* (1998).

30. *See* Gilbert M. Gaul, "The Blood Brokers: The Loose Way the FDA Regulates Blood Industry," *Philadelphia Inquirer*, Sept. 25, 1989 [hereinafter *Gaul, The Loose Way*].

31. *See* Starr, *supra* note 29.

32. *See* L. Leveton, H. Sox., & M. Stoto, *Institute of Medicine Report: Committee to Study HIV Transmission Through Blood and Blood Products, HIV and the Blood Supply: An Analysis of Crisis Decisionmaking* (1995).

33. *See, e.g.*, Titmuss, *supra* note 25.

34. *See, e.g.*, Lisa M. Korsten, Note, "The Global Market for Blood," 11 *B.U. Int'l L.J.* 227, 228 (proposing "an expansion of the

existing market for blood along with an international regulatory scheme in order to insure a safe and adequate blood supply throughout the world.").

35. *See* Kieran Healy, "Why Blood Centers Don't Need to Give You any Money for Blood Products that They Sell for Hundreds of Dollars per Donation," available at http://www.chat11.com/Emergence_Of_HIV_In_US_Blood_Supply.

36. *See, e.g.*, Paul A. Lombardo, "Taking Eugenics Seriously," 30 *Fla. St. U.L. Rev.* 191 (2003); Paul A. Lombardo, "Medicine, Eugenics, and the Supreme Court: From Coercive Sterilization to Reproductive Freedom," 13 *J. Contemp. Health L. & Pol'y* 1 (1996).

37. *See* Healy, *supra* note 36.

38. *See id.* at 533.

39. *See, e.g.*, Kevin Hopkins, "Blood, Sweat, and Tears: Toward a New Paradigm for Protecting Donor Privacy," 7 *Va. J. Soc. Pol'y & L.* 141 (2000).

40. Michael Trebilcock, et al., "Do Institutions Matter? A Comparative Pathology of the HIV-Infected Blood Tragedy," 82 *Va. L. Rev.* 1407, 1407 ("In the United States, it is estimated that at as many as 29,000 people were infected with HIV through blood transmission between 1978 and 1984 . . . ").

41. *Id.* at 1481 (noting that "private for-profit plasma and blood product sector moved much more quickly" to ensure public safety than their nonprofit counterparts).

42. *Id.*

43. *See e.g.*, Healy, *supra* note 36.

44. *See id.* at 532.

45. *See Heirs of Fruge v. Blood Services*, 506 F.2d. 841 (5th Cir. 1975) (heirs to estate suing blood supplier because decedent contracted viral hepatitis resulting from transfusion).

46. *See* Healey, *supra* note 36 at 530.

47. *See, e.g.*, Hopkins, *supra* note 40.

48. Telephone interview with Jacqueline Dillard, Director of Dialysis Services, Chicago-Area Dialysis Clinic (July 7, 2005) [hereinafter *Jacqueline Dillard Interview*].

49. *See, e.g.*, Walter E. Williams, "My Organs Are for Sale," *Freeman*, Oct. 1, 2002, at 63.

50. *Id.*

51. *See, e.g.,* Lori B. Andrews, "Harnessing the Benefit of Biobanks," 33 *J.L. Med. & Ethics* 22 (2005).

52. "Hemacare-Corp," *Business Wire,* Oct. 16, 1989.

53. *See, e.g.,* Naomi Freundlich, "All of Me," *New York Times,* March 16, 2003, at 94.

54. CNN, "Older Patients Unaware of New Medicare Law," *CNN.com,* Feb. 26, 2004, at http://www.cnn.com/2004/HEALTH/02/26/medicare.survey.ap (noting that "[a]lmost 70 percent of elderly Medicare recipients don't know the program's new prescription drug benefit has been signed into law, according to a survey by the Kaiser Family Foundation.").

55. *See, e.g.,* Margaret R. Sobota, Note, "The Price of Life, $50,000 for an Egg, Why Not $1,500 for a Kidney? An Argument to Establish a Market for Organ Procurement Similar to the Current Market for Human Egg Procurement," 82 *Wash. U.L.Q.* 1225 (2004).

56. *See, e.g.,* "Web Auction for Beauty is for Fools," *Morning Call* (Allentown, PA), Oct. 28, 1999, at A26; "Massachusetts: Photographer Plans Egg Auction," *Vero Beach Press Journal,* Oct. 24, 1999, at A16.

57. *See, e.g.,* Sharon Krum, "American Beauty," *Independent on Sunday* (UK), June 17, 2001; Hawley Fogg-Davis, "Navigating Race in the Market for Human Gametes," *The Hastings Center Report,* Sept. 1, 2001, at 13.

58. *See, e.g.,* Elizabeth E. Theran, "Free to be Arbitrary and Capricious," 11 *Cornell J. L. & Pub. Pol'y* 113, 126–27 (2001).

59. *Id.*

60. Martin D. Weiss, "The Wise Investor's Guide to Life Insurance," available at http://www.safemoneyreport.com/survey/SMR0088_Life_Insurance.pdf.

61. *See, e.g.,* Clifford Fisher, "The Role of Causation in Science as Law and Proposed Changes in the Current Common Law Toxic Tort System," 9 *Buff. Envtl L.J.* 35, 98 (2001) (noting that to "actually set a value on a life is difficult"). Although Fisher was not addressing life insurance per se, the difficulty of the matter is the same.

62. *See, e.g.,* Willy E. Rice, "'Commercial Terrorism' from the Transatlantic Slave Trade to the World Trade Center Disaster," 6 *Scholar* 1, 100, n.232 (2003) (noting that "over the centuries, British courts decided several celebrated insurance cases in which insured slave traders or their agents murdered hundreds of slaves during voyages . . ."). *Id.* at 100.

63. *See* Harris, *supra* note 1 (noting in part, nearly 150 companies have largely gone unregulated.").

64. *Id.*

65. *See* Stiglitz, *supra* note 4, at 31.

66. *Id.*

67. *See* Harris, *supra* note 1.

68. *See, e.g.,* John A. MacDonald, "Bereaved Family Wants FDA to Tighten Tissue Bank Regulations," *The Hartford Courant* (CT), May 16, 2003 (noting that as of March 2003 the Centers for Disease Control received 62 "reports of infections from these tissue products . . .").

69. *See, e.g.,* Lauren Neergaard, "Transplant Tissue Must Be Screened," *Albany Times Union* (NY), May 21, 2004, at A9; Robert Pear, "F.D.A. Delays Regulation of Tissue Transplants," *New York Times,* May 14, 2003, at A18.

70. *See* Harris, *supra* note 1.

71. *See, e.g.,* Ramirez v. Health Partners of Southern Arizona, 972 P.2d 658 (Ariz. Ct. App. 1998); Good v. Presbyterian Hosp., 934 F.Supp. 107 (S.D. N.Y. 1996); Smith v. Kurtzman, 531 N.E.2d 885 (Ill. App. Ct. 1988).

72. Travelers Ins. Co. v. Welch, 82 F.2d 799 (1936); O'Donnell v. Slack, 55 Pac. Rep.906, 907 (1899) (opining that "[t]he duty of the burial of the dead is made an express legal obligation"); Evans v. Evans, 23 Ohio Dec. 375 (Ohio Com.Pl., 1912).

8. Black Markets: The Supply of Body Parts

1. *Organ Sale: China's Growing Trade and Ultimate Violation of Prisoner's Rights, Hearing Before the Subcommittee on International Operations and Human Rights of*

the Committee on International Relations, 107th Cong. 60 (2001) (testimony of Nancy Scheper-Hughes) [hereinafter *Organ Sale*].

2. *See, e.g.,* Telephone interview with Jim Cohane, Organ Transplant Coordinator (May 4, 2004) (on file with author) [hereinafter *Cohane Interview*]; Larry Rohter, "Tracking the Sale of a Kidney on a Path of Poverty and Hope," *New York Times,* May 23, 2004, at A1.

3. *See* Joint Hearings of The House International Relations Committee and the House Government Reform and Oversight Committee, June 16, 1998; Hearing before the Subcommittee on Health and Environment of the Committee on Commerce House of Representatives, April 15, 1999; *Organ Sale, supra* note 1.

4. *See, e.g.,* Rohter, *supra* note 2.

5. *See, e.g.,* Abraham McLaughlin et al., "What is a Kidney Worth," *Christian Science Monitor,* June 9, 2004, at A1.

6. *See, e.g.,* Declan Walsh, "Transplant Tourists Flock to Pakistan, Where Poverty and Lack of Regulation Fuel Trade in Human Organs: Declan Walsh Meets the Indebted Workers who Sacrifice Their Kidneys for Cash," *The Guardian* (London), Feb. 10, 2005, at 17.

7. Cohane Interview, *supra* note 2.

8. *See* Nancy Kercheval, "U of MD School of Medicine Played Role in History of Grave Robbing," Oct. 24, 2002, *Daily Record* (Baltimore, Md.).

9. *See* Emily Bazelon, "Grave Offense," *Legal Affairs,* July-Aug. 2002, available at http://www.legalaffairs.org/issues/July-August-2002/story_bazelon-julaug2002.html.

10. *See* Kercheval, *supra* note 8.

11. *Id.*

12. University of Maryland, "Annual Circular of the Faculty of Physics of the University of Maryland. Session 1844–5," 5 (Baltimore: John Murphy, 1844), available at http://www.mdhistoryonline.net/mdmedicine/cfm/pt2.cfm (last visited Nov. 25, 2003).

13. *Id.*

14. *Id.*

15. *Id.*

16. *See* Kercheval, *supra* note 8.

17. *See* Charles Seabrook, "The Body Snatchers of Augusta; Bought as a Slave to Rob Black Graves," *Atlanta J. & Const.,* Mar. 8, 1998, at C4 (chronicling the life of Grandison Harris, the Medical College of Georgia's most invaluable grave robber or "resurrection man").

18. *See* Bazelon, *supra* note 9.

19. *Id.*

20. See "Digging up Specimens," at http://www.umich.edu/~aahist/chris1850.html (last searched March 5, 2004).

21. See Kenneth Casey, "By the Numbers: Neurology at the University of Michigan: 1890–2000" (2000), at http://www.med.umich.edu/neuro/neurology-at-michigan.pdf.

22. *See* Stephanie Hunter, "Resurrection Man' Dug Way Into History," *Augusta Chron.,* Aug. 21, 1995, at B1.

23. *Id.*

24. *Id.*

25. *See* Bazelon, *supra* note 9.

26. *Id.*

27. *See* Mark Katches, "Company Mixes Up Body Parts," *Orange County Reg.,* July 9, 2000, at http://www.ocregister.com/features/body/rti0709.shtml (last visited Nov. 25, 2003).

28. *See, e.g.,* www.cryolife.com: 1655 Roberts Blvd. NW, Kennesaw, GA; www.osteotech.com: 51 James Way, Eatown, NJ 07724.

29. William Heisel & Mark Katches, "Organ Agencies Aid For-Profit Suppliers," *Orange County Reg.,* (June 25, 2000) *at* http://www.ocregister.com/features/body/organ00625cci.shtml (last visited Nov. 25, 2003). The tissues are sold once more at a considerable mark-up. For example, a heart deemed "unviable," can generate up to $21,000 in valves and other materials.

30. *Id.*

31. *Orthopedic Technology Review,* at www.orthopedictechreview.com/issues/sepoc01/pg32.htm.

32. *Id.*

33. *Id.*

34. *See e.g.*, CryoLife, Inc., *2004 Annual Report* 8, available at http://www.cryolife.com/pdf/Annual_Report_2004.pdf.

35. *Id.*

36. *Id.*(investigating federal oversight in the tissue bank industry).

37. *Id.*

38. *Id.*

39. *Id.*

40. *See* Olympus, at http://olympus.com (last visited Jan. 3, 2003); Regeneration Technologies, at http://www.rtitechnology.com (last visited Jan. 3, 2003); CryoLife, at www.cryolife.com (last visited Jan. 3, 2003).

41. *See* Katches, *supra* note 27.

42. *Id.*

43. *See* Press Release, Olympus, "Olympus Set to Enter Tissue Engineering Field: Targeting Sales of Tissue-Engineered Bone and Automated Multi-Specimen Cell Culture Equipment" (Nov. 27, 2002), available at http://www.olympus.co.p/en/news/2002b/nr021127tissue.html (last visited Jan. 3, 2003).

44. "See RTI Receives $15.1 Million Credit Agreement" (Dec. 20, 2002), at http://www.rtitechnology.com/news/index.cfm?title=News%20Releases&11=Investor%20In (last visited Jan. 3, 2003) [hereinafter *RTI Agreement*].

45. *Id.*

46. *Id.*

47. *Id.*

48. *See* Heisel & Katches, *supra* note 29.

49. *Id.*

50. *Id.*

51. *See Moore v. Regents of California*, 793 P.2d at 496 (Cal. 1990) (declining to extend the tort of conversion to the nonconsensual removal of a special cell line from plaintiff). My point here, however, is that Moore sued on learning that his unique resources, his cell line, had been lifted, patented, and sold, earning millions for the scientists involved.

52. Julia D. Mahoney, "The Market for Human Tissue," 86 *Va. L. Rev.* 163, 189 (2000).

53. *See* "Fertility Resource Showcase," *Newsweek Magazine*, March 1, 2004 (prominently advertising several fertility and donor sources in a special centerfold, including the Diamond Institute for Infertility, which offers an egg donation program, the Huntington Reproductive Center also offering egg donation, The Donor Source, and the Southern California Reproductive Center) [hereinafter *Fertility Resource Showcase*].

54. *See* Fertility Resource Showcase, *supra* note 54.

55. *See* Tony Saavedra, "Egg Donors In Ethical Cross-Fire," *Orange County Reg.*, Dec. 20, 1999 (reporting that "student newspapers across Orange County and the nation carry ads daily seeking young egg donors, offering as much as $50,000 for eggs from tall athletes with high IQs").

56. *Id.*

57. *See* Joseph Berger, "Yale Gene Pool Seen as Route to Better Baby," *N.Y. Times*, Jan. 10, 1999, at A19; Lori Buttars, "Selling Body Parts? Americans Squeamish," *Salt Lake Trib.*, Aug. 10, 1997, at J3; Gina Kolata, "Price of Donor Eggs Soars, Setting Off a Debate on Ethics," *N.Y. Times*, Feb. 25, 1998, at A1.

58. *See, e.g.*, Carey Goldberg, "On Web, Models Auction Their Eggs to Bidders for Beautiful Children," *N.Y. Times*, Oct. 23, 1999, at A11 (scrutinizing Web-based auction, "offering up models as egg donors to the highest bidders").

59. *Id.*

60. *Id.*

61. *Id.*

62. *Id.* However, companies like eBay will not auction ova or sperm. *See* e-Bay Policies at http://www.ebay.org. Some fertility program directors have spoken out against Web-based programs, particularly those that are geared toward the Harris model program. "It's frightening and horrible, and the worst part for me is to think there might be something worse still beyond our imagination." Goldberg, *supra* note 60 (quoting Shelley Smith, director of the Egg Donor Program in Los Angeles, California).

63. *See* Matt McGrath, "Internet Rush to Buy Human Eggs," *BBC News* (Feb. 16, 2001), available at http://www.news.bbc.co.uk/1/hi/health/1172616.stm (last visited Oct. 5, 2003) (describing the plight of infertile British couples seeking human eggs). British law forbids the sale of human eggs, thereby leaving couples to wait up to 3 years for donation from an anonymous donor. *Id.*

64. *See* Kolata, *supra* note 59.

65. *See* Id. (detailing a uniform pricing structure for the sale of eggs and the changes in price since 1999).

66. *See* Sharon Lerner, "The Price of Eggs: Undercover in the Infertility Industry," *Ms.*, Mar.-Apr. 1996, at 28.

67. *See* Kolata, *supra* note 59.

68. Martha Frase-Blunt, "Ova-Compensating?; Women Who Donate Eggs to Infertile Couples Earn a Reward – But Pay a Price," *The Washington Post*, Dec. 4, 2001, at F01.

69. *Id.*

70. *Id.*

71. *Id.*

72. Gay Jervey, "Priceless; That's How Adoptive Parents Describe Their Children," *Money*, Apr., 2003, at 118.

73. *See* Id. (describing the financial transactions in adoption).

74. *See* McGrath, *supra* note 65 (suggesting that fertility clinics "are quite open" about providing information about donors and meeting the desires of their clientele).

75. *See* Id. (noting that donors "have become a little bit obsessed with what a donor looks like and what her qualities are").

76. *See, e.g.,* Mahoney *supra* note 53, at 186(concluding that pressure on women to undergo powerful drug therapies to voluntarily help couples conceive could reinforce "stereotypes of females as generous rather than self-interested").

77. *See* Gardiner Harris, "New Rules on Sperm Donations by Gays," *New York Times*, May 20, 2004, at A16.

78. Cohane Interview, *supra* note 2.

79. *Id.*

80. *Id.*

81. Cohane Interview, *supra* note 2.

82. *See* Nancy Scheper-Hughes, "Organs Without Borders"; *Prime Numbers, Foreign Policy*, Jan. 1, 2005, at http://www.foreignpolicy.com/Ning/archive/archive/146/PN146.pdf.

83. *See* Craig S. Smith, "Quandry in U.S. Over Use of Organs of Chinese Inmates," *N.Y. Times*, Nov. 11, 2001, at 1A (noting that death row inmates are the primary source of transplantable organs from China); *see also* Michael Finkel, "Complications," *N.Y. Times* (Magazine), May 27, 2001, at 26 (commenting that the organs of executed prisoners in China are most commonly used in transplantation with foreign purchasers).

84. *See, eg.,* Finkel, *supra* note 85, at 28.

85. *Id.* The organ market is international in scope. Finkel reports that although there appears to be tacit acceptance of organ selling in Israel, because of strict regulations requiring screening of nonrelative donations, most purchasers will opt for the surgeries to be performed elsewhere, including in the United States. *Id.*

86. The Organ Procurement and Transplant Network, Waitlist Data by Organ, at http://www.optn.org.

87. The Organ Procurement and Transplant Network, Data, Donors Recovered January–April 2005, at http://www.optn.org.

88. Rohter, *supra* note 2 (quoting Jane Doe).

89. *Id.*

90. *Id.*

91. *Id.*

92. *Id. See also* Finkel, *supra* note 85.

93. *Id.*

94. *Id.*

95. *Id.*

96. *Id.*

97. *Id.*

98. *Id.*

99. *Id.*

100. *Id.*

101. *Id.*

102. *See* Scheper-Hughes, *supra* note 84, at 27.

9. Critiquing the Slavery and Black Body Comparison

1. *See, e.g.,* E.C. Schneider et al., "Racial Disparities in the Quality of Care for Enrollees in Medicare Managed Care," 287 *JAMA* 1288 (2002); Ismail Jatoi et al., "Widening Disparity in Survival Between White and African American Patients with Breast Carcinoma Treated in the U.S. Department of Defense Healthcare System," 98(5) *Cancer* 894 (2003); John Stone, "Race and Healthcare Disparities: Overcoming Vulnerability," 23:6 *Theoretical Medicine and Bioethics* 499 (2002).

2. Richard Titmuss, *The Gift Relationship: From Human Blood to Social Policy* (Ann Oakley & John Ashton, eds., New Press, 1997) (1971).

3. *Dred Scott v. Sandford*, 60 U.S. 393 (1856) (holding that the United States Constitution makes clear that persons of African descent are not citizens in the United States).

4. *See* John H. Franklin, *From Slavery to Freedom* (1967).

5. *See* E. Franklin Frazier, *The Negro in the United States* (1957).

6. *See* Winthrop Jordan, *White Over Black* (1968).

7. *See* Thomas Gossett, *Race: The History of an Idea in America* (1965).

8. *See* Mary E. Goodman, *Race Awareness in Young Children* (1964).

9. *See generally* Robert William Fogel & Stanley L. Engerman, *Time on the Cross* 17 (1974). (discussing the economics of slavery).

10. *See* Phillip D. Curtain, *The Atlantic Slave Trade: A Census* (1969) (detailing census data totaling the number of Africans brought to America).

11. *See, e.g.,* Negro Women's Children to Serve According to the Condition of the Mother, Act XII, 2 Hening 170 (Virginia, December 1662) [hereinafter *Negro Women's Children's Act*]. *See* also Katherine M. Franke, "Becoming a Citizen: Reconstruction Era Regulation of African American Marriages," 11 *Yale J.L & Human.* 251 (1999).

12. Fogel & Engerman, *supra* note 9. *See also* William M. Wiecek, "Bondage, Freedom and the Constitution: The New Slavery Scholarship and Its Impact on Law and Legal Historiography: The Origins of The Law of Slavery in British North America," 17 *Cardozo L. Rev.* 1711, 1753 (1996).

13. *See* Ruth Richardson, *Death, Dissection and the Destitute* (2000); Ron Grossman, "Cemetery Trove Brings Early Chicago to Life," *Chi. Trib.*, June 19, 1991, at 1; William Hathaway, "Belief Systems are Historic Foes: Long Before Stem-Cell Debate, Medical Advances Clashed with Religion," *Hartford Courant*, Sept. 5, 2001, at A1 (noting that black markets furnished the medical community's demand for corpses well into the 19th century).

14. *See* Ruth Richardson, "Fearful Symmetry: Corpses for Anatomy, Organs for Transplantation?," in *Organ Transplantation Meanings and Realities* 68 (Stuart J. Younger et al. eds., 1996).

15. *See, e.g.,* Gloria J. Banks, "Legal and Ethical Safeguards: Protection of Society's Most Vulnerable Participants in a Commercialized Organ Transplantation System," 21 *Am. J.L. & Med.* 45 (1995); Erin P. George, "The Stem Cell Debate: The Legal, Political and Ethical Issues Surrounding Federal Funding of Scientific Research on Human Embryos," *12 Alb. J.T. Sci. & Tech.* 747 (2002); Diana Butler, "Can Science and Religion Come Together?," *Balt. Sun,* Mar. 2, 1997, at 1F; Bill Frist, "Not Ready for Human Cloning," *Wash. Post,* Apr. 11, 2002, at A29; Sheryl Gay Stolberg, "Could This Pig Save Your Life?," *N.Y. Times,* Oct. 3, 1999, § 6 (Magazine), at 46.

16. *See* Bartha M. Knoppers & Sonia LeBris, "Recent Advances in Medically Assisted Conception: Legal, Ethical and Social Issues," 17 *Am. J.L. & Med.* 329 (1991) (discussing the profit-making aspects of surrogate-motherhood and the infant as the object of sale); Sheila R. Kirschenbaum, Note, "Banking on Discord: Property Conflicts in the Transplantation of Umbilical Cord Stem Cells," 39 *Ariz. L. Rev.* 1391 (1997) (examining the property implications of open market sales of stem cells and other organs).

17. *See Moore v. Regents of Univ. of Cal.,* 499 U.S. 936 (1991); Charlotte H. Harrison, "Neither *Moore* nor the Market: Alternative Models for Compensating Contributors of Human Tissue," 28 *Am. J.L. & Med.* 77 (2002) (exploring the financial discrepancy in human organ commerce and noting researchers and biomedical companies gross substantial profits from body products of human donors, but the donors rarely see any of these proceeds); Nicholas Wade, "Scientists Make 2 Stem Cell Advances," *N.Y. Times,* June 21, 2002, at F1.

18. *See* Margaret Jane Radin, "Market-Inalienability," 100 *Harv. L. Rev.* 1849, 1936 (1987).

19. Banks, *supra* note 15, at 45 (probing the possible positive results and concurrent consequences of implementing a commercialized organ transplantation system); Kristi Ayala, "The Application of Traditional Criminal Law to Misappropriation of Gametic Materials," 24 *Am. J. Crim. L.* 503 (1997) (examining the legal status of gametic materials as property and the risks of commodifying children); Katherine B. Lieber, "Selling the Womb: Can the Feminist Critique of Surrogacy Be Answered?," 68 *Ind. L.J.* 205 (1992) (describing the societal harm that might occur to women and children as a result of commodifying pregnancy through surrogacy).

20. *See* Julia D. Mahoney, "The Market for Human Tissue," 86 *Va. L. Rev.* 163, 172 (2000) (suggesting that the "expanding usefulness of human biological materials necessitates a careful evaluation of the responsibilities of individuals in possession or control of life-saving and health-saving materials"). *Id.* at 167.

21. *See* Radin, *supra* note 19, at 1936.

22. *See generally,* E. Richard Gold, *Body Parts: Property Rights and the Ownership of Human Biological Materials* (1996)(arguing that the human body "ought not now...be treated as property"); Leon R. Kass, "Organs for Sale? Propriety, Property, and the Price of Progress," 107 *Pub. Interest* 65 (1992); Thomas H. Murray, "On the Human Body as Property: The Meaning of Embodiment, Markets and the Meaning of Strangers," 20 *U. Mich. J.L. Reform* 1055 (1987) (admonishing the use of property terms for human body parts).

23. *See* Andrew Kimbrell, "The Human Body Shop: Does America Want a 'Free Market' in Organs and Tissues?," *Wash. Post,* July 1, 1990, at B3 (examining the "fast-growing market" for human "products" in the United States and the similarities that such a market may share with slavery); Karen Wright, "The Body Bazaar: The Market in Human Organs is Growing," *Discover,* Oct. 1998 (arguing that human body product commoditization or patenting raises ethical issues akin to slavery).

24. *See* Nancy Scheper-Hughes, "The Global Traffic in Human Organs," 41 *Current Anthropology* 191 (Apr. 2000) (highlighting exploitative harvesting practices in foreign countries, including "child kidnapping, and body mutilations to procure organs for transplant surgery"); Joseph Hall, "Opening Up the Market for Organs," *Toronto Star,* Nov. 29, 2002, at F6 (scrutinizing whether organ purchases would necessarily exploit the socioeconomically disadvantaged); *see also* Organs Watch, at http://sunsite.berkeley.edu/biotech/organswatch/index.html (last visited March 2, 2003) (maintaining a database of "hot spots" where organ purchases occur and providing data on the "human rights implications of the desperate, world-wide, search for organs").

25. *See* Mark F. Anderson, "The Future of Organ Transplantation: From Where Will New Donors Come, to Whom Will Their Organs Go?," 5 *Health Matrix* 249 (1995); *see generally* Whitney Hinkle, "Giving Until it Hurts: Prisoners Are Not the Answer to the National Organ Shortage," 35 *Ind. L. Rev.* 593 (2002) (examining the discrepancy in the application of the death penalty, where African Americans are much more likely to be sentenced to death than their White counterparts. Therefore, African Americans "continue to receive a disproportionate number

of death sentences thereby providing [more] organs for the rest of society.").

26. Adam B. Wolf, "What Money Cannot Buy: A Legislative Response to C.R.A.C.K.," 33 *U. Mich. J.L. Reform* 173 (2000) (exploring the anti-organ sale legislation as a response to the exploitation of minorities for human body products).

27. *See* Craig S. Smith, "Quandry in U.S. Over Use of Organs of Chinese Inmates," *N.Y. Times*, Nov. 11, 2001, at 1A (highlighting concerns expressed by American doctors whose desperate patients have sought organs from executed Chinese prisoners as an option to languishing on domestic organ transplantation waitlists).

28. *See* Stephen J. Schnably, "Property and Pragmatism: A Critique of Radin's Theory of Property and Personhood," 45 *Stan. L. Rev.* 347 (1993) (criticizing Margaret Radin's failure to address a theory of social change in her property and personhood theory of organ sales); Michael H. Shapiro, "Is Bioethics Broke?: On the Idea of Ethics and Law "Catching Up" with Technology," 33 *Ind. L. Rev.* 17 (1999) (arguing that the discipline of bioethics avoids social change and improvement).

29. *See* Gold, *supra note 23, at 164; Khiara M. Bridges, Note,* "On The Commoditization of the Black Female Body: The Critical Implications of the Alienability of Fetal Tissue", 102 *Colum. L. Rev.* 123 (2002) (discussing the unique vulnerability of Black women as being rooted in slavery and reinvented and recast over time); Guido Calabresi & A. Douglas Melamed, "Property Rules, Liability Rules, and Inalienability: One View of the Cathedral," 85 *Harv. L. Rev.* 1089, 1111–12 (1972).

30. *See, e.g.,* Nell Irvin Painter, *Sojourner Truth: A Life, A Symbol 17* (1996) (chronicling the life of former slave, stateswoman, and abolitionist Sojourner Truth); Richard C. Wade, *Slavery in the Cities: The South 1820–1860* (1964) (scrutinizing urban slavery, race relations, violence, and the legal and social conditions under which the chattel system thrived); *see generally* William H. Harris, *The Harder We Run: Black Workers since the Civil War* (1982) (commenting on the economic rights associated with fair wages and labor.). Harris observes that the need for Black labor was apparent, but that Blacks were pacified with diminutive wages and, therefore, not treated as respected, adult laborers. *Id.* at 28. Harris also comments that when Blacks were inclined to strike in protest of their punitive treatment, Whites were known to respond with violence. *Id.* For insight into the lives of former African American slaves through narrative and detailed "visceral accounts – in recorded voice and in the printed word – of confrontations with owners, of the long hours in the field, of maintaining families without the legitimating force of law, and sustaining dignity in the most inhumane circumstances," see *Remembering Slavery: African Americans Talk About Their Personal Experiences of Slavery and Emancipation* (Ira Berlin et al. eds., 1998).

31. *See, e.g.,* Harriet Jacobs, *Incidents in the Life of a Slave Girl,* 173 (1861) (Harvard Universitytt Press, 1987) (chronicling her experiences as a slave and her disappointment at being given away as a gift to a 3-year-old rather than being set free).

32. *Id.*

33. *Id.*

34. *See* Trina Jones, "Shades of Brown: The Law of Skin Color," 49 *Duke L.J.* 1487, 1490 (2000) (exploring how "society has used skin color to demarcate lines between racial groups and to determine the relative position and treatment of individuals within racial categories"); Jonathan K. Stubbs, "Perceptual Prisms and Racial Realism: The Good News about a Bad Situation," 45 *Mercer L. Rev.* 773 (1994) (examining the development of American society around the "legacy of slavery").

35. *See* Michele Goodwin, "Deconstructing Legislative Consent Law: Organ Taking, Racial Profiling and Distributive Justice," 6 *Va. J.L. & Tech.* 2 (2001) (discussing the buying and trading of tissues removed from victims of homicide and catastrophic deaths in Los Angeles); Martin Enserink, "Physicians

Wary of Scheme to Pool Icelanders' Genetic Data," *Science*, Aug. 14, 1998, at 890 (describing Kari Stafansson's financial arrangement with Hoffman-LaRoche to name and isolate genes of Icelandic peoples); Mary Williams Walsh, "A Big Fish in a Small Gene Pool," *L.A. Times*, June 5, 1998, at A1 (highlighting social consideration in troving for genes and the financial incentives and gains of the researchers who prospect for DNA).

36. *See* Ralph Frammolino, "Harvest of Corneas at Morgue Questioned," *L.A. Times*, Nov. 2, 1997, at A1.

37. *See* Susan Okie, "Living Donor Transplants: So Successful, No Match Needed," *Wash. Post*, Dec. 11, 2001, at F8 (describing a successful kidney transplant from a White female to a Black male, noting that medical advances have made cross-racial transplants more common); Terri Williams, "Organ Donor Unites Cultures: Chinese, African-American Families Celebrate Man's Gift of Life," *Dallas Morning News*, Nov. 13, 2000, at 19A (commenting on a Chinese male, who, on death, gave the gift of life by being an organ donor to one African-American woman and two Latinos in the Dallas area).

38. Indeed, equity in the current system must be scrutinized, for without it, its harms can be as devastating as slavery, where the lives of some were valued more than others, resulting in the dissolution of families, psychological trauma, fear, poor health, and avoidable deaths. *See* Institute of Medicine, *Unequal Treatment: Confronting Racial and Ethnic Disparities in Health Care* (2002).

39. The inherent difficulties in examining the benefits and potential detriments of organ commoditization are only exacerbated by political rhetoric.

40. *See* Louise Continelli, "Out of Tragedy, Life: A Plea for Minorities to Consider Organ Donation," *Buff. News*, Nov. 3, 2002, at B2 (noting that "[t]hough African-Americans make up only 12 percent of the nation's population, of the more than 50,000 patients on the National Transplant Waiting List for a kidney, as of August 31 2002, almost half

were African-American or other minorities"); Hamil R. Harris, "For Black Patients, The Need for Organs Exceeds Availability," *Wash. Post*, Feb. 23, 2000, at M14 (noting that because of higher incidents of hypertension and diabetes among the Blacks, the African American community has a great need for kidney – and other – transplants).

41. Warren King, "DNA Analysis Boon in Battling Cancer: Technology Widens Pool of Donors for Transplants, Local Study Says," *Seattle Times*, Dec. 20, 2001, at B1 (noting that new DNA research shows promising results for a more accurate typing of bone-marrow or stem-cell donors, which will lead to a broader pool of donors for ethnic minority groups).

42. African Americans comprise about half of all patients on the kidney transplantation waitlists. This is in part due to the biological propensity of African Americans to develop kidney disease, but also due to the low donation rate of the African American community itself. *See* Sandra Blakeslee, "Studies Find Unequal Access to Kidney Transplants," *N.Y. Times*, Jan. 24, 1989, at C1; Lucille Renwick, "Minorities Wait Longer for Transplants," *L.A. Times*, May 2, 1993, at 3; *See also*, Mark Asher, "The Inside Game: With a Transplanted Kidney, Sean Elliott Takes on the Challenge of Getting Back on the Professional Basketball Court," *Wash. Post*, Apr. 4, 2000, at 12 (noting hardships that African American transplant patients have in finding matching donors).

43. Even if the institution of slavery conveyed some medical benefits to White owners, it should be recognized that there is a major distinction between slavery and organ donation. Although slavery violated our basic moral notions of human autonomy and dignity, informed organ donors can still retain these ethical principles because they have the right to choose whether they want to commodify their organs.

44. *See, e.g.*, Katherine Olukemi Bankole, "A Critical Inquiry of Enslaved African Females and the Antebellum Hospital," 31 *J. Black Stud.* 517 (2001).

45. *See Did Slavery Pay? Readings in the Economics of Black Slavery in the United States* (Hugh G.J. Aitken, ed., 1971); Alfred H. Conrad & John R. Meyer, *The Economics of Slavery, and Other Studies in Econometric History* (1964); *Working Toward Freedom: Slave Society and Domestic Economy in the American South* (Larry E. Hudson, Jr. ed., 1994).

46. *See* Brent Staples, "Monticello as the All-American Melting Pot," *N.Y. Times,* July 1, 2002, at A14 (discussing the widespread familial intertwining of slave-owning families and their slaves through sex, while also examining the DNA and other historical evidence that has proved that Thomas Jefferson had a long-term and procreative relationship with his slave – and the half-sister of his deceased wife, Martha – Sally Hemings); *see generally* Edward Ball, *Slaves in the Family* (1998) (the author explores the family history of his slave-owning ancestors and, when family records show that mixed children existed between the men and the female slaves of his family, he describes his search for his living African American relatives).

47. *See, e.g.,* Negro Women's Children's Act, *supra* note 11; Jacobs, *supra* note 32 (commenting that "at the south, a gentleman may have a shoal of colored children without any disgrace; but if he is known to purchase them, with the view of setting them free, the example is thought to be dangerous to their 'peculiar institution' and he becomes unpopular"); Leslie Espinoza & Angela P. Harris, "Afterword: Embracing the Tar-Baby-LatCrit Theory and the Sticky Mess of Race," 85 *Cal. L. Rev.* 1585 (1997) (discussing the need to complicate race further to understand the mythology of race and recognize others who are raced); Cheryl I. Harris, "Bondage, Freedom and the Constitution: The New Slavery Scholarship and Its Impact on Law and Legal Historiography: Private Law and United States Slave Regimes: Finding Sojourner's Truth: Race, Gender, and the Institution of Property," 18 *Cardozo L. Rev* 309, 330 (1996) (observing that "[r]ules of inheritance were interrelated and func-

tioned in a particularly cruel and efficient way. In general, while the rules of inheritance determined that status and property passed through the father, the status of being a slave was inherited from the mother"); Cheryl I. Harris, "Whiteness As Property," 106 *Harv. L. Rev.* 1707 (1993); Christine B. Hickman, "The Devil and the One Drop Rule: Racial Categories, African Americans and the U.S. Census," 95 *Mich. L. Rev.* 1161 (1997).

48. *See* Donna Murray Allen, "Civil War Claims Can Provide Some Fascinating Details," *St. Petersburg Times,* Oct. 3, 2002, at 2D (noting that after the Civil War, a Black slave owner who filed a claim for damages stating that he had "supported the Union," would be run out of the South); Brent Staples, "The Slave Reparations Movement Adopts the Rhetoric of Victimhood," *N.Y. Times,* Sept. 2, 2001, at 8 (arguing that a policy of widespread reparations given to individual African Americans is not sound because "[B]lack families have made and lost fortunes just as White families have." In addition, the "program would also be available to the descendants of Black slave owners, who were far more common than many people like to admit"); Brent Staples, "Wrestling with the Ghosts of New Orleans," *N.Y. Times,* Feb. 9, 1998, at A18 (noting that many Black slave owners purchased family members out of benevolence, to keep them from "being worked to death or sold into other states").

49. *See, e.g.,* Roy L. Brooks & Mary Jo Newborn, "Critical Race Theory and Classical-Liberal Civil Rights Scholarship: A Distinction Without a Difference?," 82 *Cal. L. Rev.* 787, 792 (1994) (noting that under the "institution of slavery," African Americans had no legal rights or status in their "interaction with Whites"); Jane Rutherford, "The Myth of Due Process," 72 *B.U. L. Rev.* 1 (1992) (exploring the history of due process for African Americans); James G. Wilson, "The Role of Public Opinion in Constitutional Interpretation," 1993 *BYU L. Rev.* 1037, 1075–82 (1993) (examining the public policy that allowed federal courts to rule against liberty for slaves

during the antebellum era in the United States).

50. *See* Randall Robinson, *The Debt: What America Owes to Blacks* (2001); Richard Pipes, *Property and Freedom* (2000).

51. *See generally*, Richard Pipes, *Property and Freedom* (2000) (discussing the importance of property rights to both social and economic freedom).

52. *See* Marion Crain, "Whitewashed Labor Law, Skinwalking Unions," 23 *Berkeley J. Emp. & Lab. L.* 211 (2002) (addressing racist attitudes that allowed slavery to succeed in America and its historical impact on labor unions and law); Tania Tetlow, "The Founders and Slavery: A Crisis of Conscience," 3 *Loy. J. Pub. Int. L.* 1, 3–4 (2001) (exploring the "real ideological crisis" by the founders of our nation over the "clash of slavery and political philosophy"); Wiecek, *supra note 12.*

53. *See generally* Tetlow, *supra,*note 53.

54. *See generally* John W. Blassingame, *The Slave Community: Plantation Life in the Antebellum South 257* (1972) (providing an analysis of the culture and community and life of the Black slave).

55. *Id.*

56. *See, e.g.,* Charles Johnson & Patricia Smith, *Africans in America: America's Journey Through Slavery*, 267–69 (1998) (observing that "in 1795, the first year of the cotton gin's operation, American planters produced 8 million pounds of cotton. By 1800, production increased more than 400 percent, fueling the demand for additional [slave] labor"); David Brion Davis, "Free at Last: The Enduring Legacy of the South's Civil War Victory," *N.Y. Times,* Aug. 26, 2001, at 1, (noting that slavery was a "far more stronger institution in 1880 than in 1770 – largely because of the invention of the cotton gin"); Robinson, supra note 51, (quoting Yuval Taylor) ("[T]he cotton the slaves produced had become not only the United States' leading export but exceeded in value all other exports combined.").

57. Critics argue that a compensation-based organ sale system would in effect "coerce" or "force" poor persons to sell their organs. This coercion, they claim, is akin to slavery. However, unlike slavery, persons of low economic means still have a choice – whether to sell their organs for compensation. Conversely, the institution of slavery allowed Blacks no opportunity for decision making. *See* Martha Nussbaum, "Sherman J. Bellwood Lecture, In Defense of Universal Values," 36 *Idaho L. Rev.* 379, 395 (2000) (arguing that "[p]eople are the best judges of what is good for them, and if we prevent people from acting on their own choices, we treat them like children"); Michael H. Shapiro, "Regulation as Language: Communicating Values by Altering the Contingencies of Choice," 55 *U. Pitt. L. Rev.* 681 (1994) [hereinafter *Shapiro, Regulation*] (noting that there are inconsistencies within the organ market where freedom of choice is advocated for the transplant recipient, but not the organ donor).

58. *See* Franklin, *supra* note 4; Franz Fanon, *Black Skin, White Masks* (1967); *Remembering Slavery, supra* note 31; W.E.B. Du Bois, *The Souls of Black Folk* (1903); Lerone Bennett Jr., *Forced Into Glory: Abraham Lincoln's White Dream* (1999); Painter, *supra* note 31; Wade, *supra* note 31; *See also* Harris, *supra* note 31.

59. *See* Alexander Glennie, "Sermons Preached on Plantations to Congregations of Negroes" (1844), in Blassingame, *supra* note 55, at 85.

60. *See, e.g.,* "A Search for Slavery, Through One Collection of Primary Source Photography," available at http://www.rev.net/~hmcmanus/slpage3.htm (illuminating the scars of slavery though photography, text, and image collections) (last visited Jan. 26, 2003).

61. *See* Daniel P. Black, *Dismantling Black Manhood: A Historical and Literary Analysis of the Legacy of Slavery* (1997); Nathan Irvin Huggins, *Black Odyssey: The Afro-American Ordeal in Slavery* (1990); Dorothy Schneider & Carl J. Schneider, *Slavery in America: From Colonial Times to the Civil War: An Eyewitness History* (2000).

62. *See, e.g.,* Wade, supra note 31. Wade describes how public agencies were used in cities to discipline slaves. Wade notes, "[o]rdinances provided that a master could send Blacks to the local prison for correction. He simply made out a slip for the number of lashes, gave it to the slave to be whipped and sent him off to jail for punishment . . . Increasingly . . . urban owners found it convenient. It was easy and quick; it saved the master the grim experience of wielding the whip himself." *Id.* at 94–95.

63. *See* Cathryne Schmitz et al., "The Interconnection of Childhood Poverty and Homelessness: Negative Impact/Points of Access," 82 J. *Contemp. Hum. Services* 69 (Jan. 1, 2001) (studying the effects of poverty on children, noting in particular the dynamics of poverty on African American families).

64. *See* James Bock, "Mfume Wants NAACP Gathering to Debate Education Reform: Civil Rights Group's Leader Sounds Call for Solutions to Blacks' Classroom Crisis," *Balt. Sun,* Jul. 13, 1997, at 3A (criticizing poorly maintained schools and education in urban areas); Anemona Hartocollis, "U.S. Questions the Placement of City Pupils," *N.Y. Times,* Nov. 21, 1998, at B1 (examining the discriminatory practice of New York City school districts where studies show that African American and other minority students seem to be disproportionately and wrongfully funneled into special education programs based on race, ethnicity, and language barriers); Jodie Morse & Wendy Cole, "Learning While Black," *Time,* May 27, 2002, at 50–51 (examining racial profiling and discriminatory practices within the American public school system, indicating that African American students are "more than twice as likely as their White peers to be sent to the principal's office," be suspended, and "four times as likely to be expelled").

65. *See* Thrity Umrigar, "Race and Health Care," *Chi. Trib.,* June 4, 1996, at C7. The author reports findings from a study conducted by the National Cancer Institute that revealed death rates among Blacks were "disproportionately higher than for Whites." *Id.*

Umrigar also reports that when the study "matched people for socioeconomic status, education and income, the [death rates] were no different between the races". *Id. See also* Michael Weisskopf, "Minorities' Pollution Risk is Debated: Some Activists Link Exposure to Racism," *Wash. Post,* Jan. 16, 1992, at A25 (arguing that minorities in low-income areas are subject to "environmental racism," because "industry consciously locates its most polluting plants in low-income minority areas and . . . government willingly approves and goes easy on regulating them").

66. *See* Rhonda Y. Williams, "'We're Tired of Being Treated Like Dogs:' Poor Women and Power Politics in Black Baltimore," 31 *Black Scholar* 31 (2001) (following the struggle of low-income African American women in Baltimore to receive adequate housing).

67. *See* Shapiro, *Regulation, supra* note 58, at 773 (arguing that the ban on organ sales within the United States "demands some explanation, in the face of the acute shortage of organs for transplantation and the significant loss of life it entails"); *see also* Richard A. Epstein, "Organ Transplants: Is Relying on Altruism Costing Lives?," 4 *Am. Enterprise,* 4, 50 (Nov.–Dec. 1993).

68. *See* Remigius N. Nwabueze, "Biotechnology and the New Property Regime in Human Bodies and Body Parts," 24 *Loy. L.A. Int'l & Comp. L. Rev.* 19, 61 (2002) (noting that "[m]arket transactions in regenerative body parts like blood, hair, fingernails, toenails, and bone marrow are already well known, though in the case of blood it is sometimes regarded as a 'service' rather than a sale"); Stephen J. Hedges, "U.S. Urges Overhaul for Human Tissue Trade: Report Identifies Safety Lapses, Lack of Oversight in Burgeoning Industry," *Chi. Trib.,* Jan. 6, 2001, at N1 (observing that the market in tissue sales had grown from 6,000 donations in 1994 to 20,000 donations in 1999, and that what once was a "local community endeavor" has grown to a "booming, near-billion-dollar-a-year national industry"); Rick Weiss, "A Look At . . . The Body Shop: At the Heart of

an Uneasy Commerce," *Wash. Post*, June 27, 1999, at B3 (exposing the inconsistency in American tissue regimes, where sperm, ova, human embryos, placentas, foreskins, and hair can be sold, but "[i]t's illegal ... to sell a lobe of your liver to someone in liver failure, even though your body would regenerate the missing lobe at least as quickly as your hair would grow back").

69. *See* Barbara A. Noah, *Racial Disparities in the Delivery of Health Care*, 35 *San Diego L. Rev.* 135, 143 (1998).

70. Studies taking a critical stand against the organ referral and allocation system in the United States seemingly imply not only a greater need among black Americans because many patients are never referred onto transplantation waitlists, but also racial discrimination.

10. Conclusion

1. *See* Komesar, *Law's Limits* at 38–39 (noting that "greater substantive competence" in some institutions "is often purchased by increased systemic bias").

2. See James Lindemann Nelson, "Transplantation Through a Glass Darkly," 22:5 *Hastings Center Rep.* 6 (Sept.–Oct. 1992).

3. The market in human body parts is expected to reach $1 billion this year. *See e.g.*, Mark Katches, William Heisel, & Ronald Campbell, "Body Donors Fueling a Booming Business," *Orange County Register*, April 17, 2000; Andrew Kimbrell, *The Human Body Shop* (1997).

4. See *Brotherton v. Cleveland* 173 F.3d 552 (6th Cir) (1999) (permitting widowed plaintiff to pursue civil claim against a physician for nonconsensual removal of her deceased's husband's corneas); *Newman v. Sathyavaglswaran*, 287 F.3d 786 (9th Cir) (2002) (reversing district court's dismissal of plaintiff's suit against coroner for nonconsensual removal of their children's corneas).

See also, Michele Goodwin, "Deconstructing Legislative Consent Law: Organ Taking, Racial Profiling and Distributive Justice," 6 *Va. J. L & Tech.* 2 (2001).

5. *See* Margaret Jane Radin, "Market-Inalienability," 100 *Harv. L. Rev.* 1849, 1879–81 (1987) (arguing that personhood is threatened by certain forms of human alienation).

6. Julia D. Mahoney, "The Market for Human Tissue," 86 *Va. L. Rev.* 163, 165 (2000).

7. *Id.*

8. *Id.*

9. *Id.*

10. *See generally* James F. Childress, "Ethical Criteria for Procuring and Distributing Organs for Transplantation," in *Organ Transplantation Policy: Issues and Prospects* 87 (James F. Blumsetin & Frank A. Sloan eds., 1989) (providing an ethical examination of organ procurement); E. Richard Gold, *Body Parts: Property Rights and the Ownership of Human Biological Materials* 177 (1996) (concluding that the human body should not be analyzed under property law). *See also United States v. Garber*, 607 F.2d 92 (5th Cir. 1979) (recognizing indirectly the permissibility of plasma sales).

11. *See* OPTN at http://www.optn.org/latestData/rptData.asp (last searched March 5, 2004); "Politics & Policy – Organ Donation: Pilot Program Would Compensate Families," *Am. Health Line*, Apr. 30, 2002, available at http://www.nationaljournal.com.

12. *See* OPTN, *supra* note 80. Of the 56,864 candidates awaiting kidney transplants, 20,225 are African American. These statistics are based on OPTN data as of February 27, 2004.

13. *See* OPTN at http://www.optn.org; see also Goodwin, *supra* note 16, at 9.

14. *Id.*

15. *See* Barbara A. Noah, "Racial Disparities in the Delivery of Health Care," 35 *San Diego L. Rev.* 135, 145 (1998).

16. Id.

Bibliography

I. Books

Abraham, Laurie Kaye. *Mama Might Be Better Off Dead: The Failure of Health Care in Urban America*. Chicago: University of Chicago Press, 1993.

Aitken, Hugh. *Did Slavery Pay? Readings in the Economics of Black Slavery in the United States*. Boston: Houghton Mifflin, 1971.

Ball, Edward. *Slaves in the Family*. New York: Ballantine Books, 1998.

Barker, Ernest. *Introduction to Social Contract: Essays by Locke, Hume, and Rousseau*. New York: Oxford University Press, 1947.

Bell, Derrick. *Faces at the Bottom of the Well: The Permanence of Racism*. New York: Basic Books, 1992.

Bennett Jr., Lerone. *Forced into Glory: Abraham Lincoln's White Dream*. Chicago: Johnson Publishing Co., 1999.

Berlin, Ira et al. eds. *Remembering Slavery: African Americans Talk about Their Personal Experiences of Slavery and Emancipation*. New York: W. W. Norton & Company, 1998.

Berridge, Virginia. "AIDS and the Gift Relationship in the UK," in Richard Titmuss, *The Gift Relationship*. New York: New Press, 1997.

Black, Daniel P. *Dismantling Black Manhood: A Historical and Literary Analysis of the Legacy of Slavery*. New York: Garland Publishing, 1997.

Blassingame, John W. *The Slave Community: Plantation Life in the Antebellum South*. New York: Oxford University Press, 1972.

Burch, Jane S. et al. eds. *Institute of Medicine: Improving Health in the Community: A Role for Performance Monitoring*. Washington, D.C.: National Academy Press, 1997.

Calabresi, Guido & Philip Bobbit. *Tragic Choices*. New York: W. W. Norton & Company, 1978.

Caplan, Arthur L. *If I Were a Rich Man Could I Buy a Pancreas? and Other Essays on the Ethics of Health Care*. Bloomington: Indiana University Press, 1992.

Cerelli, G. James. *Organ Transplantation and Replacement*. Philadelphia: Lippincott Williams & Wilkins, 1998.

Childress, James F. "Ethical Criteria for Procuring and Distributing Organs for Transplantation." *Organ Transplantation Policy: Issues and Prospects* by James F. Blumsetin & Frank A. Sloan. Durham: Duke University Press, 1989.

Conley, Dalton. *Being Black, Living in the Red: Race, Wealth, and Social Policy in America*. Berkeley: University of California Press, 1999.

269

Conrad, Alfred H. & John R. Meyer. *The Economics of Slavery, and Other Studies in Econometric History*. Chicago: Aldine Publishing Co., 1954.

Curtain, Phillip D. *The Atlantic Slave Trade: A Census*. Madison: The University of Wisconsin Press, 1969.

DuBois, W. E. B. *Black Reconstruction in America 1860–1880*. New York: New Press, 1935.

DuBois, W. E. B. *The Souls of Black Folk*. New York: Penguin Books, 1903.

Fanon, Franz. *Black Skin, White Masks*. New York: Grove Press, 1967.

Fogel, Robert William & Stanley L. Engerman. *Time on the Cross*. New York: W. W. Norton & Company, 1974.

Franklin, John H. *From Slavery to Freedom*. New York: Alfred A. Knopf, 1967.

Frazier, Edward Franklin. *The Negro in the United States*. New York: Macmillan, 1957.

Fuller, Lon L. *The Morality of Law*. New Haven: Yale University Press, 1994.

Glennie, Alexander. *Sermons Preached to Congregations on Negroes*. Manchester: Ayer Co Pub., 1844.

Gold, Richard. E. *Body Parts: Property Rights and the Ownership of Human Biological Materials*. Washington D.C.: Georgetown University Press, 1996.

Goodin, Robert E. & Philip Pettit. *A Companion to Contemporary Political Philosophy*. Malden: Blackwell Publishers, 1993.

Goodman, Mary Ellen. *Race Awareness in Young Children*. New York: Collier Books, 1964.

Gossett, Thomas. *Race: The History of an Idea in America*. New York: Shocken, 1965.

Gray, Fred. D. *The Tuskegee Syphilis Study: The Real Story and Beyond*. Revelstoke: River City Pub., 1998.

Harris, William H. *The Harder We Run: Black Workers since the Civil War*. Oxford: Oxford University Press, 1982.

Hudson, Larry E. *Working Toward Freedom: Slave Society and Domestic Economy in the American South*. Rochester: University of Rochester Press, 1994.

Huggins, Nathan Irvin. *Black Odyssey: The Afro-American Ordeal in Slavery*. New York: Pantheon Books, 1990.

Institute of Medicine. *Xenotransplantation: Science, Ethics, and Public Policy*. Washington D.C.: National Academy Press, 1996.

Jacobs, Harriet. *Incidents in the Life of a Slave Girl*. Cambridge: Harvard University Press, 1987.

Jennings, Francis. *The Invasion of America: Indians, Colonialism, and the Cant of Conquest*. New York: W. W. Norton & Company, 1975.

Johnson, Charles & Patricia Smith. *Africans in America: America's Journey Through Slavery*. Fort Washington: Harvest Books, 1998.

Jones, James H. *Bad Blood: The Tuskegee Syphilis Experiment*. Detroit: Free Press, 1981.

Jordan, Winthrop D. *White over Black: American Attitudes toward the Negro, 1550–1812*. Chapel Hill: University of North Carolina Press, 1968.

Kass, Leon R., "Organs for Sale? Propriety, Property, and the Price of Progress," in *Politics and the Human Body: Assault on Dignity* 153, (Jean Bethke Elstain & Timothy Cloyd eds., Vanderbelt University Press, Tennessee, U.S.A., 1995).

Komesar, Neil. *Law's Limits: Rule of Law and the Supply and Demand of Rights*. Cambridge: Cambridge University Press, 2002.

Kimbrell, Andrew. *The Human Body Shop*. New York: Harper Collins, 1997.

Kymlicka, Will. "The Social Contract Tradition," in Peter Singer, *A Companion to Ethics*. Malden: Blackwell Publishers, 1991.

Lessnoff, Michael. *Social Contract*. New York: New York University Press, 1986.

Leveton, Lauren B. et al. eds. *Institute of Medicine Report: Committee to Study HIV Transmission Through Blood and Blood Products, HIV and the Blood Supply: An Analysis of Crisis Decisionmaking*. Washington D.C.: National Academy Press, 1995.

Lubiano, Wahneema, et al. *The House that Race Built*. New York: Vintage Books USA, 1997.

Marmot, Micheal & Richard Wilkinson eds. *Social Determinants of Health: The Solid Facts*. Copenhagen: World Health Organization, 1999.

Martlew, Vanessa. "Transfusion Medicine Toward the Millenium," in Richard Titmuss, *The Gift Relationship*. New York: New Press, 1997.

Mauer, Marc. *Race to Incarcerate*. New York: New Press, 1999.

McKinnon, Catherine. *Sexual Harassment of Working Women: A Case of Sex Discrimination*. New Haven: Yale University Press, 1979.

Mills, Charles W. *The Racial Contract*. Ithaca: Cornell University Press, 1997.

Oliver, Melvin L. & Thomas M. Shapiro. *Black Wealth/White Wealth: A New Perspective on Racial Inequality*. New York: Routledge, 1997.

Painter, Nell Irvin. *Sojourner Truth: A Life, A Symbol*. New York: W. W. Norton & Company, 1996.

Pipes, Richard. *Property and Freedom*. New York: Vintage Books USA, 2000.

Radin, Margaret Jane. *Contested Commodities*. Cambridge: Harvard University Press, 1996.

Rawls, John. *A Theory of Justice*. Cambridge: Belknap Press, 1971.

Richardson, Ruth. *Death, Dissection, and the Destitute*. Chicago: University of Chicago Press, 2000.

Richardson, Ruth. "Fearful Symmetry: Corpses for Anatomy, Organs for Transplantation?" By Stuart J. Younger et al., ed. *Organ Transplantation Meanings and Realities*. Madison: University of Wisconsin, 1996.

Roberts, Dorothy. *Killing the Black Body: Race, Reproduction, and the Meaning of Liberty*. New York: Vintage Books USA, 1997.

Robinson, Randall. *The Debt: What America Owes to Blacks*. New York: Plume Books, 2000.

Rotherberg, Paula, Nicolaus Schnafhausen, & Caroline Schneider. *Race, Class, and Gender in the United States*. New York: Worth Publishing Inc., 1998.

Rousseau, Jean-Jacques. *The Social Contract or Principles of Political Right*. Knoxville: Wordsworth Classics, 1998.

Schneider, Dorothy & Carl J. Schneider. *Slavery in America: From Colonial Times to the Civil War: An Eyewitness History*. New York: Facts on File, 2000.

Smedley, Brian D. et al. eds., *Institute of Medicine: Unequal Treatment: Confronting Racial and Ethnic Disparities in Health Care*. Washington D.C.: National Academy Press, 2002.

Stannard, David E. *American Holocaust: Columbus and the Conquest of the New Worlds*. Philadelphia: American Philological Association, 1992.

Starr, Douglas. *Blood: An Epic History of Medicine and Commerce*. New York: Alfred A. Knopf, 1998.

Steinberg, Stephen. *Turning Back: The Retreat from Racial Justice in American Thought and Policy*. Boston: Beacon Press, 1995.

Stiglitz, Joseph E. *Whither Socialism?* Cambridge: MIT Press, 1996.

Titmuss, Richard. *The Gift Relationship: From Human Blood to Social Policy*. New York: New Press, 1971.

Wade, Richard. *Slavery in the Cities: The South 1820–1860*. Oxford: Oxford University Press, 1964.

Wicker, Tom. *Tragic Failure: Racial Integration in America*. New York: William Morrow & Company, 1996.

Woodward, Vann C. *The Strange Career of Jim Crow*. Oxford: Oxford University Press, 1955.

II. Law Review and Journal Articles

Allen, Anita. "Social Contract Theory in America Case Law," 51 *Fla. L. Rev.* 1 (1999).

Anderson, Mark F. "The Future of Organ Transplantation: From Where Will New Donors Come, to Whom Will Their Organs Go?," 5 *Health Matrix* 249 (1995).

Andrews, Lori B. "Harnessing the Benefit of Biobanks," 33 *J.L. Med. & Ethics* 22 (2005).

Andrews, Lori B. "Is There a Right to Clone? Constitutional Challenges to Bans on Human Cloning," 11 *Harv. J.L. & Tech.* 643 (1998).

Ayala, Kristi. "The Application of Traditional Criminal Law to Misappropriation of Gametic Materials," 24 *Am. J. Crim. L.* 503 (1997).

Ayres, Ian et al. "Unequal Racial Access to Kidney Transplantation," 46 *Vand. L. Rev.* 805 (1993).

Bailey, Ronald. "Warning: Bioethics May Be Hazardous to Your Health," 31 *Reason* 24 (1999).

Bankole, Katherine Olukemi. "A Critical Inquiry of Enslaved African Females and the Antebellum Hospital," 31 *J. Black Stud.* 517 (2001).

Banks, Gloria J. "Legal and Ethical Safeguards: Protection of Society's Most Vulnerable Participants in a Commercialized Organ Transplantation System," 21 *Am. J. L. & Med.* 45 (1995).

Bernier, Barbara L. "Class, Race, and Poverty: Medical Technologies and Socio-Political Choices," 11 *Harv. Blackletter L.J.* 115 (1994).

Blair, Roger D., & David L. Kaserman. "The Economics and Ethics of Alternative Cadaveric Organ Procurement Policies," 8 *Yale J. of Reg.* 403 (1991).

Boyd, S. Gregory. Comment, "Considering a Market in Human Organs," 4 *N.C. J.L. & Tech.* 417 (2003).

Brandon, Beth. Note, "Anencephalic Infants as Organ Donors: A Question of Life or Death," 40 *Case West. Res. L. Rev.* 781 (1989–90).

Bridges, Khiara M. Note, "On the Commodification of the Black Female Body: The Critical Implications of the Alienability of Fetal Tissue," 102 *Colum. L. Rev.* 123 (2002).

Brooks, Roy L. & Mary Jo Newborn. "Critical Race Theory and Classical-Liberal Civil Rights Scholarship: A Distinction Without a Difference?," 82 *Cal. L. Rev.* 787 (1994).

Buffone, Douglas C. "Sperm, Spleens, and Other Valuables: The Need to Recognize Property Rights in Human Body Parts," 23 *Hofstra L. Rev.* 693 (1995).

Calabresi, Guido. "An Introduction to Legal Thought: Four Approaches to Law and to the Allocation of Body Parts," 55 *Stan. L. Rev.* 2113 (2003).

Calabresi, Guido & A. Douglas Melamed. "Property Rules, Liability Rules, and Inalienability: One View of the Cathedral," 85 *Harv. L. Rev.* 1089 (1972).

Caplan, Arthur L. "Organ Procurement: It's Not in the Cards," *The Hastings Center Report*, Oct. 1984.

Cohen, Lloyd R. "Increasing the Supply of Transplant Organs: The Virtues of a Futures Market," 58 *Geo. Wash. L. Rev.* 1 (1989).

Coleman, Phyllis. "'Brother Can You Spare a Liver?': Five Ways to Increase Organ Donation," 31 *Val. U. L. Rev.* 1 (1996).

Coucie, Michael et al. "Race and Sex Differences in the Identification of Candidates for Renal Transplantation," 19 *Am. J. Kidney Diseases* 414 (1992).

Crain, Marion. "Whitewashed Labor Law, Skinwalking Unions," 23 *Berkeley J. Emp. & Lab. L.* 211 (2002).

Crespi, Gregory S. "Overcoming the Legal Obstacles to the Creation of a Futures Market in Bodily Organs," 55 *Ohio St. L.J.* 1 (1994).

De Costa, Caroline M. "James Marion Sims: Some Speculations and a New Position," 178 *MJA* 660 (2003).

Delmarco, Francis L. et al. "Ethical Incentives – Not Payment – for Organ Donation, *New Eng. J. Med.* Vol. 346 No. 25 (June 20, 2002).

"Developments in the Law – Medical Technology and the Law," 103 *Harv. L. Rev.* 1519 (1990).

Dolgin, Janet L. "Personhood, Discrimination, and the New Genetics," 66 *Brook L. Rev.* 755 (2001).

Dukeminier, Jesse. "Supplying Organs for Transplantation," 68 *Mich. L. Rev.* 811 (1970).

Editorial, "Institutionalized Racism in Health Care," *The Lancet*, Vol. 353 No. 9155, Mar. 6, 1999.

Espinoza, Leslie & Angela P. Harris. "Afterword: Embracing the Tar-Baby-LatCrit Theory and the Sticky Mess of Race," 85 *Cal. L. Rev.* 1585 (1997).

Fauci, Cara A. "Racism and Health Care in America: Legal Responses to Racial Disparities in the Allocation of Kidneys," 21 *B.C. Third World L.J.* 35 (2001).

Farley, Anthony Paul. "The Black Body as Fetish Object," 76 *Ore. L. Rev.* 457 (1997).

Fentiman, Linda. "Organ Donation as National Service: A Proposed Federal Organ Donation Law," 27 *Suffolk U. L. Rev.* 1593 (1993).

Fisher, Clifford. "The Role of Causation in Science as Law and Proposed Changes in the Current Common Law Toxic Tort System," 9 *Buff. Envtl. L. J.* 35 (2001).

Fogg-Davis, Hawley. "Navigating Race in the Market for Human Gametes," *The Hastings Center Report*, Sept. 1, 2001, at 13.

Franke, Katherine M. "Becoming a Citizen: Reconstruction-Era Regulation of African American Marriages," 11 *Yale J. L. Human.* 251 (1999).

Gaston, Robert S. et al. "Racial Equity in Transplantation: The Disparate Impact of HLA-Based Allocation," 270 *JAMA* 1352 (1993).

George, Erin P. "The Stem Cell Debate: The Legal, Political and Ethical Issues Surrounding Federal Funding of Scientific Research on Human Embryos," 12 *Alb. J.T. Sci & Tech.* 747 (2002).

Gill, Michael B. & Sade, Robert M. "Paying for Kidneys: The Case Against Prohibition," 12 *Kennedy Inst. Ethics J.* 17 (2002).

Goodwin, Michele. "Altruism's Limits: Law, Capacity and Organ Commodification," 56 *Rutgers L. Rev.* 305 (2004).

Goodwin, Michele. "Deconstructing Legislative Consent Law: Organ Taking, Racial Profiling and Distributive Justice," 6 *Va. J.L. & Tech.* 2 (2001).

Hall, Mark A. "Rationing Health Care at the Bedside," 69 *N.Y.U.L. Rev.* 693 (1994).

Hansmann, Henry. "The Economics and Ethics of Markets for Human Organs," 14 *J. Health Pol. Pol'y & Law* 57 (1989).

Harris, Cheryl. Bondage, Freedom and the Constitution: The New Slavery Scholarship and Its Impact on Law and Legal Historiography: Private Law and United States Slave Regimes: Finding Sojourner's Truth: Race, Gender, and the Institution of Property," 18 *Cardozo L. Rev.* 309 (1996).

Harris, Cheryl. "Whiteness as Property," 106 *Harv. L. Rev.* 1707 (1993).

Harrison, Charlotte H. "Neither *Moore* nor the Market: Alternative Models for Compensating Contributors of Human Tissue," 28 *Am. J.L. & Med.* 77 (2002).

Harrison, Jeffrey L. "Pier cing Pareto Superiority: Real People and the Obligations of Legal Theory," 39 *Ariz. L. Rev.* 1 (1997).

Hazard Jr., Geoffrey C. "Communitarian Ethics and Legal Justification," 59 *U. Col. L. Rev.* 721 (1988).

Hickman, Christine. "The Devil and the One Drop Rule: Racial Categories, African Americans and the U.S. Census," 95 *Mich. L. Rev.* 1161 (1997).

Hill, John Lawrence. "Exploitation," 79 *Cornell L. Rev.* 631 (1994).

Hinkle, Whitney. "Giving Until it Hurts: Prisoners Are Not the Answer to the National Organ Shortage," 35 *Ind. L. Rev.* 593 (2002).

Hopkins, Kevin. "Blood, Sweat, and Tears: Toward a New Paradigm for Protecting Donor Privacy," 7 *Va. J. Soc. Pol'y & L.* 141 (2000).

Jatoi, Ismail. "Widening Disparity in Survival Between White and African-American Patients with Breast Carcinoma Treated in the U.S. Department of Defense Healthcare System," 98(5) *Cancer* 894 (2003).

Jefferies, David E. "The Body as Commodity: The Use of Markets to Cure the Organ Deficit," 5 *Ind. J. Global Legal Stud.* 621 (1998).

Jones, Trina. "Shades of Brown: The Law of Skin Color," 49 *Duke L.J.* 1487, 1490 (2000).

Justice, J. Steven. "Personhood and Death – The Proper Treatment of Anencephalic Organ Donors Under the Law: In re T.A.C.P.," 62 *U. Cin. L. Rev.* 1227 (1994).

Kass, Leon R. "Organs for Sale? Propriety, Property, and the Price of Progress," 107 *Pub. Interest* 65 (1992).

Kelly, Mayor Sharon Pratt. "Thurgood Marshall Commemorative Issue: Keynote Address," 35 *How. L. J.* 61 (1991).

Kenn, Deborah. "Institutionalized, Legal Racism: Housing Segregation and Beyond," 11 *B.U. Pub. Int. L.J.* 35 (2001).

Khauli, Raja B. "Issues and Controversies Surrounding Organ Donation and Transplantation: The Need for Laws that Ensure Equity and Optimal Utility of a Scarce Resource," 27 *Suffolk U.L. Rev.* 1225 (1993).

Kilner, John F. "Selecting Patients when Resources are Limited: A Study of U.S. Medical Directors of Kidney Dialysis and Transplantation Facilities," 78 *Am. J. of Pub. Health* 144, 144–47 (1988).

Kirschenbaum, Sheila R. Note, "Banking on Discord: Property Conflicts in the Transplantation of Umbilical Cord Stem Cells," 39 *Ariz. L. Rev.* 1391 (1997).

Kjellstrand, Carl M. "Age, Sex, and Race Inequality in Renal Transplantation," 148 *Archives of Internal Med.* 1305, 1309 (1988).

Knoppers, Bartha M. & Sonia LeBris. "Recent Advances in Medically Assisted Conception: Legal, Ethical and Social Issues," 17 *AM. J.L. & Med.* 329 (1991).

Kolber, Adam J. "A Matter of Priority: Transplanting Organs Preferentially to Registered Donors," 55 *Rutgers. L. Rev.* 671, 704 (2005).

Korsten, Lisa M. Note, "The Global Market for Blood," 11 *B.U. Int'l. L.J.* 227 (1993).

Kress, Jack M. "Xenotransplantation: Ethics and Economics," 53 *Food Drug L.J.* 353 (1998).

Leiber, Katherine B. "Selling the Womb: Can the Feminist Critique of Surrogacy be Answered?," 68 *Ind. L.J.* 205 (1992).

Lombardo, Paul. "'The American Breed': Nazi Eugenics and the Origins of the Pioneer Fund," 65 *Alb. L. Rev.* 743 (2002).

Lombardo, Paul. "Medicine, Eugenics, and the Supreme Court: From Coercive Sterilization to Reproductive Freedom," 13 *J. Contemp. Health L. & Pol'y.* 1 (1996).

Lombardo, Paul. "Taking Eugenics Seriously," 30 *Fla. St. L. Rev.* 191 (2003).

Mahoney, Julia D. "The Market for Human Tissue," 86 *Va. L. Rev.* 163, 172 (2000).

McKinnon, Catherine. "Feminism, Marxism, and the State: An Agenda for Theory," 7 *Signs* 541 (1982).

Meier, Benjamin Mason. "International Protection of Persons Undergoing Medical Experimentation: Protecting the Right of Informed Consent," 20 *Berkeley J. Int'l L.* 513 (2002).

Mintz, Benjamin. Note, "Analyzing the OPTN Under State Action Doctrine – Can UNOS's Organ Allocation Criteria Survive Strict Scrutiny?," 28 *Colum. J.L. & Soc. Probs.* 339, 340–41 n.9 (1995).

Editorial, "Mistrust Limits Minority Representation in U.S. Biomedical Research," *Drug Week*, March 5, 2004.

Motley, Constance Baker. "Thurgood Marshall," 68 *N.Y.U.L. Rev.* 208 (1993).

Munroe, Maurice E. R. "Unamerican Tail: Of Segregation and Multicultural Education," 64 *Alb. L. Rev.* 241 (2000).

Murray, Thomas H. "On the Human Body as Property: The Meaning of Embodiment, Markets and the Meaning of Strangers," 20 *U. Mich. J.L. Reform* 1055 (1987).

Nelson, James Lindemann. "Transplantation Through a Glass Darkly," 22 *Hastings Center Rep.* 6 (Sept.–Oct. 1992).

Noah, Barbara A. "Racial Disparities in the Delivery of Health Care," 35 *San Diego L. Rev.* 135 (1998).

Note, "Regulating the "Gift of Life" – The 1987 Uniform Anatomical Gift Act," 65 *Wash. L. Rev.* 171 (1990).

Note, "Regulating the Sale of Human Organs," 71 *Virginia L. Rev.* 1015 (1985).

Note, "The Sale of Human Body Parts," 72 *Mich. L. Rev.* 1182 (1974).

Nussbaum, Martha. "Sherman J. Bellwood Lecture, In Defense of Universal Values," 36 *Idaho L. Rev.* 379, 395 (2000).

Nwabueze, Remigius N. "Biotechnology and the New Property Regime in Human Bodies and Body Parts," 24 *Loy. L.A. Int'l & Comp. L. Rev.* 19, 61 (2002).

Pendleton, Annie. "Ethical Implications of Organ Transplantation," 4 *Plastic Surgical Nursing* 18 (1998).

Peppin, Patricia & Elaine Carty. "Innovation, Myths, and Equality: Constructing Drug Knowledge in Research and Advertising," 23 *Sydney L. Rev.* 543 (2001).

Pilarczyk, Ian C. "Organ Donor Trusts and Durable Powers of Attorney for Organ Donation: New Trusts on the Living Trust and Living Will," 13 *Prob. L.J.* 29 (1995).

Pollitt, Daniel H. "Reflection on the Bicentennial of the Bill of Rights: The Flag Burning Controversy: A Chronology," 70 *N.C.L. Rev.* 553 (1992).

Powhida, Alexander. "Force Organ Donation: The Presumed Consent to Organ Donation Laws of the Various States and the United States Constitution," 9 *Alb. L.J. Sci. Tech.* 349 (1999).

Rao, Radhika. "Property, Privacy, and the Human Body," 80 *B.U.L. Rev.* 359 (2000).

Radin, Margaret Jane. "Market Inalienability," 100 *Harv. L. Rev.* 1849 (1987).

Rice, Willy E. "'Commercial Terrorism' from the Transatlantic Slave Trade to the World Trade Center Disaster," 6 *Scholar* 1 (2003).

Robinson, Shelby E. "Organs for Sale? An Analysis of Proposed Systems for Compensating Organ Providers," 70 *U. Colo. L. Rev.* 1019 (1999).

Rutherford, Jane. "The Myth of Due Process," 72 *B.U.L. Rev.* 1 (1992).

Sanders, David & Jesse Dukeminier Jr. "Medical Advance and Legal Lag: Hemodialysis and Kidney Transplantation," 15 *UCLA L. Rev.* 357 (1968).

Scheper-Hughes, Nancy. "The Global Traffic in Human Organs," 41 *Current Anthropology* 191 (Apr. 2000).

Schmitz, Cathryne et al. "The Interconnection of Childhood Poverty and Homelessness: Negative Impact/Points of Access," 82 *J. Contemp. Hum. Services* 69 (2001).

Schnably, Stephen J. "Property and Pragmatism: A Critique of Radin's Theory of Property and Personhood," 45 *Stan. L. Rev.* 347 (1993).

Schneider, E. C. et al. "Racial Disparities in the Quality of Care for Enrollees in Medicare Managed Care," 287 *JAMA* 1288 (2002).

Schwartz, Howard S. "Bioethical and Legal Considerations in Increasing the Supply of Transplantable Organs: From UAGA to 'Baby Fae'," 10 *Am. J.L. & Med.* 397 (1985).

Shalala, Donna E. "Message from the Secretary," 1 *Healthy People* 2010 18 (2000).

Shapiro, Michael H. "Is Bioethics Broke?: On the Idea of Ethics and Law "Catching Up" with Technology," 33 *Ind. L. Rev.* 17 (1999).

Shapiro, Michael H. "Regulation as Language: Communicating Values by Altering the Contingencies of Choice," 55 *U. Pitt. L. Rev.* 681 (1994).

Silver, Jessica Dunsay. "From Baby Doe to Grandpa Doe: The Impact of the Federal Age Discrimination Act on the "Hidden" Rationing of Medical Care," 37 *Cath. U. L. Rev.* 993 (1988).

Sobota, Margaret R. Note, "The Price of Life, $50,000 for an Egg, Why Not $1,500 for a Kidney? An Argument to Establish a Market for Organ Procurement Similar to the Current Market for Human Egg Procurement," 82 *Wash. U.L. Q.* 1225 (1988).

Soucie, Michael et al. "Race and Sex Differences in the Identification of Candidates for Renal Transplantation," 19 *AM. J. Kidney Disease* 414 (1992).

Spurr, Stephen J. "The Shortage of Transplantable Organs: An Analysis and a Proposal," 15 *Law & Policy* 355 (1993).

Statson, E. B. "The Uniform Anatomical Gift Act," 23 *Bus. Law.* 919 (1968).

Stone, John. "Race and Healthcare Disparities: Overcoming Vulnerability," 23:6 *Theoretical Medicine and Bioethics* 499 (2002).

Stubbs, Jonathan K. "Perceptual Prisms and Racial Realism: The Good News about a Bad Situation," 45 *Mercer L. Rev.* 773 (1994).

Takemoto, Steve et al. "Equitable Allocation of HLA-Compatible Kidneys for Local Pools and for Minorities," 331 *New. Eng. J. Med.* 760 (1994).

Tetlow, Tania. "The Founders and Slavery: A Crisis of Conscience," 3 *Loy. J. Pub. Int. L.* 1 (2001).

Theran, Elizabeth E. "Free to be Arbitrary and . . . Capricious," 11 *Cornell J. L. Pub. Pol'y* 113 (2001).

Trebilcock, Michael et al. "Do Institutions Matter? A Comparative Pathology of the HIV-Infected Blood Tragedy," 82 *Va. J. Soc. Pol'y & L.* 1407 (2000).

Watson, Sidney. "Race, Ethnicity and Quality of Care: Inequalities and Incentives," 27 *Am. J.L. & Med.* 203 (2001).

Whitehead, Angela T. "Rejecting Organs: The Organ Allocation Process and the Americans with Disabilities Act," 24 *Am. J.L. & Med.* 481 (1998).

Wiecek, William M. "Bondage Freedom and the Constitution: The New Slavery Scholarship and Its Impact on Law and Legal Historiography: The Origins of the Law of Slavery in British North America," 17 *Cardozo L. Rev.* 1711 (1996).

Williams, Christian. Note, "Combating the Problems of Human Rights Abuses and Inadequate Supply Through Presumed Donative Consent," 26 *Case W. Res. J. Int'l L.* 315 (1994).

Williams, Rhonda Y. "'We're Tired of Being Treated Like Dogs:' Poor Women and Power Politics in Black Baltimore," 31 *Black Scholar* 31 (2001).

Williams, Walter E. "My Organs Are for Sale," *Freeman: Ideas on Liberty*, Oct. 1, 2002, at 63.

Wilson, James G. "The Role of Public Opinion in Constitutional Interpretation," 1993 *BYU L. Rev.* 1037 (1993).

Wiltgen, Janet S. "Understanding the Issues of Organ and Tissue Donation, Allocation and Payment," 19 *Whittier L. Rev.* 29 (1997).

Wolf, Adam B. "What Money Cannot Buy: A Legislative Response to C.R.A.C.K.," 33 *U. Mich. J.L. Reform* 173 (2000).

World Health Org. "Guiding Principles on Human Organ Transplantation," 337 *Lancet* 1470 (1991).

III. Cases

Bonner v. Moran, 126 F.2d 121 (D.C. Cir. 1941).

Brotherton v. Cleveland, 923 F.2d 477, 481 (6th Cir. 1991).

Brotherton v. Cleveland, 173 F.3d 552 (6th Cir.)(1999).

Buck v. Bell, 274 U.S. 200 (1927).

Cahill v. Cahill, 757 So. 2d 465 (Ala. Civ. App. 2000).

Christensen v. Superior Court, 820 P.2d 181 (Cal. 1991).

Cryolife, Inc. v. Superior Court of Santa Cruz County, 110 Cal. App. 4th 1145 (Cal. Ct. App. 2003).

Curran v. Bosze, 566 N.E.2d 1319 (Ill. 1990).

Diamond v. Chakhabarty, 447 U.S. 303 (1980).

Doe v. Cutter Biological, 852 F. Supp. 909 (D. Ida. 1994).

Doe v. Travenol Laboratories, Inc., 698 F. Supp. 780 (D. Minn., 1988).

Dred Scott v. Sandford, 60 U.S. 393 (1856).

Employment Div, Dept. of Human Res. of Oregon v. Smith, 494 U.S. 872 (1990).

Evans v. Evans, 23 Ohio Dec. 375 (Ohio Com.Pl. 1912).

Ex parte Whitebread, (1816) 2 Meriv 99, 35 Eng Reprint 878 (Ch).

Foster v. Harrison, No. 68674, Eq. Mass. Sup. Jud. Ct. (Nov. 20, 1957).

Good v. Presbyterian Hosp., 934 F. Supp. 107 (S.D. N.Y. 1996).

Hart v. Brown, 29 Conn. Supp. 368, 289 A.2d 386 (Super. 1972).

Heirs of Fruge v. Blood Services, 506 F.2d 841 (5th Cir. 1975).

Hurdle et. al. v. Currier et. al., 5 Va. Cir. 509 (1977).

Hushey v. Harrison, No. 68666, Eq. Mass. Sup. Jud. Ct. (Aug. 30, 1957).

In Re Estate of Moyer, 577 P.2d 108 (Utah 1978).
In Re Guardianship of Pescinski, 67 Wis.2d 226, 226 N.W.2d 180 (1975).
In Re Richardson, 284 So.2d 185 (L.A. App. 1973).
Jacobson v. Massachusetts, 197 U.S. 11 (1905).
J.B. v. M.B., 170 N.J. 9, 783 A.2d 707 (2001).
Kass v. Kass, 91 N.Y.2d 554, 673 N.Y.S.2d 350 (1998).
Litowitz v. Litowitz, 146 Wash.2d 514, 48 P.3d 261 (2002).
Little v. Little, 576 S.W.2d 493 (Tex. Civ. 1979).
Madsen v. Harrison, No. 68651, Eq. Mass. Sup. Jud. Ct. (June 12, 1957).
McFall v. Shimp, 10 Pa. D. & C.3d 90 (Ch. Ct. 1978).
Moore v. Regents of Univ. of Cal., 499 U.S. 936 (1991).
Michigan v. Moye, 491 N.W.2d 232 (Michigan, 1992).
Newman v. Sathyavaglswaran, 287 F.3d 786 (9th Cir.)(2002).
O'Donnell v. Slack, 55 Pac. Rep. 906, 907 (1899).
Prince v. Massachusetts, 321 U.S. 158, 64 S.Ct. 438, 88 L. Ed. 645 (1945).
Ramirez v. Health Partners of Southern Arizona, 972 P.2d 658 (Ariz. Ct. App. 1998).
Re Baby K, 16 F.3d 590, 598 (4th Cir. 1994).
Re Earl of Carysfort, (1840) Craig & Ph 76, 41 Eng Reprint 418.
Skinner v. Oklahoma, 316 U.S. 535 (1942).
Smith v. Kurtzman, 531 N.E.2d 885 (Ill. App. Ct. 1988).
State v. McKnight, 576 S. E.3d 168 (2003).
Strunk v. Strunk, 445 S.W.2d 145 (KY. App. 1969).
Travelers Ins. Co. v. Welch, 82 F.2d 799 (1936).
United States v. Garber, 607 F.2d 92 (5th Cir. 1979).
Vossler v. Richards Manufacturing Company, 143 Cal. App. 3d 952 (1983).
You Vang Yang v. Sturner, 728 F.Supp. 845 (D.R.I. 1990).

IV. Statutes

1968 Unif. Anatomical Gift Act (1987) § 2(h).
1968 Unif. Anatomical Gift Act (1987) § 5.
1968 Unif. Anatomical Gift Act (1987) § 10.
42 U.S.C.A. §273.
42 U.S.C. §273 (2000).
42 U.S.C. §274(e) (2000).
42 U.S.C. §274 (a)-(b) (2000).
42 U.S.C. §1320b-8.
Act of June 12, 1967, ch. 353, 1967 Mass. Acts 202, 202 (repealed 1971).
ARK. CODE ANN. 12-12-320 (1987).
ARIZ. REV. STAT. ANN. 36-851 to 852 (1986 & Supp. 1989).
CAL. GOV'T CODE 27491.46-.47 (West 1988).
CAL. PENAL CODE § 367f.
COLO. REV. STAT. 30-10-621 (1986).
CONN. GEN. STAT. ANN. 732.9185 (West Supp. 1989).
DEL. CODE ANN. Tit. 29, 4712 (Supp. 1988).
FLA. STAT. ANN. 732.9185 (West Supp. 1989).
GA. CODE ANN. 31-23-6 (1985).
HAW. REV. STAT. ANN. 327-4 (1988).
IDAHO CODE 39-3405 (Supp.1989).
ILL. ANN. STAT. CH. 110 $^{1}/_{2}$, 351-354 (Smith-Hurd Supp. 1989).

KY. REV. STAT. ANN. 311.187 (Michie Supp. 1989).

LA. REV. STAT. ANN. 17:2354.1-3, 33:1565 (West 1982, 1988 & Supp. 1989).

MD.EST. & TRUSTS CODE ANN. 4-509.1 (Supp.1989).

MASS. ANN. LAWS CH. 113, 12 (Law.Co-op.Supp.1989).

MICH.COMP. LAWS. ANN. 333.10202 (1989).

MISS. CODE ANN. 41-61-71 (Supp.1989).

MO.ANN.STAT. 58.770 (Vernon 1989).

MONT. CODE ANN. 72-12-215 (1989).

N.C.GEN.STAT. 130A-391 (1989).

N.D.CENT. CODE 23-06.2-04 (Supp.1989).

OHIO REV. CODE ANN. 2108.60 (Baldwin 1987).

OKLA.STAT.ANN. tit. 63, 944.1 (West Supp. 1990).

R.I. GEN. LAWS 23-18.6-4 (1989).

TENN. CODE ANN. 68-30-204 (Supp.1989).

TEX. HEALTH & SAFETY CODE ANN. 693.012 (Vernon pamphlet 1990).

UTAH CODE ANN. 26-4-23 (1989).

WASH. REV. CODE ANN. 68.50.280 (Supp.1989).

WIS. LAWS 157.06 (1989).

W.VA. CODE 16-19-3a (1985).

K.Y. REV. STAT. ANN. §311.187 (1988).

KY. REV. STAT. ANN. §508.110 (Michie 2002)

Law of April 22, 1964, ch. 702, § 1, 1964 N.Y. Laws 1827, 1828 (repealed 1971).

Law of April 24, 1961, ch. 315, § 1, 11961 Md. Laws 397, 398 (repealed 1968).

Law of Aug. 1, 1968, ch. 429, § 7, 56 Del. Laws, 1773, 1773 (1967) (repealed 1970).

Law of May 20, 1967, ch. 94, § 1, 1967 Hawaii Laws 91, 91 (repealed 1969).

MD. HEALTH-GENERAL CODE ANN. § 5.408.

MICH. COMP. LAWS. ANN. § 333.

N.Y. PUB. HEALTH LAW § 4307.

OHIO REV. CODE ANN. 2108.60 (1987).

S.C. CODE ANN. §16-3-85 (2002).

State of Wisconsin Statutes 157.06 Uniform Anatomical Gift Act.

TEX. HEALTH AND SAFETY 693.012.

The Organ Donation and Recovery Act. S. 573, 108th Cong. (2003).

UAGA (1968) § 1(e).

UAGA (1968) § 2(b).

UAGA (1968) §3.

UAGA (1968) § 7(d).

Unif. Anatomical Gift Act § 5(b), 8A U.L.A. 47 (amend 1987).

UTAH CODE ANN. §75-5-109 (2000)

UTAH CODE ANN. §76-208 (2000)

VA. CODE § 32.1-289.1 (1985).

W.VA. CODE 16-19-3s (1985).

V. Websites

"A Search for Slavery, Through One Collection of Primary Source Photography," available at http://www.rev.net/~hmcmanus/slpage3.htm (last visited Jan. 26, 2003).

America's Blood Centers, at http://www.americasblood.org (last visited June 26, 2004).

Andrulis, Dennis P., The National Public Health and Hospital Institute, "New Dimensions and Directions in Inner-City Health Care," at http://www/acponline.orh/hpp/pospaper/andrulis.htm, *citing* Satcher Rivo, "Improving access to health care through physician workforce reform," *JAMA*, 1993 at 270.

Casey, Kenneth. "By the Numbers: Neurology at the University of Michigan: 1890-2000" (2000). http://www.med.umich.edu/neuro/neurology-at-michigan.pdf.

CNN, "Older Patients Unaware of New Medicare Law," CNN.com, Feb. 26, 2004, at http://www.cnn.com/2004/HEALTH/02/06/medicare.survey.ap.

"Cryolife," at http://www.cryolife.com (Jan. 3, 2003).

"Digging Up Specimens," http://www/umich.edu/~aahist/chris1850.html (last searched Mar. 5, 2004).

Emily Bazelon, "Grave Offense," *Legal Affairs*, July–Aug. 2002, available at http://www.legalaffairs.org/issues/July-August-2002/story_bazelon-julaug2002.html.

Healy, Kieran, "Why Blood Centers Don't Need to Give You any Money for Blood Products that They Sell for Hundreds of Dollars per Donation," available at http://www.chat11.com/Emergence_Of_HIV_In_US_Blood_Supply.

Heisel, William & Mark Katches. "Organ Agencies Aid For-Profit Suppliers," *Orange County Reg.*, (June 25, 2000) at http://www.ocregister.com/features/body/organ00625cci.shtml (Nov. 25, 2003).

"Improving Fairness and Effectiveness in Allocating Organs for Transplantation," available at http://www/hhs.gov/news/press/1998pres/980326b.html (Mar. 26, 1998).

Katches, Mark. "Company Mixes Up Body Parts," *Orange County Reg.*, (July 9, 2000) at http://www.ocregister.com/features/body/rti0709.shtml (Nov. 25, 2003).

Meckler, Laura. "Congress Examines Tissue Banks," *AP Press* (May 24, 2001), available at http://organtx.org/tissuebanks.htm (Oct. 5, 2003).

McGrath, Matt. "Internet Rush to Buy Human Eggs." *BBC News* (Feb. 16, 2001), available at http://www.news.bbc.com.uk/1/hi/health/1172616.stm (Oct. 5, 2003).

"Olympus," at http://olympus.com (Jan. 3, 2003).

Olympus Press Release, "Olympus Set to Enter Tissue Engineering Field: Targeting Sales of Tissue-Engineered Bone and Automated Multi-Specimen Cell Culture Equipment," (Nov. 27, 2002), at http://www.olympus.co.p/en/news/2002/nr021127tissue.html (Jan. 3, 2003).

OPTN at http://www.optn.org/latestData/rptData.asp (last searched March 5, 2004).

OPTN, "Deceased Donors Recovered in the U.S. by State of OPO Headquarters," available at http://optn.org/data/annualreport.asp (Jan. 3, 2003).

"Organ Procurement Transplantation Network, Current U.S. Waiting List by Ethnicity," at http://www.optn.org/latestdata/rptData.asp (Oct. 3, 2003).

"Organs Watch," at http://sunsite.berkeley.edu/biotech.organswatch/index.html (March 2, 2003).

"Politics and Policy – Organ Donation: Pilot Program Would Compensate Families," *Am. Health Line*, Apr. 30, 2002, available at http://www.nationaljournal.com.

Radoes, Carol. "Inside Clinical Trials: Testing Medical Products in People," *FDA Consumer*, Sept. 9, 2003, available at http://www.fda.gov.fdsc/features/2003/503_trial.html.

"Red Cross," at http://www.redcross.org.

"Regeneration Technologies," at http://www.rtechnology.com (Jan. 3, 2003).

"RTI Receives $15.1 Million Credit Agreement" (Dec. 20, 2002), at http://www.rtitechnology.com/news/index.cfm?title=News%20In (Jan. 3, 2003).

"Surgeons Say Paying for Organ Donations Should Not Be Pursued," *PR Newswire*, June 28, 2002, available at http://www.facs.org/news/organdonation.html.

United Network for Organ Sharing (UNOS) at http://www.unos.org (Nov. 25, 2003).

University of Maryland, "Annual Circular of the Faculty of Physics of the University of Maryland. Session 1844–5," 5 (Baltimore: John Murphy, 1844), available at http://www.mdhistoryonline.net/mdmedicine/cfm/pt2.cfm (last visited Nov. 25, 2003).

Weiss, Martin D., "The Wise Investor's Guide to Life Insurance," available at http://www.safemoneyreport.com/survey/SMR0088_Life_Insurance.pdf.

VI. Newspaper Articles

Allen, Arthur. "God and Science," *Wash. Post.* (Magazine), Oct. 15, 2000, at W8.

Allen, Donna Murray. "Civil War Claims Can Provide Some Fascinating Details," *St. Petersburg Times*, Oct. 3, 2002, at 2D.

Asher, Mark. "The Inside Game: With a Transplanted Kidney, Sean Elliot Takes on the Challenge of Getting Back on the Professional Basketball Court," *Wash. Post.* Apr. 4, 2000, at 12.

"Autopsy Through the Ages: Competition for Cadavers so Intense that Doctors Hired Body Snatchers," *The Independent* (London), Nov. 21, 2002, at 3 (reviewing Jeremy Laurence William Hogarth, *The Four Stages of Cruelty* [1751]).

Batz, Jr., Bob. "Illegal, Fattening and Moral: Local Group Dispenses Marijuana Brownies as an Act of Compassion," *Pittsburgh Post-Gazette*, Nov. 13, 1994, at M1.

Belkin, Lisa. "Fairness Debated in Quick Transplant," *N.Y. Times*, June 16, 1993, at A16.

Berger, Joseph. "Yale Gene pool Seen as Route to Better Baby," *N.Y. Times*, Jan. 10, 1999, at A19.

Blake, Catherine. "Survey to Deal with Transplantation Needs," *L.A. Times*, March 9, 2000, at 3.

Blakeslee, Sandra. "Studies Find Unequal Access to Kidney Transplants," *N.Y. Times*, Jan. 24, 1989, at C1.

Bock, James. "Mfume Wants NAACP Gathering to Debate Education Reform: Civil Rights Group's Leader Sounds Call for Solutions to Black's Classroom Crisis," *Balt. Sun*, July 13, 1997, at 3A.

Bor, Jonation. "Dead Men Tell Tales for Medical Students," *Chic. Trib.*, Sept. 21, 2003 at 10.

Broder, John M. "U.C.L.A. Suspends Donations of Cadavers, Pending Inquiry," *N.Y. Times*, Mar. 10, 2004, at A1.

Brown, Tom. "Keep Your Hands Off My Body: The Voice of Authority with the Body to Match," *Daily Record* (Scotland, UK), July 8, 1999, at 13.

Butgereit, Betsy. "Mother Feels Corneas Were Stolen," *Birmingham News* (Alabama), Feb. 16, 1998, at A1.

Butler, Diana. "Can Science and Religion Come Together?" *Balt. Sun*, Mar. 2, 1997, at 1F.

Buttars, Lori. "Selling Body Parts? Americans Squeamish," *Salt Lake Trib.*, Aug. 10, 1997, at J13.

Carpenter, Mackenzie. "Presumed Donor Bill Aired," *Pittsburgh Post-Gazette*, July 14, 1993, at A10.

Carlstrom, Charles T. & Christy D. Rollow. "Organ Transplant Shortages: A Matter of Life and Death," *USA Today*, Nov. 1, 1999, at 50.

Ceccoli, Stephen. "Open Purse to Boost Organ Donations," *The Commercial Appeal*: (Memphis, TN), July 12, 2002, at B5.

Collins, Denis. "'Harvest of Dead' Bill Advances in Richmond," *Wash. Post*, Jan. 23, 1981, at C1.

Continelli, Louise. "Out of Tragedy, Life: A Plea for Minorities to Consider Organ Donation," *Buff. News*, Nov. 3, 2002, at B2.

Corbella, Licia, "Don't Put Children Near Front Air Bags," *The Calgary Sun*, March 16, 2001, at 4.

Corwin, Tom. "Doctors Face Culture Issues with Patients," *Augusta Chronical* (Georgia) Feb. 9, 2000 at C6.

Davis, David Brion. "Free at Last: The Enduring Legacy of the South's Civil War Victory," *N.Y. Times*, Aug. 26, 2001, at 1.

Editorial, "Accepted for Too Long the Disparity in Health of White and Black Won't Disappear by Itself, *Des Moines Register*, Feb. 25, 2000, at 12.

Escobar, Gabriel. "Deaths Pose Continuing D.C. Mystery: City Carries Hundreds of Undetermined Cases, Muddying Vital Statistics," *Wash. Post*, Dec. 22, 1997 at A1.

Fears, Darryl. "Urban Spotlight: Is Atlanta the Next Detroit?" *The Atlanta Journal and Constitution*, Dec. 18, 1994 at D1.

Fegelman, Andrew. "Guardian Allowed to Talk to Twins," *Chic. Trib.*, Aug. 24, 1990, at C4.

Fischer, Meredith & Will Jones. "Some Roads are Deadly: Deficient Design, Driver Inattention Can Be Fatal Mix," *Richmond Times Dispatch* (Virginia), at A1.

Foster, Dick. "Little Brother Adam is Sister Molly's Hero," *Denver Rocky Mtn. News*, Oct. 4, 2000, at 4A.

Frammolino, Ralph. "Harvest of Corneas at Morgue Questioned," *L.A. Times*, Nov. 2, 1997, at A1.

Frase-Blunt, Martha. "Ova-Compensating?; Women who Donate Eggs to Infertile Couples Earn a Reward – But Pay a Price," *Wash. Post*, Dec. 4, 2001 at F1.

Freundlich, Naomi. "All of Me," *N.Y. Times*, March 16, 2003, at 94.

Frist, Bill. "Not Ready for Human Cloning," *Wash. Post*, Apr. 11, 2002, at A29.

Gaul, Gilbert M. "The Blood Brokers: How Blood, The 'Gift of Life,' Became a Billion-Dollar Business," *Philadelphia Inquirer*, Sept. 24, 1989 at A1.

Gaul, Gilbert M. "The Blood Brokers: Red Cross – From Disaster Relief to Blood," *Philadelphia Inquirer*, Sept. 27, 1989 at A1.

Gaul, Gilbert M. "The Blood Brokers: The Loose Way the FDA Regulates Blood Industry," *Philadelphia Inquirer*, Sept. 25, 1989 at A1.

Glaberson, William. "Lawyers Math in Sept. 11 Deaths Shows Varying Values for Life," *N.Y. Times*, Nov. 11, 2001, at B1.

Ellen, Goodman. "Life for Sale," *Washington Post*, Oct. 1, 1983, at A15, col.1.

Goldberg, Carey. "On Web, Models Auction their Eggs to Bidders for Beautiful Children," *N.Y. Times*, Oct. 23, 1999, at A11.

Grady, Denise. "Discrimination is Painful, It can Also be Agonizing," *N.Y. Times*, Apr. 9, 2000, 4, at 2.

Greene, Jay. "More Med Students Bone Up on Diversity Issues," *San Diego Union-Trib.*, Nov. 22, 1999, at E3.

Green, Reg. "A Child's Legacy of Love," *L.A. Times*, May 15, 2002, at §5 at 2.

Grossman, Ron. "Cemetery Trove Brings Early Chicago to Life," *Chicago Tribune*, June 19, 1991, § 1, at 1.

Hall, Joseph. "Opening up the Market for Organs," *Toronto Star*, Nov. 29, 2002, at F6.

Harper, Pat. "Savoring a Role in Workplace," *Chicago Tribune*, May 11, 1999, at 3.

Harris, Gardiner, "New Rules on Sperm Donation by Gays," *N.Y. Times*, May 20, 2004, at A16.

Harris, Hamil R. "For Black Patients, the Need for Organs Exceeds Availability," *Wash. Post*, Feb. 23, 2000, at M14.

Hartocollis, Anemona, "U.S. Questions the Placement of City Pupils," *N.Y. Times*, Nov. 21, 1998, at B1.

Hathaway, William. "Belief Systems are Historic Foes: Long Before Stem-Cell Debate, Medical Advances Clashed with Religion," *Hartford Courant*, Sept. 5, 2001, at A1.

Hawkes, Nigel. "Doctors Question Morality of Ban on Willing Sales," *Times* (London), Aug. 31, 2002, §9 at 7.

Hedges, Stephen J. "U.S. Urges Overhaul for Human Tissue Trade: Report Identifies Safety Lapses, Lack of Oversight in Burgeoning Industry," *Chi. Trib.*, Jan. 6, 2001, at N1.

Hedges, Stephen J. & William Gaines. "Donor Bodies Milled into Growing Profits," *Chi. Trib.*, May 21, 2000, at C1.

Hopfensperger, Jean. "Study Offers a Hand on Welfare-to-Work," *Star Tribune*, March 17, 2000, at 1A.

Hopper, Leigh. "His Dying Wish: Body of Executed Inmate was Milled, then Rendered into 1800 Photos Used for Medical Training," *The Houston Chronicle*, July 17, 2002 at A1.

Hudson, Christopher. "Theatres of Horror," *Daily Mail* (London), Nov. 23, 2002, at 44.

Hunter, Stephanie. "'Resurrection Man' Dug Way into History," *Augusta Chron.*, Aug. 21, 1995, at B1.

Jimenez, Marina & Stewart Bell. "Americans Buying Kidneys in Manilla," *Chic. Sun-Times*, July 22, 2001, at 10.

Katches, Mark, William Heisel, & Ronald Campbell. "Body Donors Fueling a Booming Business," *Orange County Register*, April 17, 2000.

Kercheval, Nancy. "U of MD School of Medicine Played Role in History of Grave Robbing," *The Daily Record* (Baltimore, MD), October 24, 2002.

Kerr, Kathleen. "PA May OK Pay for Organ Donations/$300 Toward Funeral Costs," *Newsday*, June 8, 1999, at A6.

Kimbrell, Andrew. "The Human Body Shop: Does America Want a 'Free Market' in Organs and Tissues?," *Wash. Post*, July 1, 1990, at B3.

King, Warren. "DNA Analysis Boon in Battling Cancer: Technology Widens Pool of Donors for Transplants, Local Study Says," *Seattle Times*, Dec. 20, 2001, at B1.

Kolata, Gina. "Price of Donor Eggs Soars, Setting Off a Debate on Ethics," *N.Y. Times*, Feb. 25, 1998, at A1.

Kowalsi, Jo Anna. "Blow for Couple in 'Designer Baby Bid,'" *Nottingham Evening Post*, December 11, 2003, at 13.

Krum, Sharon, "American Beauty," *Independent on Sunday* (London), June 17, 2001, at 1.

MacDonald, John A. "Bereaved Family Wants FDA to Tighten Tissue Bank Regulations," *Hartford Courant* (CT), May 16, 2003.

Mackenzie, Carpenter. "'Presumed' Donor Bill Aired," *Pittsburgh Post-Gazette*, July, 14, 1999 at A10.

"Massachusetts: Photographer Plans Egg Auction," *Vero Beach Press Journal*, Oct. 24, 1999, at A16.

McCoy, Kevin. "Deadly Disparity in Transplants: Blacks and Hispanics Deprived," *Daily News*, Aug. 8, 1996, at 6.

Meadows, Karin. "Cornea Policy OK by Commissioners," *Birmingham News* (Alabama), Feb. 19, 1998 at B1.

Neergaard, Lauren. "Transplant Tissue Must be Screened," *Albany Times Union* (NY), May 21, 2004, at A9.

Noonan, Erica. "Sprinkler Bill Stirs Some Debate," *Boston Globe*, Feb. 25, 2001 at 3.

Norton, Cherry & Ian Herbert. "How a Dead Man Provoked an Ethical Dilemma that Has Convulsed the NHS," *Independent* (London), July 8, 1999, at 3.

Okie, Susan. "Surgeons Back Study of Payment for Organs: Plan Aimed at Boosting Donor Rates," *Wash. Post*, Apr. 30, 2002, at A3.

Okie, Susan. "Living Donor Transplants: So Successful, No Match Needed," *Wash. Post*, Dec. 11, 2001, at F8.

Pear, Roberts, "F.D.A. Delays Regulation of Tissue Transplants," *N.Y. Times*, May 14, 2003, at A18.

Pinsley, Elliot. "Routine Donation of Organs Pushed: Ethics Group Seeks 'Presumed Consent,'" *Record*, Dec. 22, 1992, at A1.

Price, Joyce Howard. "Organ Donations Aren't Keeping Up; Serious Shortage Has Experts Searching for Solutions," *Wash. Times*, May 17, 1999, at A9.

Renwick, Lucille, "Minorities Wait Longer for Transplants," *L.A. Times*, May 2, 1993, at 3.

Richardson, Lisa. "Praise for His Art Keeps Young Muralist from Being Walled in by Harsh Gang Life," *Los Angeles Times*, Nov. 27, 1992, at B1.

Roan, Shari. "A Medical Imbalance," *L.A. Times*, Nov. 1, 1994, at E1.

Rohter, Larry, "Desperation and Sympathy Impel the Illegal Purchase of a Kidney," *Int'l Herald Tribune*, May 24, 2004, at 6.

Rosenbaum, David E. "Senate Panel Votes Organ Transplant Policy," *N.Y. Times*, Apr. 13, 2000, at A24.

Russakoff, Dale. "The Heart that Didn't Die: One Evening, Mike Lucas Lay Beaten on the Ground. A Week Later, the Governor was Saved," *Wash. Post*, Aug. 9, 1993 at B1.

Saavedra, Tony. "Egg Donors in Ethical Cross-Fire," *Orange County Reg.*, Dec. 20, 1999.

Schmeck Jr., Harold M. "Issue and Debate: Should Life Always he Prolonged?," *N.Y. Times*, June 28, 1983, at C2.

Schmickle, Sharon. "Under the Skin We're All Alike – Except Medically, Science Says," *Minneapolis Star Trib.*, Mar. 26, 2002, at 1A.

Schoofs, Mark. "Man-Man Made: Will We Transform Ourselves into a New Species by Manipulating DNA?," *Village Voice*, Dec. 30, 1997, at 34.

Schulte, Brigid. "Minorities Face Unequal Health in U.S.: Statistics Show Ethnicities Encounter Higher Illness Rates," *Ft. Worth Star-Telegram*, Aug. 2, 1998, at 1.

Schwartz. "Providing Incentives for Organ Donations," *Wall Street Journal*, July 25, 1983, at 10.

Scott, Gale. "From Pigs to People," *N.Y. Times*, Oct. 2, 2001, at F5.

Seabrook, Charles. "The Body Snatchers of Augusta; Bought as a Slave to Rob Black Graves," *Atlanta J. & Const.*, Mar. 8, 1998, at C4.

Shontz, Lori. "Healing Rock: Process of Moving on after Earnhardt's Death Begins," *N.C., Pittsburgh Post-Gazette*, Feb. 25, 2001, at D1.

Simple, Peter. "Comment: Dilemma," *Daily Telegraph* (London), July 9, 1999, at 28.

Smith, Craig S. "Quandry in U.S. Over Use of Organs of Chinese Inmates," *N.Y. Times*, Nov. 11, 2001, at 1A.

Smith, Tammie. "Payment for Organs Weighed: Agency Seeking Way to Motivate Donors," *Rich Times. Dispatch*, June 24, 2002, at A1.

Snyder, Jodie. "Race Disparity in Transplants Questioned: Time Not on Minorities' Side," *Ariz. Republic*, May 11, 1999, at A1.

Srikameswaran, Anita. "A Great Divide: Institutional Racism on One Side, Misinformation on the Other Mean Minorities Lag in Receiving Transplants and Heart Surgeries," *Pittsburgh Post-Gazette*, July 23, 2002, at F1.

Staples, Brent. "Monticello as the All-American Melting Pot," *N.Y. Times*, July 1, 2002, at A14.

Staples, Brent. "The Slave Reparations Movement Adopts the Rhetoric of Victimhood," *N.Y. Times*, Sept. 2, 2001, at 8.

Staples, Brent. "Wrestling with the Ghosts of New Orleans," *N.Y. Times*, Feb. 9, 1998, at A18.

Stolberg, Sheryl Gay. "Could this Pig Save Your Life?," *N.Y. Times*, Oct. 3, 1999. § 6 (Magazine), at 46.

Stolberg, Sheryl Gay. "On Medicine's Frontier: The Last Journey of James Quinn," *N.Y. Times*, Oct. 8, 2002, at F1.

Stolberg, Sheryl Gay. "Race Gap Seen in Health Care of Equally Insured Patients." *N.Y. Times*, Mar. 21, 2002, at A1.

Strom, Stephanie. "An Organ Donor's Generosity Raises the Question of How Much Is Too Much," *N.Y. Times*, Aug. 17, 2003, at 14.

Swanson, Marie G. "Variables for Unbiased Medical Research," *Chi. Trib.*, Dec. 17, 1995, at 21.

Tanner, Lindsey. "Blacks' Mental Care Lags that of Whites," *Chi. Sun Times*, Mar. 13, 2002, at 22.

Turay, Ismail. "Reps Press Minority Health Research," *Dayton Daily News* (Ohio), Feb. 3, 2000, at 3A.

Umrigar, Thrity. "Race and Health Care," *Chi. Trib.*, June 4, 1996, at C7.

Wade, Nicholas. "Scientists Make 2 Stem Cell Advances," *N.Y. Times*, June 21, 2002, at F1.

Walsh, Williams. "A Big Fish in a Small Gene Pool," *L.A. Times*, June 5, 1998, at A1.

Warren, Jim. "As Support Grows for Studying Financial Incentives to Increase Donation, Top Surgeon's Group Not Buying In," *Transplant News*, June 30, 2002, at 1.

Warren, Jim. "Passage of Much Needed Transplant Bill May Depend on Finding Compromise on Financial Incentives Trial Commentary," *Transplant News*, June 27, 2003, at No. 12, Vol. 13.

Watson, Rod. "In Blacks, Tragic Mistrust of Medicine," *Buffalo News*, Feb. 22, 2001, at 1B.

"Web Auction for Beauty is for Fools," *Morning Call* (Allentown, PA), Oct. 28, 1999, at A26.

Weiss, Jeffrey. "Doctors Soul-Searching After Bias Study; Unconscious Sexism and Racism May Be Killing Patients," *Hous. Chron.*, June 6, 1999, at A19.

Weiss, Rick. "A Look at . . . The Body Shop: At the Heart of an Uneasy Commerce," *Wash. Post*, June 27, 1999, at B3.

Weiss, Rick. "Gene Alteration Boosts Pig-Human Transplant Feasibility," *Wash. Post*, Jan. 4, 2002, at A11.

Weiss, Rick. "Demand Growing for Anthrax Vaccine," *Wash. Post*, Oct. 3, 2001, at A1.
Weisskopf, Michael. "Minorities' Pollution Risk is Debated: Some Activists Link Exposure to Racism," *Wash. Post*, Jan. 16, 1992, at A25.
Wheelen, Charles. "Lives Changed in a Split Second," *N.Y. Times*, Jan. 10, 2001, at A19.
Wickham, DeWayne. "To Save Country, Save Kids from Violence, AIDS," *USA Today*, May 26, 1998.
Williams, Terri. "Organ Donor Unites Cultures: Chinese, African American Families Celebrate Man's Gift of Life," *Dallas Morning News*, Nov. 13, 2000, at 19A.

VII. Magazine Articles

Andrews, Lori. "My Body, My Property," *Hastings Center Rep.*, April 1987.
Barnett II, William et al. "A Free Market in Kidneys: Efficient and Equitable," *Indep. Rev.*, Winter, 2001, at 373.
Boston, Gabriella. "Emory Addresses Reluctance of Black Organ Donors," *Atlanta J. and Constitution*, May 6, 1999, at 9JA.
Campbell, Roger. "Too Many Blacks Await Lifesaving Donations," *Essence*, Apr. 1999, at 45.
Easterbrook, Gregg. "Medical Evolution: Will Homo Sapiens Become Obsolete?," *New Republic*, Mar. 1, 1999, at 21.
Epstein, Richard A. "Organ Transplants: Is Relying on Altruism Costing Lives?," *Am. Enterprise*, Nov.–Dec. 1993, at 50.
Enserink, Martin. "Physicians Wary of Scheme to Pool Icelanders' Genetic Data," *Science*, Aug. 14, 1998 at 890.
Jervey, Gay. "Priceless," *Money Magazine*, April 2003, at 118.
Loury, Glen. "The Impossible Dilemma," *The New Republic*, Jan. 1, 1996, at 21.
Lerner, Sharon. "The Price of Eggs: Undercover in the Infertility Industry," *Ms.*, Mar.–Apr. 1996, at 28.
MacKenzie, Debora. "A Cure for Quacks," *New Scientist*, Aug. 22, 1998, at 18.
Morrow, Lance. "When One Body Can Save Another; A Family's Act of Lifesaving Conception Was on the Side of Angels, but Hovering in the Wings is the Devilish Ghost of Dr. Mengele," *Time*, June 17, 1992, at 54.
Morse, Jodie & Wendy Cole. "Learning While Black," *Time*, May 27, 2002, at 50.
Newsweek Magazine, "Fertility Resource Showcase," March 1, 2004.
Scheper-Hughes, Nancy. "The Organ of Last Resort," *UNESCO Courier*, July/Aug. 2001.
Scheper-Hughes, Nancy. "Postmodern Cannibalism: Black Market Trade of Human Organs," *Whole Earth*, June 22, 2000.
Wright, Karen. "The Body Bazaar: The Market in Human Organs is Growing." *Discover*, Oct. 1998.

VIII. Interviews

Interview in person with Mark Larson, Executive Director of the Eyebank of Wisconsin, in Madison Wis. (Feb. 21, 2000).
Interview in person with Dr. Jim Martin, Executive Director of the Louisville Eye Bank (Mar. 1999 and Aug. 1999).
Telephone interview with Tom Buckley, Executive Director of New England Eye and Tissue Transplant Bank (Apr. 6, 2000).

Telephone interview with Jim Cohan, May 5, 2004 and Mar. 30, 2004.

Telephone interview with Donica Davis, Hospital Development Coordinator, Tennessee Eye Bank (Apr. 5, 2000).

Telephone interview of Jacqueline Dillard, Director of Dialysis Services, Chicago-Area Dialysis Clinic (June 7, 2005).

Telephone interview with Dr. Michael Dreis, Administrator, Health Resources and Services Administration, Office of Special Programs, Division of Transportation (Apr. 21, 2000).

Telephone interview with Dr. Mary D. Ellison, Representative, UNOS (July and Aug. 1999).

Telephone interview with Dr. Ellison, Representative, United Network of Organ Sharing (July, 1999 and Aug., 1999).

Telephone interview with Scott Helm (Apr. 20, 2000).

Telephone interview with Scott Helm, Spokesperson, UNOS (Apr. 21, 2000).

Telephone interview with Florence Johnston, President & CEO, Midwest Eyebank (Apr. 6, 2000).

Telephone interview with Kristen McCoy, Laboratory Director, Illinois Eye Bank, (Feb. 21, 2000).

Telephone interview with Mary Jane O'Neil, Executive Director, Eye Bank Sight Restoration in New York, N.Y. (Feb. 21, 2000).

Telephone interview with David Sierra, Hospital Development Technical Director for North Florida Lions Eye Banks (Feb. 23, 2000).

Telephone interview with David Weisstub, May 27, 2003.

Telephone interview with Doyce Williams, Executive Director of the Alabama Eye Bank (Feb. 21, 2000).

Telephone interview with Doyce Williams, Executive Director of the Alabama Eye Bank (Feb. 23, 2000).

Telephone interview with Maurice Van Zance, Executive Director of the Indiana Eye Bank (Feb. 22, 2000).

IX. Congressional Hearings

Hearings before the House Appropriations Subcommittee on Labor, Health and Human Services, and Education. 105th Cong., 2d. Sess. (1998). Testimony of Benjamin F. Payton.

Hearings before the House Appropriations Subcommittee on Labor, Health and Human Services, and Education, Federal Document Clearing House Congressional Testimony (Feb. 5, 1998). Testimony of Benjamin Payton, President of Tuskegee University.

National Organ Transplant Act: Hearings on H.R. 4080 before the Subcommittee on Health and Environment of the House Committee on Energy and Commerce, 98th Cong, 1st Sess. 224 (1983).

Putting Patients First – Allocation of Transplant Organ: Hearings before the House Commerce Comm. Subcomm. on Health and the Environment and the Senate Labor and Human Resources Comm., 105th Cong., 2d Sess. 215 (1998).

Putting Patients First – Allocation of Transplant Organ: Hearings before the House Commerce Comm. Subcomm. on Health and the Environment and the Senate Labor and Human Resources Comm., 106th Cong., 2nd Sess. (1998).

Sale of Human Organs in China: Hearings before the House Comm. On Int'l Relations, Subcommittee On Int'l Operations and Human Rights, Federal Documents Clearing House Congressional Testimony (June 27, 2001). Testimony of Professor Nancy Scheper-Hughes.

The Importance of Studying Motivation for Organ Donation: Hearings before the House Committee on Energy and the House Commerce Subcommittee on Oversight and Investigations, Federal News Service (June 3, 2003). Testimony of Robert M. Sade, M.D.

Fox, Claude E. Administrator of Health Resources and Services Administration's letter to L. G. Hunsicker. http://www.hrsa.gov/osp/fox/tr.htm (last visited August 8, 1999)

X. Transcripts

ABC Nightline: America in Black and White (ABC Television Broadcast, Feb. 24, 1999).

CBS News: Governor Tommy Thompson, Republican, Wisconsin and Dr. Jean Emond, UNOS, Discuss the Organization of Organ Transplantations Within the Country (CBS Television Broadcast, Mar. 16, 2000).

NPR Weekend Saturday: Race Relations (NPR Radio Broadcast, Oct. 31, 1998).

XI. Empirical Studies

African American Organ Transplant Study I (2002–2003)

African American Organ Transplant Study II (2003)

Presumed Consent Survey (2000)

XII. UNOS and UPTN Materials

2003 OPTN/SRTR Annual Report, Tables 1.1, 5.1, 6.1, and 9.1.

OPTN data, Donors Recovered in the U.S. by Donor Type. February 27, 2004.

OPTN, Death Removals by Ethnicity by Year: Removed from Waiting List, January 1995–December 31, 2003.

2003 Annual Report, Living Donor Characteristics, 1993 to 2002, Table 2.8.

2003 Annual Report of the U.S. Scientific Registry of Transplant Recipients and the Organ Procurement and Transplantation Network: Transplant Data 1993–2002. (2003, Feb. 16) Rockville, MD and Richmond, VA: HHS/HRSA/OSP/DOT and UNOS. Available online at www.optn.org/AR2003/208_don_relation_ty_dc.htm (Mar. 21, 2004).

United Network for Organ Sharing, *2000 Ann. Rep., The U.S. Sci. Registry of Transplant Recipients and the Organ Procurement and Transplantation Network* (2000).

XIII. Unpublished Manuscripts

Goodwin, Michele. *Organ Transplant Survey Analysis* (Feb. 16, 2000) (unpublished manuscript, on file with author).

Larson, Mark E. *Use of Tissue Recovered Using Medical Examiner/Corner Laws* (Mar. 5, 1998) (unpublished manuscript, on file with author).

Index